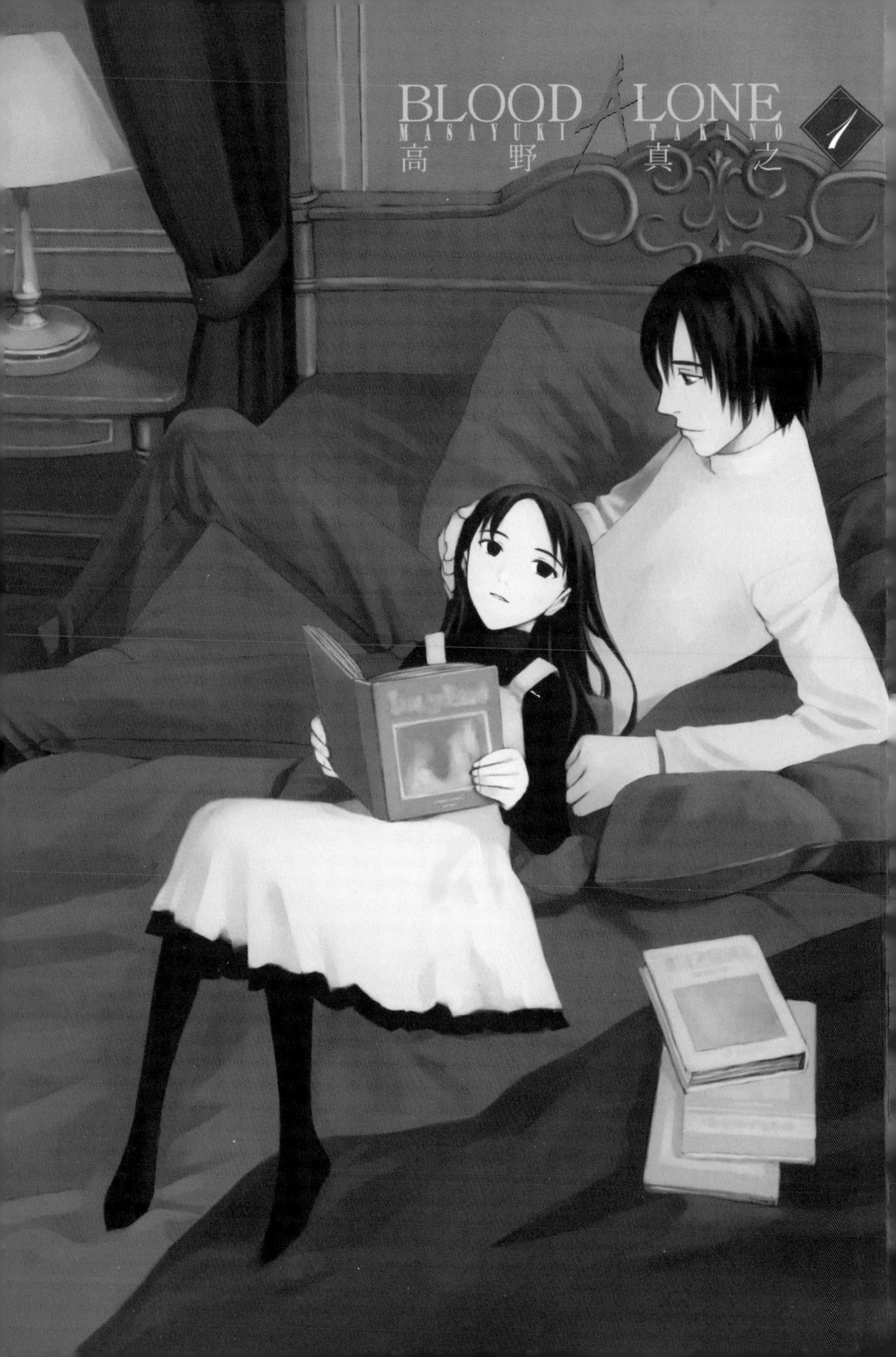
BLOOD ALONE
MASAYUKI TAKANO
高野真之
1

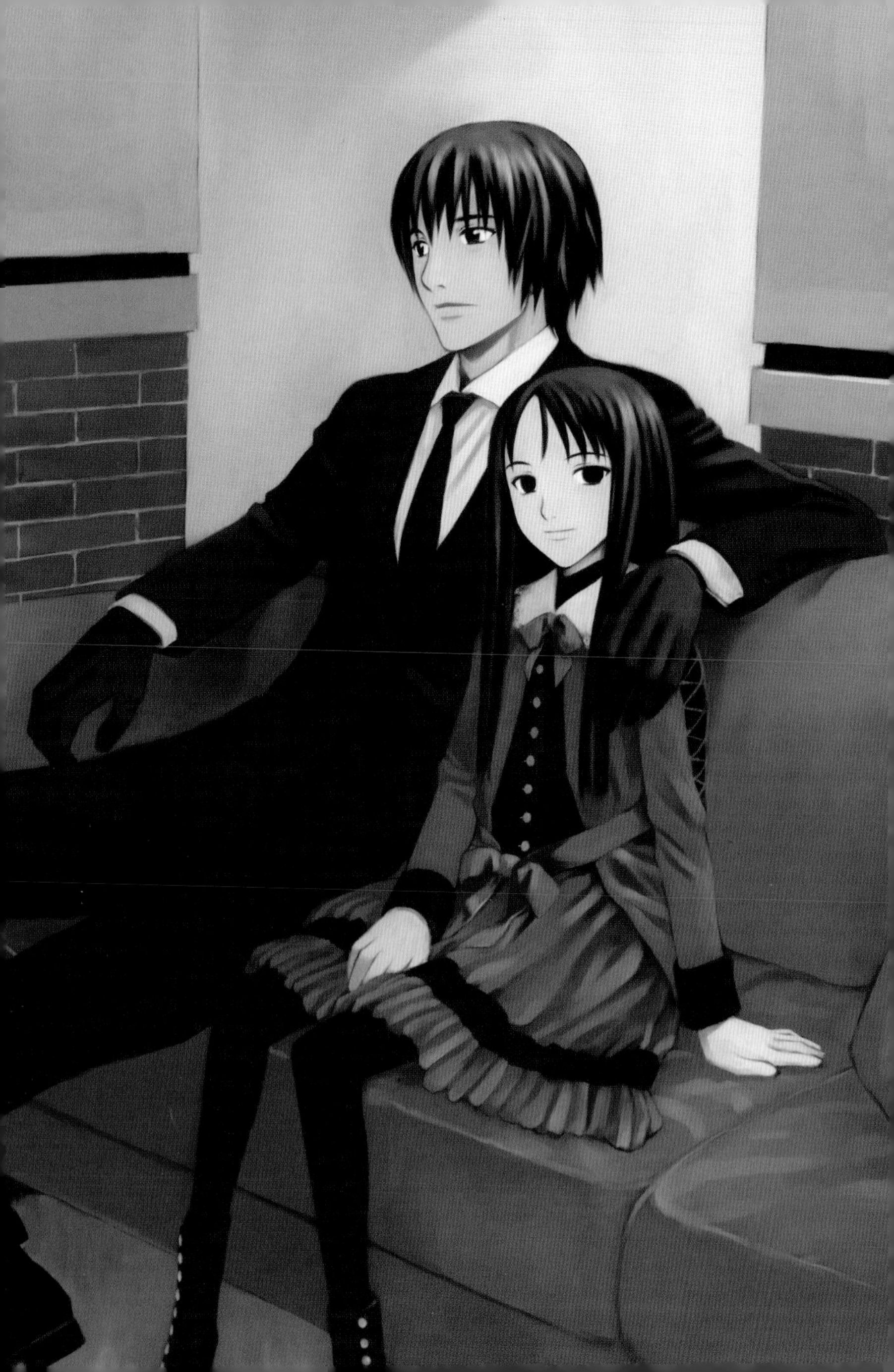

BLOOD ALONE ◆ *1*

Contents

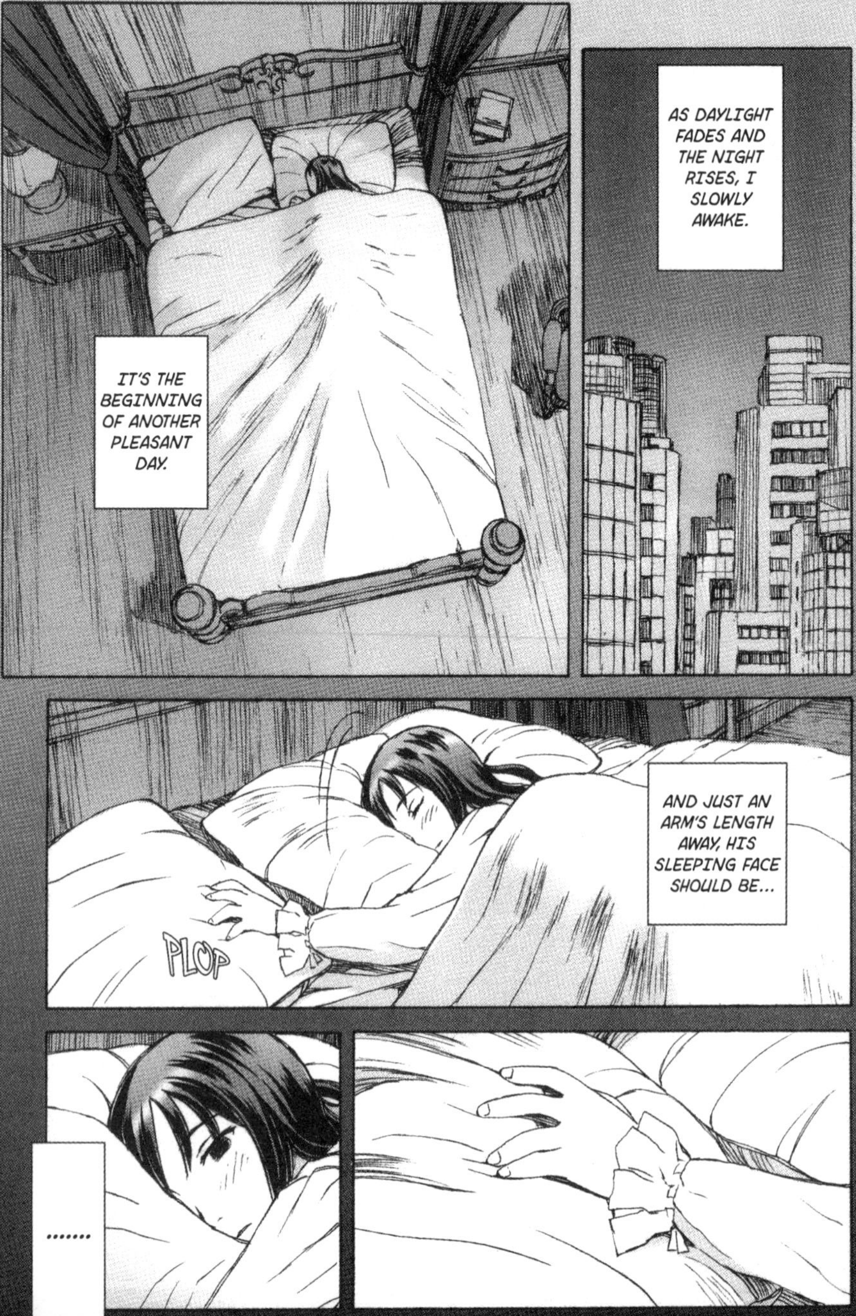
AS DAYLIGHT FADES AND THE NIGHT RISES, I SLOWLY AWAKE.
IT'S THE BEGINNING OF ANOTHER PLEASANT DAY.
AND JUST AN ARM'S LENGTH AWAY, HIS SLEEPING FACE SHOULD BE...
PLOP
....

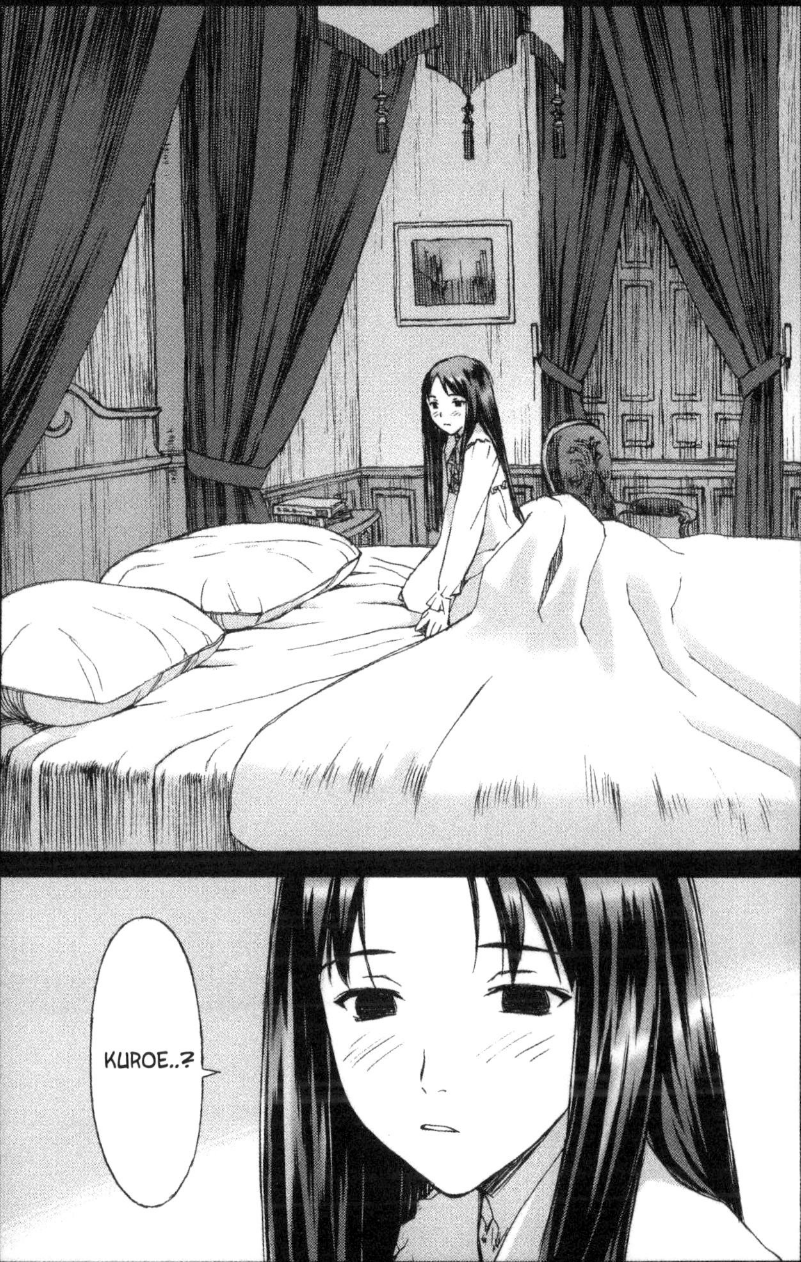
KUROE..?

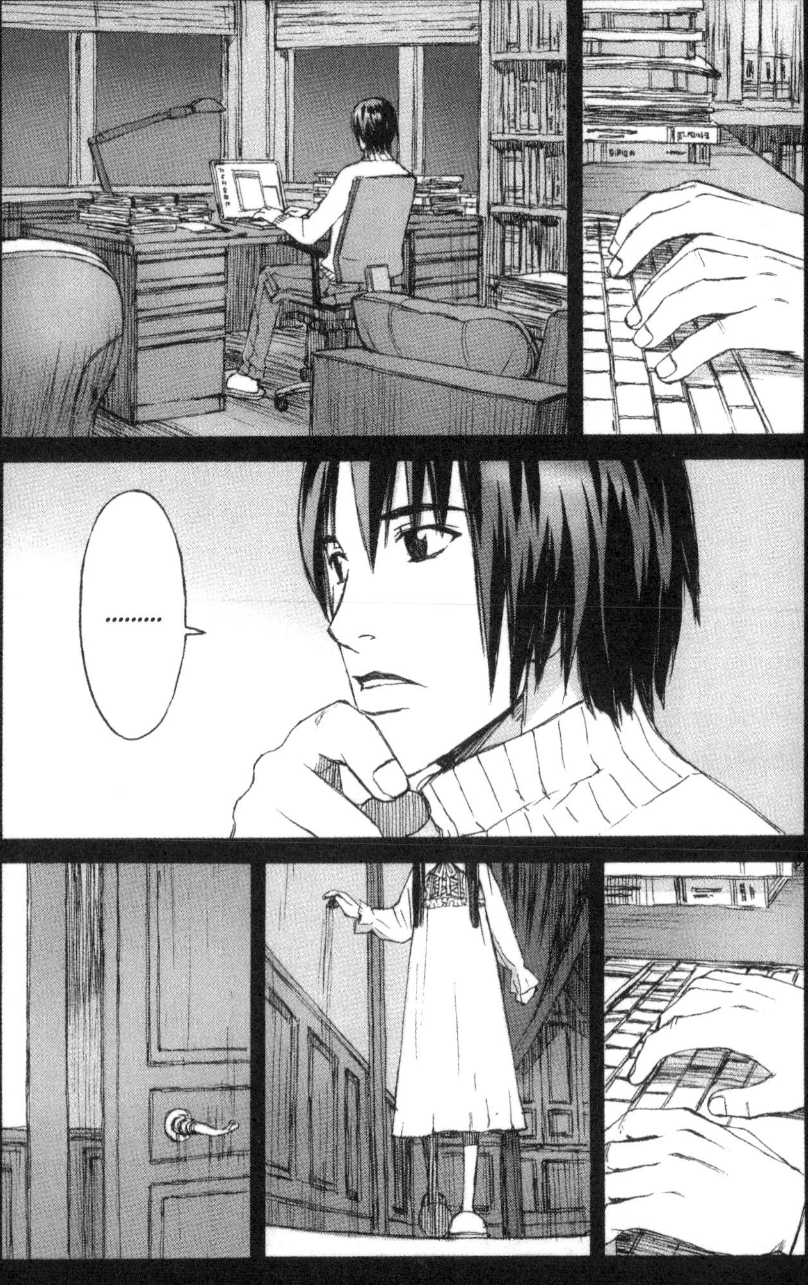
....

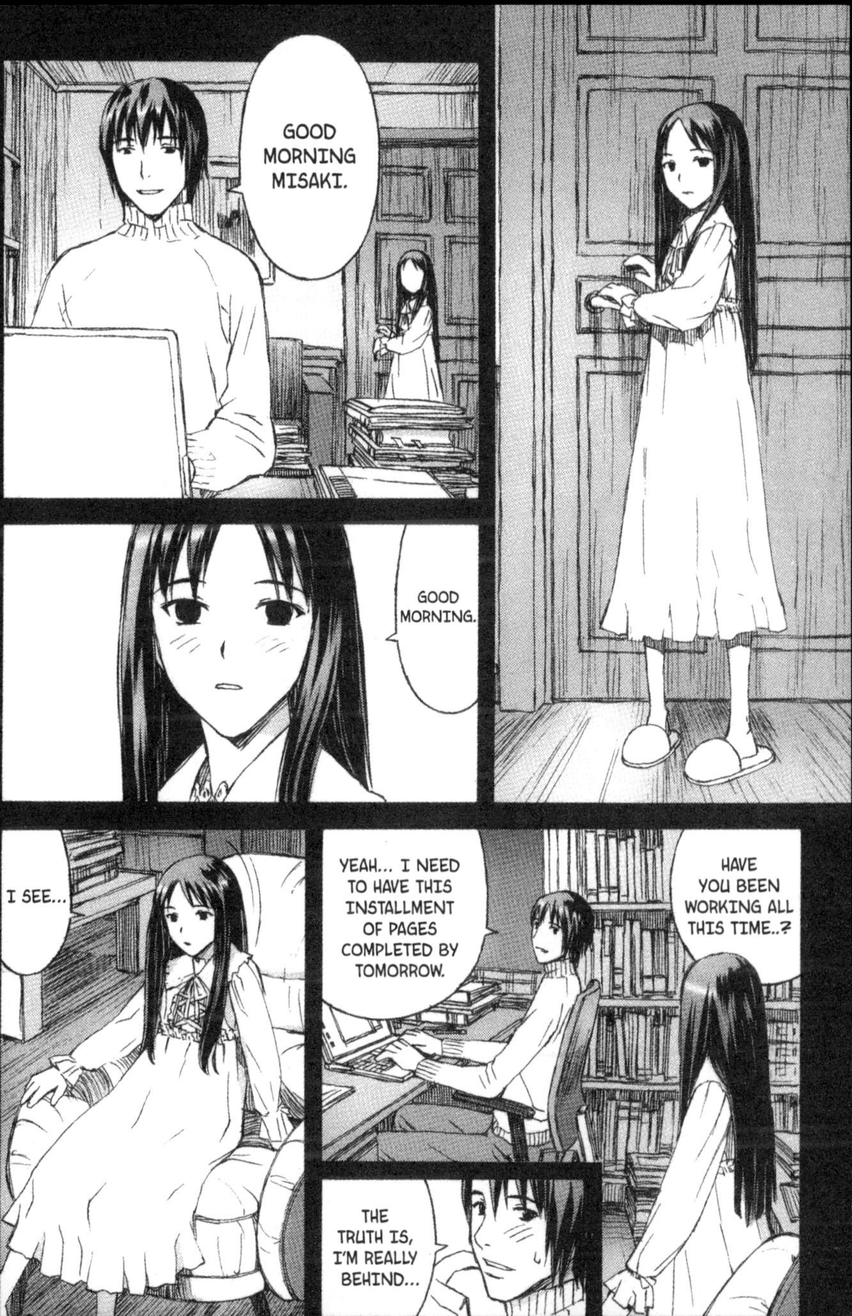

GOOD MORNING MISAKI.
GOOD MORNING.
HAVE YOU BEEN WORKING ALL THIS TIME..?
YEAH... I NEED TO HAVE THIS INSTALLMENT OF PAGES COMPLETED BY TOMORROW.
THE TRUTH IS, I'M REALLY BEHIND...
I SEE...

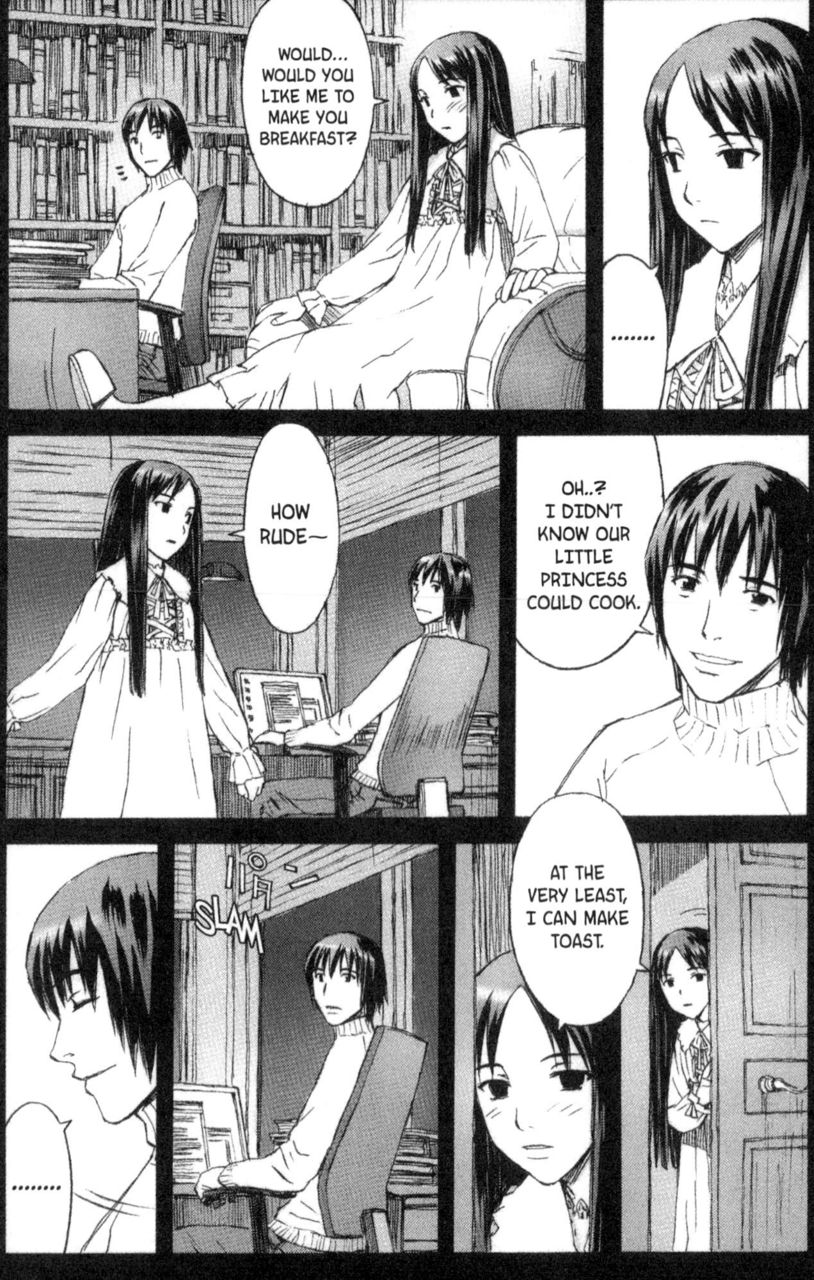
....
WOULD... WOULD YOU LIKE ME TO MAKE YOU BREAKFAST?
OH..? I DIDN'T KNOW OUR LITTLE PRINCESS COULD COOK.
HOW RUDE~
AT THE VERY LEAST, I CAN MAKE TOAST.
SLAM
....

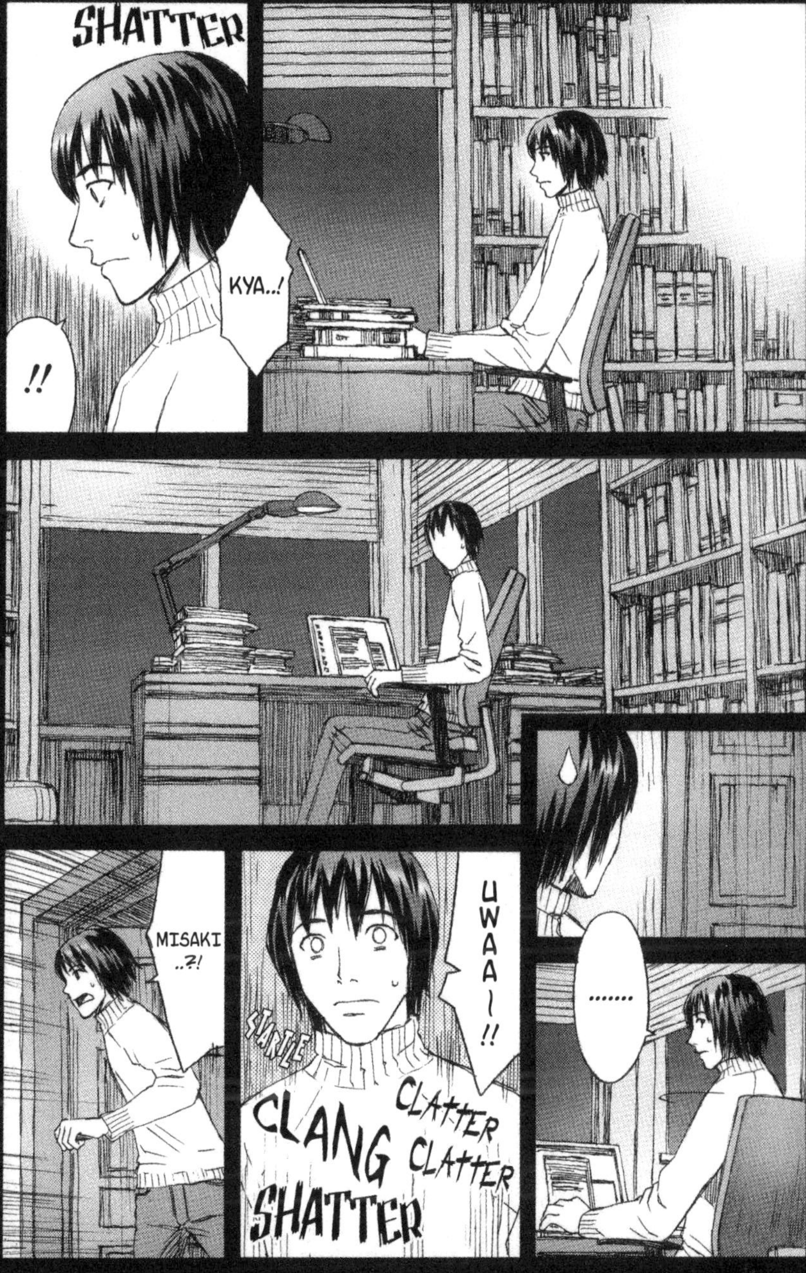
SHATTER
KYA..!
!!
....
UWAAA!!
STARTLE
CLATTER
CLATTER
CLANG
SHATTER
MISAKI ..?!

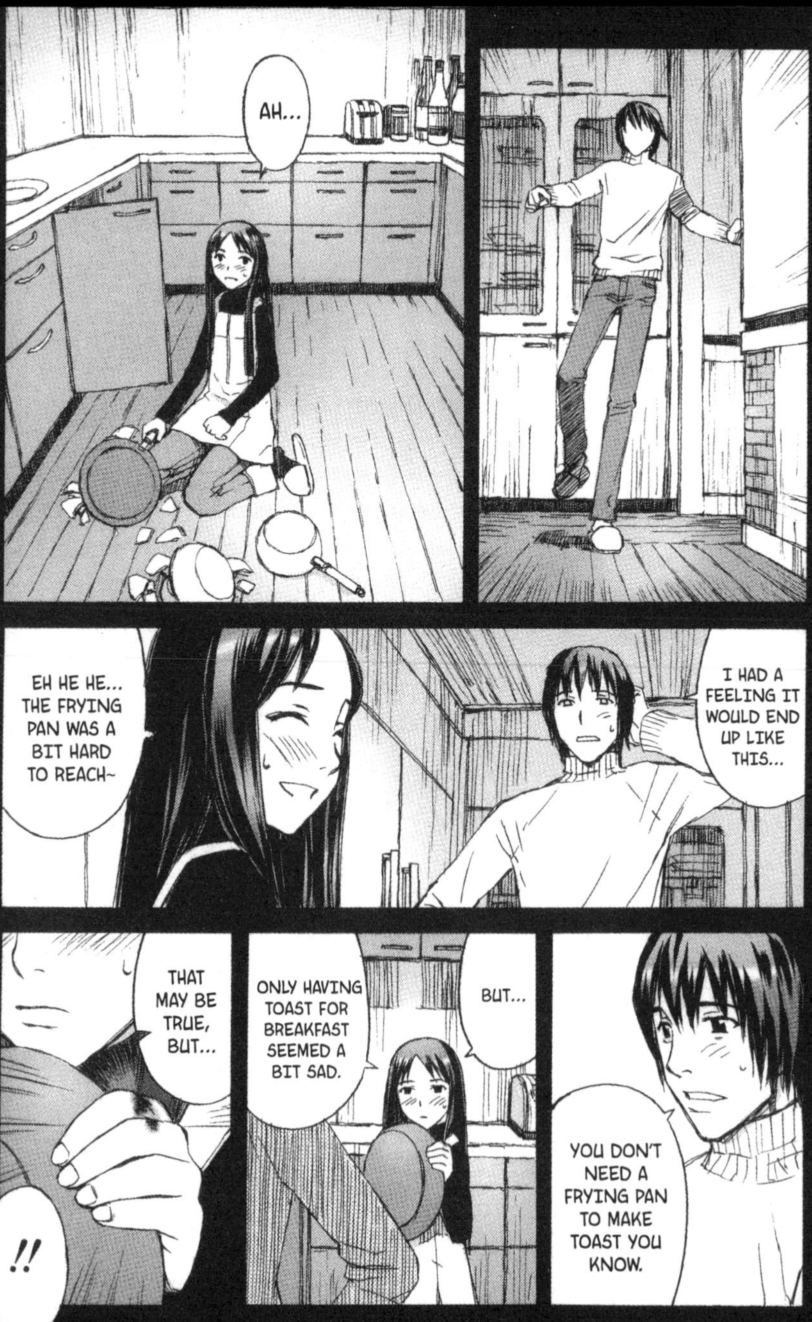
AH...
I HAD A FEELING IT WOULD END UP LIKE THIS...
EH HE HE... THE FRYING PAN WAS A BIT HARD TO REACH~
YOU DON'T NEED A FRYING PAN TO MAKE TOAST YOU KNOW.
BUT...
ONLY HAVING TOAST FOR BREAKFAST SEEMED A BIT SAD.
THAT MAY BE TRUE, BUT...
!!

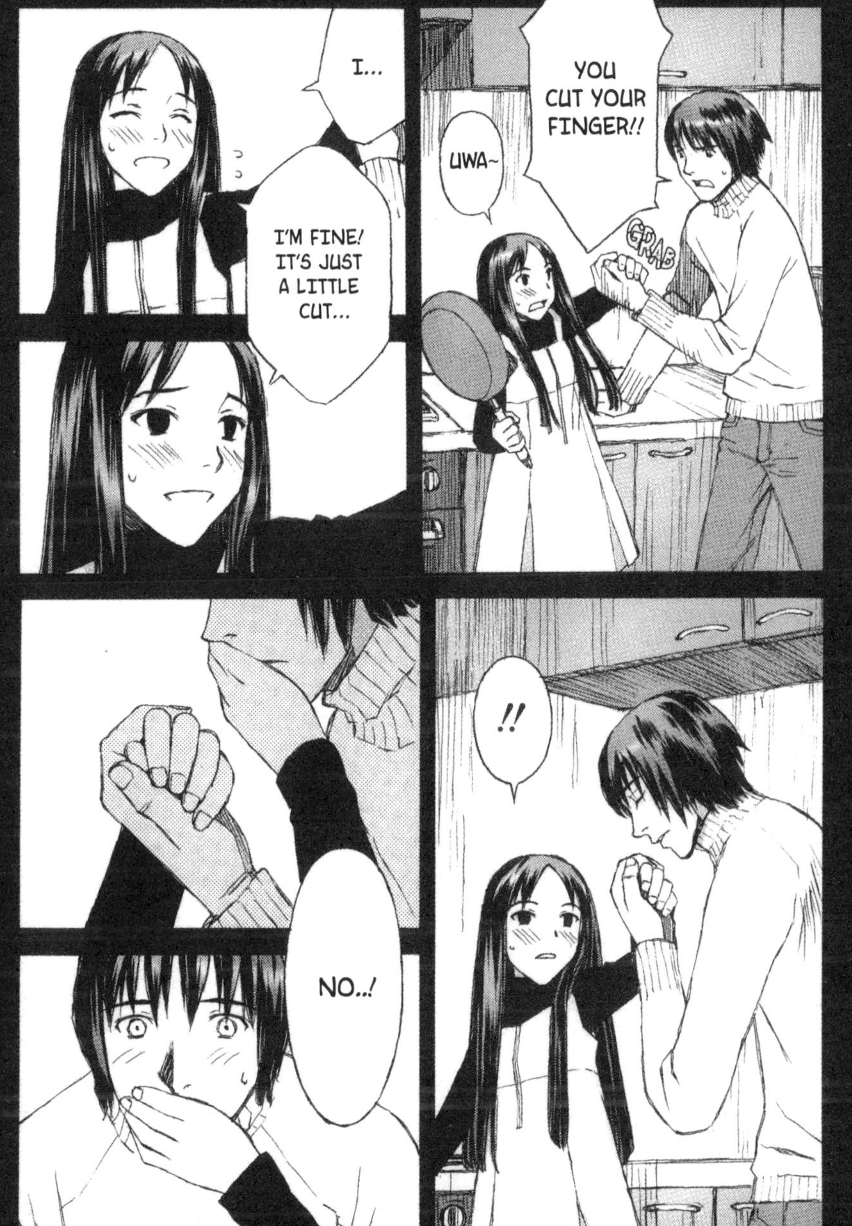
YOU CUT YOUR FINGER!!
UWA~
GRAB
I...
I'M FINE! IT'S JUST A LITTLE CUT...
!!
NO..!

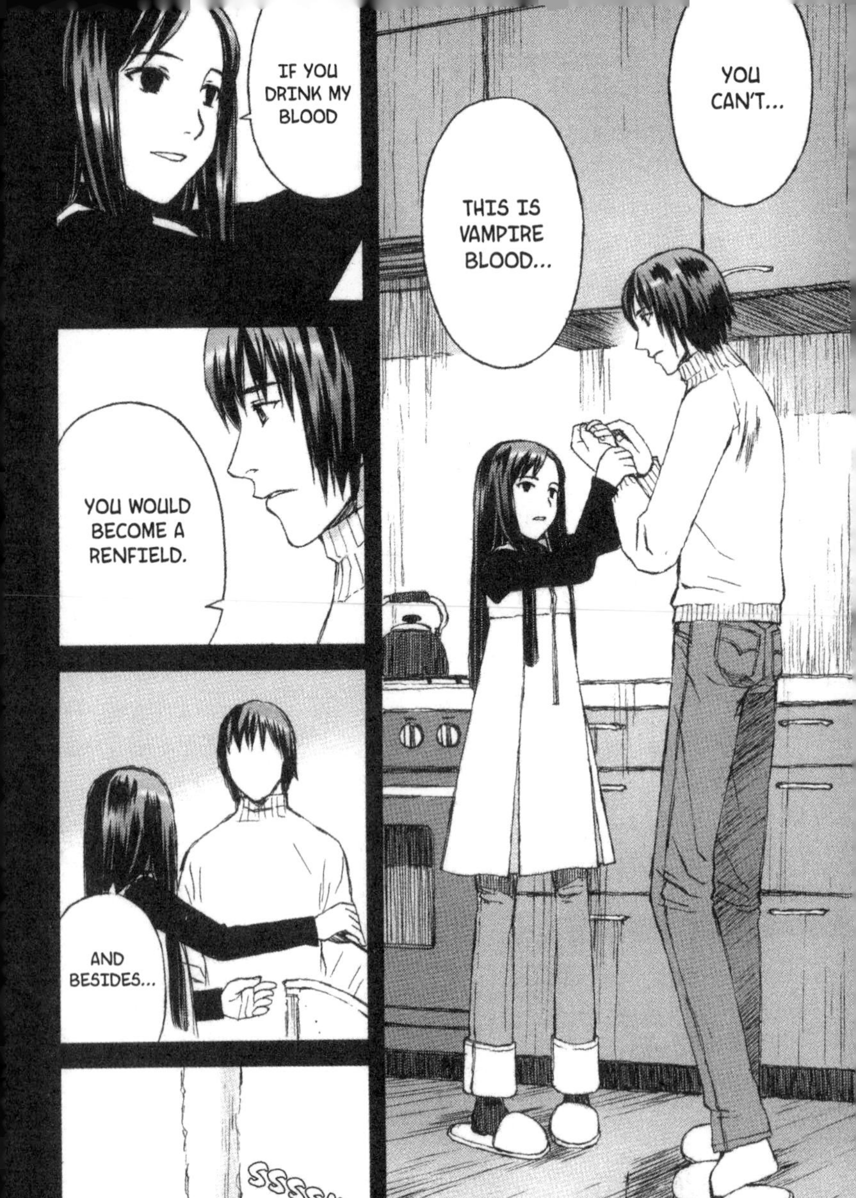
YOU CAN'T...
THIS IS VAMPIRE BLOOD...
IF YOU DRINK MY BLOOD
YOU WOULD BECOME A RENFIELD.
AND BESIDES...
SSSSHH

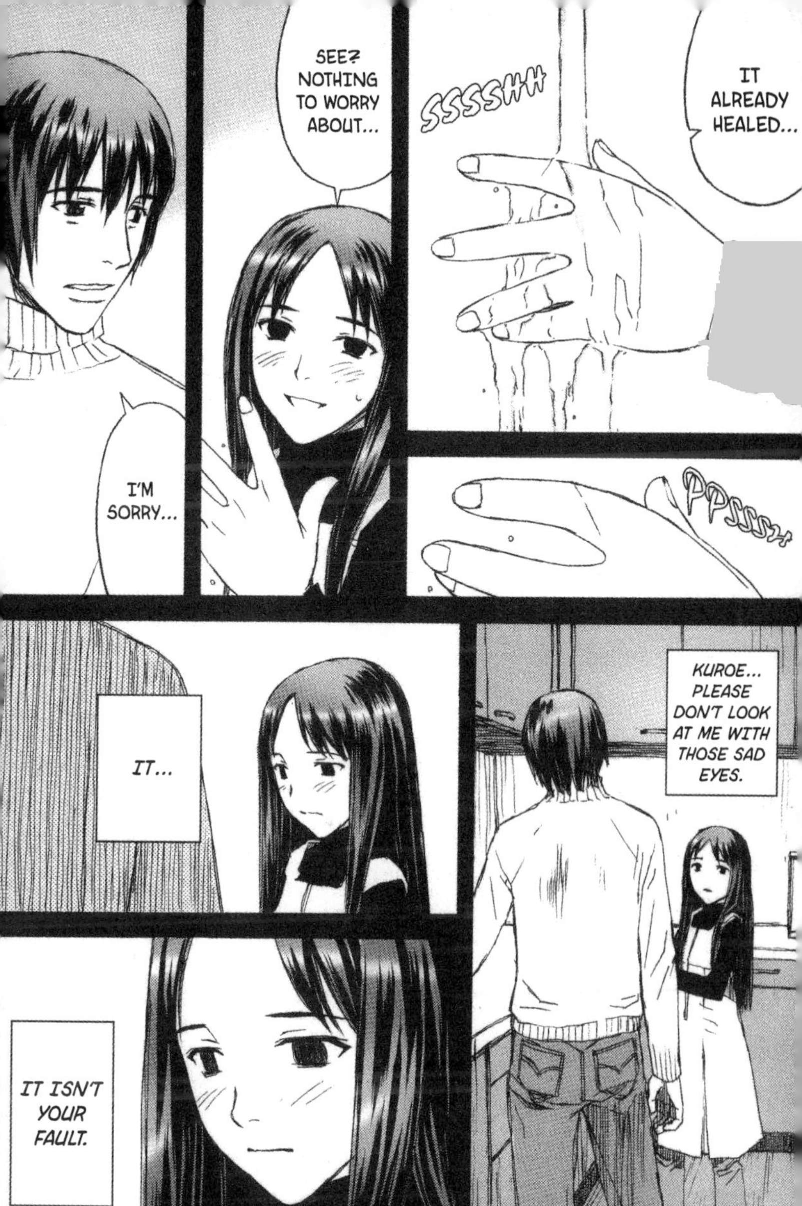
IT ALREADY HEALED...
SSSSHH
PPSSSH
SEE? NOTHING TO WORRY ABOUT...
I'M SORRY...
KUROE... PLEASE DON'T LOOK AT ME WITH THOSE SAD EYES.
IT...
IT ISN'T YOUR FAULT.

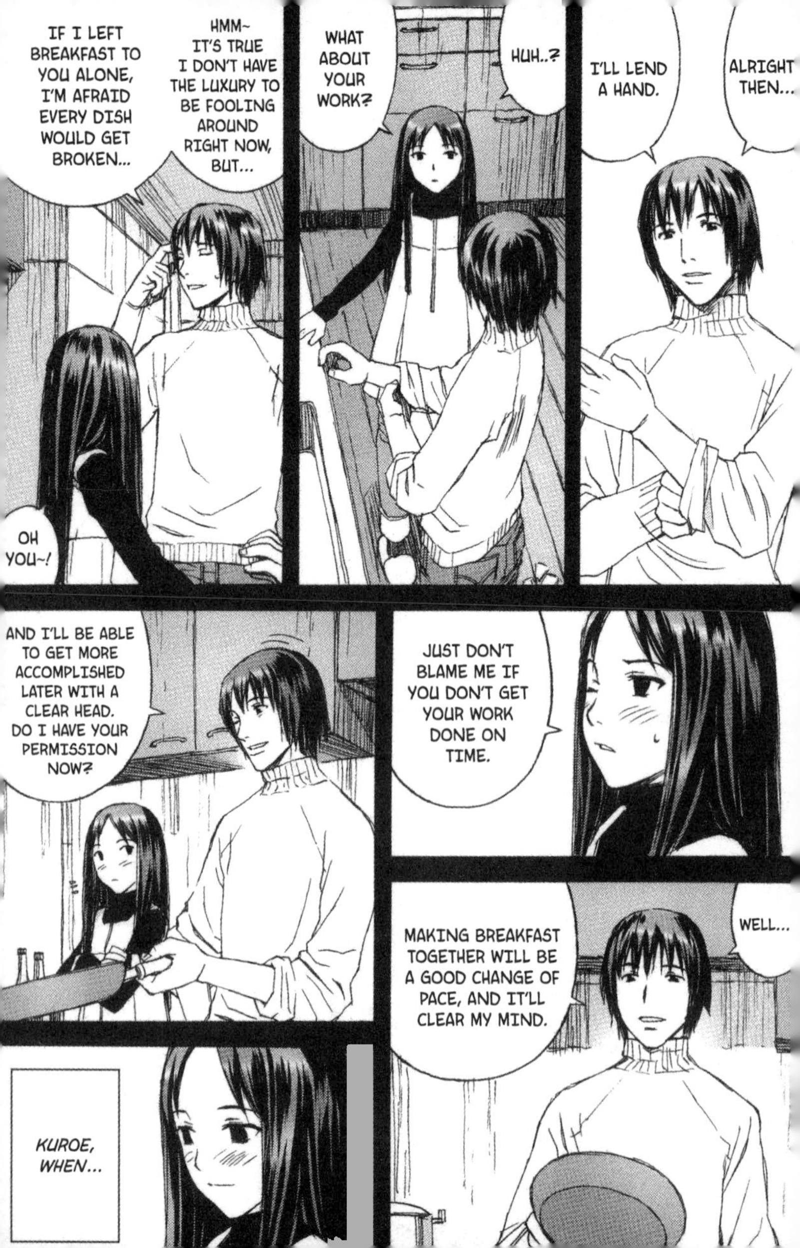

ALRIGHT THEN...
I'LL LEND A HAND.
HUH..?
WHAT ABOUT YOUR WORK?
HMM~ IT'S TRUE I DON'T HAVE THE LUXURY TO BE FOOLING AROUND RIGHT NOW, BUT...
IF I LEFT BREAKFAST TO YOU ALONE, I'M AFRAID EVERY DISH WOULD GET BROKEN...
OH YOU~!
WELL...
MAKING BREAKFAST TOGETHER WILL BE A GOOD CHANGE OF PACE, AND IT'LL CLEAR MY MIND.
AND I'LL BE ABLE TO GET MORE ACCOMPLISHED LATER WITH A CLEAR HEAD. DO I HAVE YOUR PERMISSION NOW?
JUST DON'T BLAME ME IF YOU DON'T GET YOUR WORK DONE ON TIME.
KUROE, WHEN...

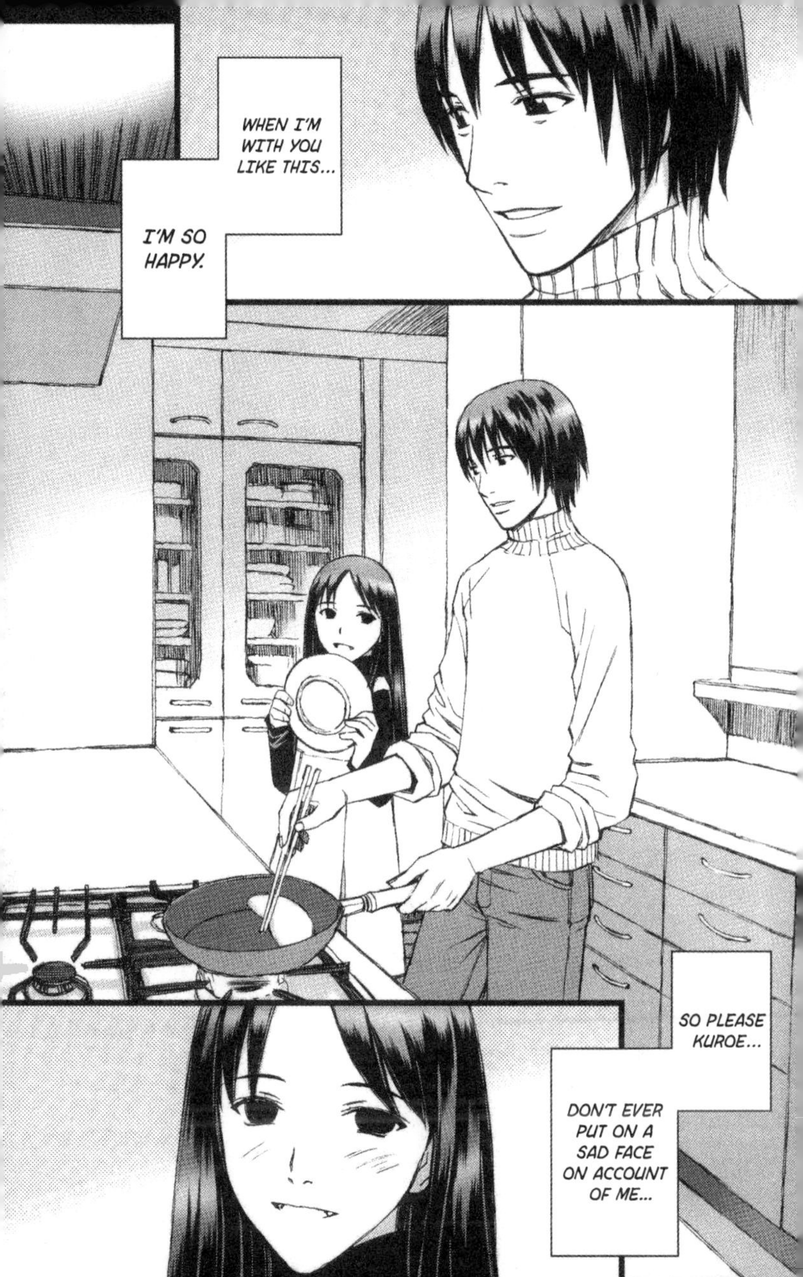
WHEN I'M WITH YOU LIKE THIS...
I'M SO HAPPY.
SO PLEASE KUROE...
DON'T EVER PUT ON A SAD FACE ON ACCOUNT OF ME...

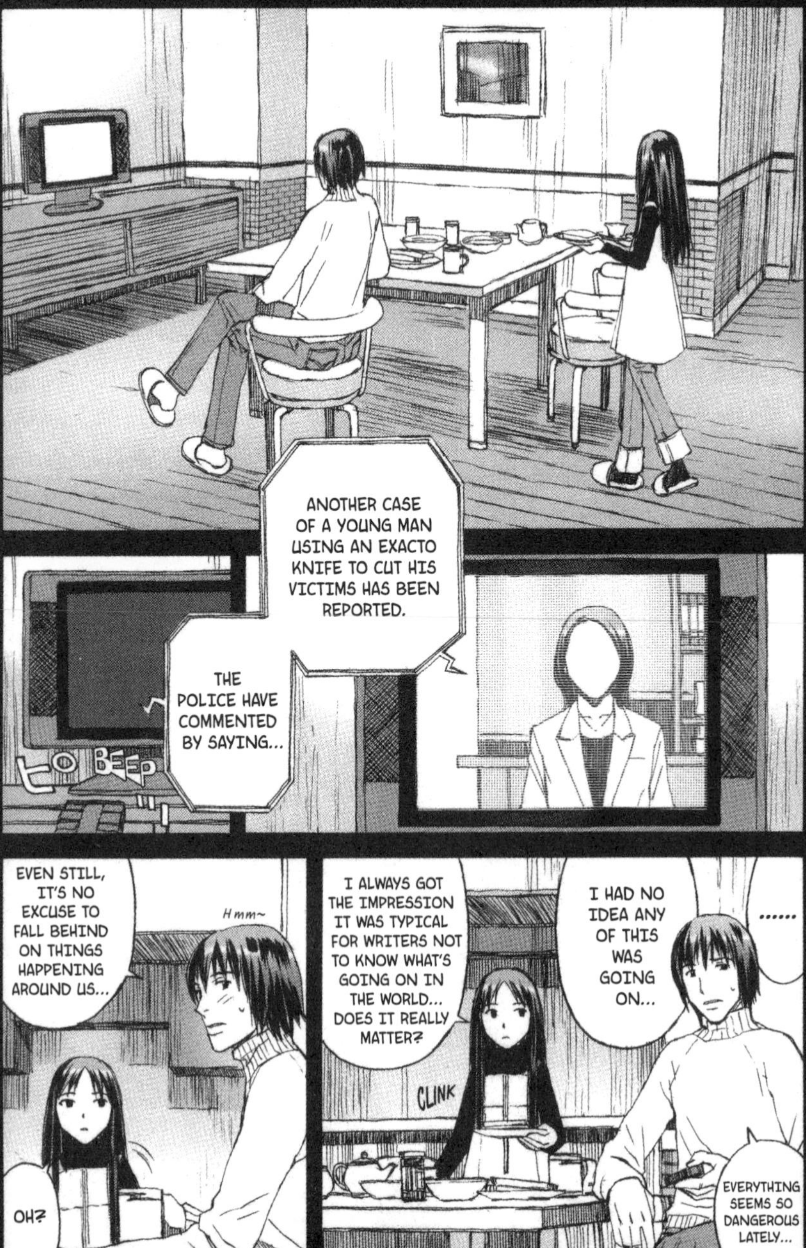
ANOTHER CASE OF A YOUNG MAN USING AN EXACTO KNIFE TO CUT HIS VICTIMS HAS BEEN REPORTED.
THE POLICE HAVE COMMENTED BY SAYING...
ヒ〇 BEEP
......
I HAD NO IDEA ANY OF THIS WAS GOING ON...
I ALWAYS GOT THE IMPRESSION IT WAS TYPICAL FOR WRITERS NOT TO KNOW WHAT'S GOING ON IN THE WORLD... DOES IT REALLY MATTER?
CLINK
EVERYTHING SEEMS SO DANGEROUS LATELY...
EVEN STILL, IT'S NO EXCUSE TO FALL BEHIND ON THINGS HAPPENING AROUND US...
Hmm~
OH?

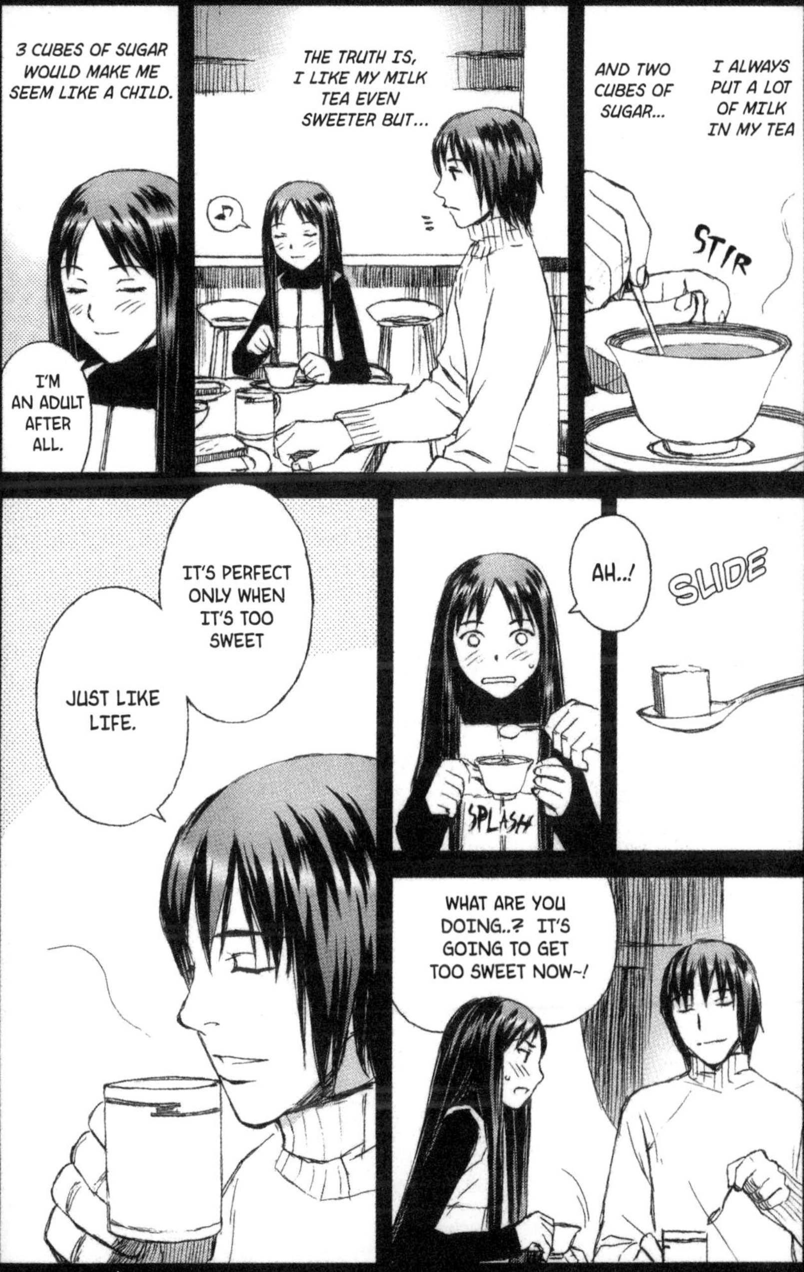
I ALWAYS PUT A LOT OF MILK IN MY TEA
AND TWO CUBES OF SUGAR...
STIR
THE TRUTH IS, I LIKE MY MILK TEA EVEN SWEETER BUT...
3 CUBES OF SUGAR WOULD MAKE ME SEEM LIKE A CHILD.
I'M AN ADULT AFTER ALL.
SLIDE
AH..!
SPLASH
WHAT ARE YOU DOING..? IT'S GOING TO GET TOO SWEET NOW~!
IT'S PERFECT ONLY WHEN IT'S TOO SWEET
JUST LIKE LIFE.

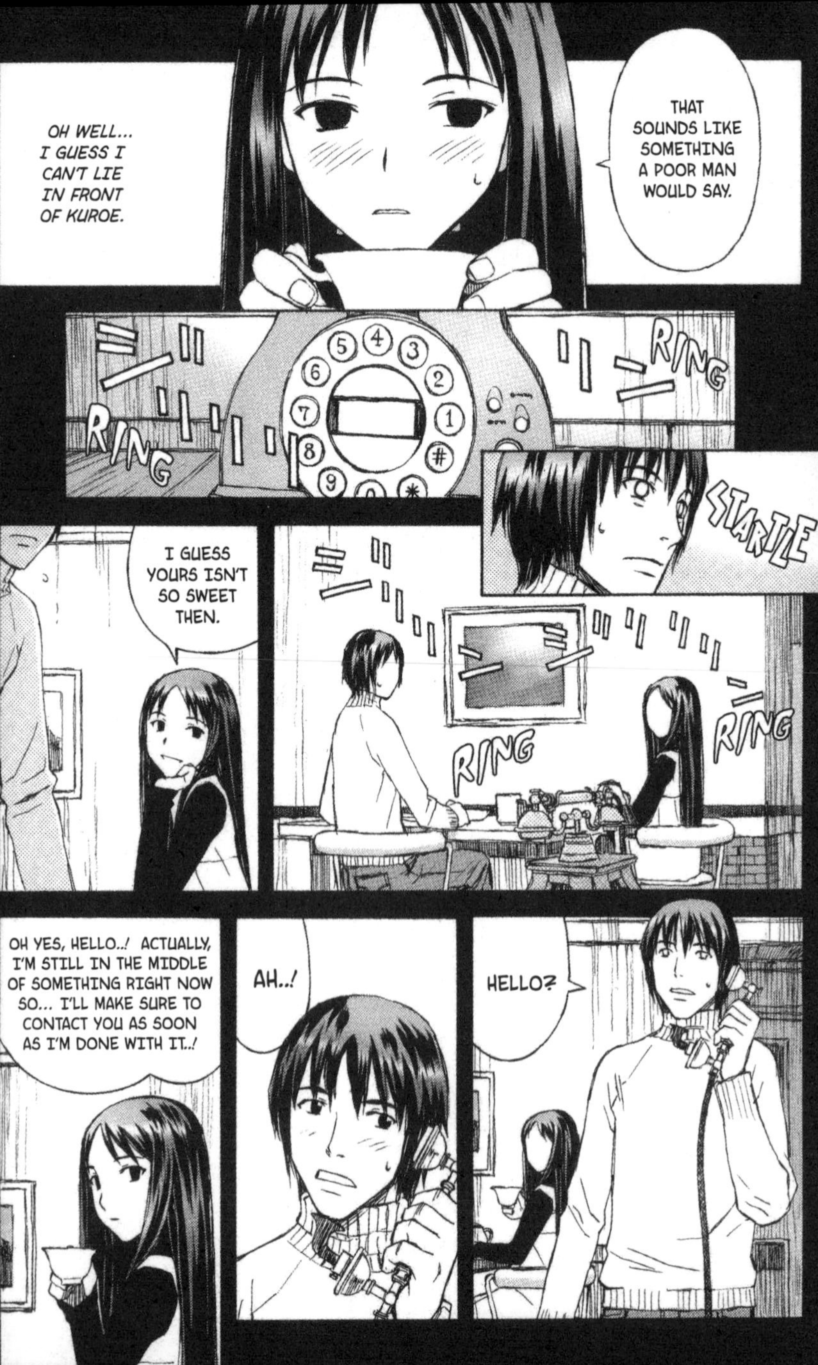
THAT SOUNDS LIKE SOMETHING A POOR MAN WOULD SAY.
OH WELL... I GUESS I CAN'T LIE IN FRONT OF KUROE.
RING
RING
STARTLE
RING
RING
I GUESS YOURS ISN'T SO SWEET THEN.
HELLO?
AH..!
OH YES, HELLO..! ACTUALLY, I'M STILL IN THE MIDDLE OF SOMETHING RIGHT NOW SO... I'LL MAKE SURE TO CONTACT YOU AS SOON AS I'M DONE WITH IT..!

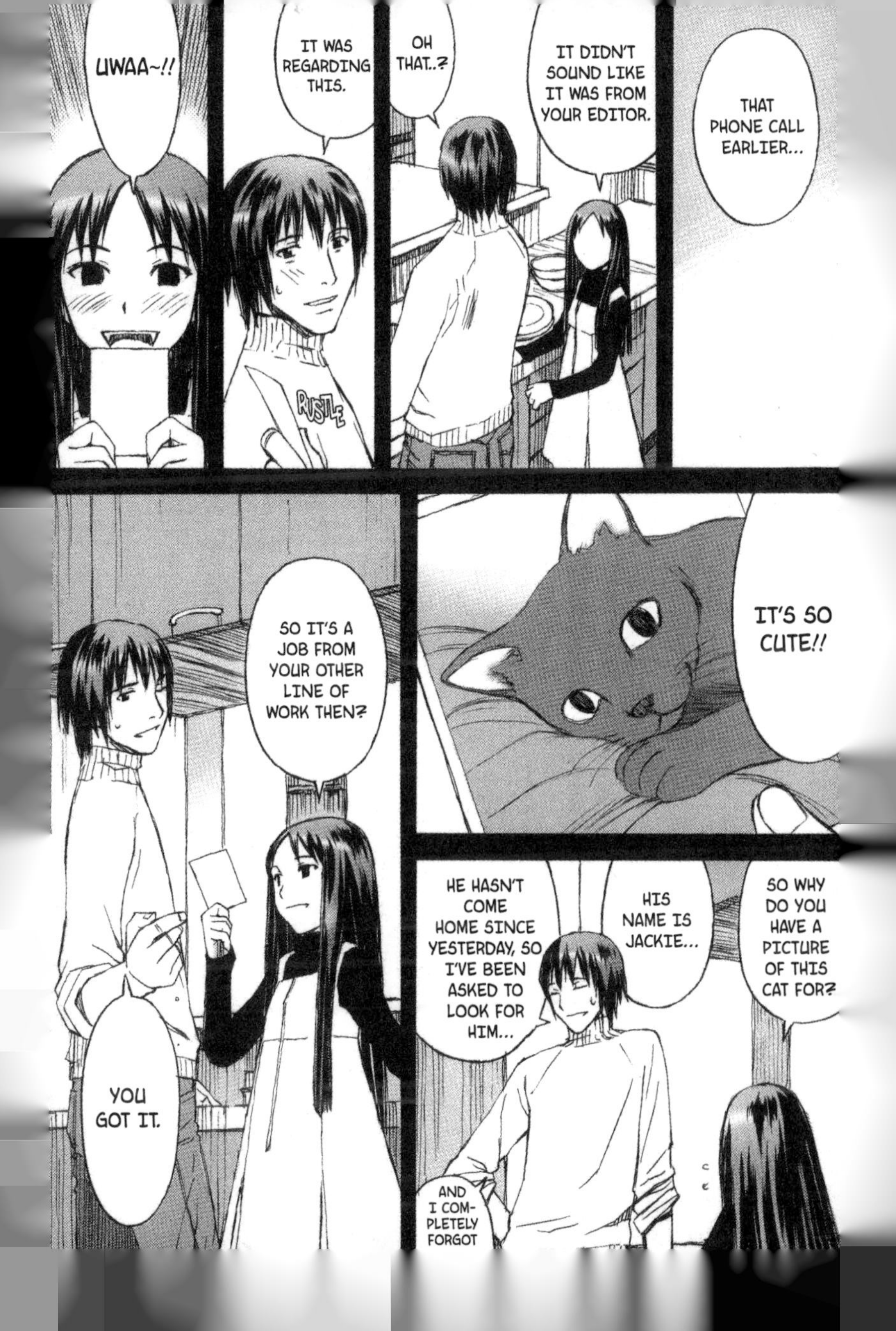
THAT PHONE CALL EARLIER...
IT DIDN'T SOUND LIKE IT WAS FROM YOUR EDITOR.
OH THAT..?
IT WAS REGARDING THIS.
RUSTLE
UWAA~!!
IT'S SO CUTE!!
SO WHY DO YOU HAVE A PICTURE OF THIS CAT FOR?
HIS NAME IS JACKIE...
HE HASN'T COME HOME SINCE YESTERDAY, SO I'VE BEEN ASKED TO LOOK FOR HIM...
AND I COM-PLETELY FORGOT
SO IT'S A JOB FROM YOUR OTHER LINE OF WORK THEN?
YOU GOT IT.

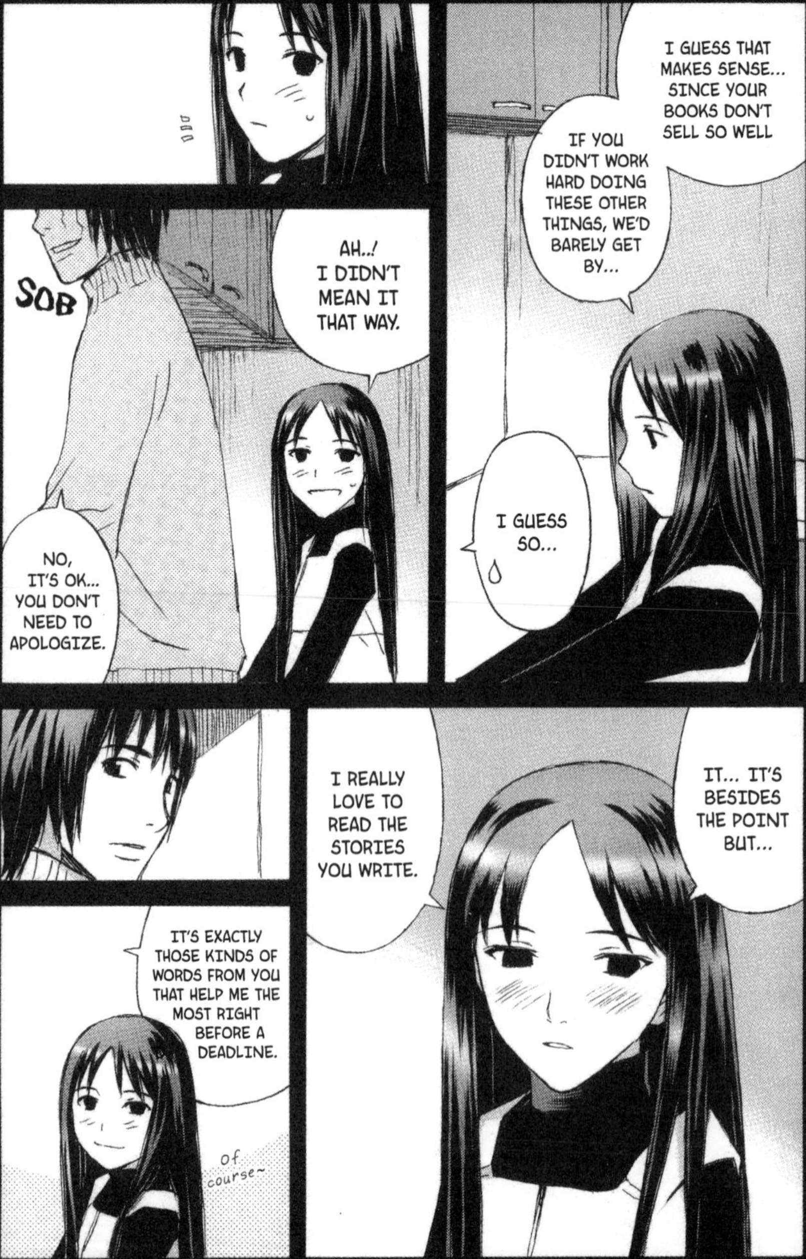
I GUESS THAT MAKES SENSE... SINCE YOUR BOOKS DON'T SELL SO WELL
IF YOU DIDN'T WORK HARD DOING THESE OTHER THINGS, WE'D BARELY GET BY...
I GUESS SO...
AH..! I DIDN'T MEAN IT THAT WAY.
SOB
NO, IT'S OK... YOU DON'T NEED TO APOLOGIZE.
IT... IT'S BESIDES THE POINT BUT...
I REALLY LOVE TO READ THE STORIES YOU WRITE.
IT'S EXACTLY THOSE KINDS OF WORDS FROM YOU THAT HELP ME THE MOST RIGHT BEFORE A DEADLINE.
Of course~

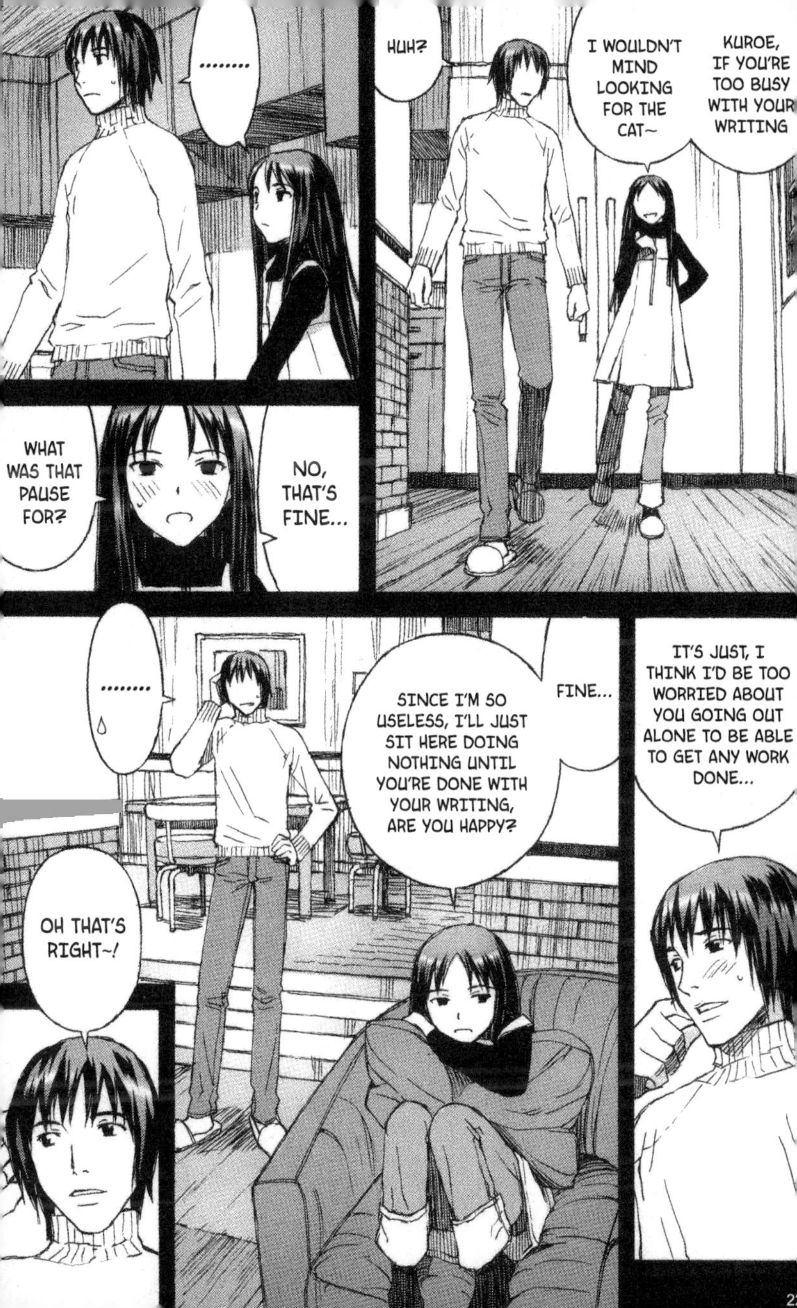
KUROE, IF YOU'RE TOO BUSY WITH YOUR WRITING
I WOULDN'T MIND LOOKING FOR THE CAT~
HUH?
....
NO, THAT'S FINE...
WHAT WAS THAT PAUSE FOR?
IT'S JUST, I THINK I'D BE TOO WORRIED ABOUT YOU GOING OUT ALONE TO BE ABLE TO GET ANY WORK DONE...
FINE...
SINCE I'M SO USELESS, I'LL JUST SIT HERE DOING NOTHING UNTIL YOU'RE DONE WITH YOUR WRITING, ARE YOU HAPPY?
....
OH THAT'S RIGHT~!

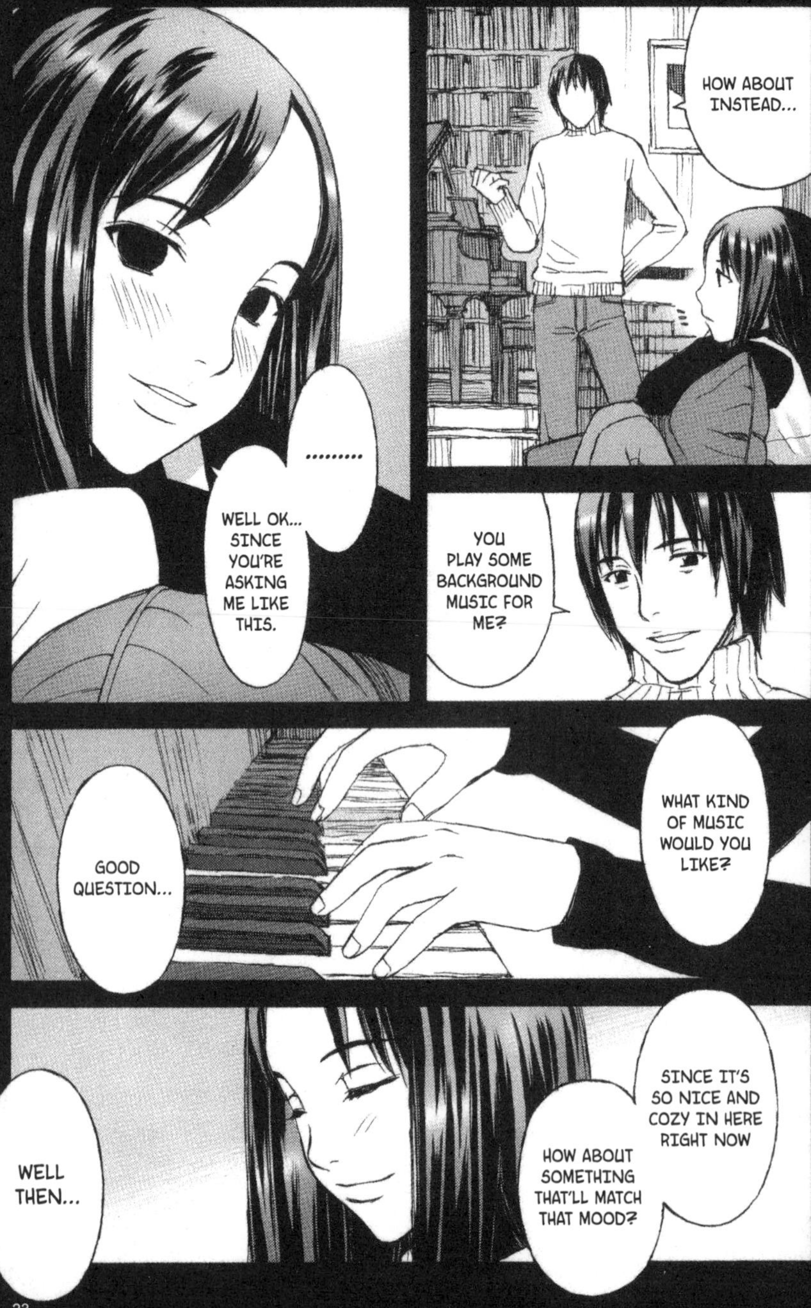
HOW ABOUT INSTEAD...
YOU PLAY SOME BACKGROUND MUSIC FOR ME?
....
WELL OK... SINCE YOU'RE ASKING ME LIKE THIS.
WHAT KIND OF MUSIC WOULD YOU LIKE?
GOOD QUESTION...
SINCE IT'S SO NICE AND COZY IN HERE RIGHT NOW
HOW ABOUT SOMETHING THAT'LL MATCH THAT MOOD?
WELL THEN...

Episode 1

ORDINARY LIFE

ありふれた日常 – An Ordinary Day

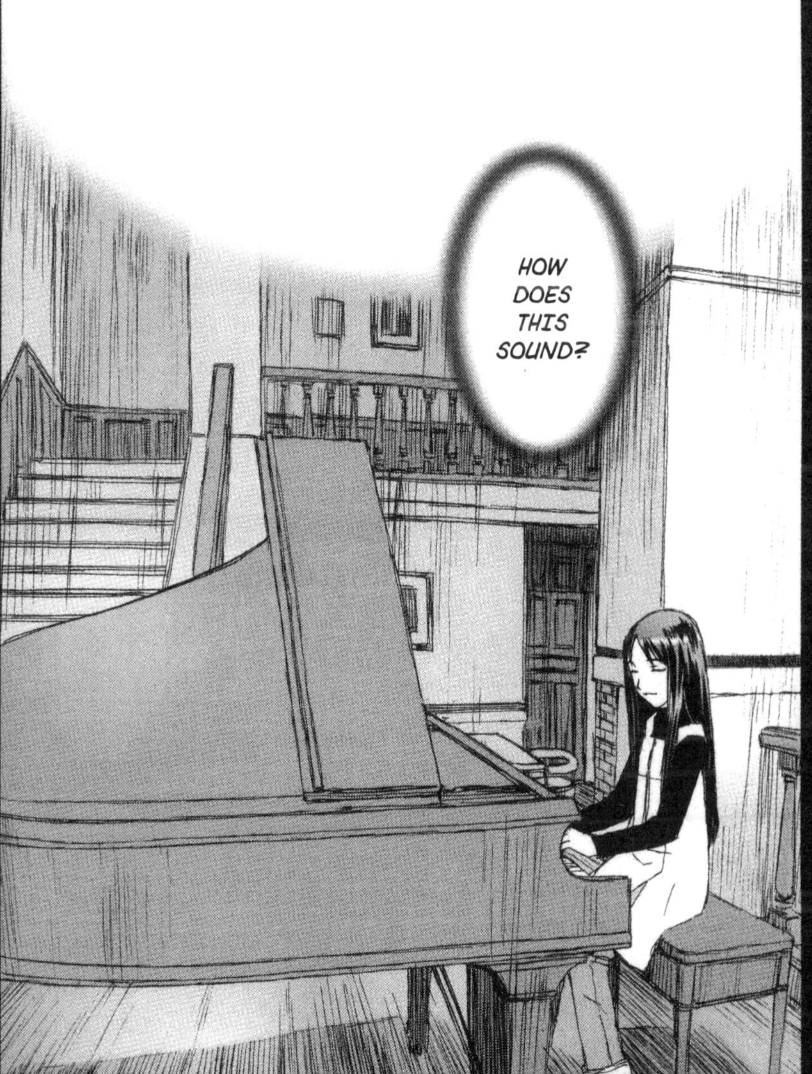
HOW DOES THIS SOUND?

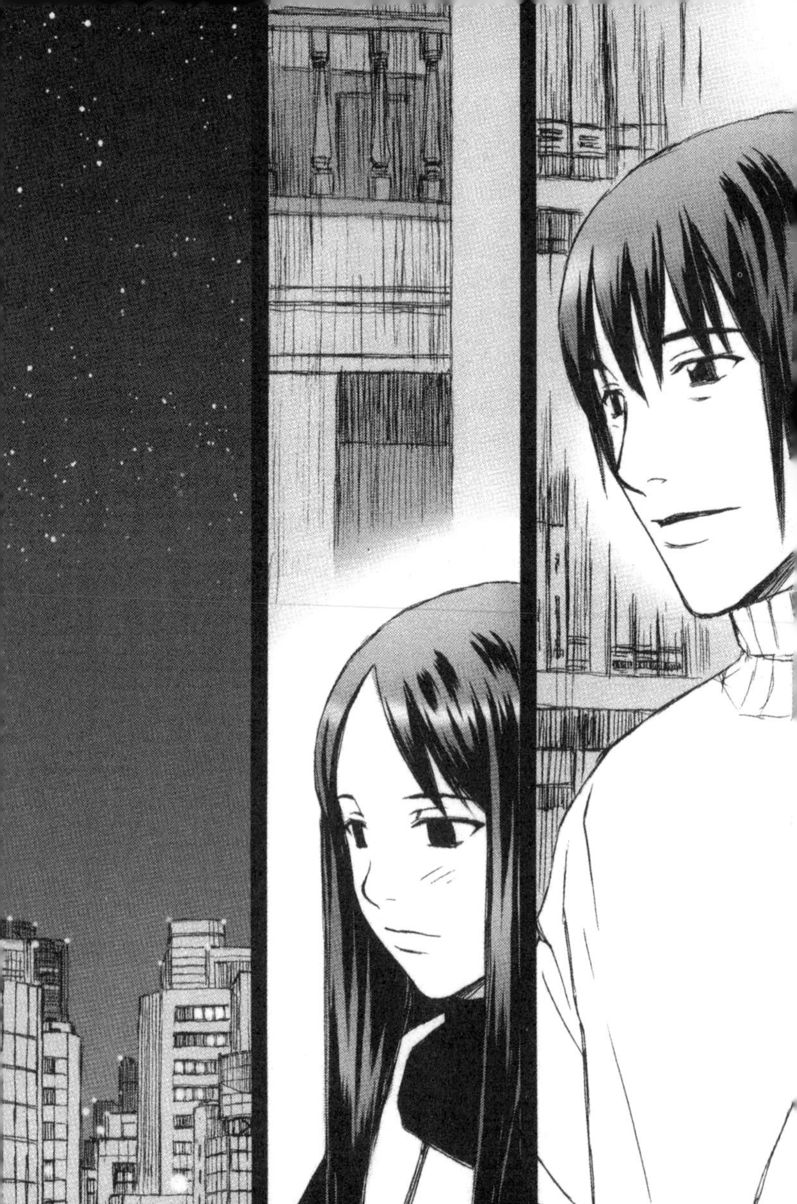

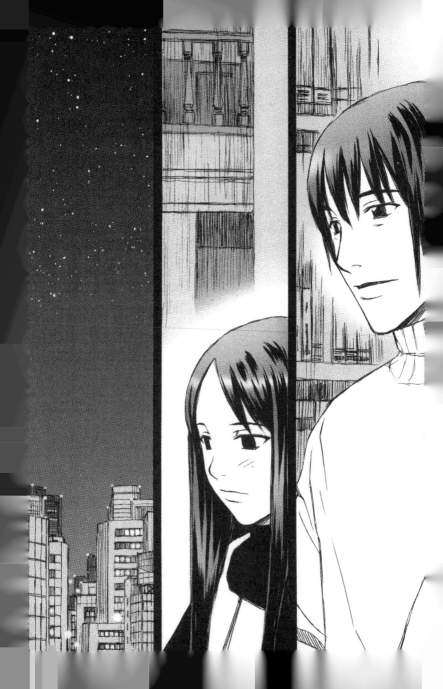

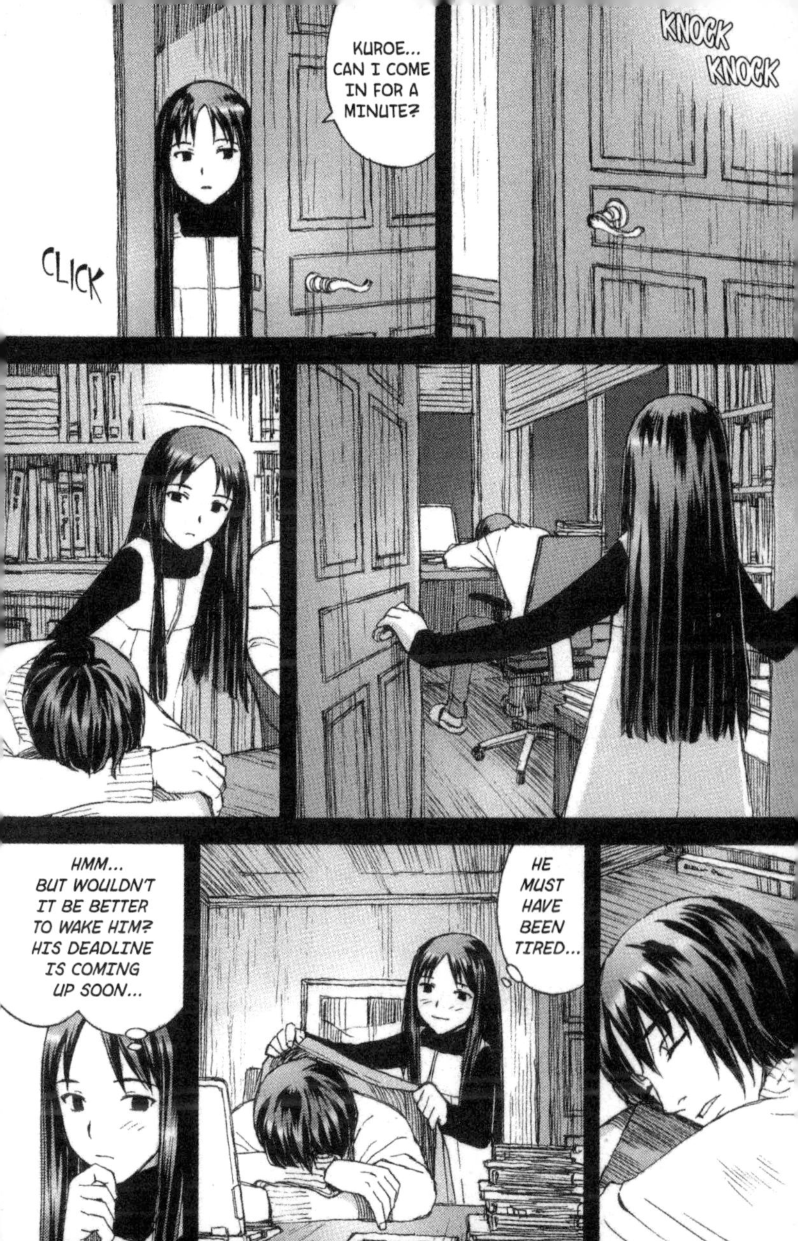
KNOCK KNOCK
CLICK
KUROE... CAN I COME IN FOR A MINUTE?
HE MUST HAVE BEEN TIRED...
HMM... BUT WOULDN'T IT BE BETTER TO WAKE HIM? HIS DEADLINE IS COMING UP SOON...

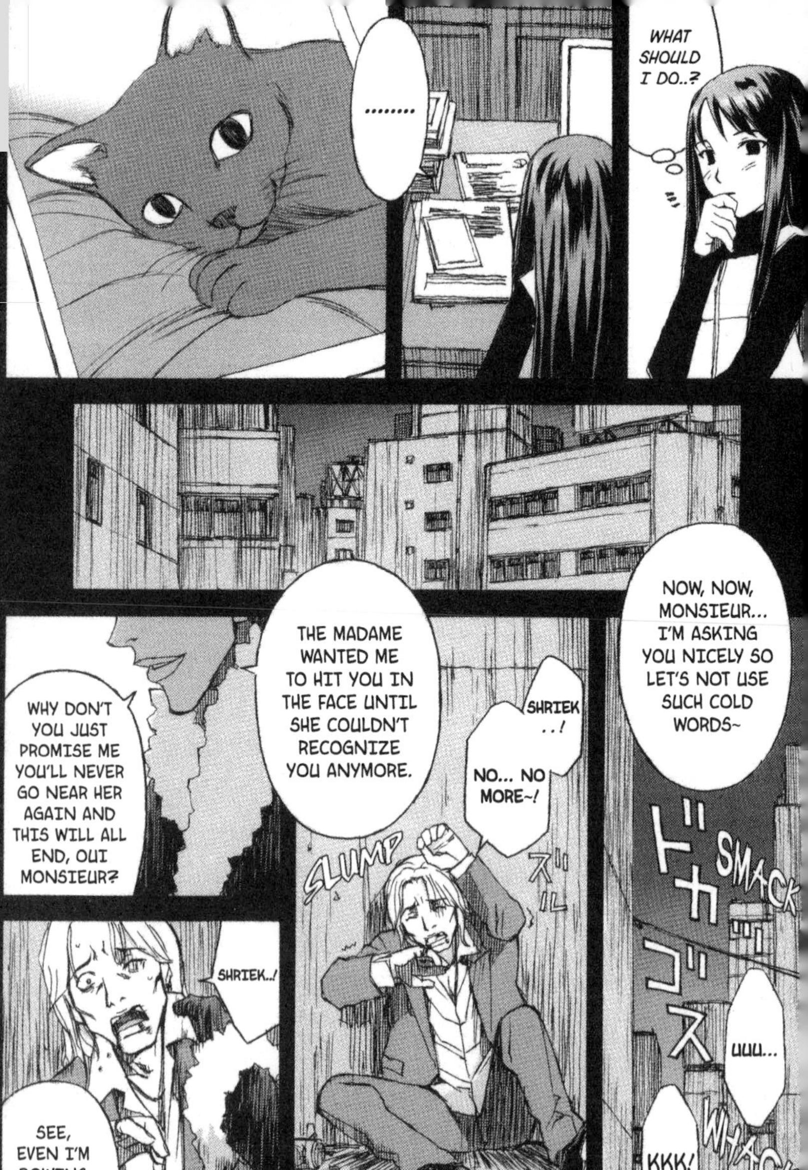
WHAT SHOULD I DO..?
....
NOW, NOW, MONSIEUR... I'M ASKING YOU NICELY SO LET'S NOT USE SUCH COLD WORDS~
ドカッ
SMACK
ゴス
UUU...
KKK!
WHACK
SHRIEK..!
NO... NO MORE~!
ズル
SLUMP
THE MADAME WANTED ME TO HIT YOU IN THE FACE UNTIL SHE COULDN'T RECOGNIZE YOU ANYMORE.
WHY DON'T YOU JUST PROMISE ME YOU'LL NEVER GO NEAR HER AGAIN AND THIS WILL ALL END, OUI MONSIEUR?
SHRIEK..!
SEE, EVEN I'M BOWING MY HEAD LIKE THIS...

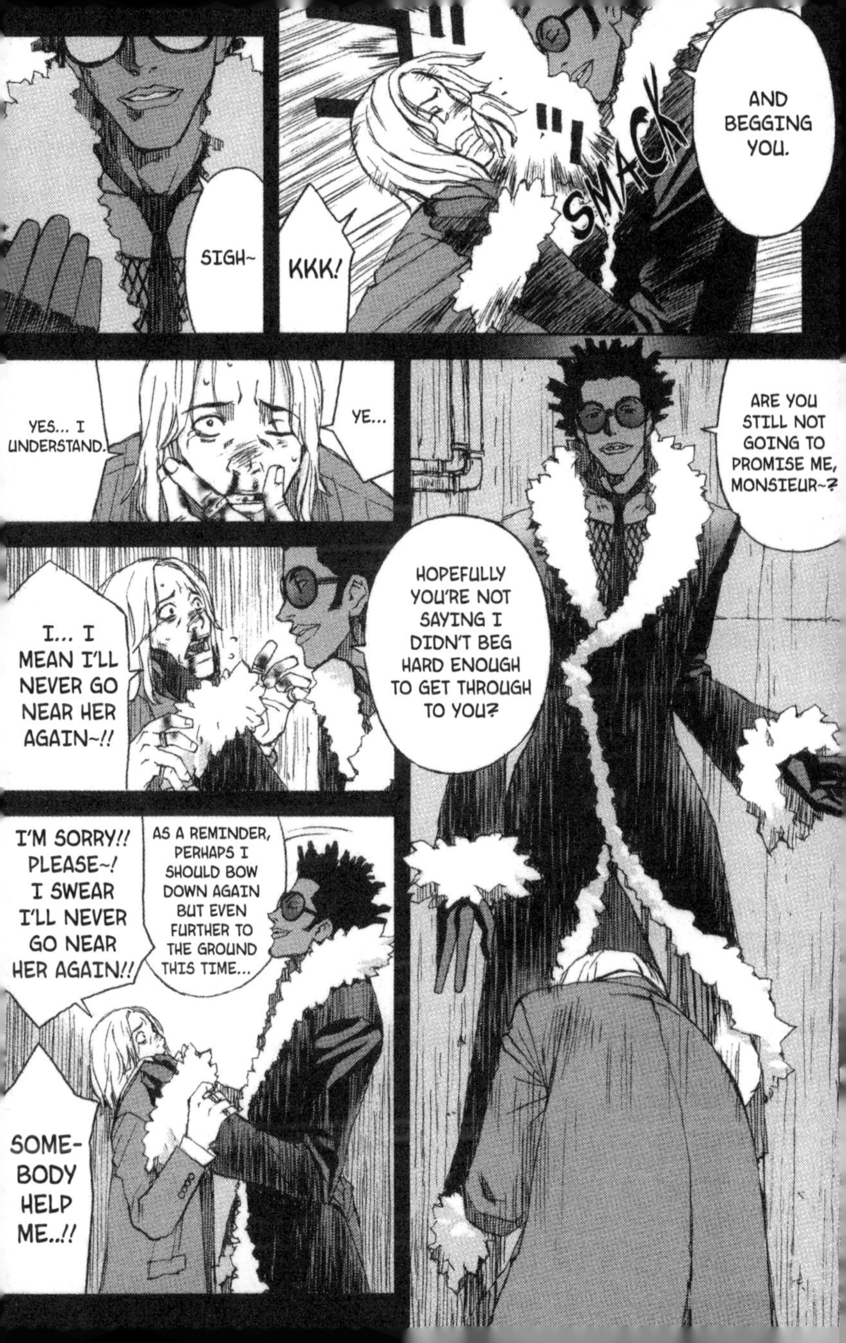
AND BEGGING YOU.
SMACK
KKK!
SIGH~
ARE YOU STILL NOT GOING TO PROMISE ME, MONSIEUR~?
HOPEFULLY YOU'RE NOT SAYING I DIDN'T BEG HARD ENOUGH TO GET THROUGH TO YOU?
YE...
YES... I UNDERSTAND.
I... I MEAN I'LL NEVER GO NEAR HER AGAIN~!!
AS A REMINDER, PERHAPS I SHOULD BOW DOWN AGAIN BUT EVEN FURTHER TO THE GROUND THIS TIME...
I'M SORRY!! PLEASE~! I SWEAR I'LL NEVER GO NEAR HER AGAIN!!
SOME-BODY HELP ME..!!

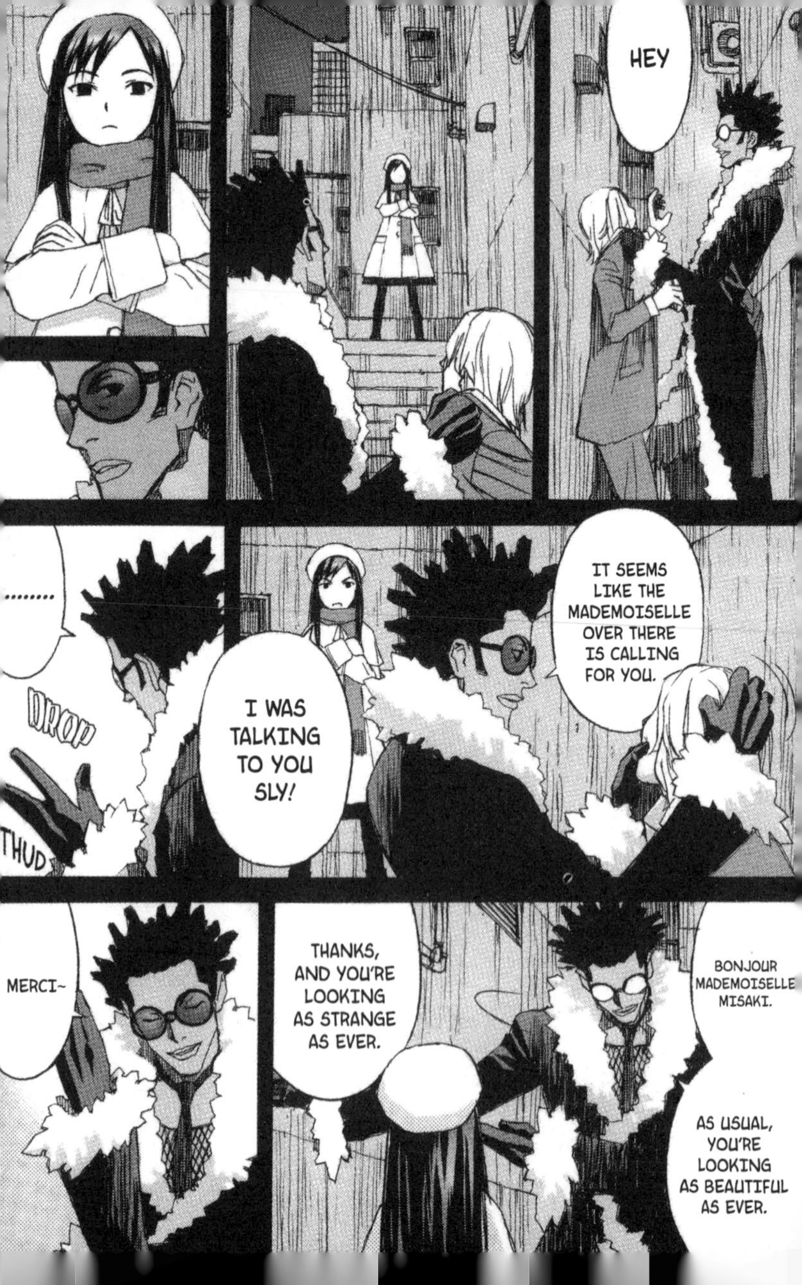
HEY
IT SEEMS LIKE THE MADEMOISELLE OVER THERE IS CALLING FOR YOU.
I WAS TALKING TO YOU SLY!
....
DROP
THUD
BONJOUR MADEMOISELLE MISAKI.
AS USUAL, YOU'RE LOOKING AS BEAUTIFUL AS EVER.
THANKS, AND YOU'RE LOOKING AS STRANGE AS EVER.
MERCI~

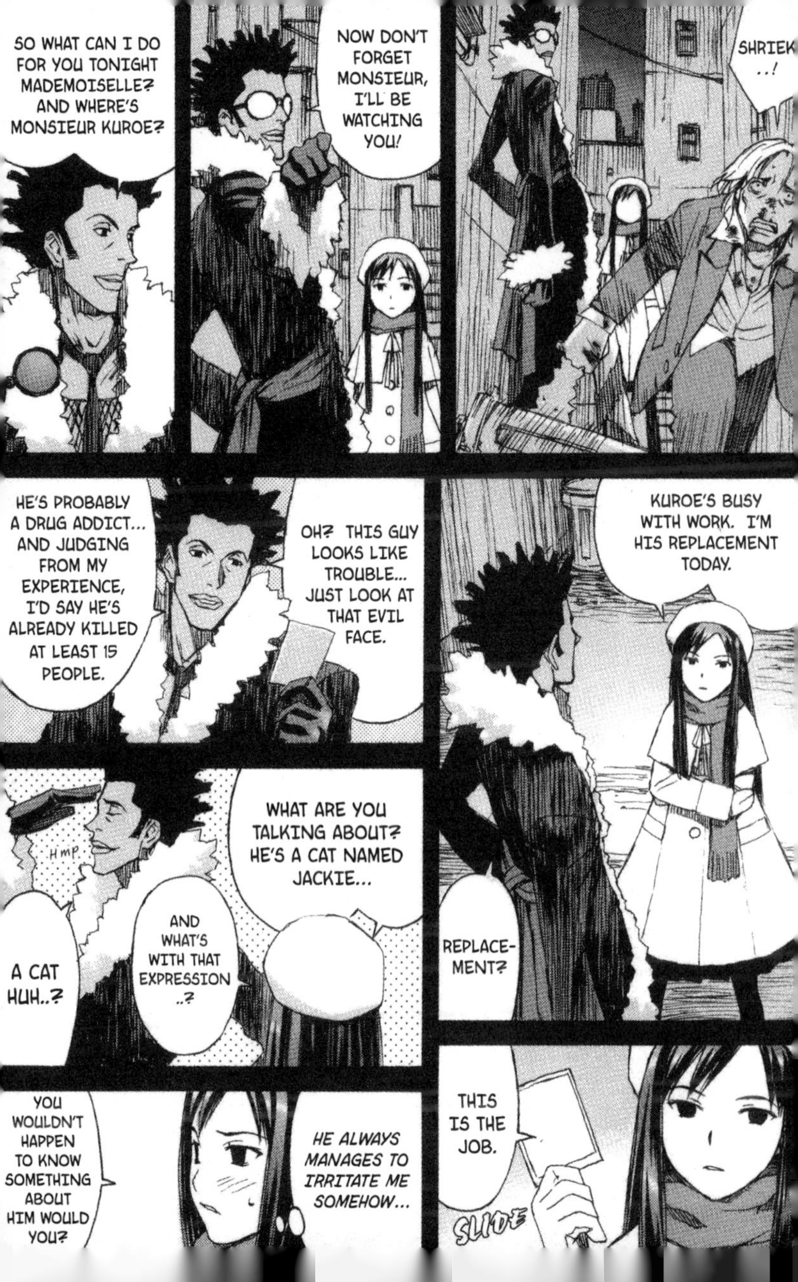
SHRIEK ..!
NOW DON'T FORGET MONSIEUR, I'LL BE WATCHING YOU!
SO WHAT CAN I DO FOR YOU TONIGHT MADEMOISELLE? AND WHERE'S MONSIEUR KUROE?
KUROE'S BUSY WITH WORK. I'M HIS REPLACEMENT TODAY.
REPLACE-MENT?
OH? THIS GUY LOOKS LIKE TROUBLE... JUST LOOK AT THAT EVIL FACE.
HE'S PROBABLY A DRUG ADDICT... AND JUDGING FROM MY EXPERIENCE, I'D SAY HE'S ALREADY KILLED AT LEAST 15 PEOPLE.
WHAT ARE YOU TALKING ABOUT? HE'S A CAT NAMED JACKIE...
Hmp.
A CAT HUH..?
AND WHAT'S WITH THAT EXPRESSION ..?
THIS IS THE JOB.
SLIDE
HE ALWAYS MANAGES TO IRRITATE ME SOMEHOW...
YOU WOULDN'T HAPPEN TO KNOW SOMETHING ABOUT HIM WOULD YOU?

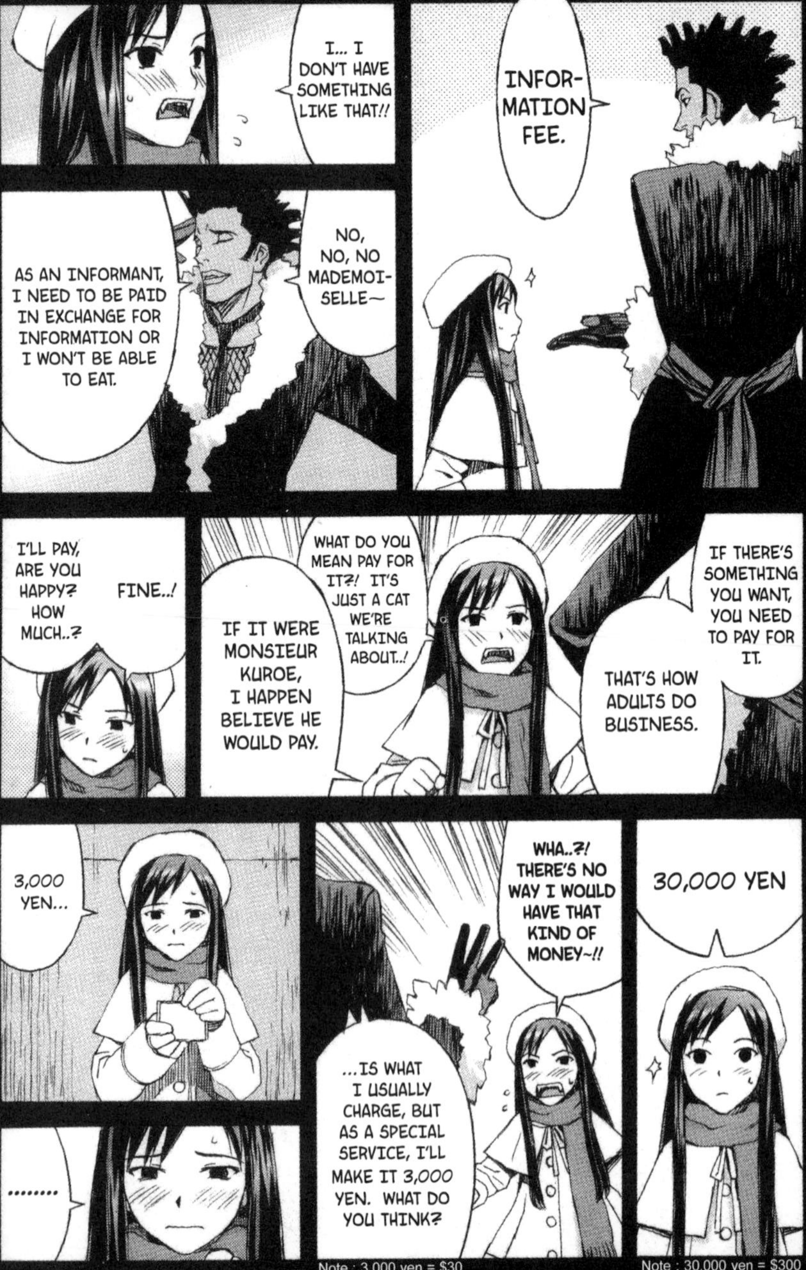
INFOR-MATION FEE.
I... I DON'T HAVE SOMETHING LIKE THAT!!
NO, NO, NO MADEMOI-SELLE~
AS AN INFORMANT, I NEED TO BE PAID IN EXCHANGE FOR INFORMATION OR I WON'T BE ABLE TO EAT.
IF THERE'S SOMETHING YOU WANT, YOU NEED TO PAY FOR IT.
THAT'S HOW ADULTS DO BUSINESS.
WHAT DO YOU MEAN PAY FOR IT?! IT'S JUST A CAT WE'RE TALKING ABOUT..!
IF IT WERE MONSIEUR KUROE, I HAPPEN BELIEVE HE WOULD PAY.
FINE..!
I'LL PAY, ARE YOU HAPPY? HOW MUCH..?
30,000 YEN
WHA..?! THERE'S NO WAY I WOULD HAVE THAT KIND OF MONEY~!!
...IS WHAT I USUALLY CHARGE, BUT AS A SPECIAL SERVICE, I'LL MAKE IT 3,000 YEN. WHAT DO YOU THINK?
3,000 YEN...
....

Note : 30,000 yen = $300

Note : 3,000 yen = $30

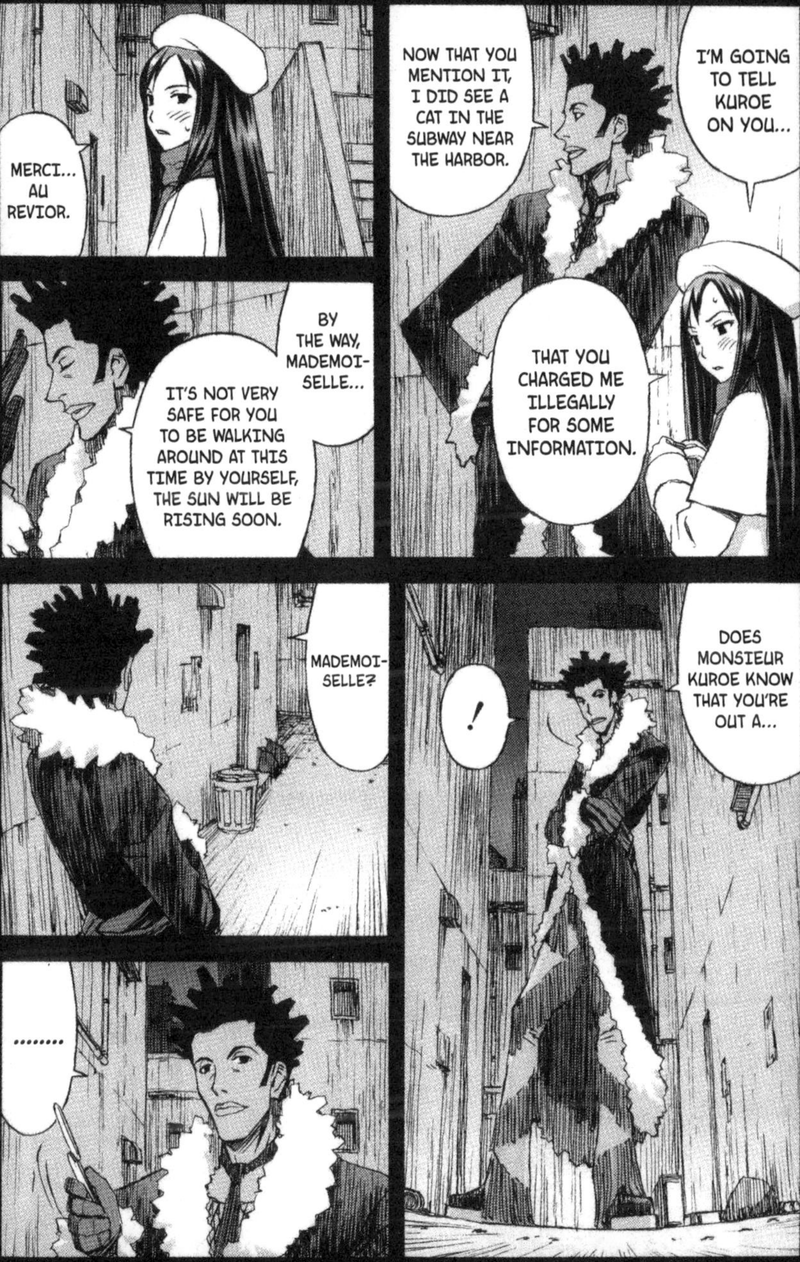
I'M GOING TO TELL KUROE ON YOU...
NOW THAT YOU MENTION IT, I DID SEE A CAT IN THE SUBWAY NEAR THE HARBOR.
THAT YOU CHARGED ME ILLEGALLY FOR SOME INFORMATION.
MERCI... AU REVIOR.
BY THE WAY, MADEMOI-SELLE...
IT'S NOT VERY SAFE FOR YOU TO BE WALKING AROUND AT THIS TIME BY YOURSELF, THE SUN WILL BE RISING SOON.
DOES MONSIEUR KUROE KNOW THAT YOU'RE OUT A...
!
MADEMOI-SELLE?
....

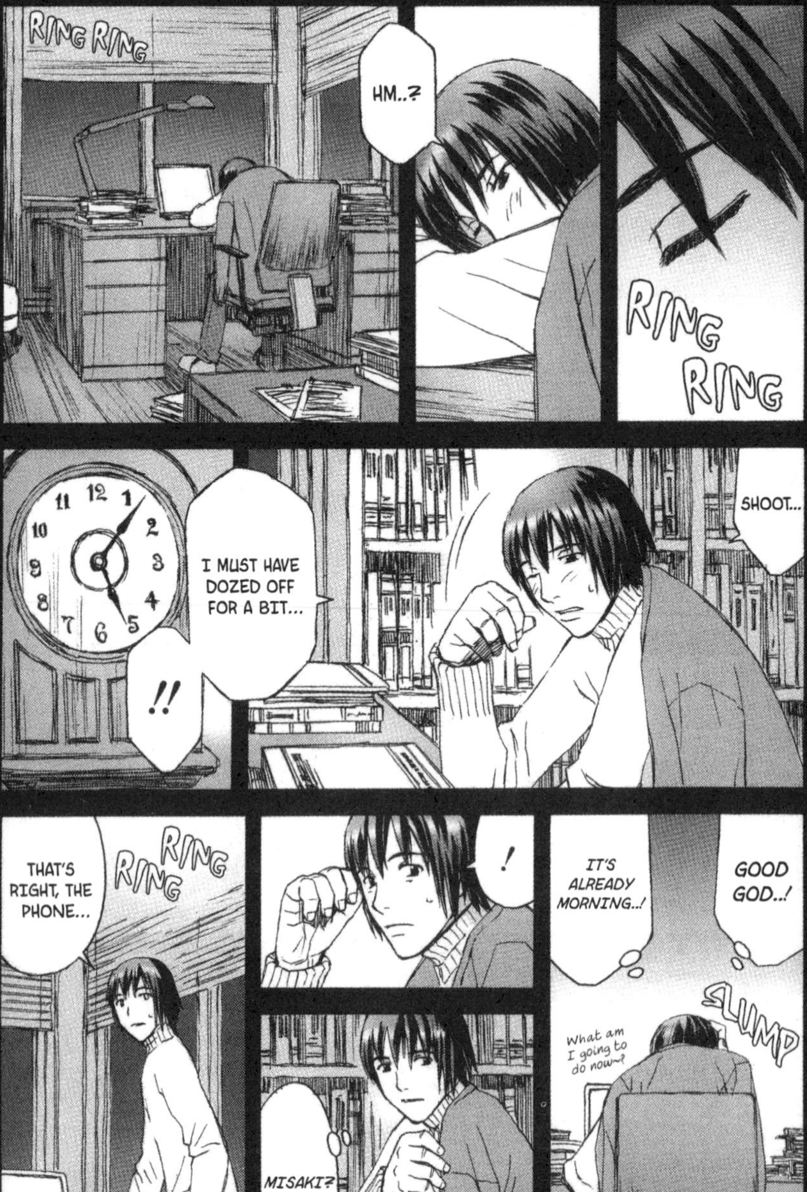
RING RING
HM..?
RING RING
RING RING
SHOOT...
I MUST HAVE DOZED OFF FOR A BIT...
!!
GOOD GOD..!
IT'S ALREADY MORNING..!
SLUMP
What am I going to do now~?
!
MISAKI?
RING RING
THAT'S RIGHT, THE PHONE...

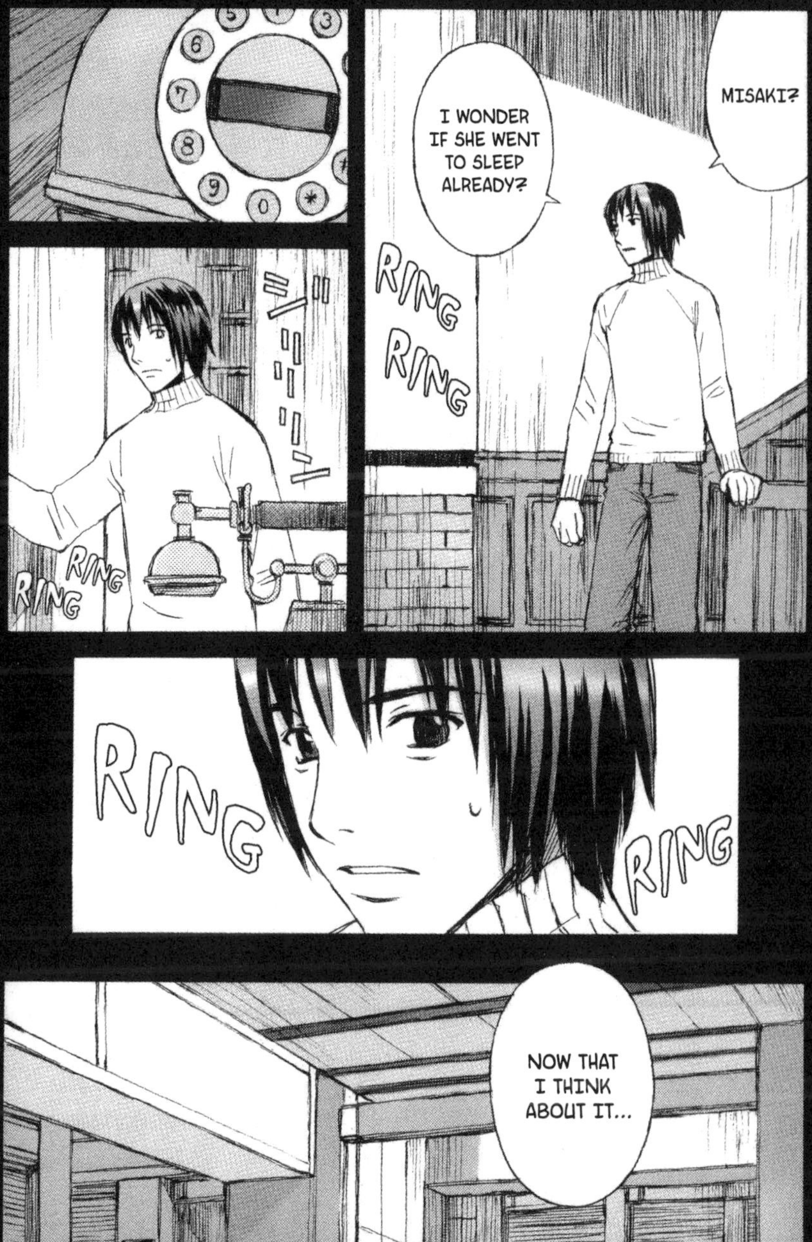
MISAKI?
I WONDER IF SHE WENT TO SLEEP ALREADY?
RING RING
RING RING
RING
RING
NOW THAT I THINK ABOUT IT...

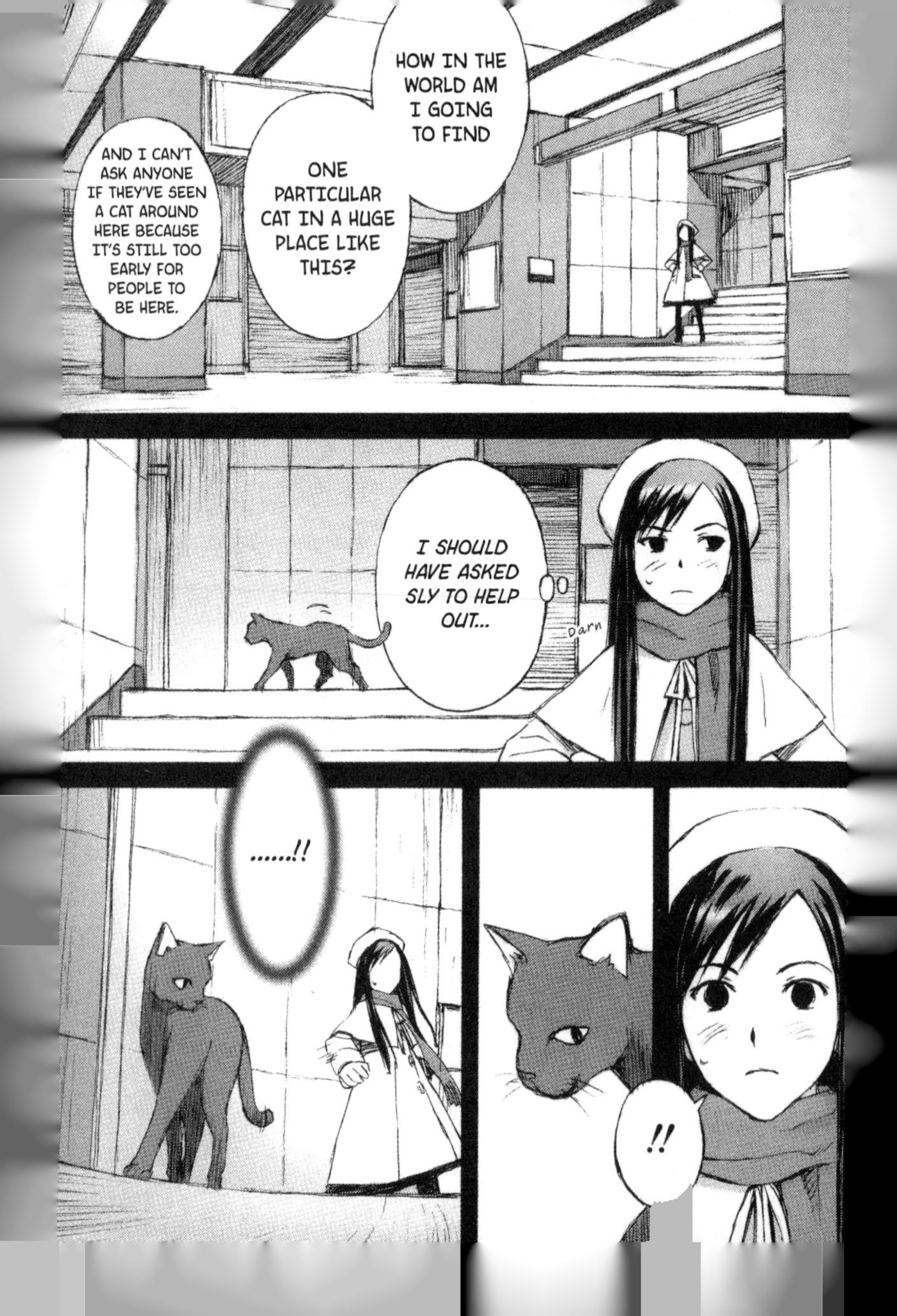
HOW IN THE WORLD AM I GOING TO FIND
ONE PARTICULAR CAT IN A HUGE PLACE LIKE THIS?
AND I CAN'T ASK ANYONE IF THEY'VE SEEN A CAT AROUND HERE BECAUSE IT'S STILL TOO EARLY FOR PEOPLE TO BE HERE.
I SHOULD HAVE ASKED SLY TO HELP OUT...
Darn
!!
......!!

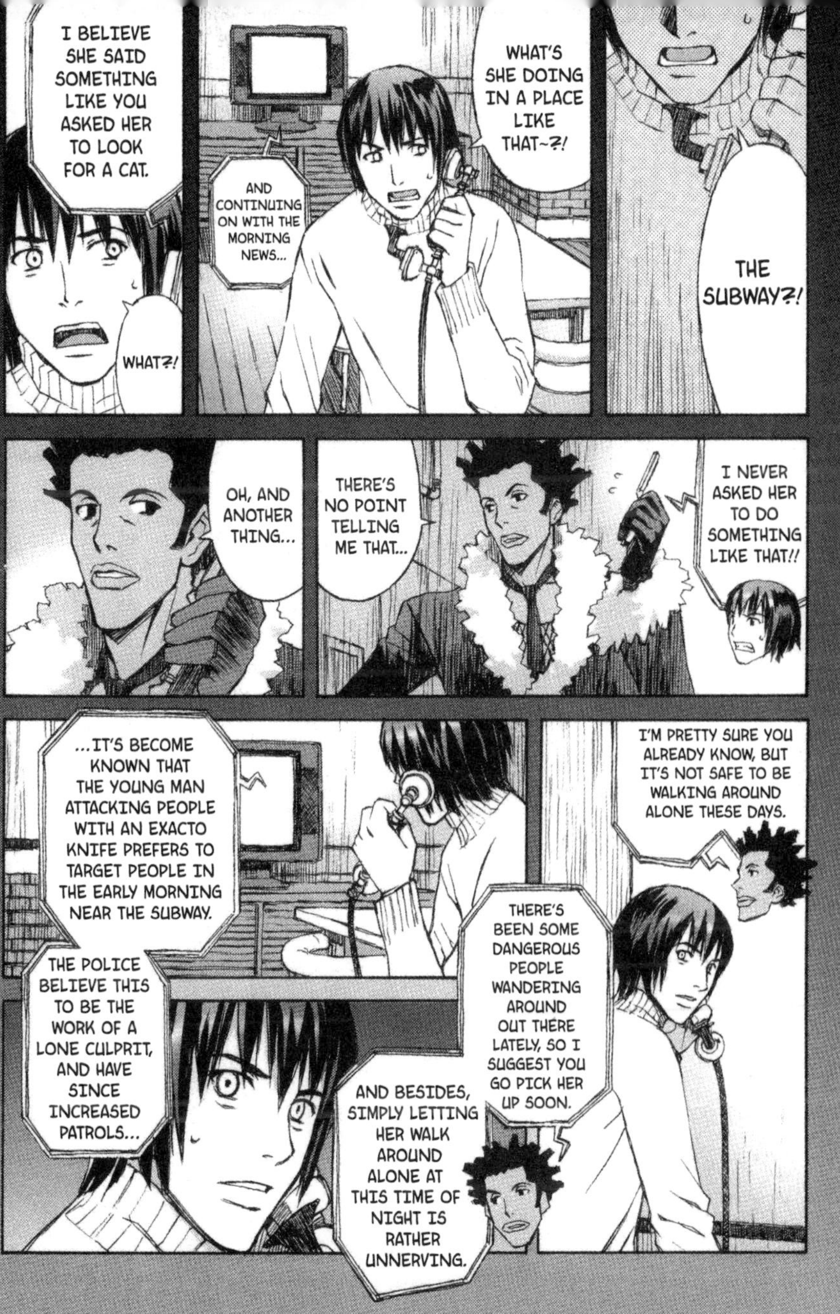
THE SUBWAY?!
WHAT'S SHE DOING IN A PLACE LIKE THAT~?!
AND CONTINUING ON WITH THE MORNING NEWS...
I BELIEVE SHE SAID SOMETHING LIKE YOU ASKED HER TO LOOK FOR A CAT.
WHAT?!
I NEVER ASKED HER TO DO SOMETHING LIKE THAT!!
THERE'S NO POINT TELLING ME THAT...
OH, AND ANOTHER THING...
I'M PRETTY SURE YOU ALREADY KNOW, BUT IT'S NOT SAFE TO BE WALKING AROUND ALONE THESE DAYS.
THERE'S BEEN SOME DANGEROUS PEOPLE WANDERING AROUND OUT THERE LATELY, SO I SUGGEST YOU GO PICK HER UP SOON.
AND BESIDES, SIMPLY LETTING HER WALK AROUND ALONE AT THIS TIME OF NIGHT IS RATHER UNNERVING.
...IT'S BECOME KNOWN THAT THE YOUNG MAN ATTACKING PEOPLE WITH AN EXACTO KNIFE PREFERS TO TARGET PEOPLE IN THE EARLY MORNING NEAR THE SUBWAY.
THE POLICE BELIEVE THIS TO BE THE WORK OF A LONE CULPRIT, AND HAVE SINCE INCREASED PATROLS...

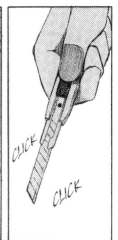

CLICK

CLICK

HAAA

HAAA

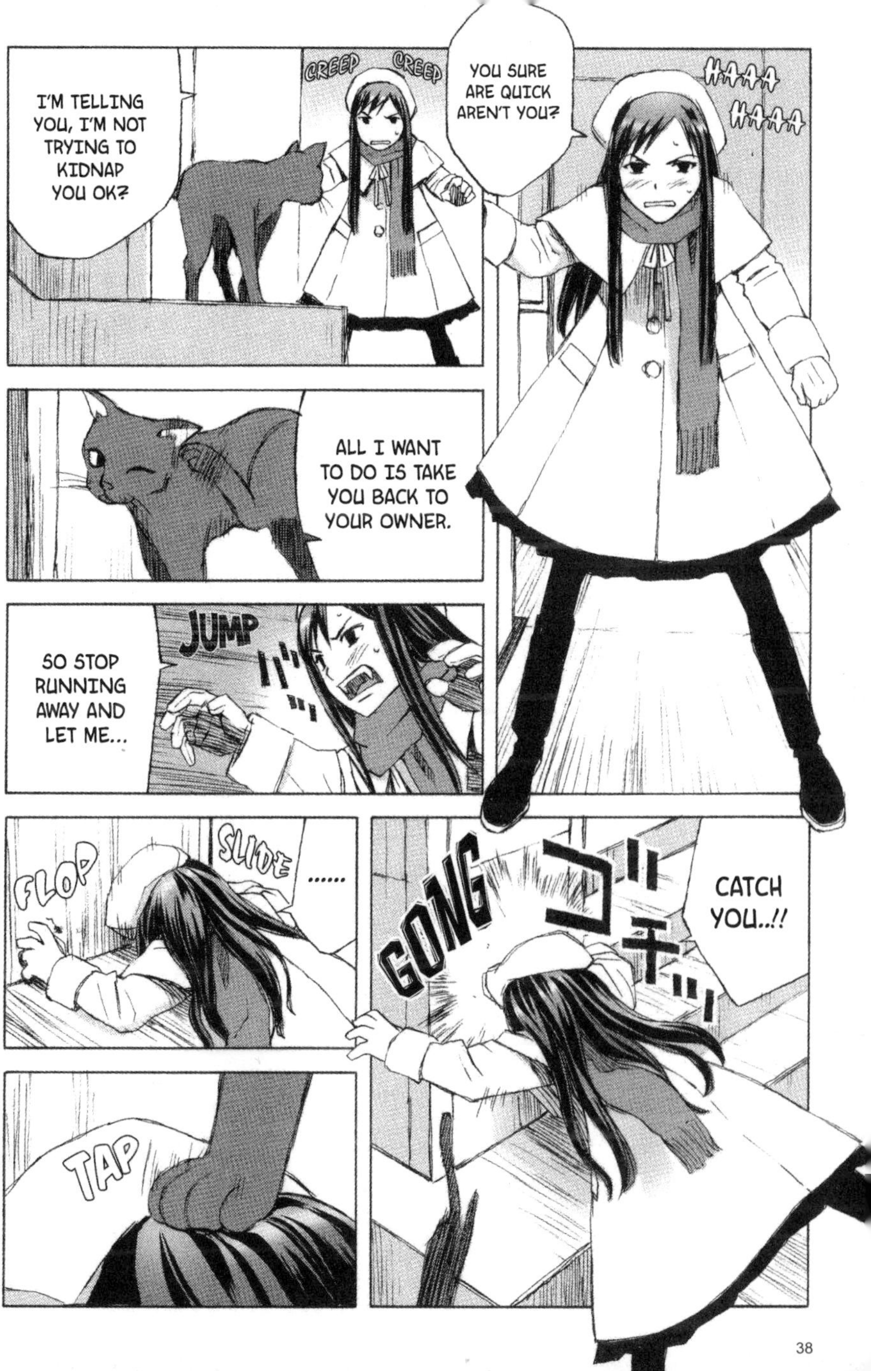
HAAA HAAA
YOU SURE ARE QUICK AREN'T YOU?
CREEP CREEP
I'M TELLING YOU, I'M NOT TRYING TO KIDNAP YOU OK?
ALL I WANT TO DO IS TAKE YOU BACK TO YOUR OWNER.
JUMP
SO STOP RUNNING AWAY AND LET ME...
CATCH YOU..!!
GONG
......
SLIDE
FLOP
TAP

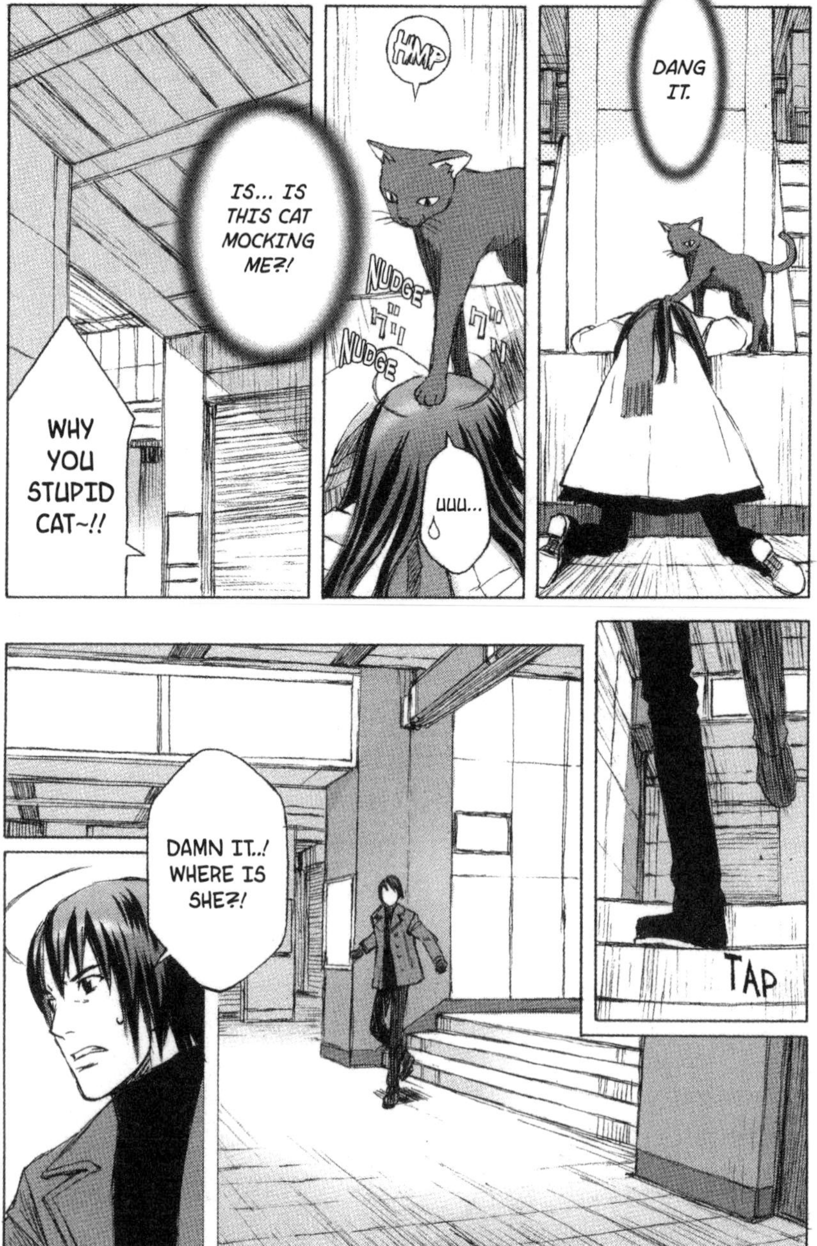
DANG IT.
HMP
IS... IS THIS CAT MOCKING ME?!
NUDGE
NUDGE
uuu...
WHY YOU STUPID CAT~!!
TAP
DAMN IT..! WHERE IS SHE?!

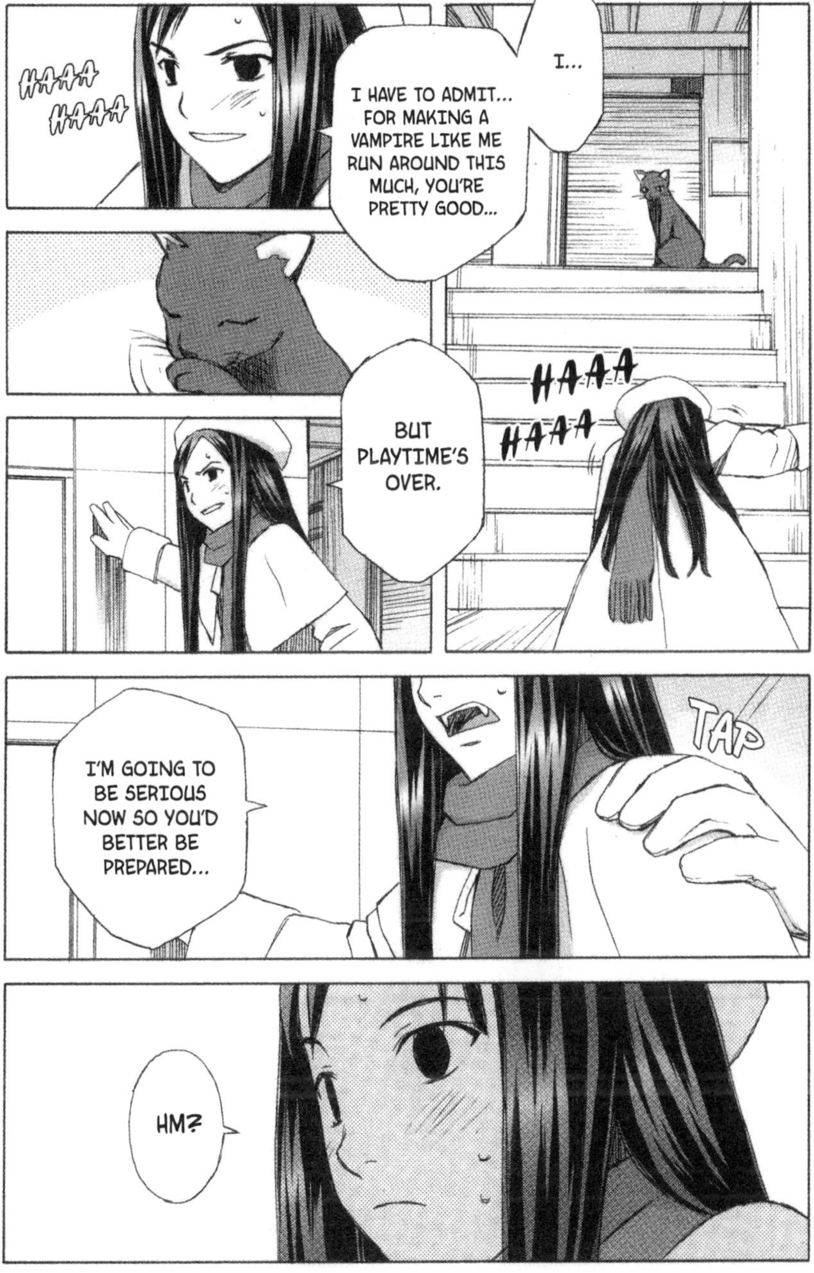
I...
HAAA HAAA
HAAA HAAA
I HAVE TO ADMIT... FOR MAKING A VAMPIRE LIKE ME RUN AROUND THIS MUCH, YOU'RE PRETTY GOOD...
BUT PLAYTIME'S OVER.
TAP
I'M GOING TO BE SERIOUS NOW SO YOU'D BETTER BE PREPARED...
HM?

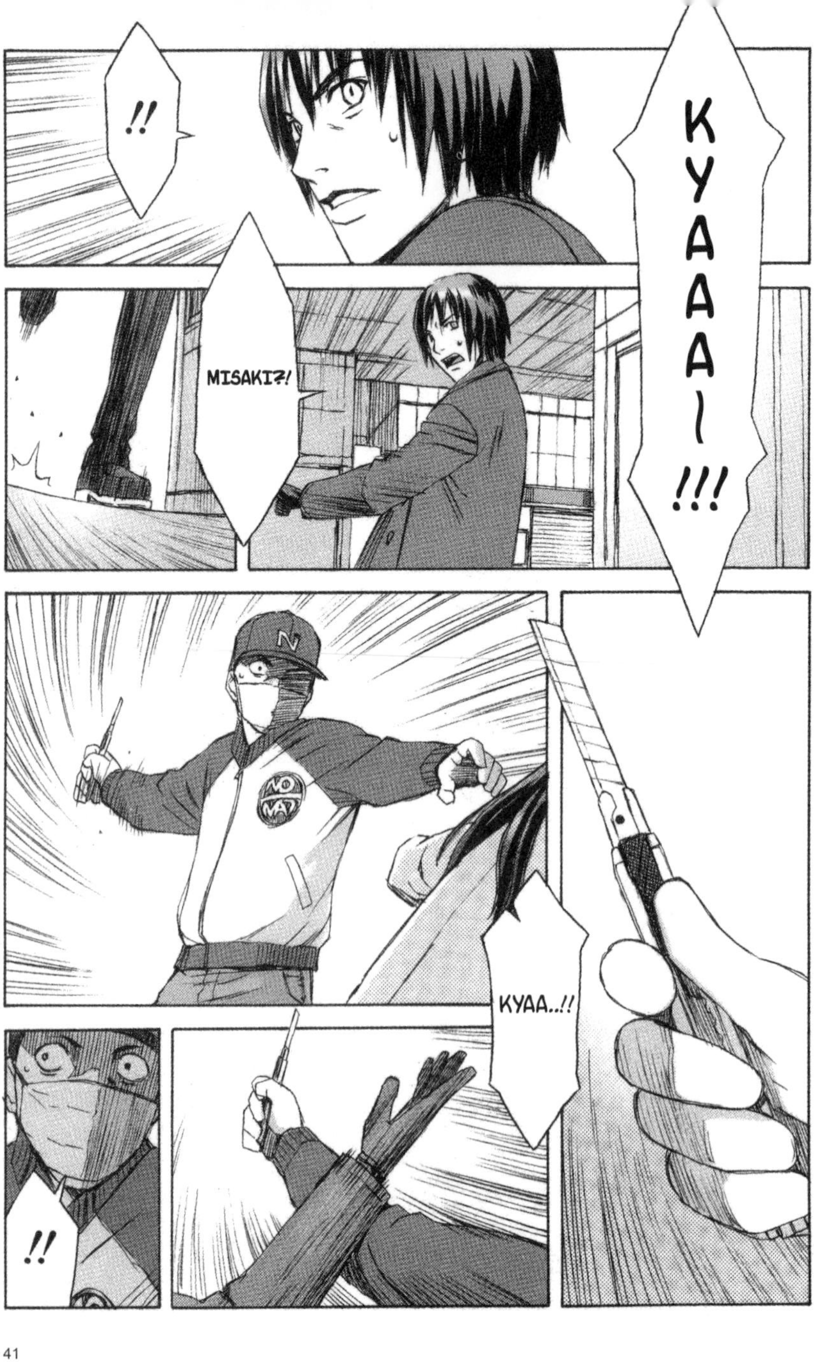

KYAAAI!!!
!!
MISAKI?!
KYAA..!!
!!

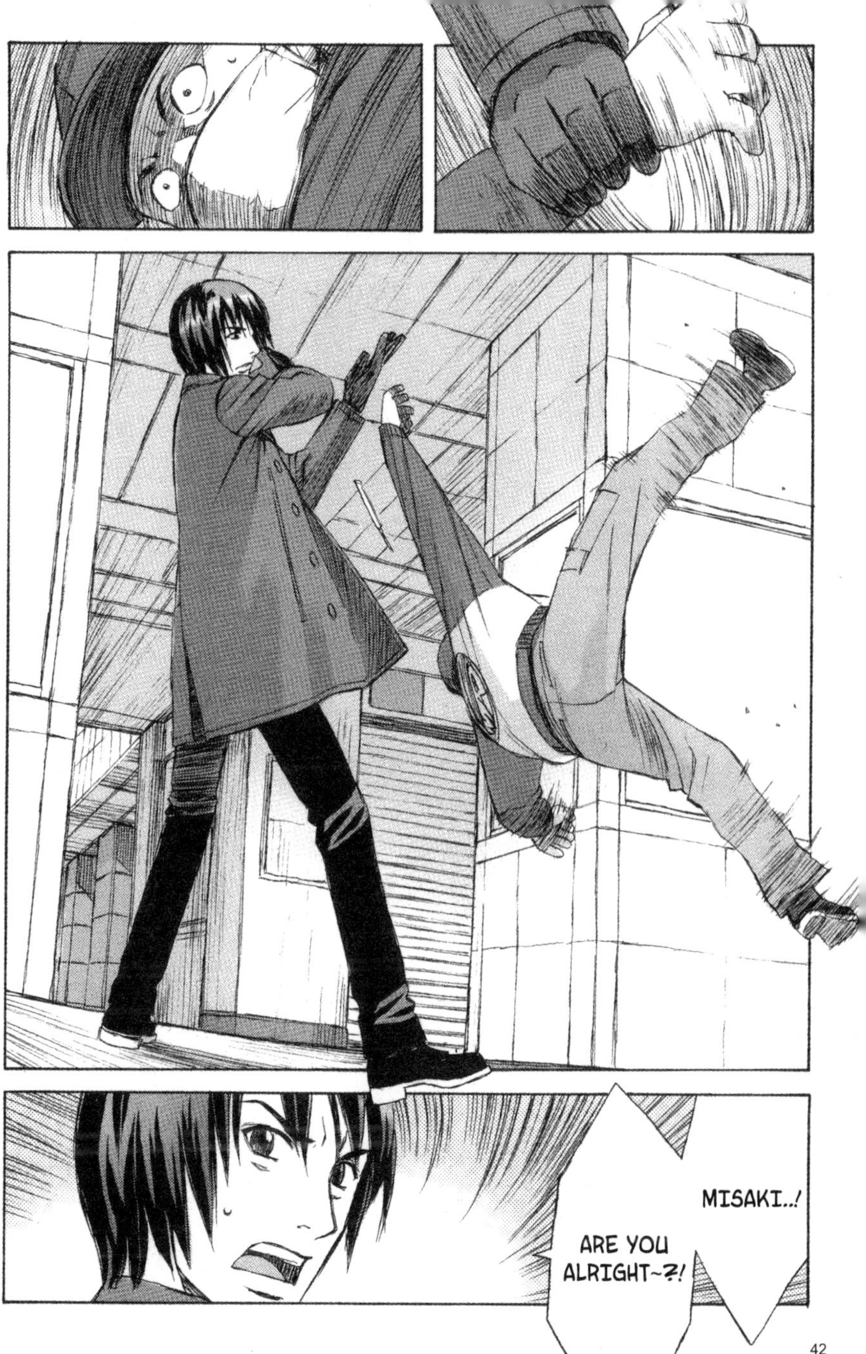
MISAKI..!
ARE YOU ALRIGHT~?!

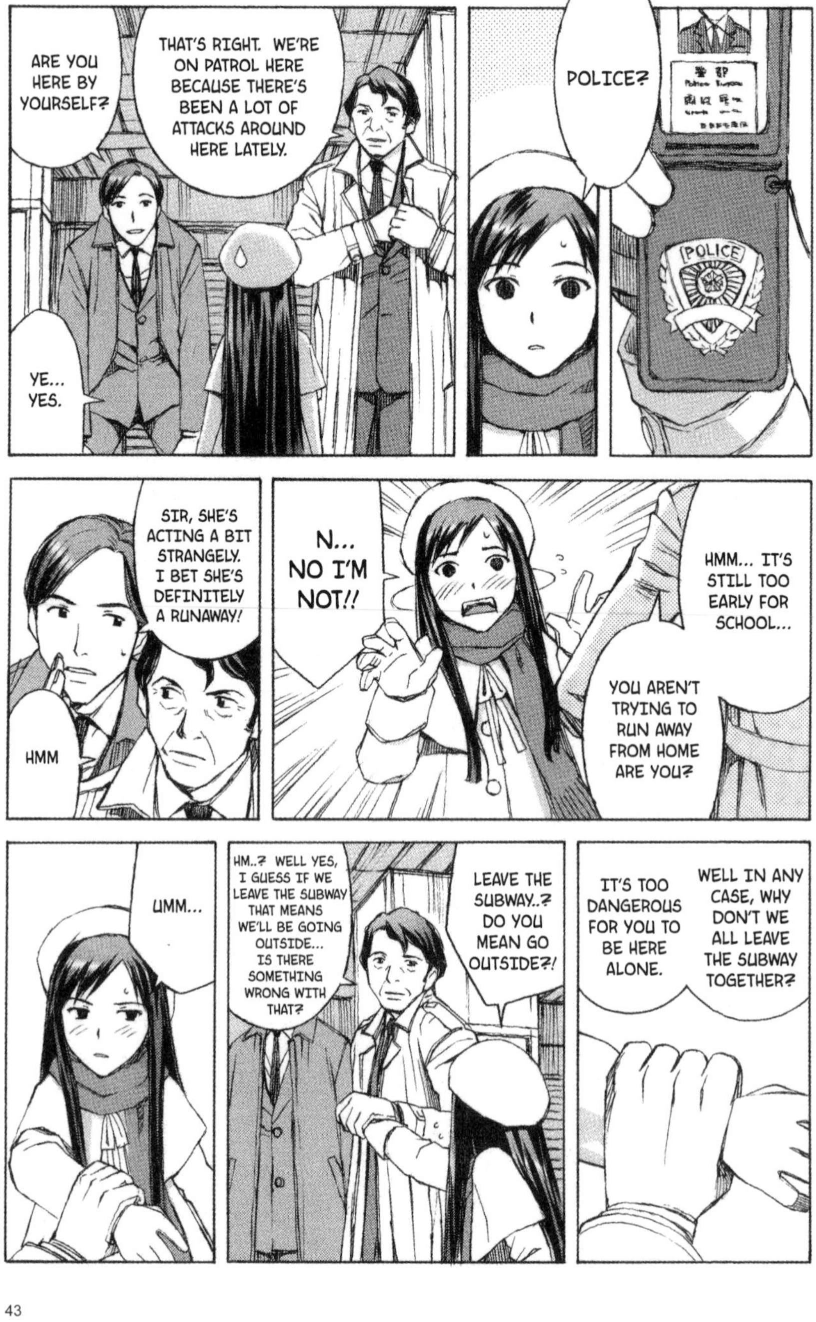
POLICE
POLICE?
THAT'S RIGHT. WE'RE ON PATROL HERE BECAUSE THERE'S BEEN A LOT OF ATTACKS AROUND HERE LATELY.
ARE YOU HERE BY YOURSELF?
YE... YES.
HMM... IT'S STILL TOO EARLY FOR SCHOOL...
YOU AREN'T TRYING TO RUN AWAY FROM HOME ARE YOU?
N... NO I'M NOT!!
SIR, SHE'S ACTING A BIT STRANGELY. I BET SHE'S DEFINITELY A RUNAWAY!
HMM
WELL IN ANY CASE, WHY DON'T WE ALL LEAVE THE SUBWAY TOGETHER?
IT'S TOO DANGEROUS FOR YOU TO BE HERE ALONE.
LEAVE THE SUBWAY..? DO YOU MEAN GO OUTSIDE?!
HM..? WELL YES, I GUESS IF WE LEAVE THE SUBWAY THAT MEANS WE'LL BE GOING OUTSIDE... IS THERE SOMETHING WRONG WITH THAT?
UMM...

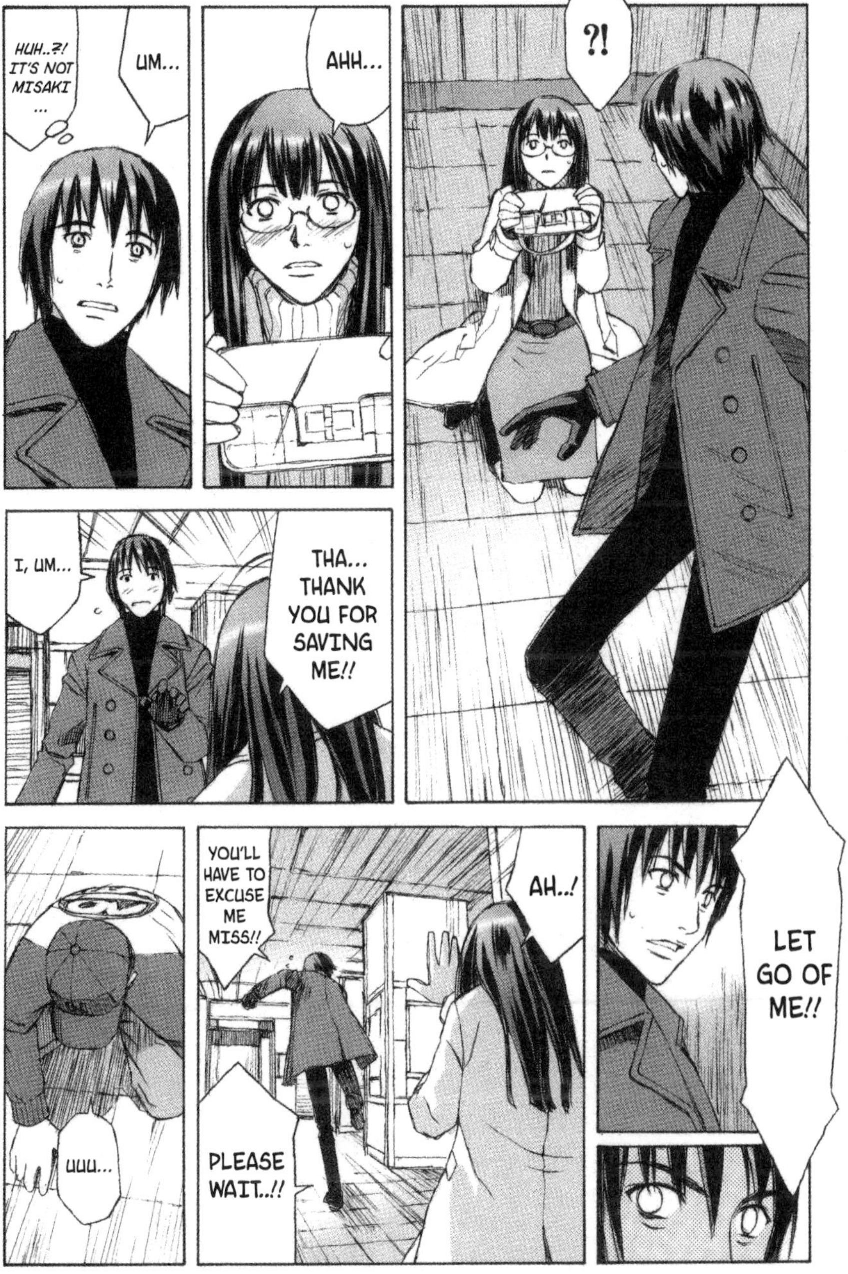
?!
AHH...
UM...
HUH..?! IT'S NOT MISAKI ...
THA... THANK YOU FOR SAVING ME!!
I, UM...
LET GO OF ME!!
AH..!
YOU'LL HAVE TO EXCUSE ME MISS!!
PLEASE WAIT..!!
UUU...

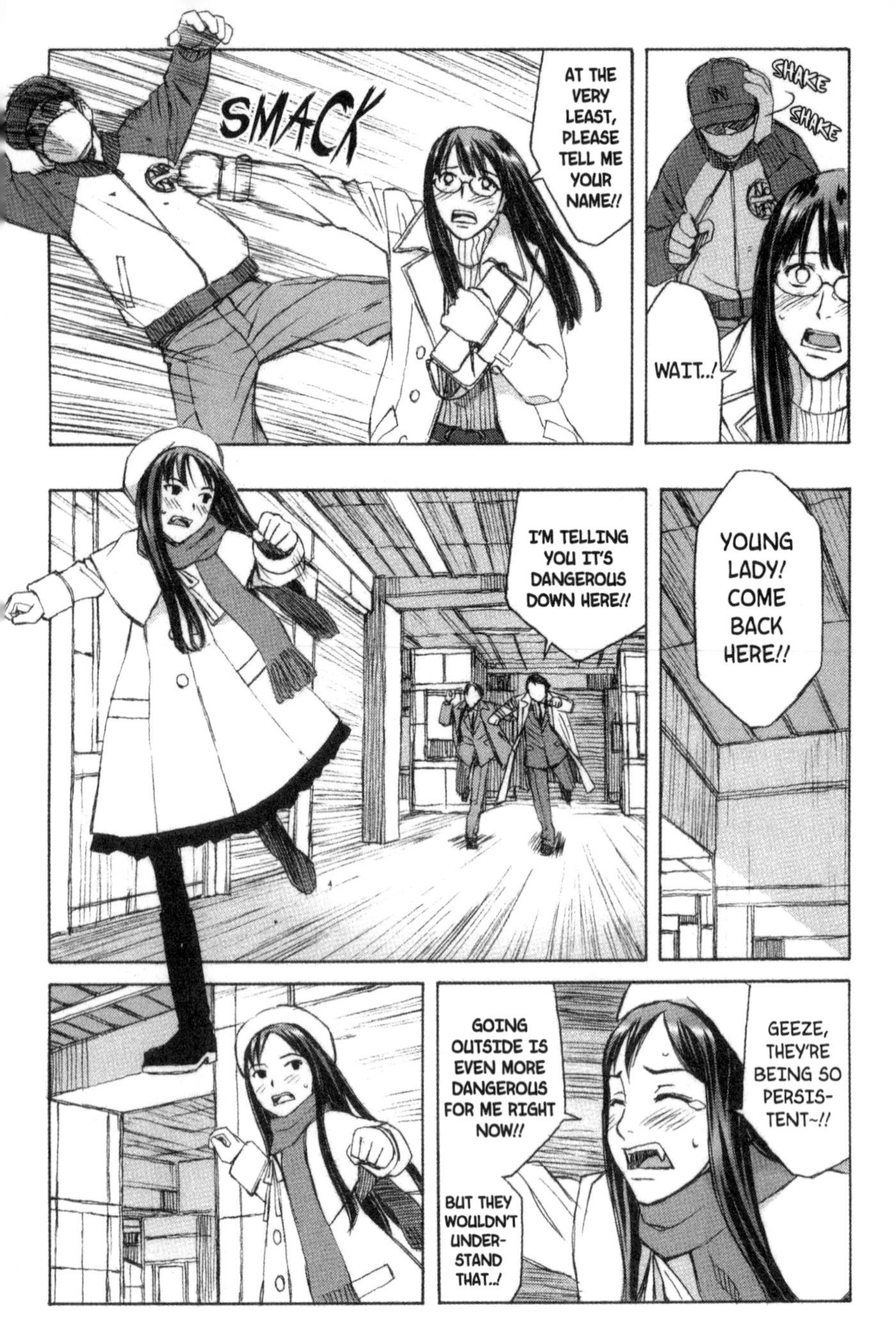
SHAKE
SHAKE
WAIT..!
AT THE VERY LEAST, PLEASE TELL ME YOUR NAME!!
SMACK
YOUNG LADY! COME BACK HERE!!
I'M TELLING YOU IT'S DANGEROUS DOWN HERE!!
GEEZE, THEY'RE BEING SO PERSIS-TENT~!!
GOING OUTSIDE IS EVEN MORE DANGEROUS FOR ME RIGHT NOW!!
BUT THEY WOULDN'T UNDER-STAND THAT..!

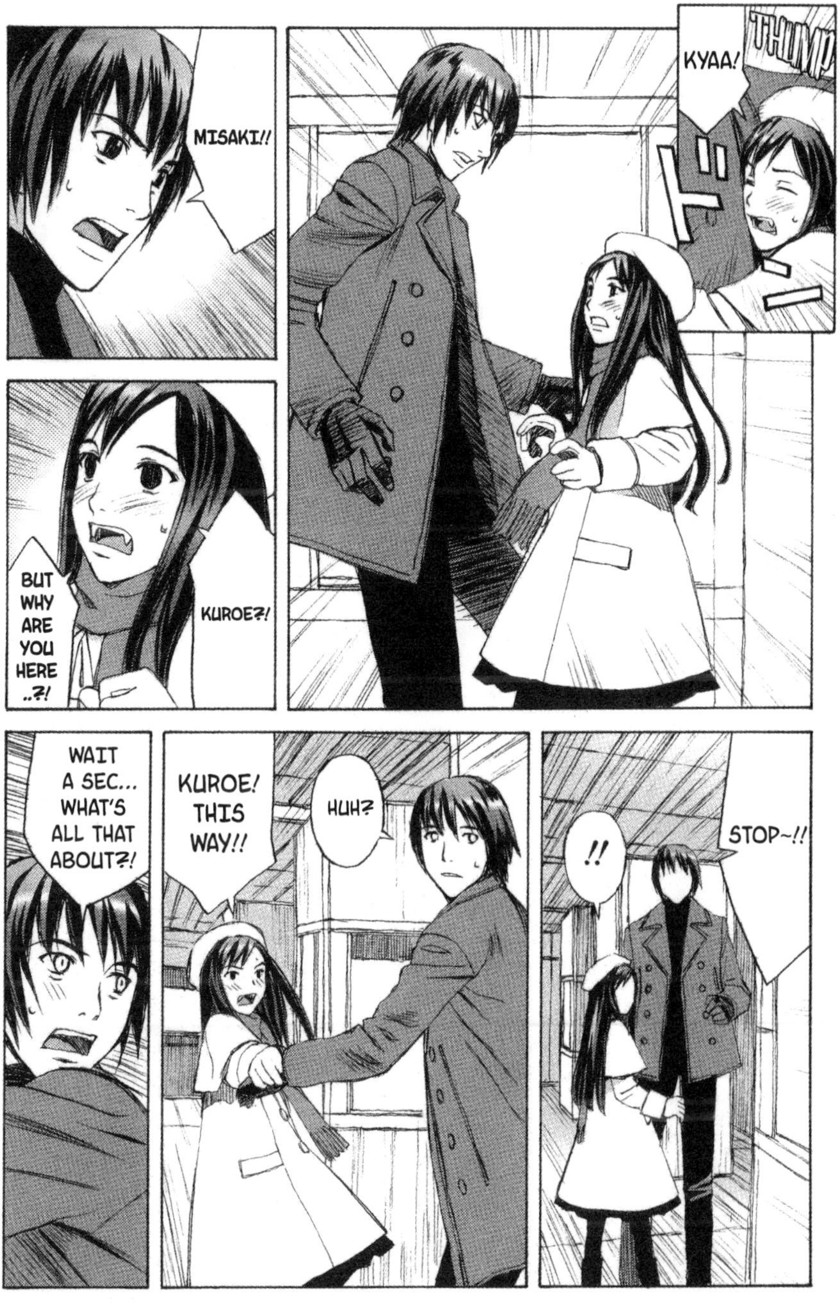
KYAA!
THUMP
MISAKI!!
KUROE?!
BUT WHY ARE YOU HERE..?!
STOP~!!
!!
HUH?
KUROE! THIS WAY!!
WAIT A SEC... WHAT'S ALL THAT ABOUT?!

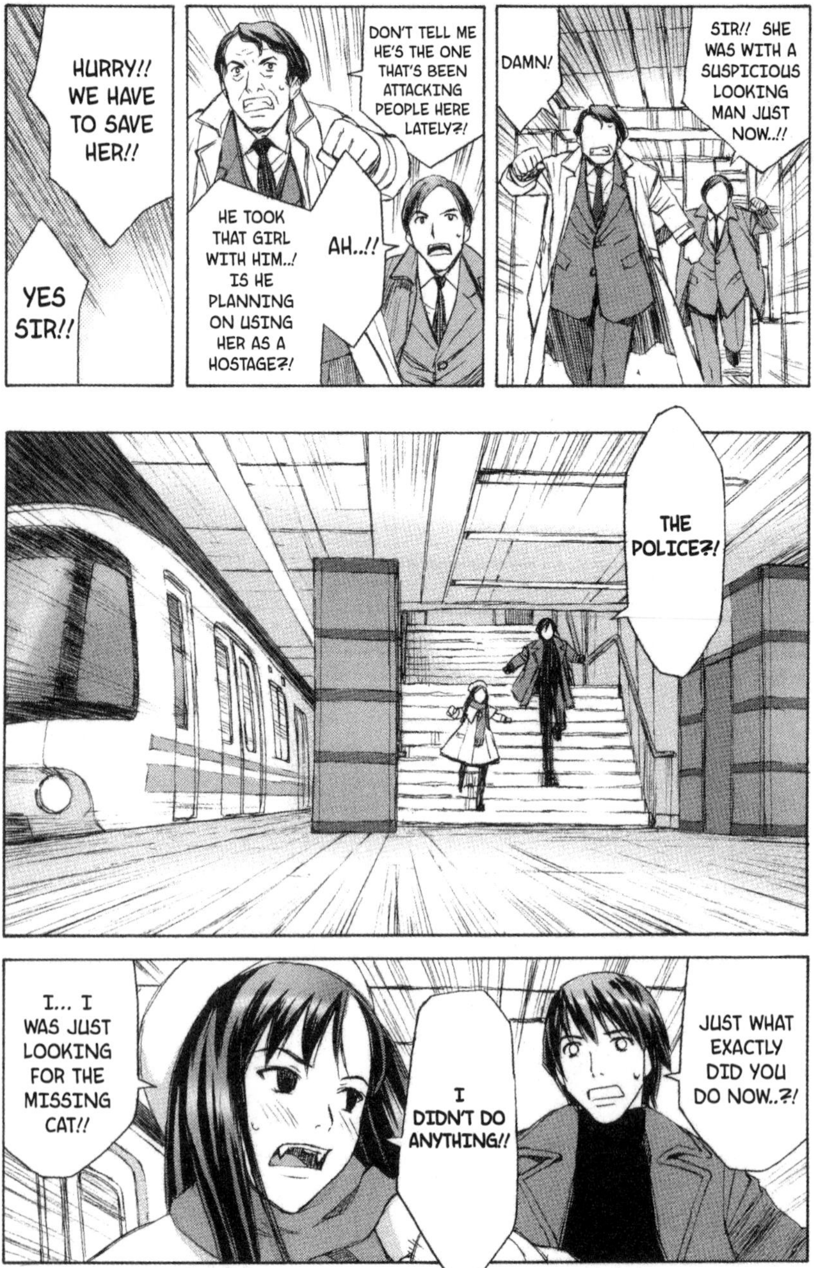
SIR!! SHE WAS WITH A SUSPICIOUS LOOKING MAN JUST NOW..!!
DAMN!
DON'T TELL ME HE'S THE ONE THAT'S BEEN ATTACKING PEOPLE HERE LATELY?!
AH..!!
HE TOOK THAT GIRL WITH HIM..! IS HE PLANNING ON USING HER AS A HOSTAGE?!
HURRY!! WE HAVE TO SAVE HER!!
YES SIR!!
THE POLICE?!
JUST WHAT EXACTLY DID YOU DO NOW..?!
I DIDN'T DO ANYTHING!!
I... I WAS JUST LOOKING FOR THE MISSING CAT!!

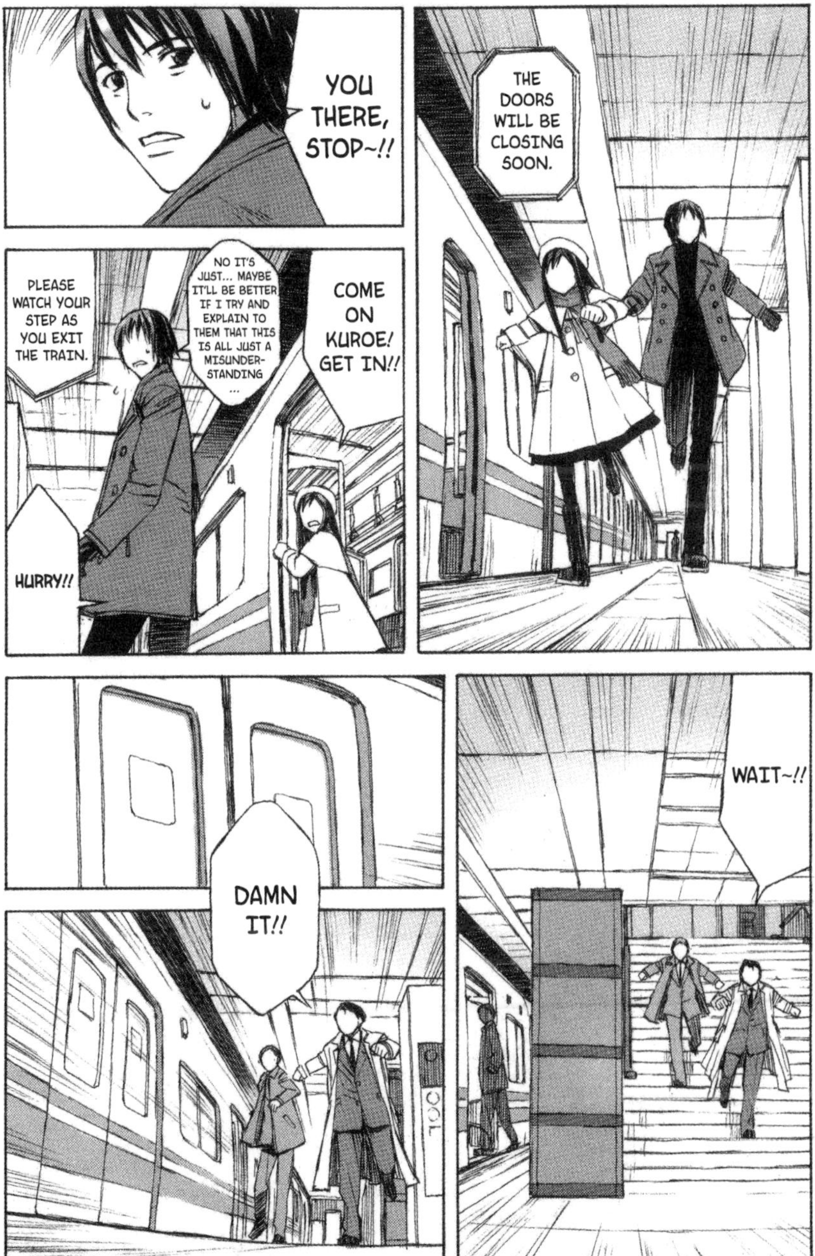
THE DOORS WILL BE CLOSING SOON.
YOU THERE, STOP~!!
COME ON KUROE! GET IN!!
NO IT'S JUST... MAYBE IT'LL BE BETTER IF I TRY AND EXPLAIN TO THEM THAT THIS IS ALL JUST A MISUNDER-STANDING ...
PLEASE WATCH YOUR STEP AS YOU EXIT THE TRAIN.
HURRY!!
WAIT~!!
DAMN IT!!

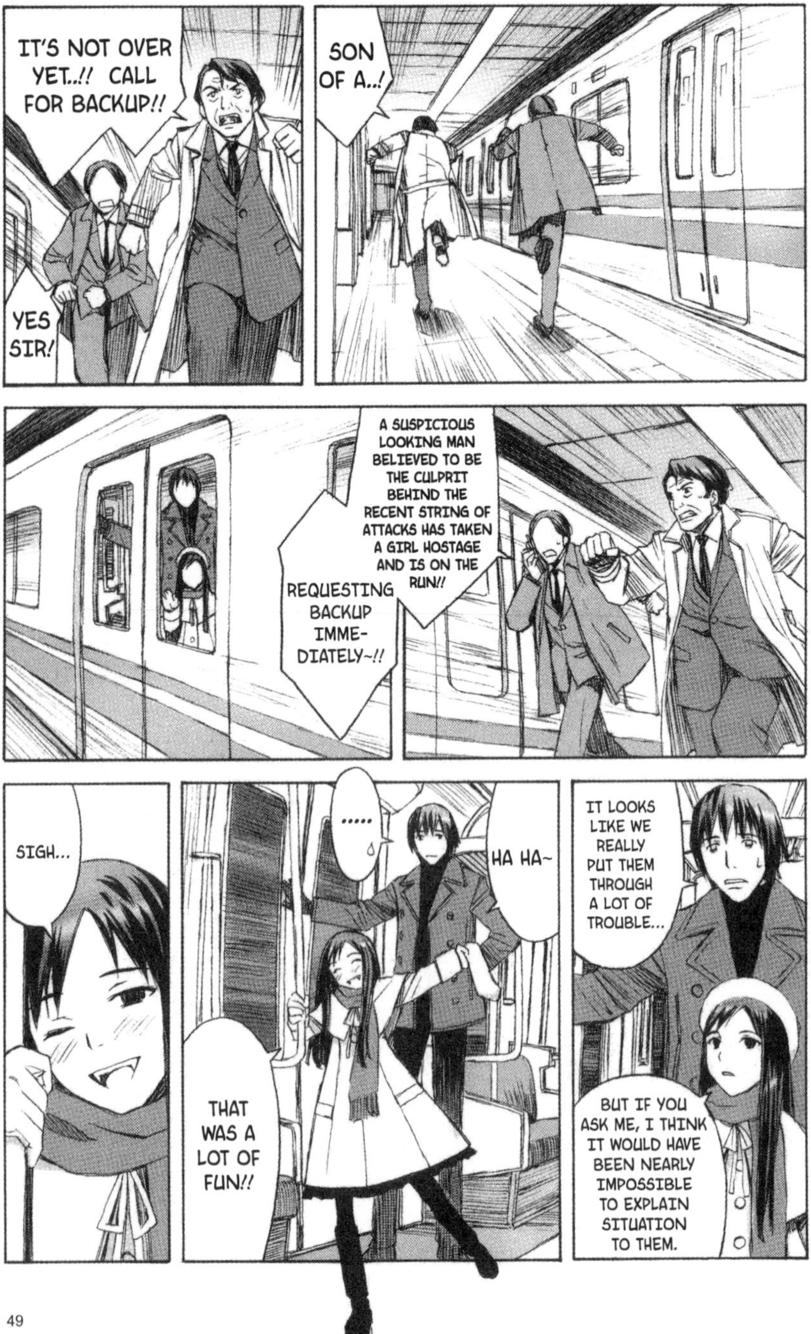
SON OF A..!
IT'S NOT OVER YET..!! CALL FOR BACKUP!!
YES SIR!
A SUSPICIOUS LOOKING MAN BELIEVED TO BE THE CULPRIT BEHIND THE RECENT STRING OF ATTACKS HAS TAKEN A GIRL HOSTAGE AND IS ON THE RUN!!
REQUESTING BACKUP IMME-DIATELY~!!
IT LOOKS LIKE WE REALLY PUT THEM THROUGH A LOT OF TROUBLE...
BUT IF YOU ASK ME, I THINK IT WOULD HAVE BEEN NEARLY IMPOSSIBLE TO EXPLAIN SITUATION TO THEM.
......
HA HA~
THAT WAS A LOT OF FUN!!
SIGH...

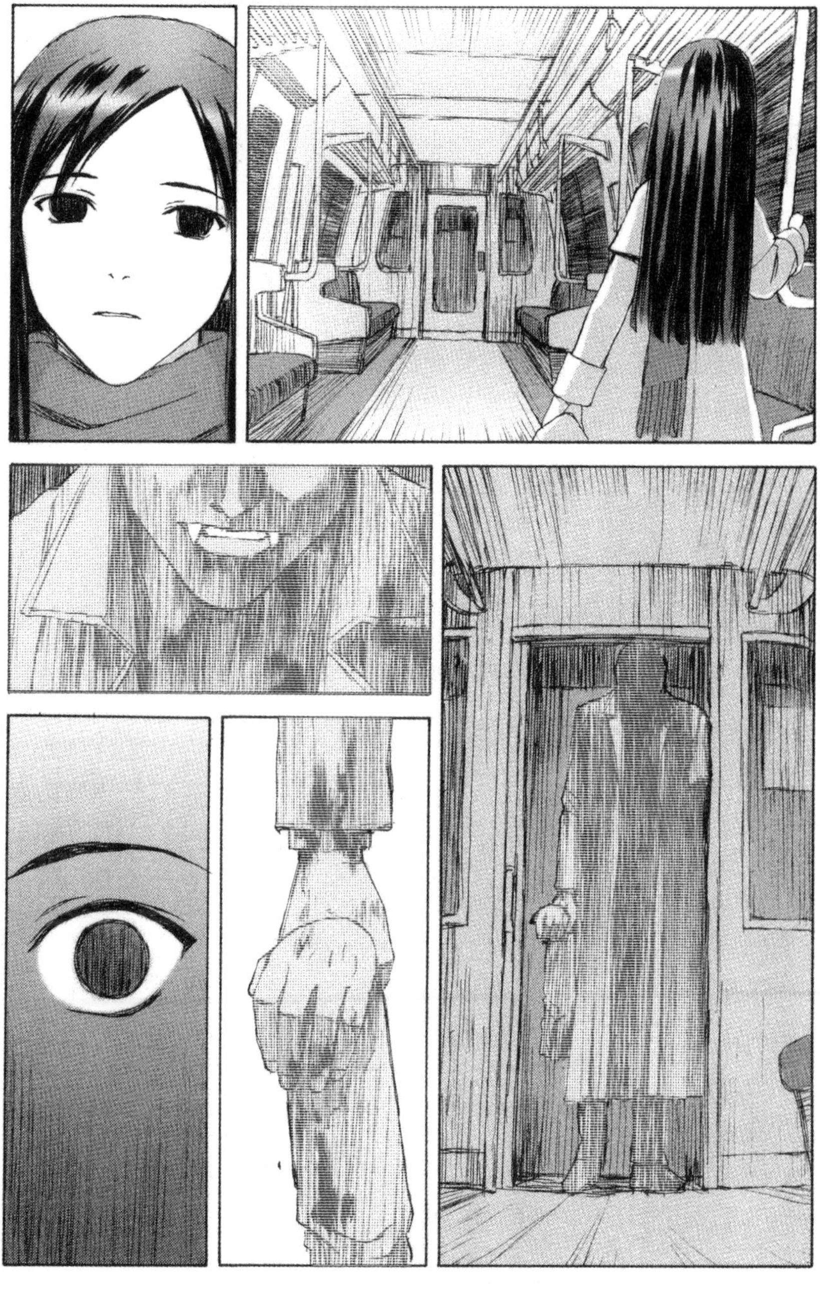

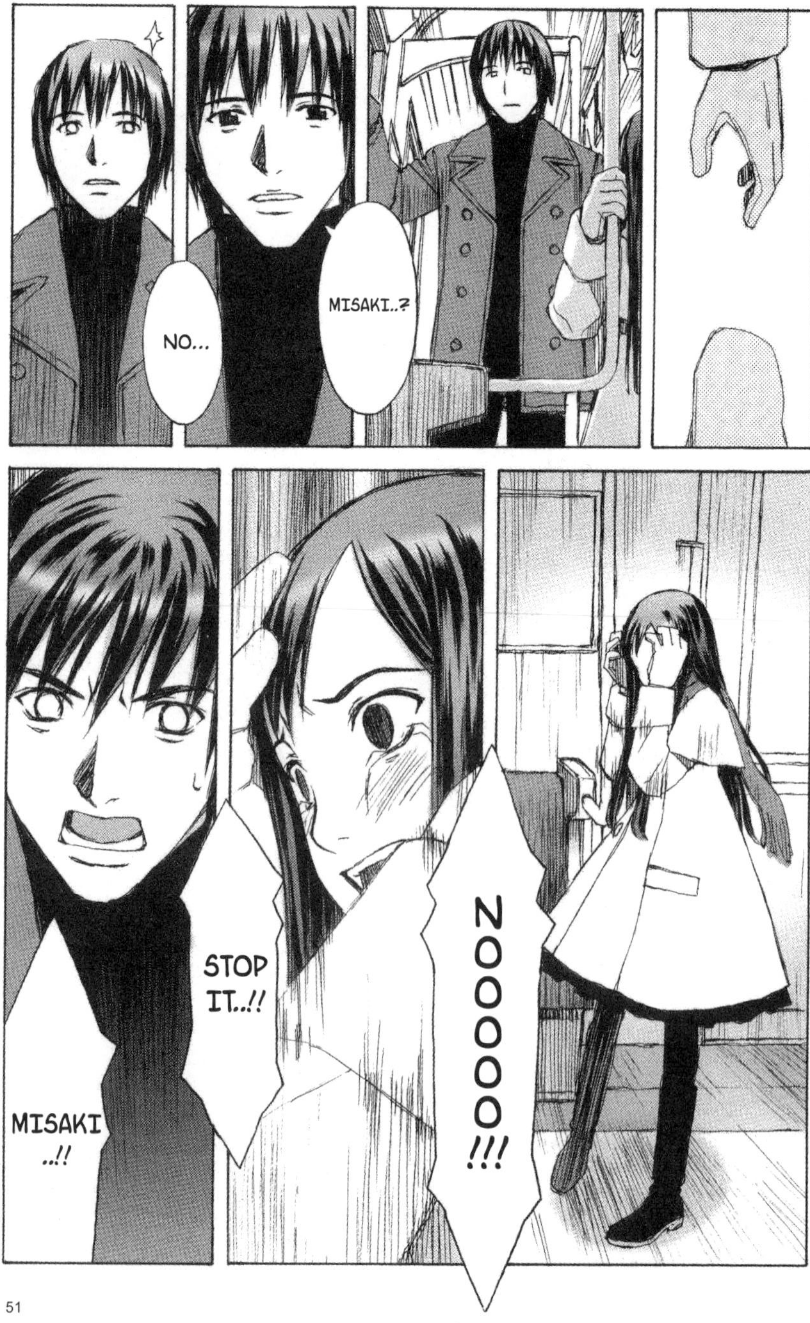
MISAKI..?
NO...
NOOOOOO!!!
STOP IT..!!
MISAKI ..!!

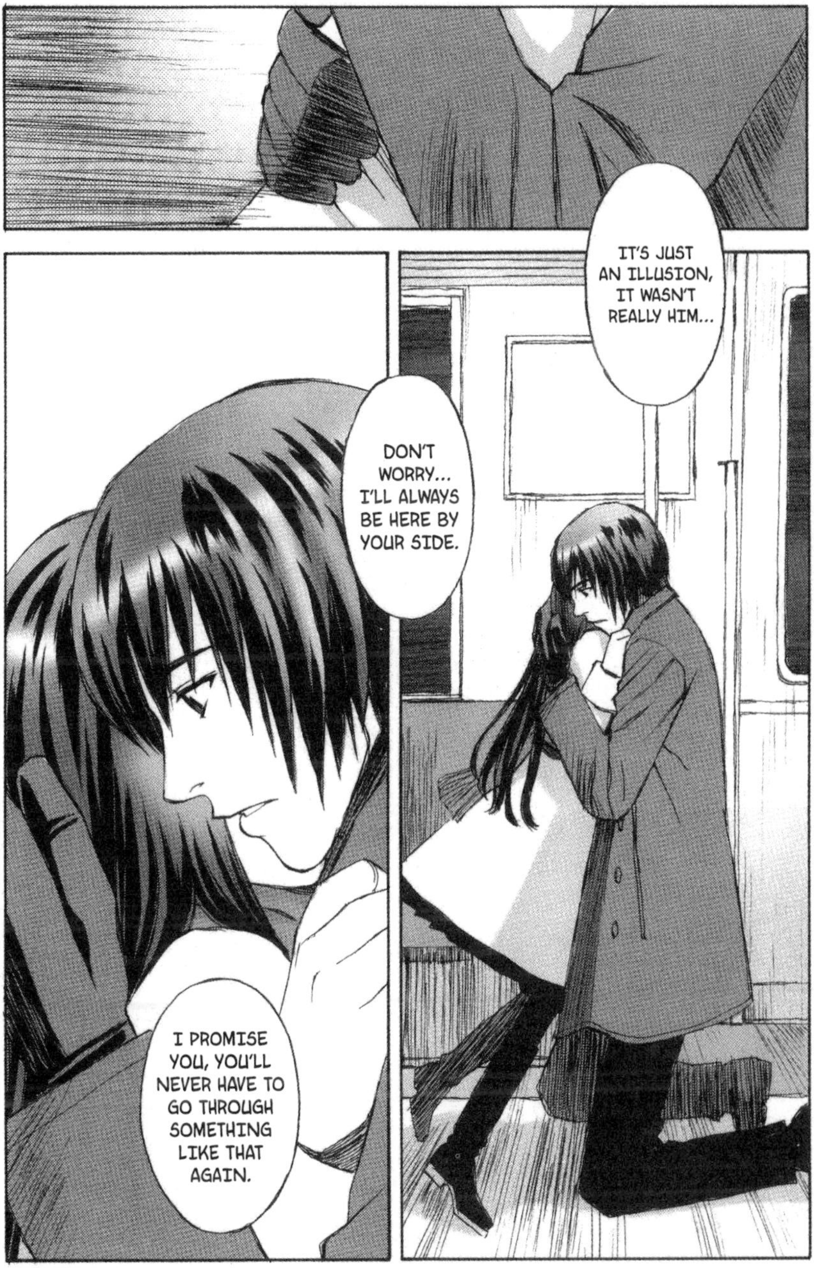
IT'S JUST AN ILLUSION, IT WASN'T REALLY HIM...
DON'T WORRY... I'LL ALWAYS BE HERE BY YOUR SIDE.
I PROMISE YOU, YOU'LL NEVER HAVE TO GO THROUGH SOMETHING LIKE THAT AGAIN.

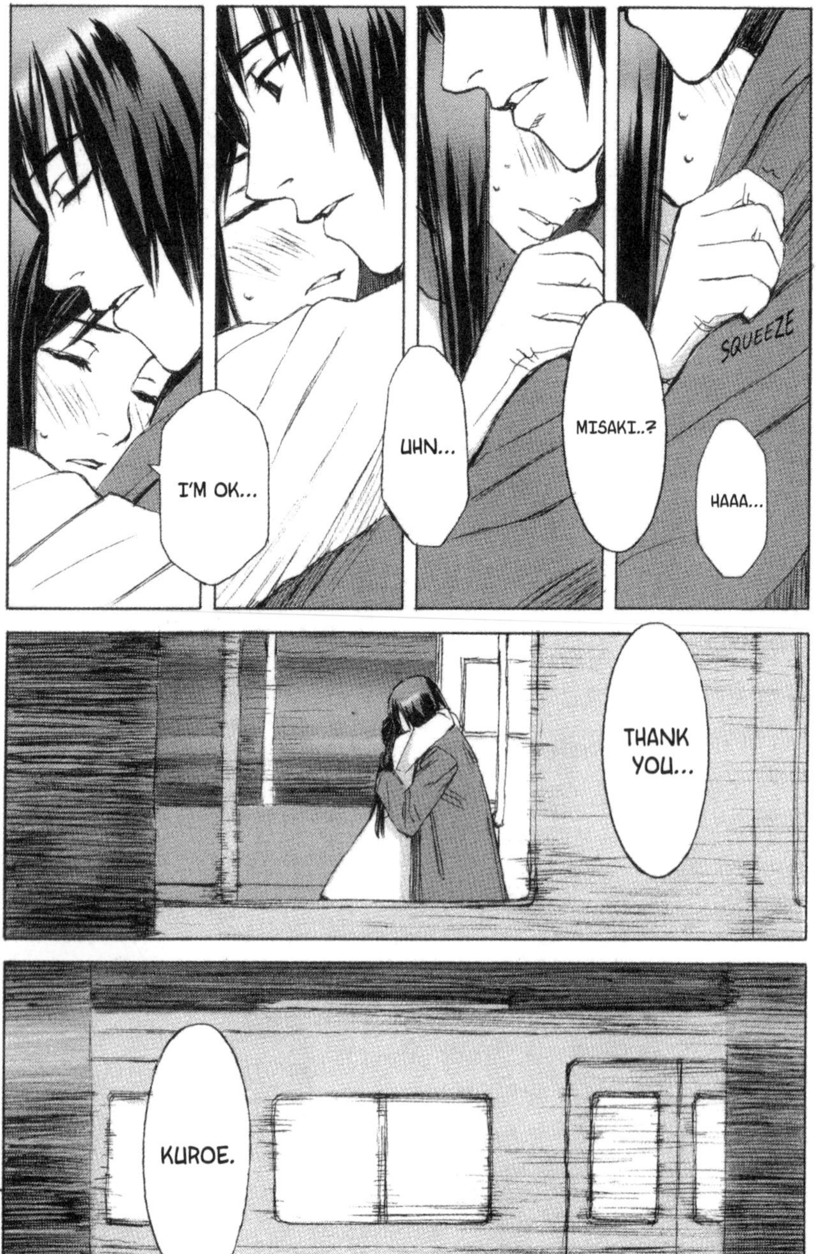
SQUEEZE
HAAA...
MISAKI..?
UHN...
I'M OK...
THANK YOU...
KUROE.

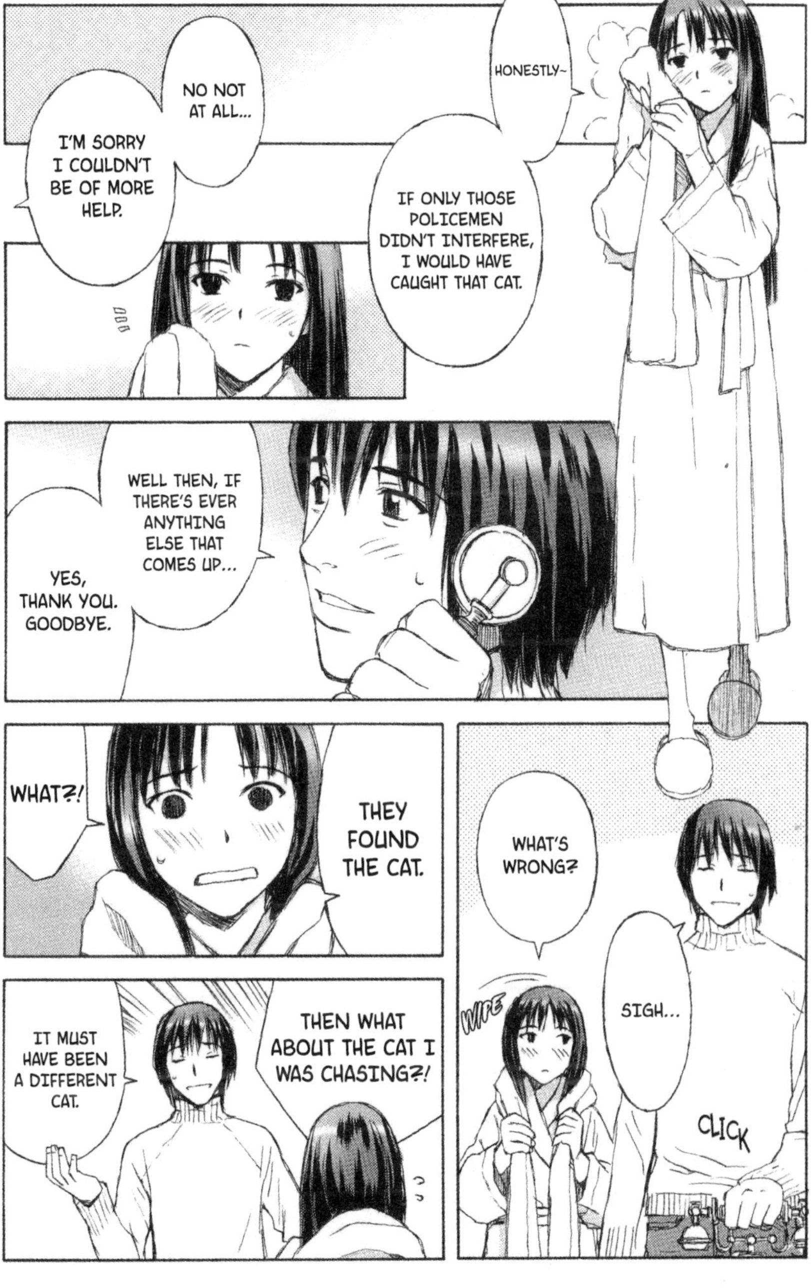
HONESTLY~
IF ONLY THOSE POLICEMEN DIDN'T INTERFERE, I WOULD HAVE CAUGHT THAT CAT.
NO NOT AT ALL...
I'M SORRY I COULDN'T BE OF MORE HELP.
WELL THEN, IF THERE'S EVER ANYTHING ELSE THAT COMES UP...
YES, THANK YOU. GOODBYE.
WHAT'S WRONG?
SIGH...
WIPE
CLICK
THEY FOUND THE CAT.
WHAT?!
THEN WHAT ABOUT THE CAT I WAS CHASING?!
IT MUST HAVE BEEN A DIFFERENT CAT.

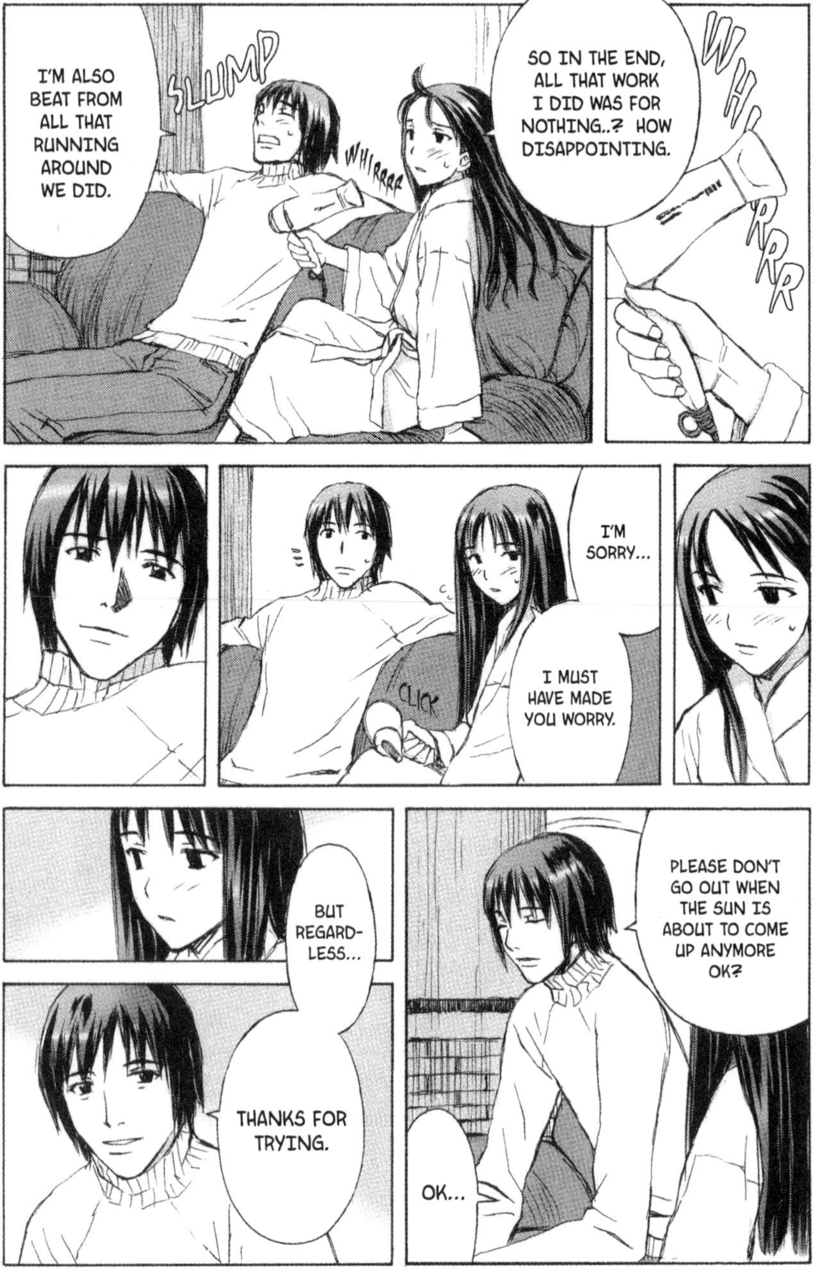
WHIRRRR
SO IN THE END, ALL THAT WORK I DID WAS FOR NOTHING..? HOW DISAPPOINTING.
SLUMP
WHIRRRR
I'M ALSO BEAT FROM ALL THAT RUNNING AROUND WE DID.
I'M SORRY...
I MUST HAVE MADE YOU WORRY.
CLICK
PLEASE DON'T GO OUT WHEN THE SUN IS ABOUT TO COME UP ANYMORE OK?
OK...
BUT REGARDLESS...
THANKS FOR TRYING.

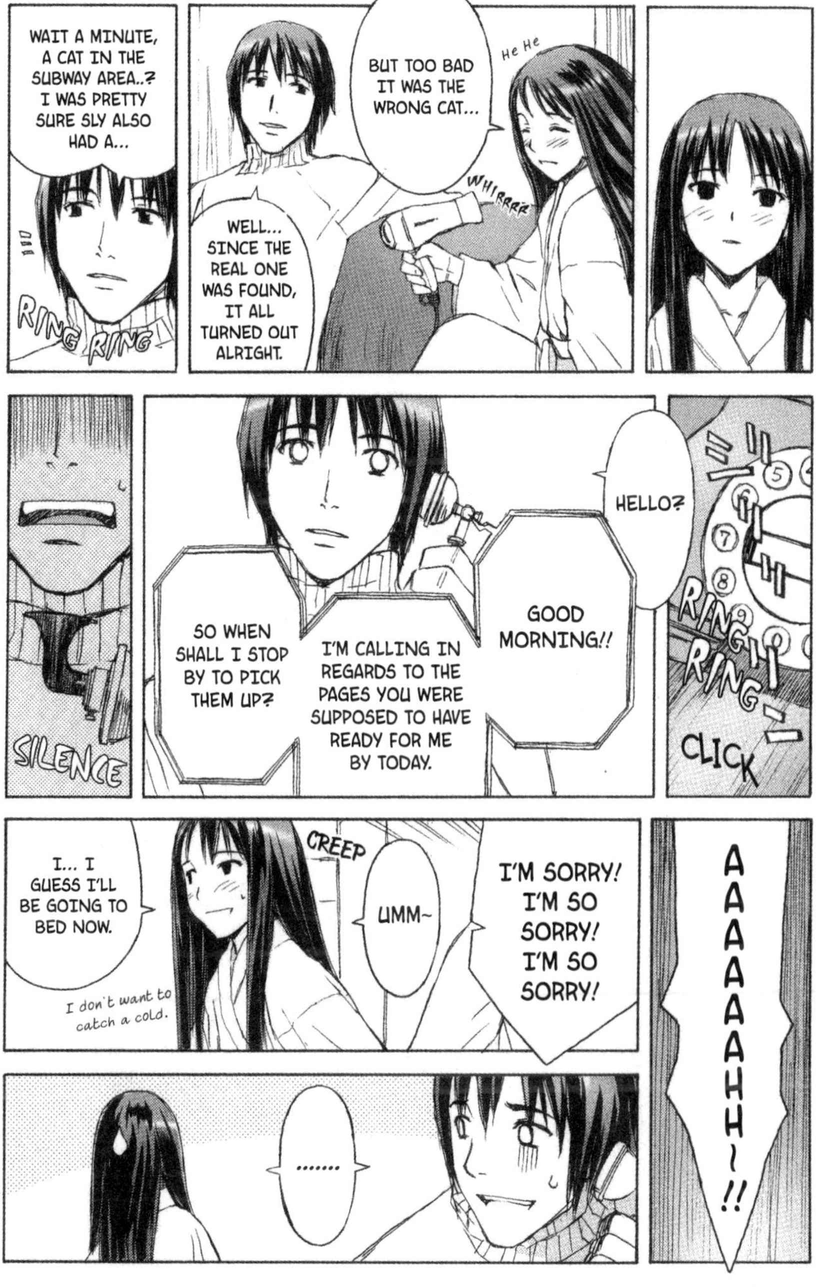

BUT TOO BAD IT WAS THE WRONG CAT...
He He
WHIRRRR
WELL... SINCE THE REAL ONE WAS FOUND, IT ALL TURNED OUT ALRIGHT.
WAIT A MINUTE, A CAT IN THE SUBWAY AREA..? I WAS PRETTY SURE SLY ALSO HAD A...
RING RING
RING RING
CLICK
HELLO?
GOOD MORNING!!
I'M CALLING IN REGARDS TO THE PAGES YOU WERE SUPPOSED TO HAVE READY FOR ME BY TODAY.
SO WHEN SHALL I STOP BY TO PICK THEM UP?
SILENCE
AAAAAAAH~!!
I'M SORRY! I'M SO SORRY! I'M SO SORRY!
UMM~
CREEP
I... I GUESS I'LL BE GOING TO BED NOW.
I don't want to catch a cold.
....

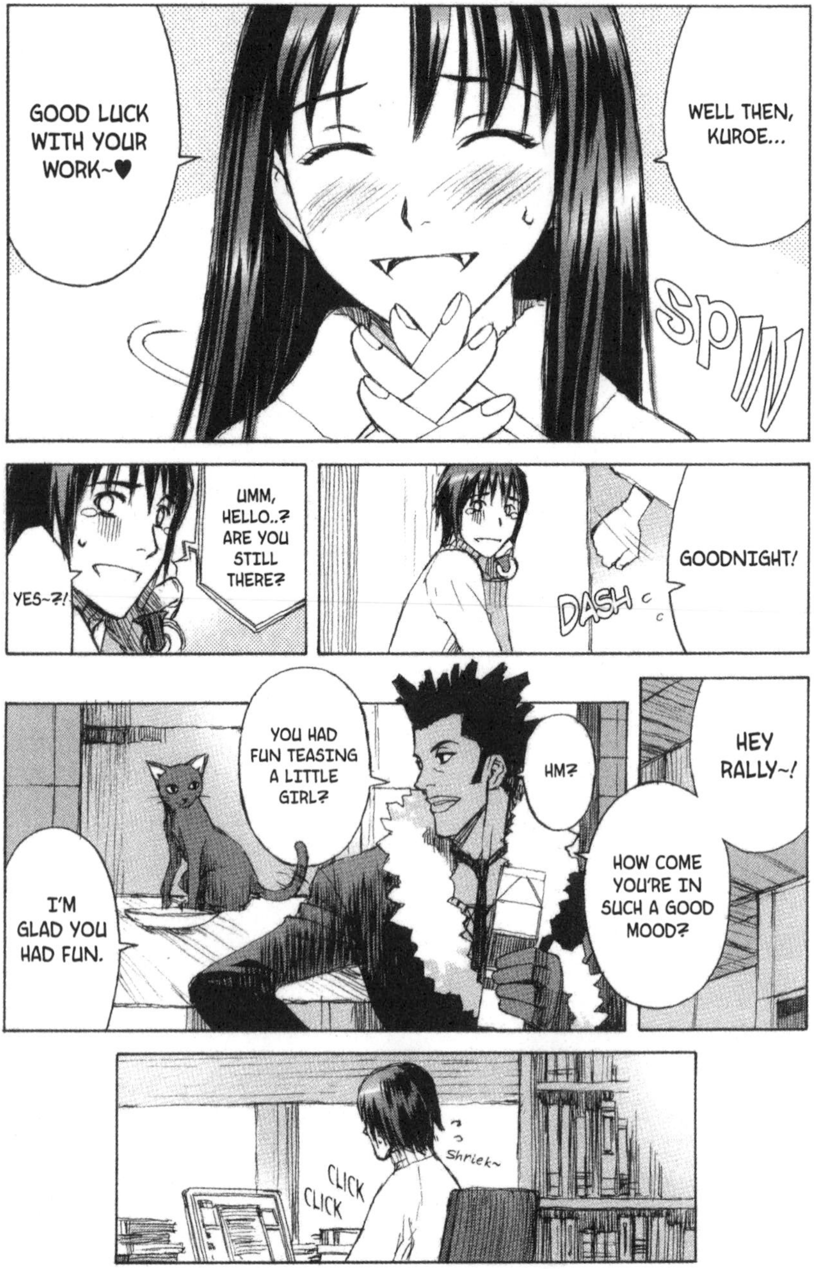
WELL THEN, KUROE...
SPIN
GOOD LUCK WITH YOUR WORK~♥
GOODNIGHT!
DASH
UMM, HELLO..? ARE YOU STILL THERE?
YES~?!
HEY RALLY~!
HM?
HOW COME YOU'RE IN SUCH A GOOD MOOD?
YOU HAD FUN TEASING A LITTLE GIRL?
I'M GLAD YOU HAD FUN.
Shriek~
CLICK
CLICK

Episode 2
LIVING THROUGH THE TWILIGHT
黄昏に生きて

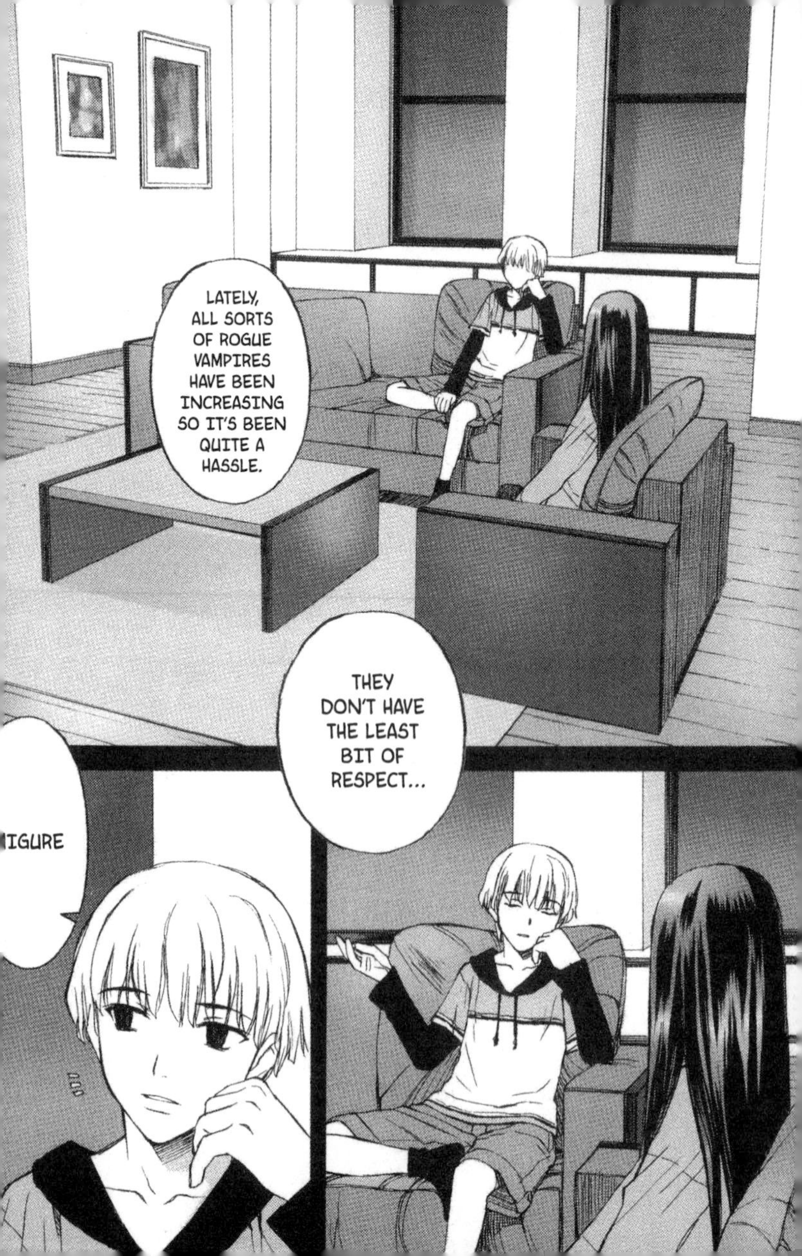
LATELY, ALL SORTS OF ROGUE VAMPIRES HAVE BEEN INCREASING SO IT'S BEEN QUITE A HASSLE.
THEY DON'T HAVE THE LEAST BIT OF RESPECT...
IGURE
...

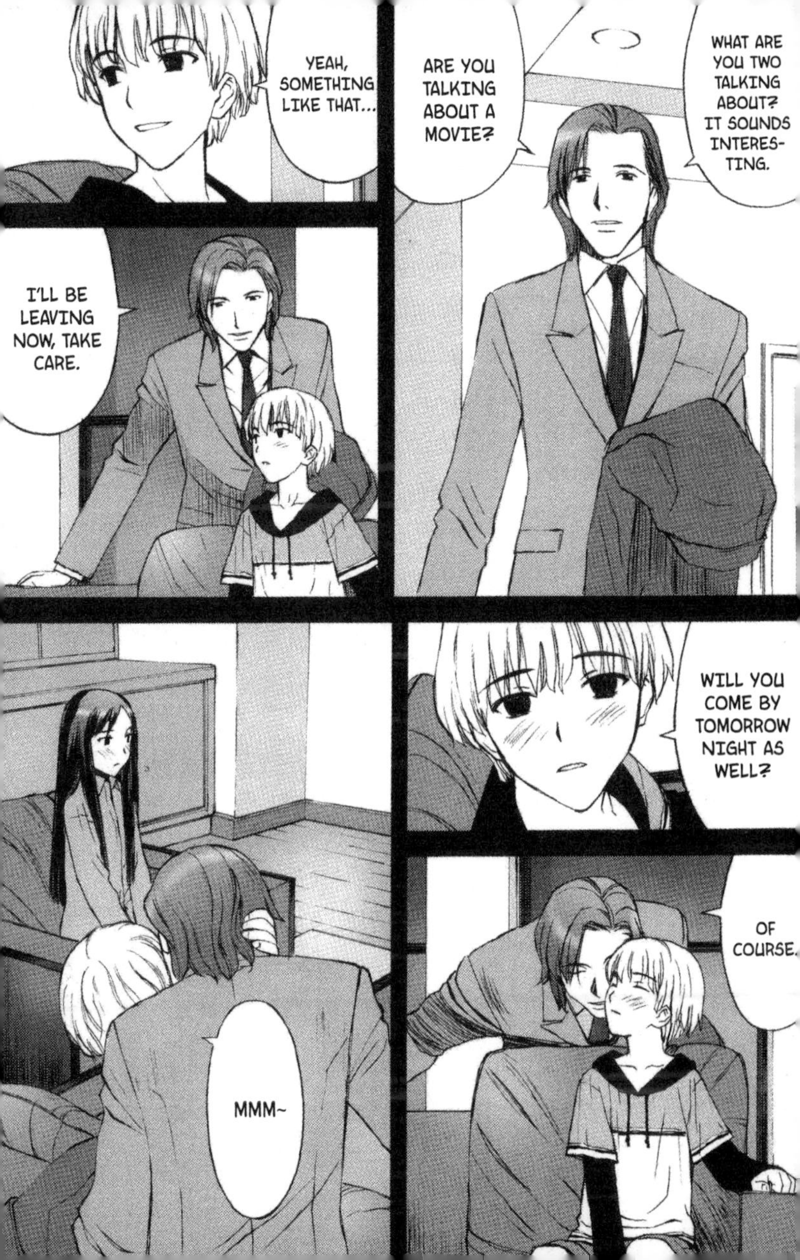
WHAT ARE YOU TWO TALKING ABOUT? IT SOUNDS INTERESTING.
ARE YOU TALKING ABOUT A MOVIE?
YEAH, SOMETHING LIKE THAT...
I'LL BE LEAVING NOW, TAKE CARE.
WILL YOU COME BY TOMORROW NIGHT AS WELL?
OF COURSE.
MMM~

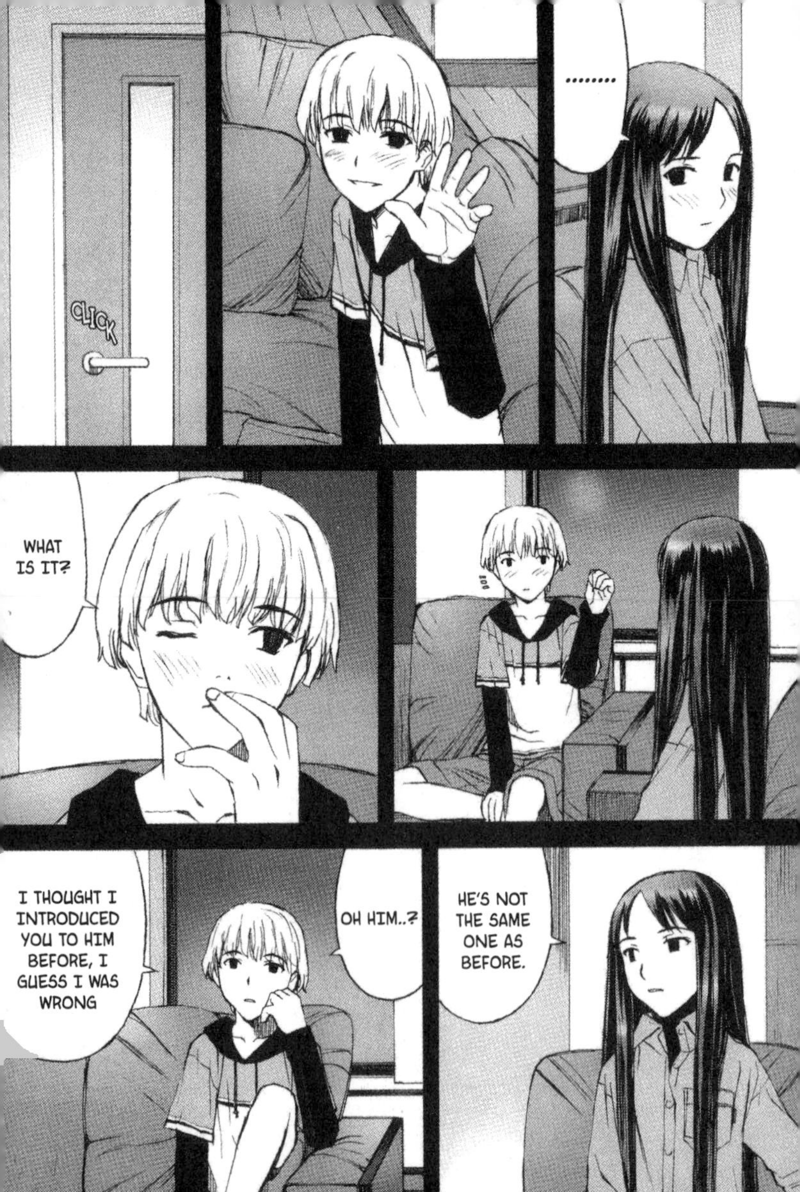
....
CLICK
WHAT IS IT?
HE'S NOT THE SAME ONE AS BEFORE.
OH HIM..?
I THOUGHT I INTRODUCED YOU TO HIM BEFORE, I GUESS I WAS WRONG

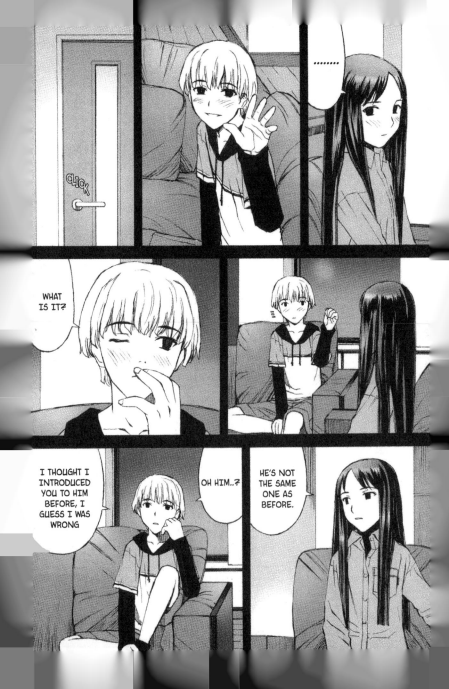

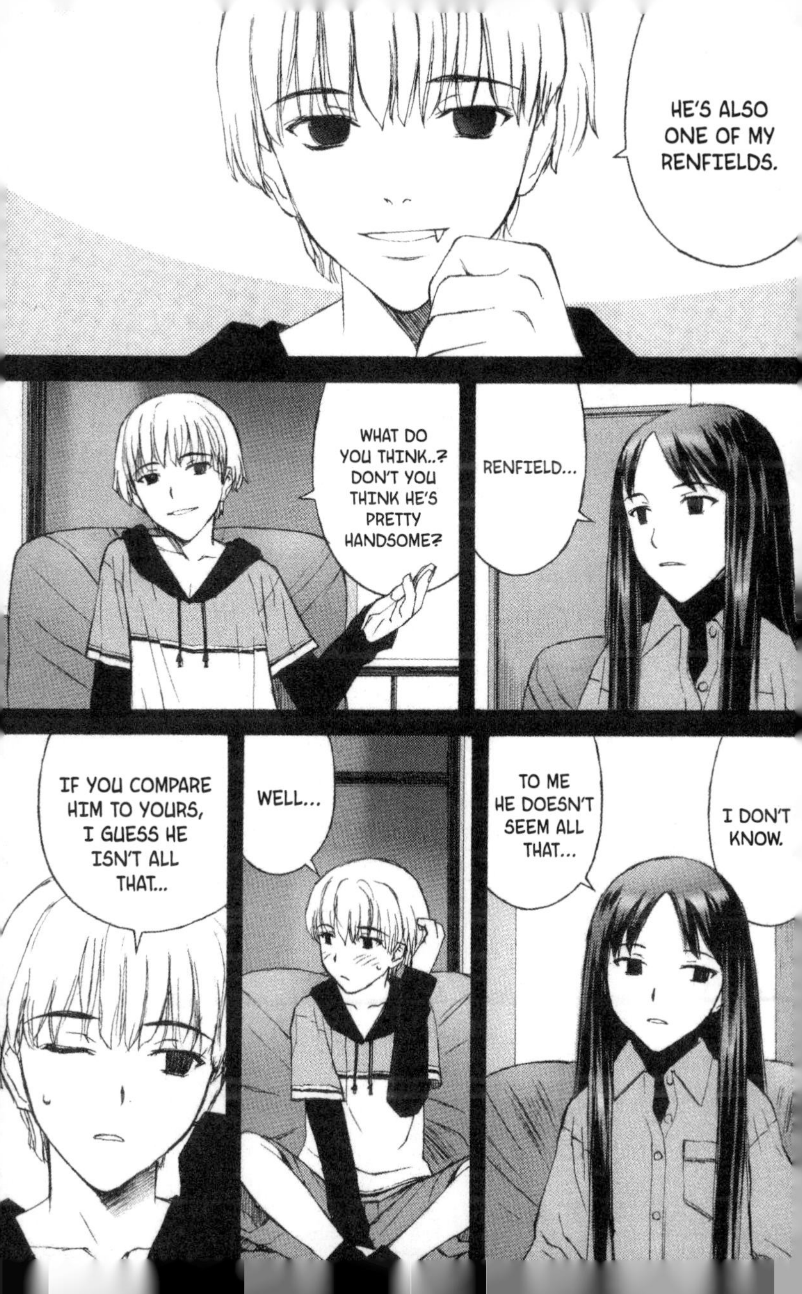
HE'S ALSO ONE OF MY RENFIELDS.
RENFIELD...
WHAT DO YOU THINK..? DON'T YOU THINK HE'S PRETTY HANDSOME?
I DON'T KNOW.
TO ME HE DOESN'T SEEM ALL THAT...
WELL...
IF YOU COMPARE HIM TO YOURS, I GUESS HE ISN'T ALL THAT...

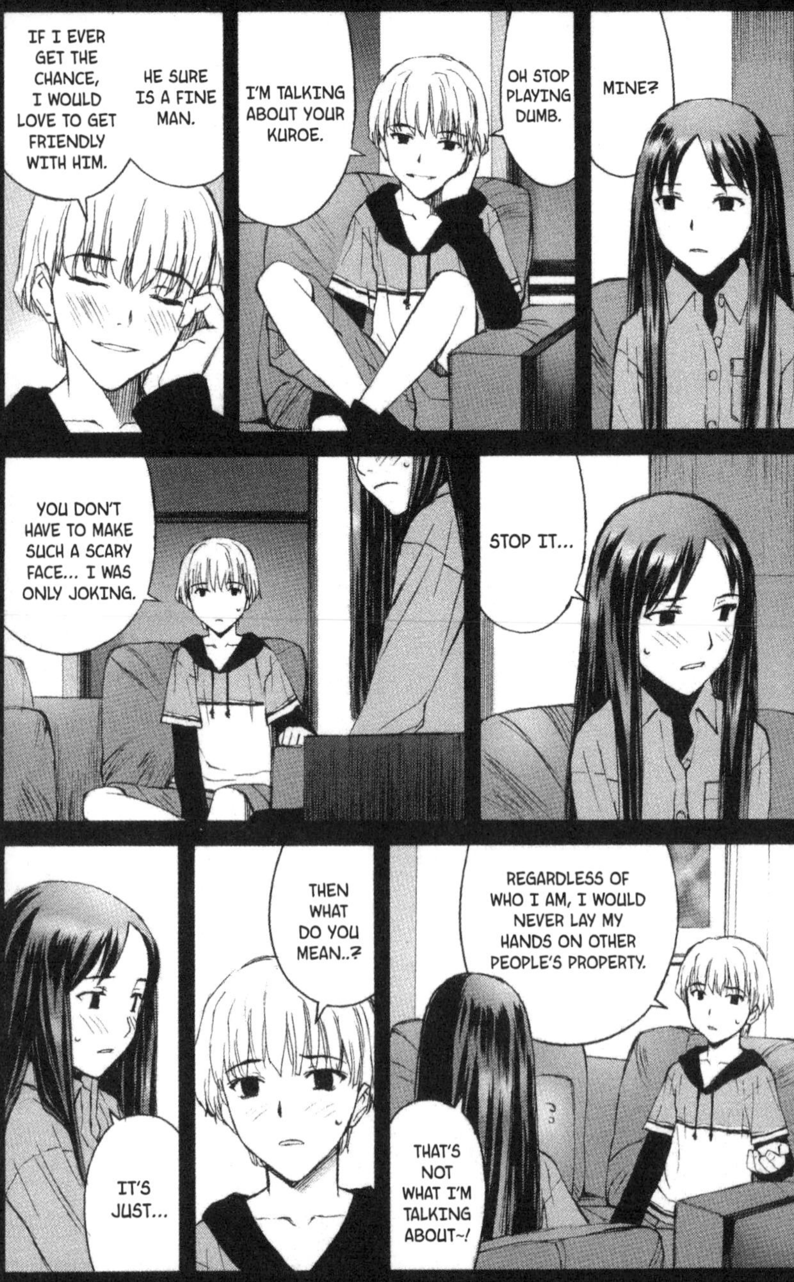
MINE?
OH STOP PLAYING DUMB.
I'M TALKING ABOUT YOUR KUROE.
HE SURE IS A FINE MAN.
IF I EVER GET THE CHANCE, I WOULD LOVE TO GET FRIENDLY WITH HIM.
STOP IT...
YOU DON'T HAVE TO MAKE SUCH A SCARY FACE... I WAS ONLY JOKING.
REGARDLESS OF WHO I AM, I WOULD NEVER LAY MY HANDS ON OTHER PEOPLE'S PROPERTY.
THAT'S NOT WHAT I'M TALKING ABOUT~!
THEN WHAT DO YOU MEAN..?
IT'S JUST...

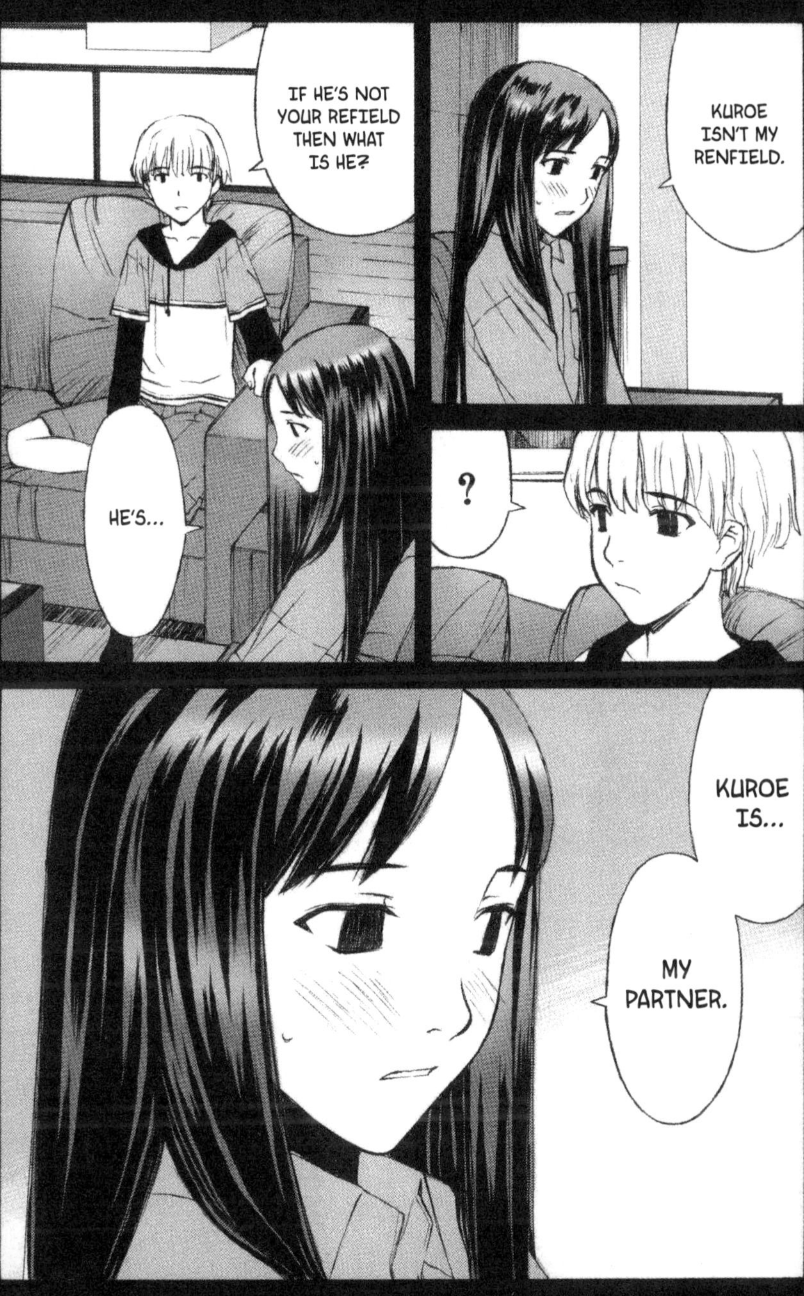
KUROE ISN'T MY RENFIELD.
?
IF HE'S NOT YOUR REFIELD THEN WHAT IS HE?
HE'S...
KUROE IS...
MY PARTNER.

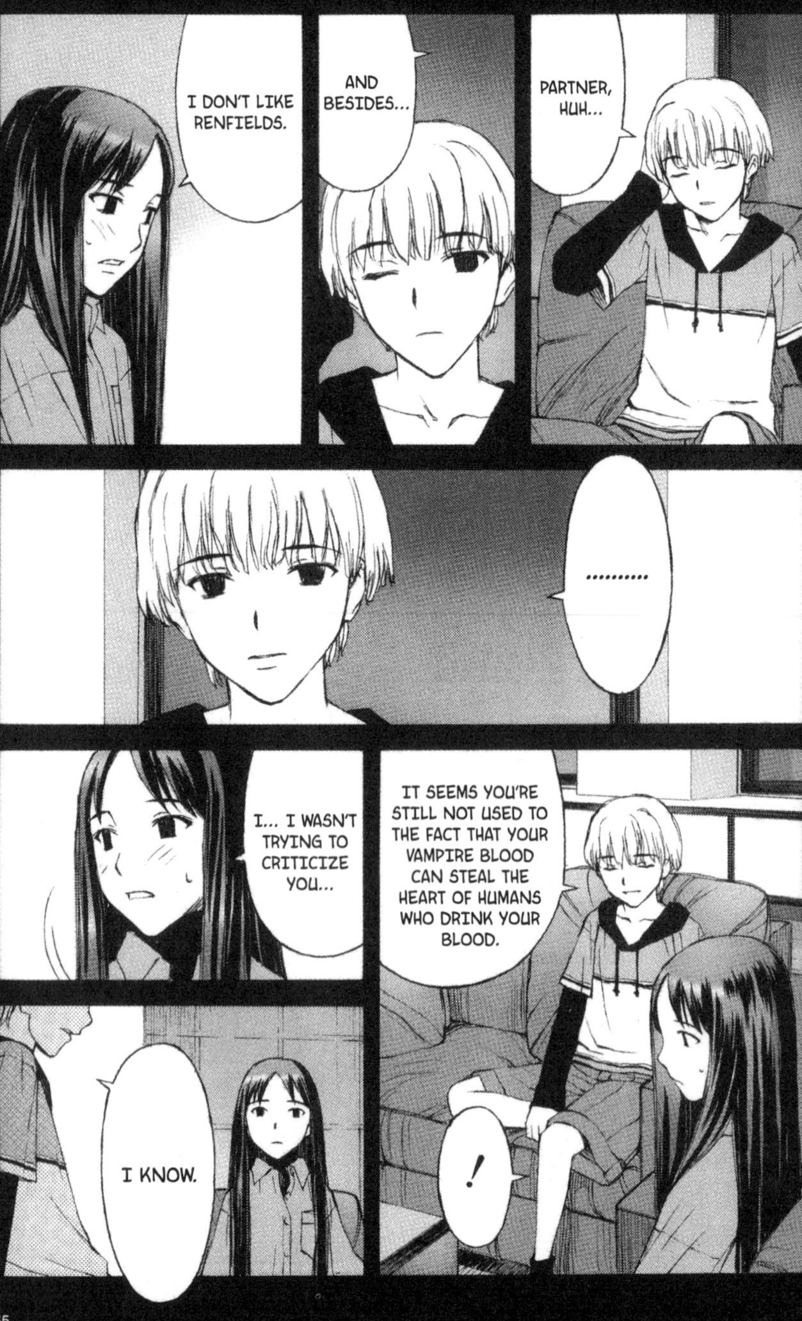
PARTNER, HUH...
AND BESIDES...
I DON'T LIKE RENFIELDS.
....
IT SEEMS YOU'RE STILL NOT USED TO THE FACT THAT YOUR VAMPIRE BLOOD CAN STEAL THE HEART OF HUMANS WHO DRINK YOUR BLOOD.
!
I... I WASN'T TRYING TO CRITICIZE YOU...
I KNOW.

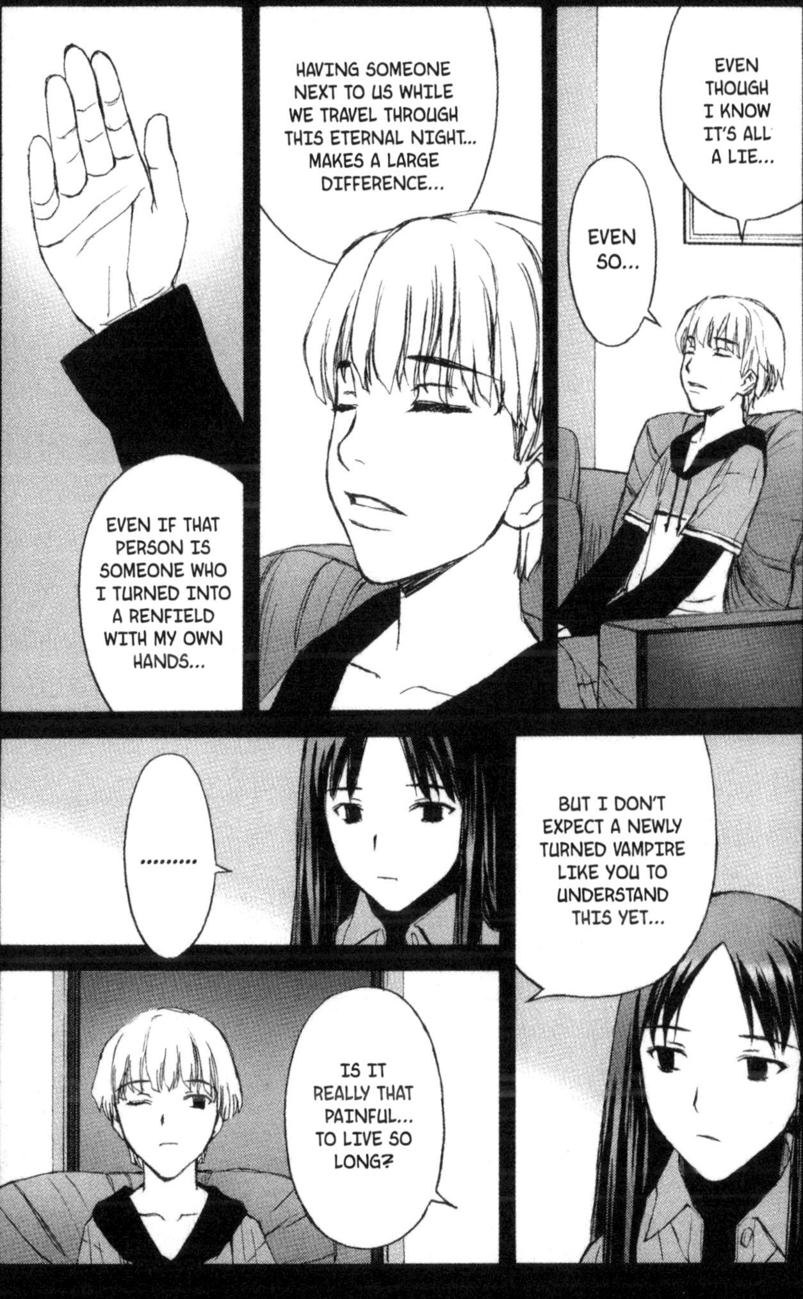
EVEN THOUGH I KNOW IT'S ALL A LIE...
EVEN SO...
HAVING SOMEONE NEXT TO US WHILE WE TRAVEL THROUGH THIS ETERNAL NIGHT... MAKES A LARGE DIFFERENCE...
EVEN IF THAT PERSON IS SOMEONE WHO I TURNED INTO A RENFIELD WITH MY OWN HANDS...
BUT I DON'T EXPECT A NEWLY TURNED VAMPIRE LIKE YOU TO UNDERSTAND THIS YET...
....
IS IT REALLY THAT PAINFUL... TO LIVE SO LONG?

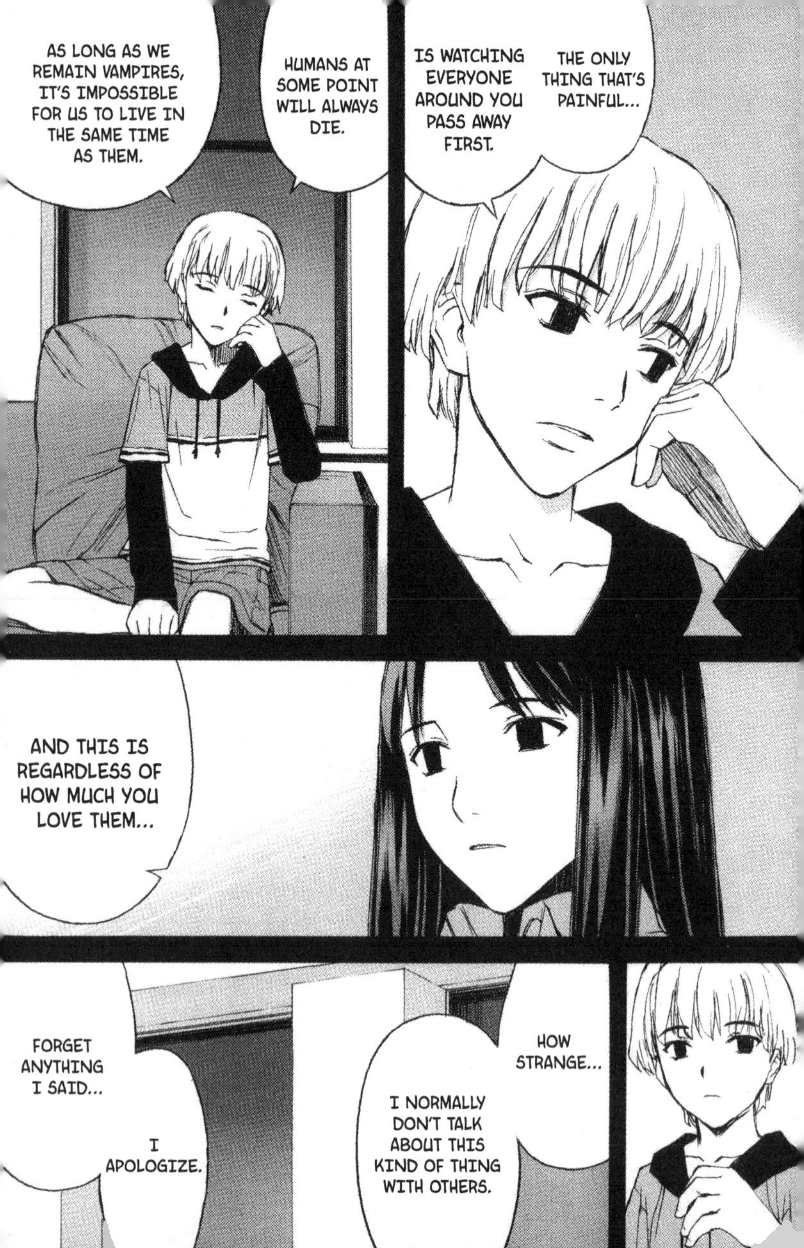
THE ONLY THING THAT'S PAINFUL...
IS WATCHING EVERYONE AROUND YOU PASS AWAY FIRST.
HUMANS AT SOME POINT WILL ALWAYS DIE.
AS LONG AS WE REMAIN VAMPIRES, IT'S IMPOSSIBLE FOR US TO LIVE IN THE SAME TIME AS THEM.
AND THIS IS REGARDLESS OF HOW MUCH YOU LOVE THEM...
HOW STRANGE...
I NORMALLY DON'T TALK ABOUT THIS KIND OF THING WITH OTHERS.
FORGET ANYTHING I SAID...
I APOLOGIZE.

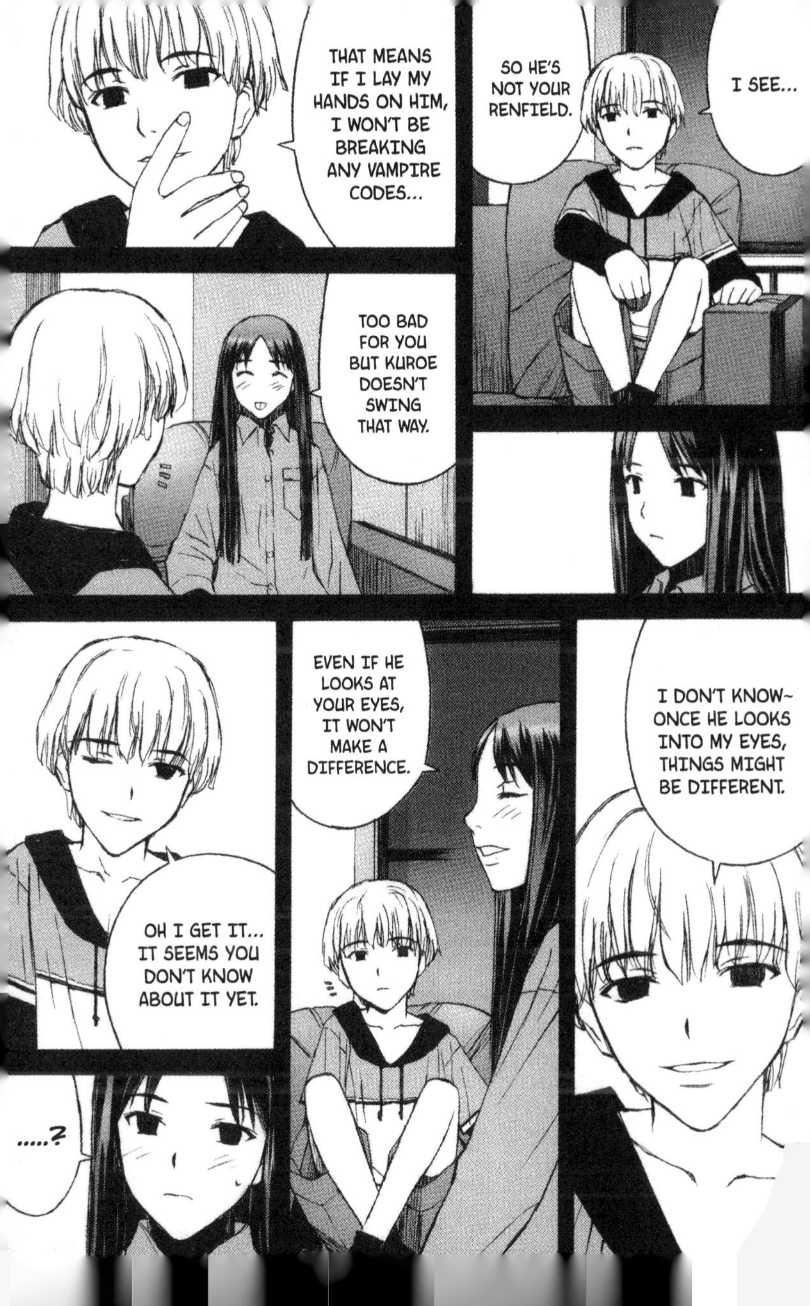
I SEE...
SO HE'S NOT YOUR RENFIELD.
THAT MEANS IF I LAY MY HANDS ON HIM, I WON'T BE BREAKING ANY VAMPIRE CODES...
TOO BAD FOR YOU BUT KUROE DOESN'T SWING THAT WAY.
I DON'T KNOW~ ONCE HE LOOKS INTO MY EYES, THINGS MIGHT BE DIFFERENT.
EVEN IF HE LOOKS AT YOUR EYES, IT WON'T MAKE A DIFFERENCE.
OH I GET IT... IT SEEMS YOU DON'T KNOW ABOUT IT YET.
.....?

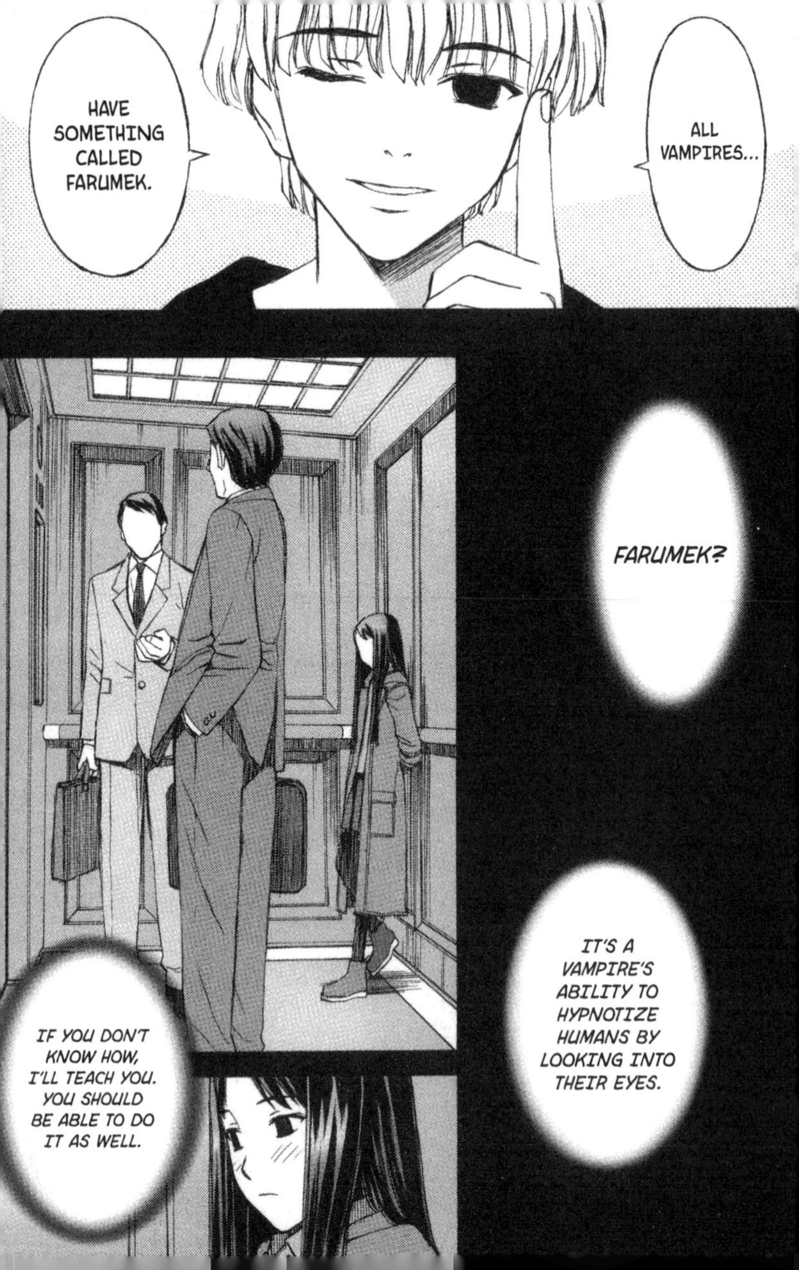
ALL VAMPIRES...
HAVE SOMETHING CALLED FARUMEK.
FARUMEK?
IT'S A VAMPIRE'S ABILITY TO HYPNOTIZE HUMANS BY LOOKING INTO THEIR EYES.
IF YOU DON'T KNOW HOW, I'LL TEACH YOU. YOU SHOULD BE ABLE TO DO IT AS WELL.

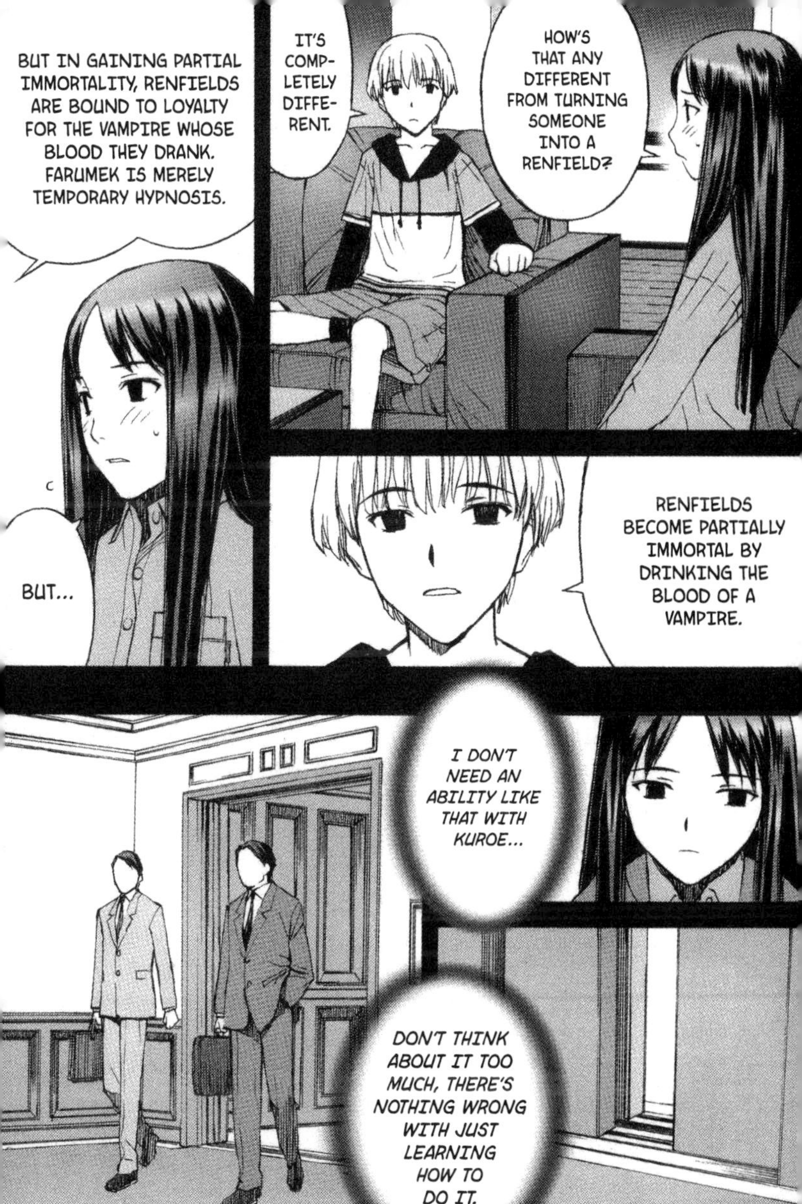
HOW'S THAT ANY DIFFERENT FROM TURNING SOMEONE INTO A RENFIELD?
IT'S COMPLETELY DIFFERENT.
RENFIELDS BECOME PARTIALLY IMMORTAL BY DRINKING THE BLOOD OF A VAMPIRE.
BUT IN GAINING PARTIAL IMMORTALITY, RENFIELDS ARE BOUND TO LOYALTY FOR THE VAMPIRE WHOSE BLOOD THEY DRANK. FARUMEK IS MERELY TEMPORARY HYPNOSIS.
BUT...
I DON'T NEED AN ABILITY LIKE THAT WITH KUROE...
DON'T THINK ABOUT IT TOO MUCH, THERE'S NOTHING WRONG WITH JUST LEARNING HOW TO DO IT.

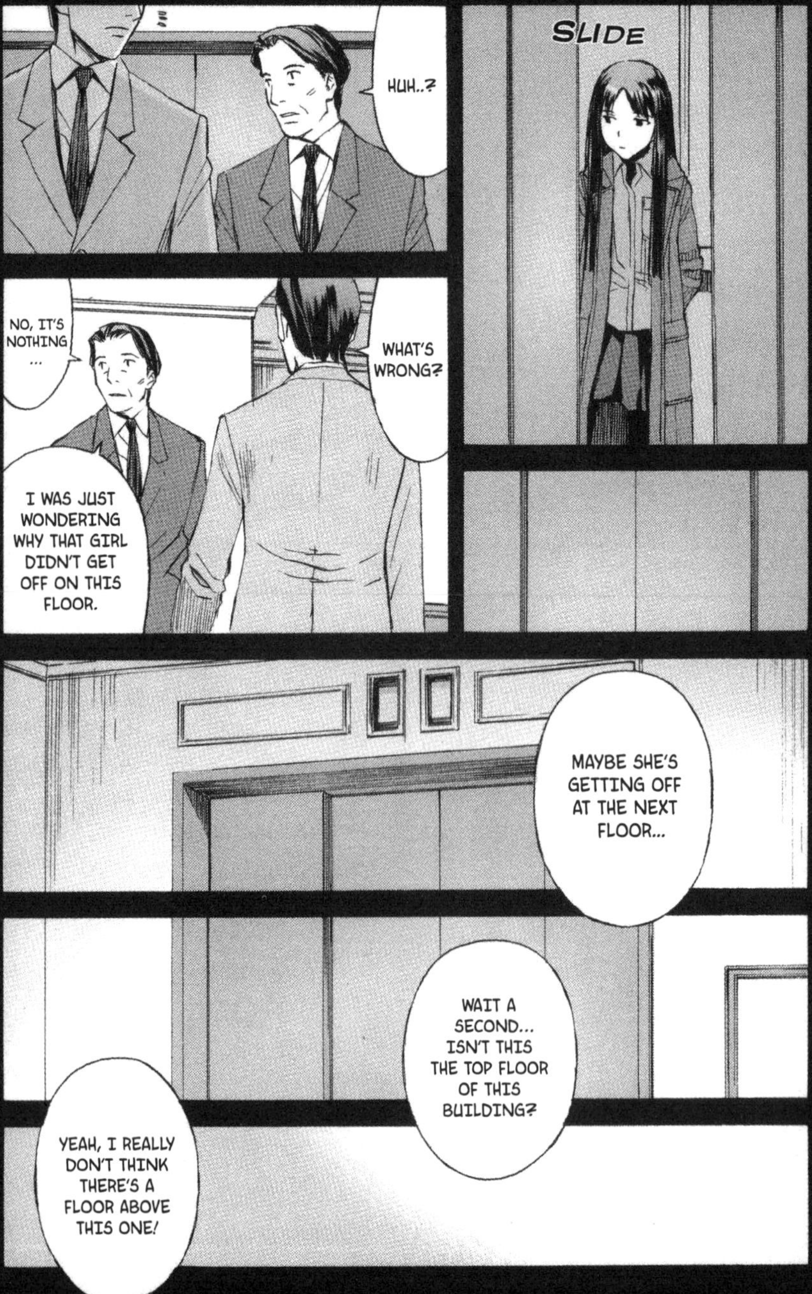
SLIDE
HUH..?
WHAT'S WRONG?
NO, IT'S NOTHING ...
I WAS JUST WONDERING WHY THAT GIRL DIDN'T GET OFF ON THIS FLOOR.
MAYBE SHE'S GETTING OFF AT THE NEXT FLOOR...
WAIT A SECOND... ISN'T THIS THE TOP FLOOR OF THIS BUILDING?
YEAH, I REALLY DON'T THINK THERE'S A FLOOR ABOVE THIS ONE!

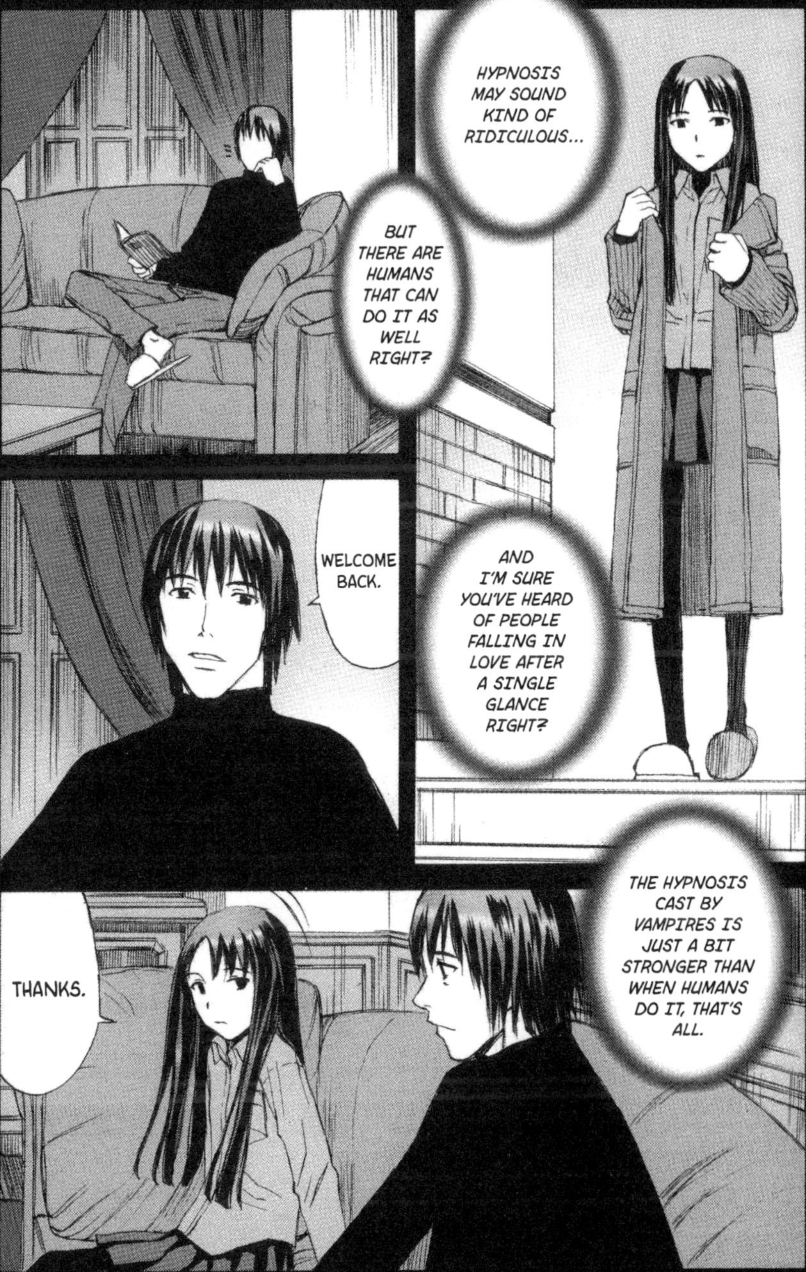
HYPNOSIS MAY SOUND KIND OF RIDICULOUS...
BUT THERE ARE HUMANS THAT CAN DO IT AS WELL RIGHT?
AND I'M SURE YOU'VE HEARD OF PEOPLE FALLING IN LOVE AFTER A SINGLE GLANCE RIGHT?
WELCOME BACK.
THE HYPNOSIS CAST BY VAMPIRES IS JUST A BIT STRONGER THAN WHEN HUMANS DO IT, THAT'S ALL.
THANKS.

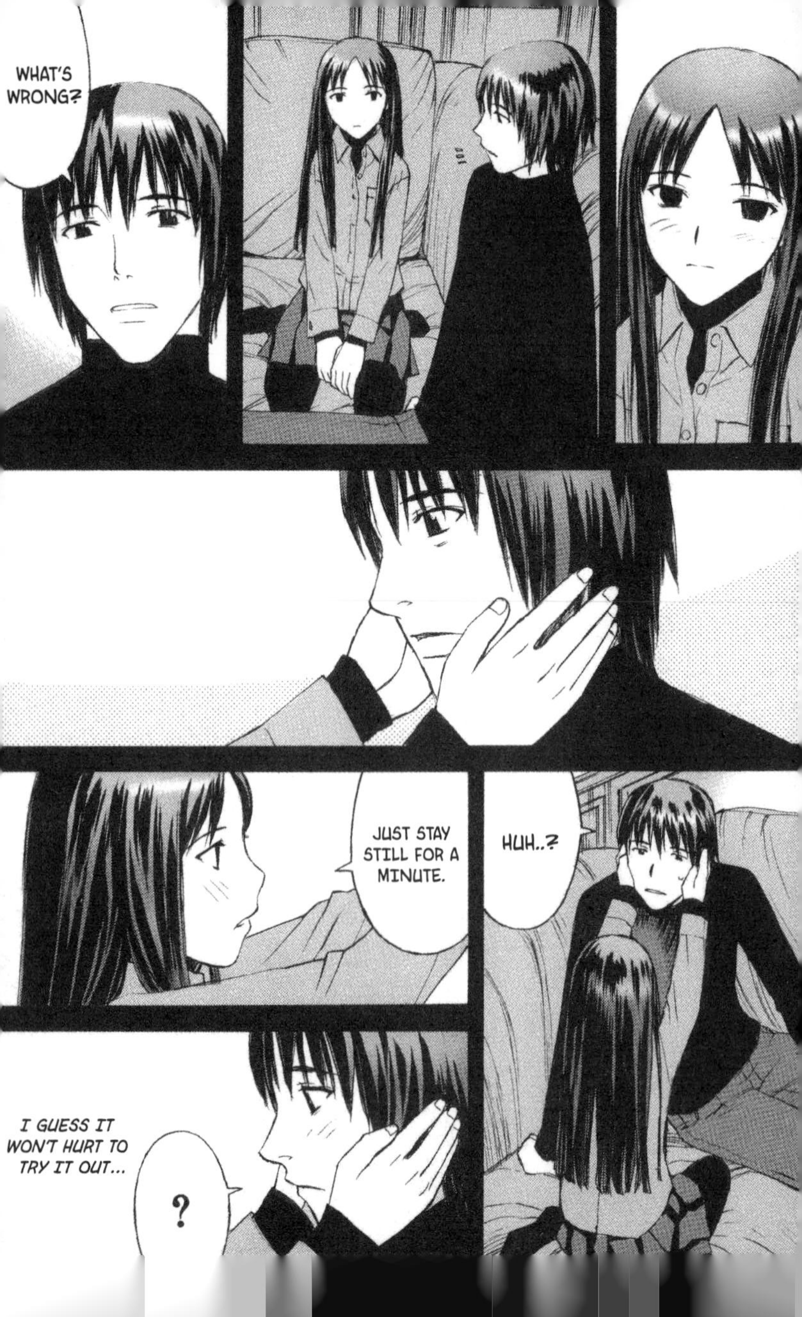
WHAT'S WRONG?
HUH..?
JUST STAY STILL FOR A MINUTE.
I GUESS IT WON'T HURT TO TRY IT OUT...
?

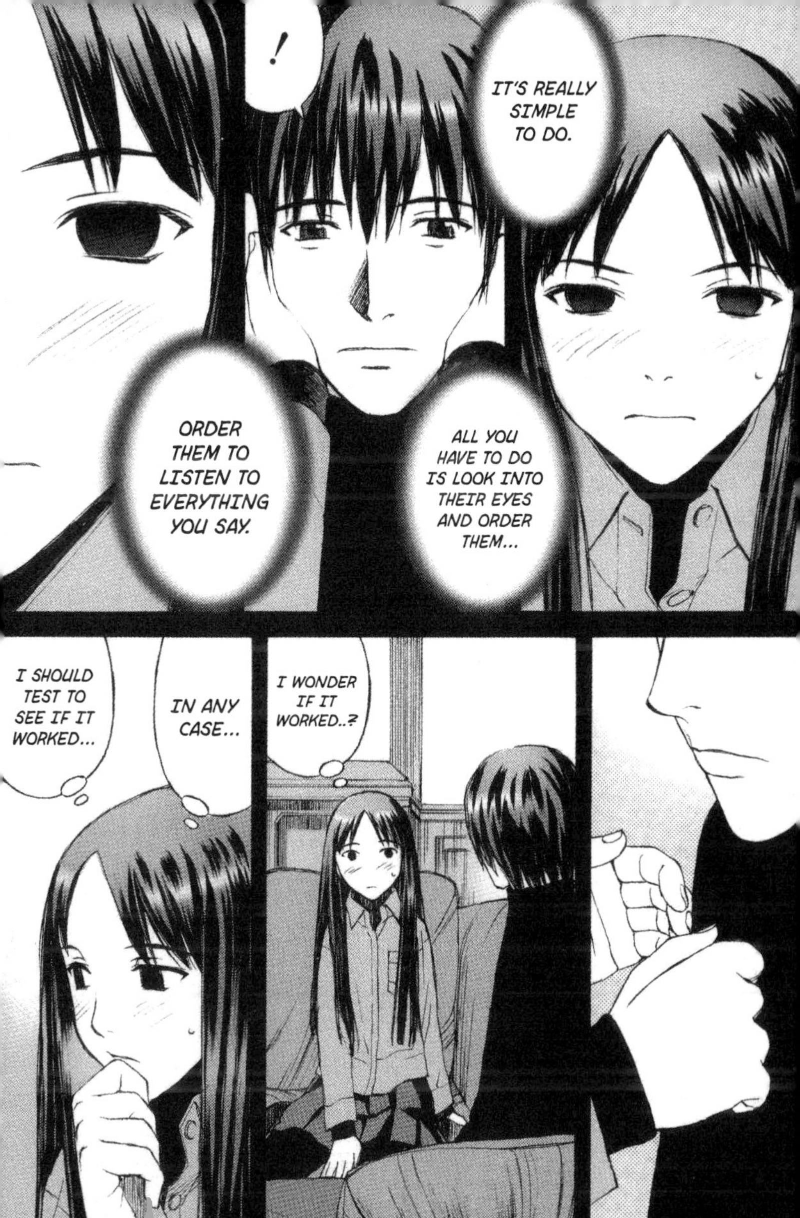
IT'S REALLY SIMPLE TO DO.
!
ALL YOU HAVE TO DO IS LOOK INTO THEIR EYES AND ORDER THEM...
ORDER THEM TO LISTEN TO EVERYTHING YOU SAY.
I WONDER IF IT WORKED..?
IN ANY CASE...
I SHOULD TEST TO SEE IF IT WORKED...

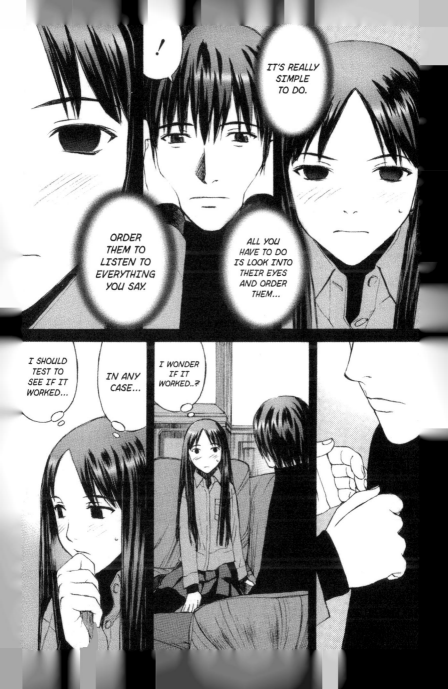

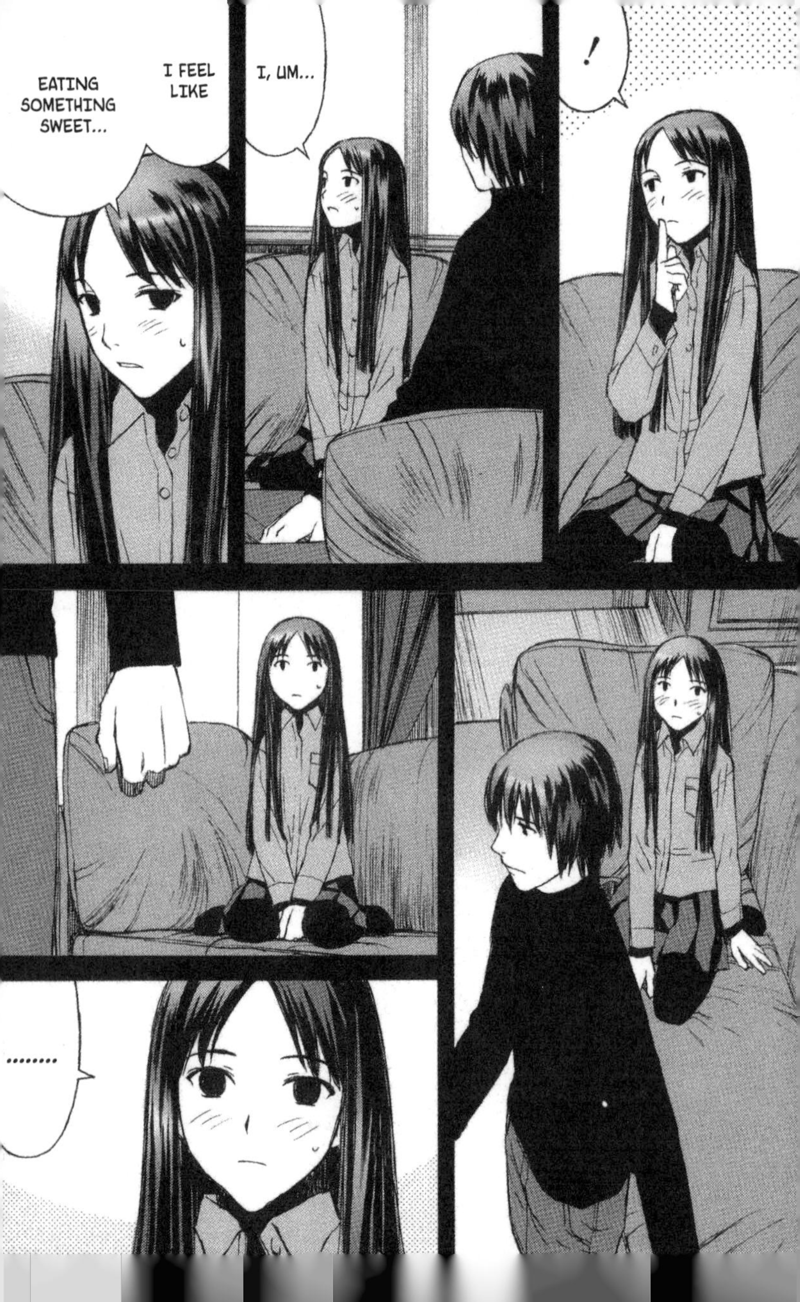
!
I, UM...
I FEEL LIKE
EATING SOMETHING SWEET...
....

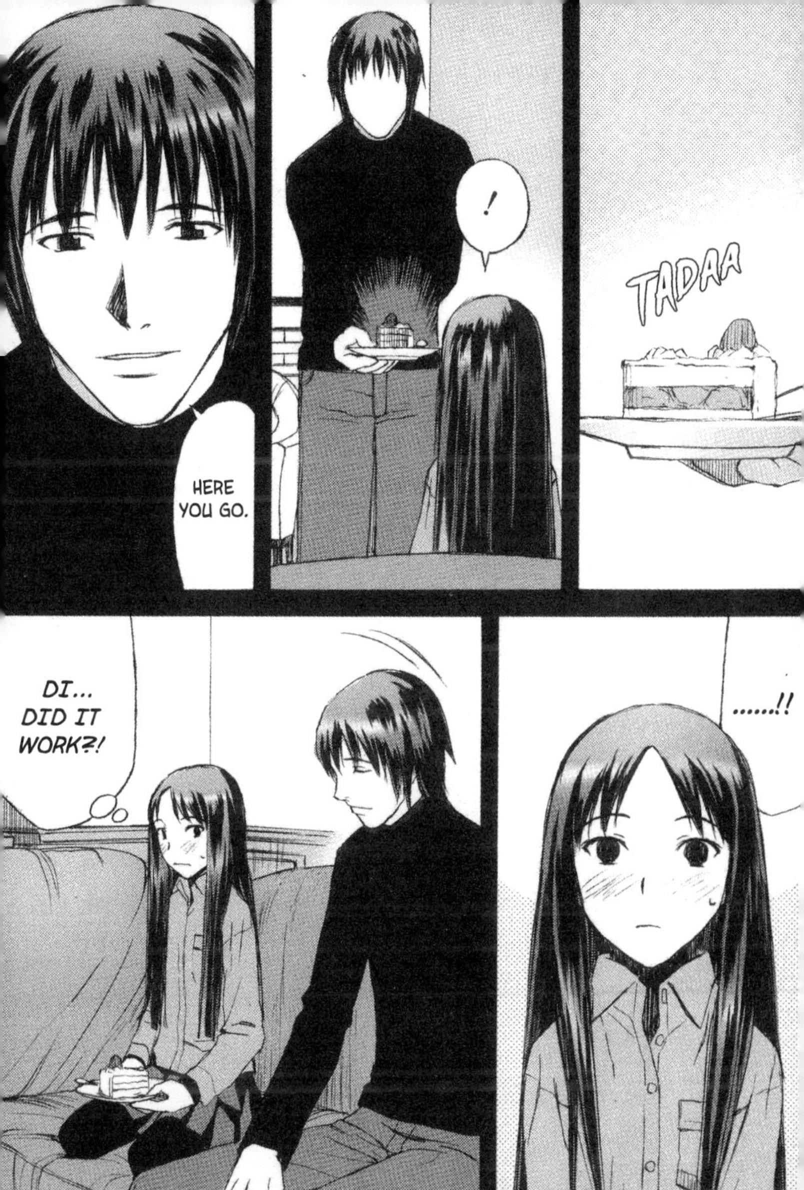
TADAA
!
HERE YOU GO.
......!!
DI... DID IT WORK?!

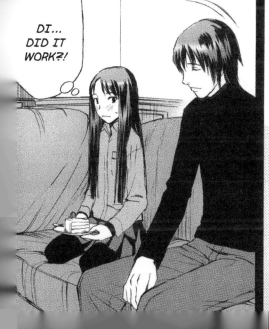

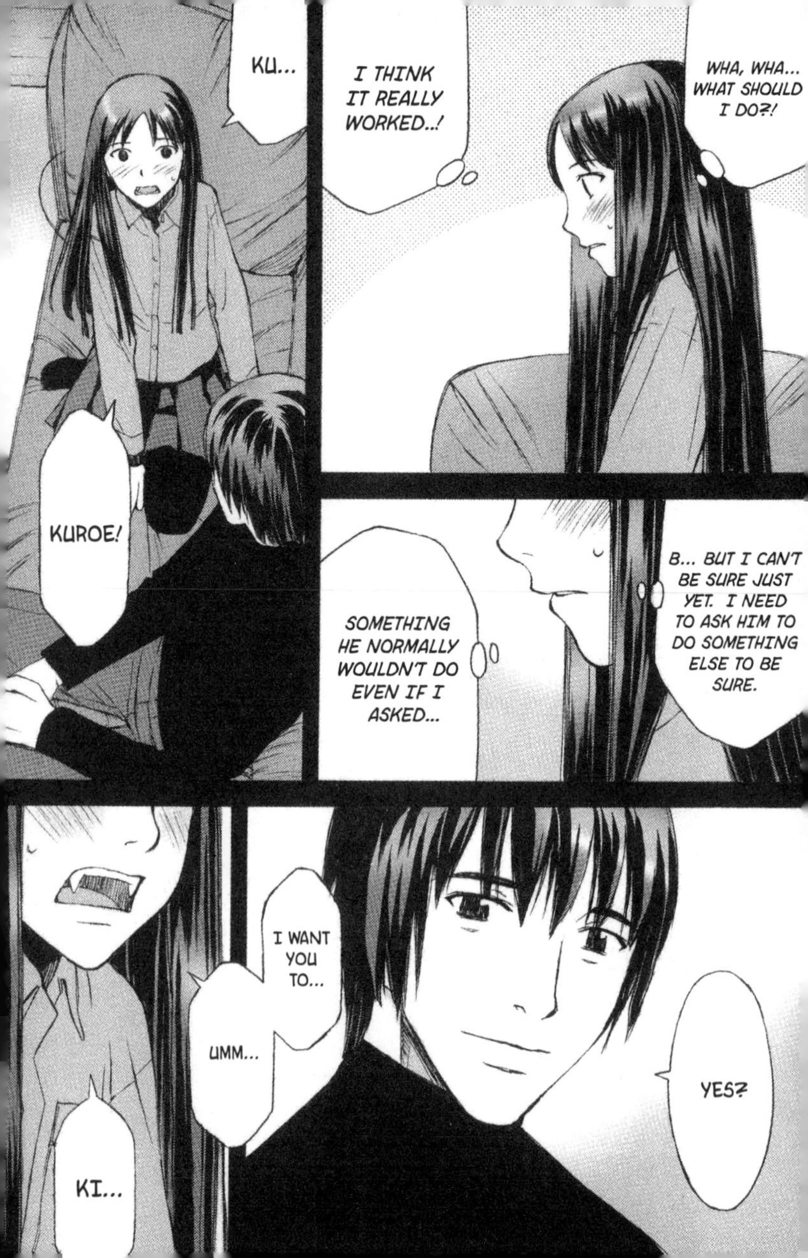
WHA, WHA... WHAT SHOULD I DO?!
I THINK IT REALLY WORKED..!
B... BUT I CAN'T BE SURE JUST YET. I NEED TO ASK HIM TO DO SOMETHING ELSE TO BE SURE.
SOMETHING HE NORMALLY WOULDN'T DO EVEN IF I ASKED...
KU...
KUROE!
YES?
I WANT YOU TO...
UMM...
KI...

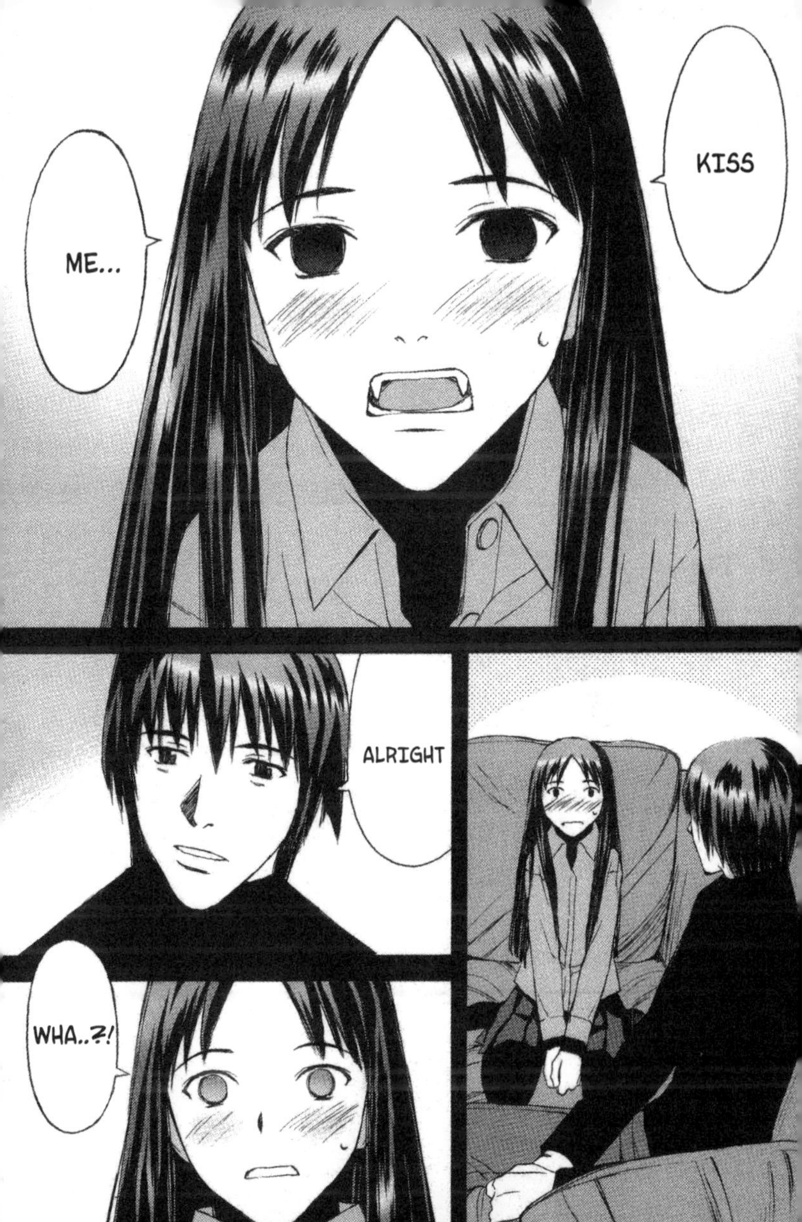
KISS
ME...
ALRIGHT
WHA..?!

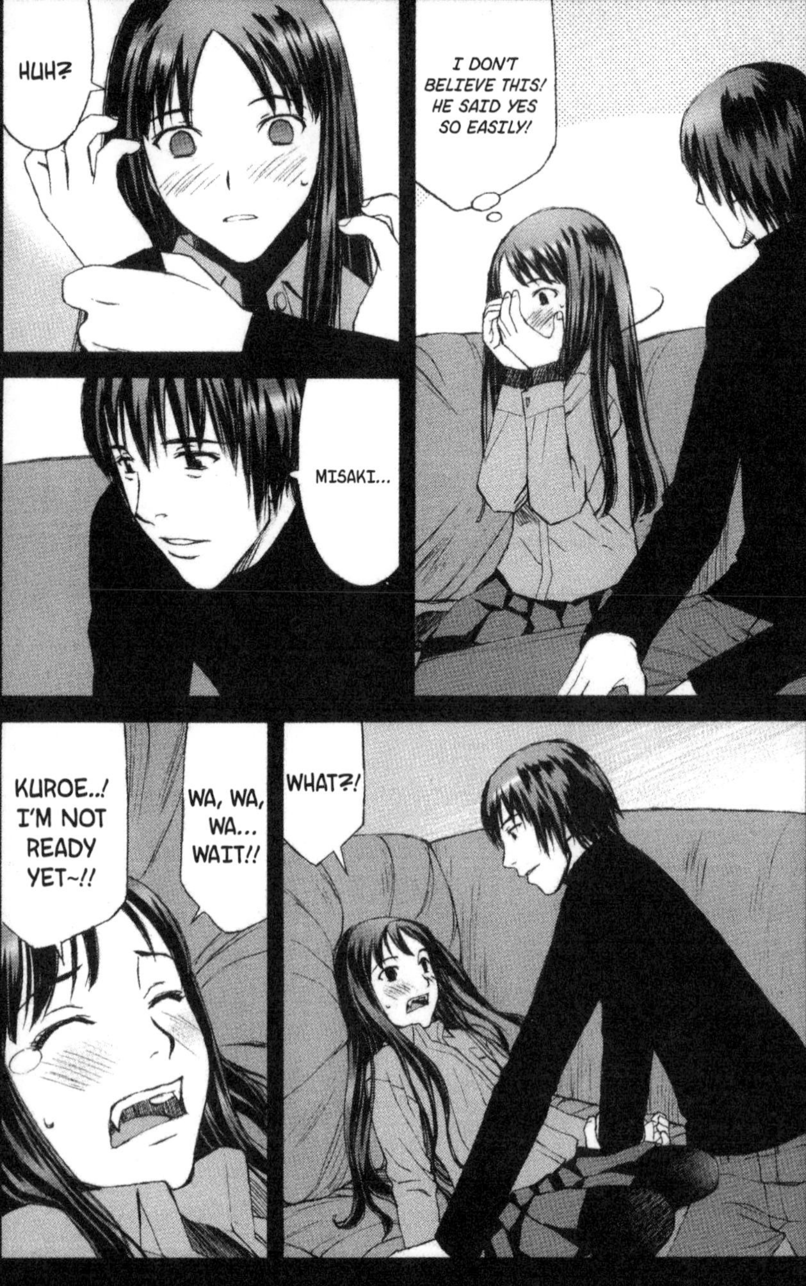
I DON'T BELIEVE THIS! HE SAID YES SO EASILY!
HUH?
MISAKI...
WHAT?!
WA, WA, WA... WAIT!!
KUROE..! I'M NOT READY YET~!!

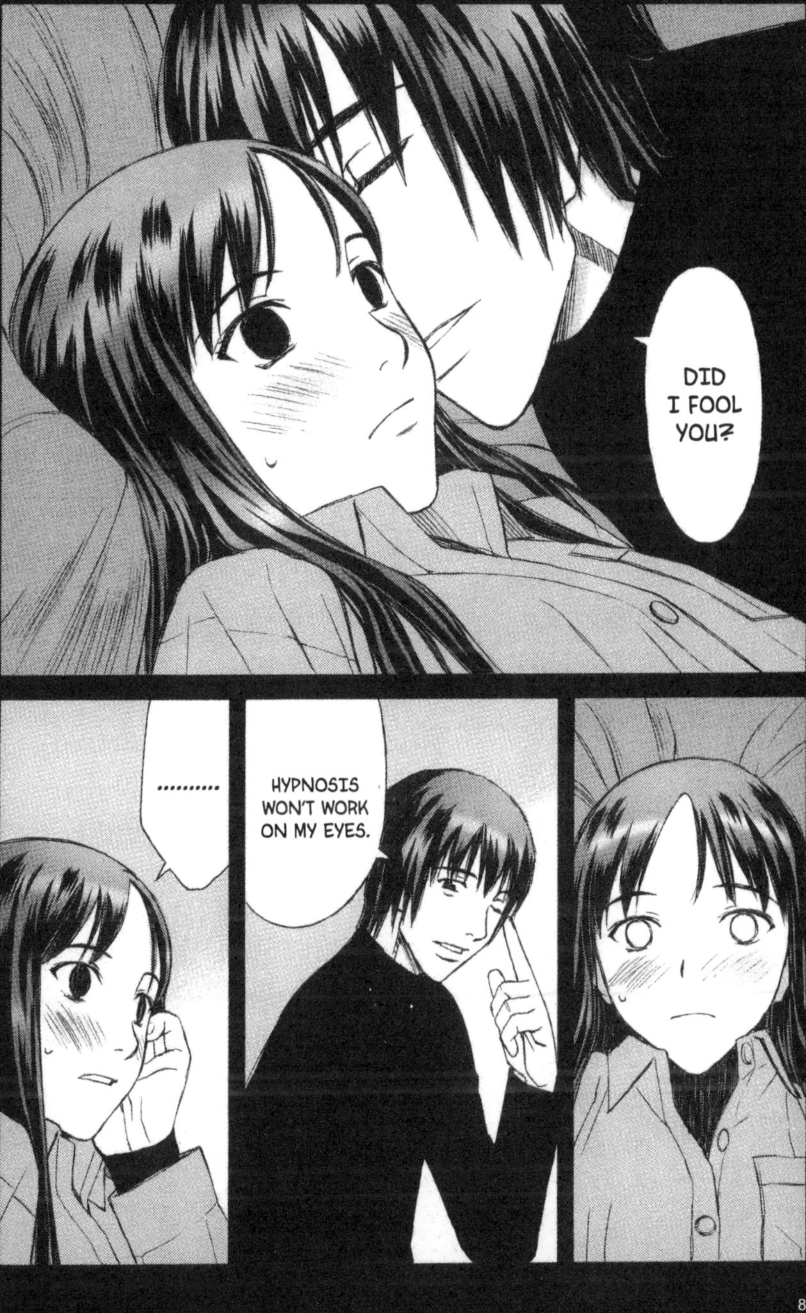
DID I FOOL YOU?
HYPNOSIS WON'T WORK ON MY EYES.
....

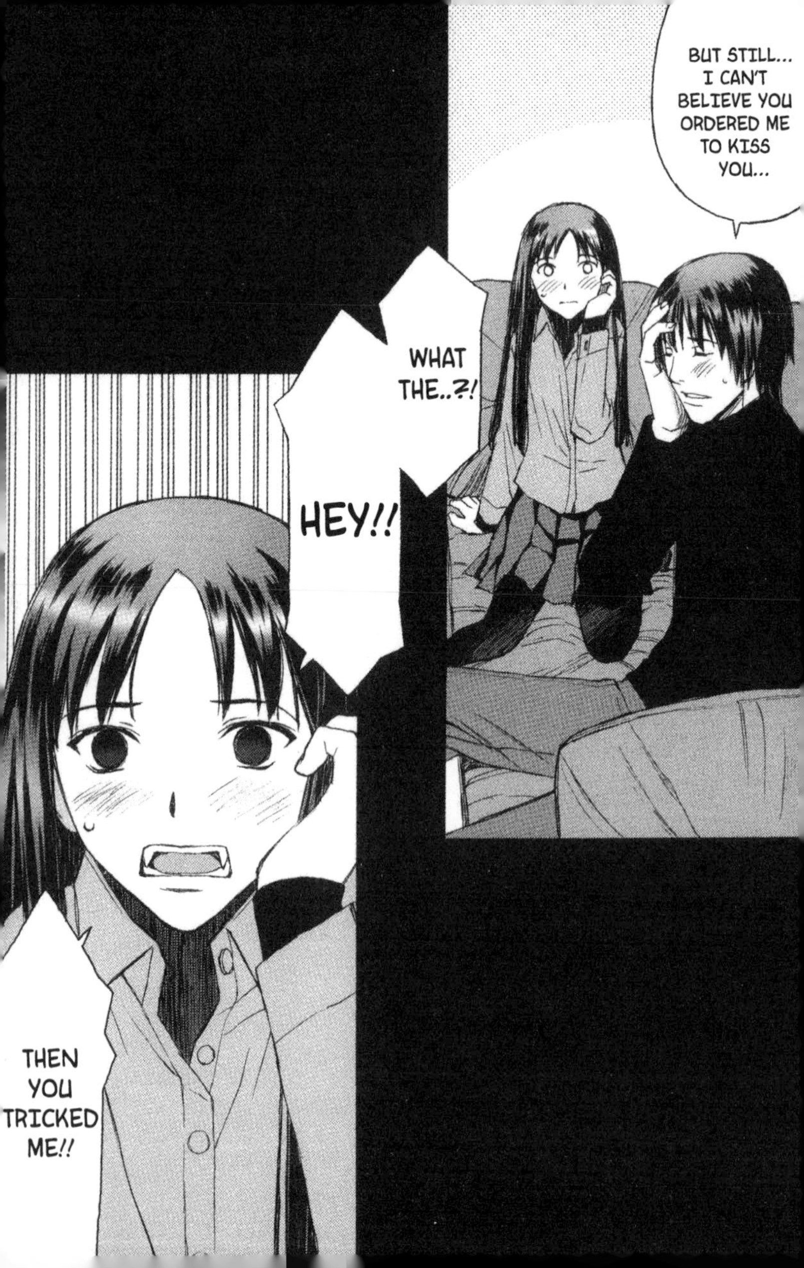
BUT STILL... I CAN'T BELIEVE YOU ORDERED ME TO KISS YOU...
WHAT THE..?!
HEY!!
THEN YOU TRICKED ME!!

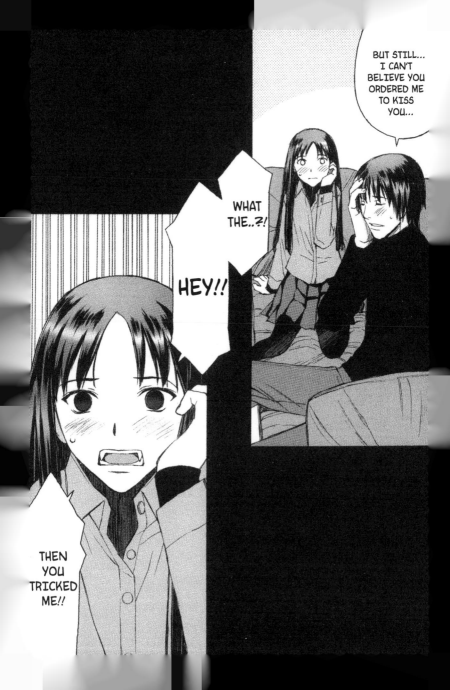

Episode 3

SOUL SLAVE part 1

魂の奴隷

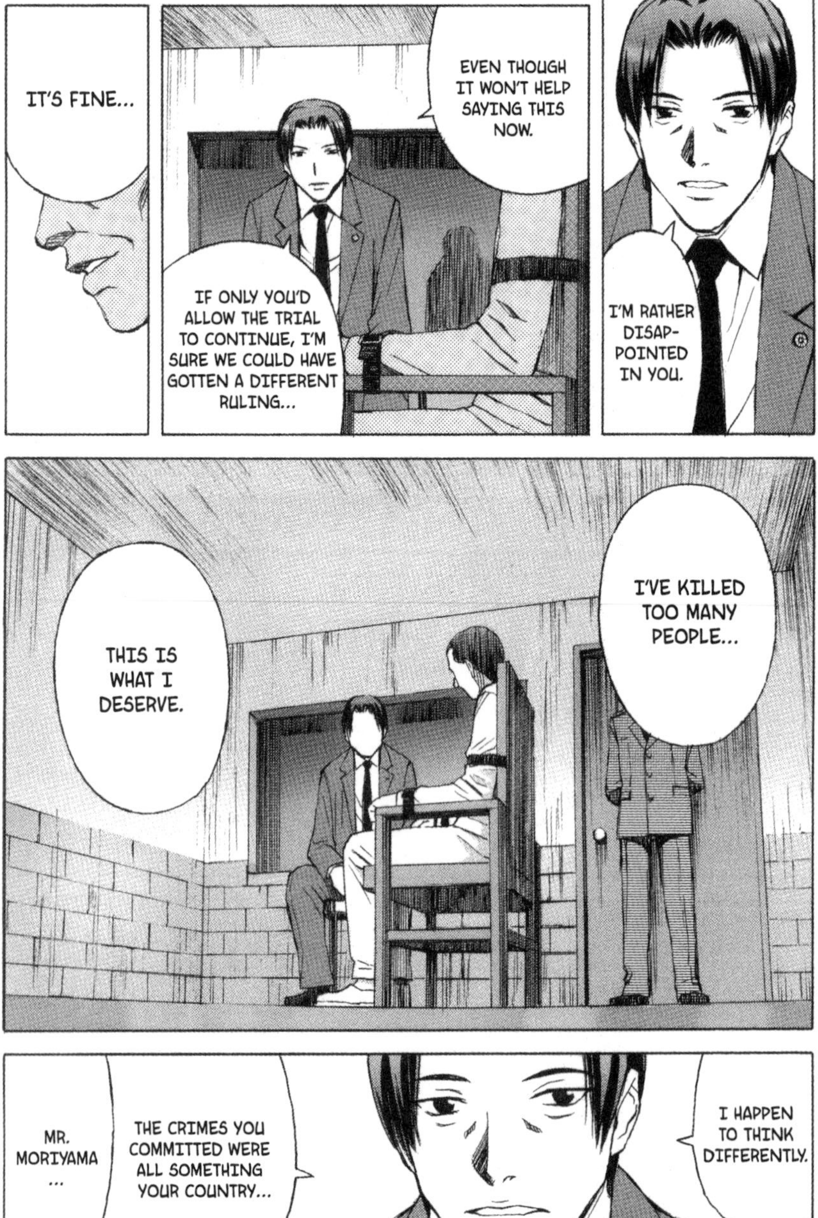
I'M RATHER DISAPPOINTED IN YOU.
EVEN THOUGH IT WON'T HELP SAYING THIS NOW.
IF ONLY YOU'D ALLOW THE TRIAL TO CONTINUE, I'M SURE WE COULD HAVE GOTTEN A DIFFERENT RULING...
IT'S FINE...
I'VE KILLED TOO MANY PEOPLE...
THIS IS WHAT I DESERVE.
I HAPPEN TO THINK DIFFERENTLY.
THE CRIMES YOU COMMITTED WERE ALL SOMETHING YOUR COUNTRY...
MR. MORIYAMA ...

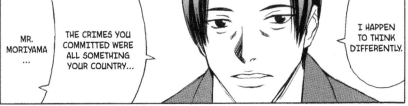

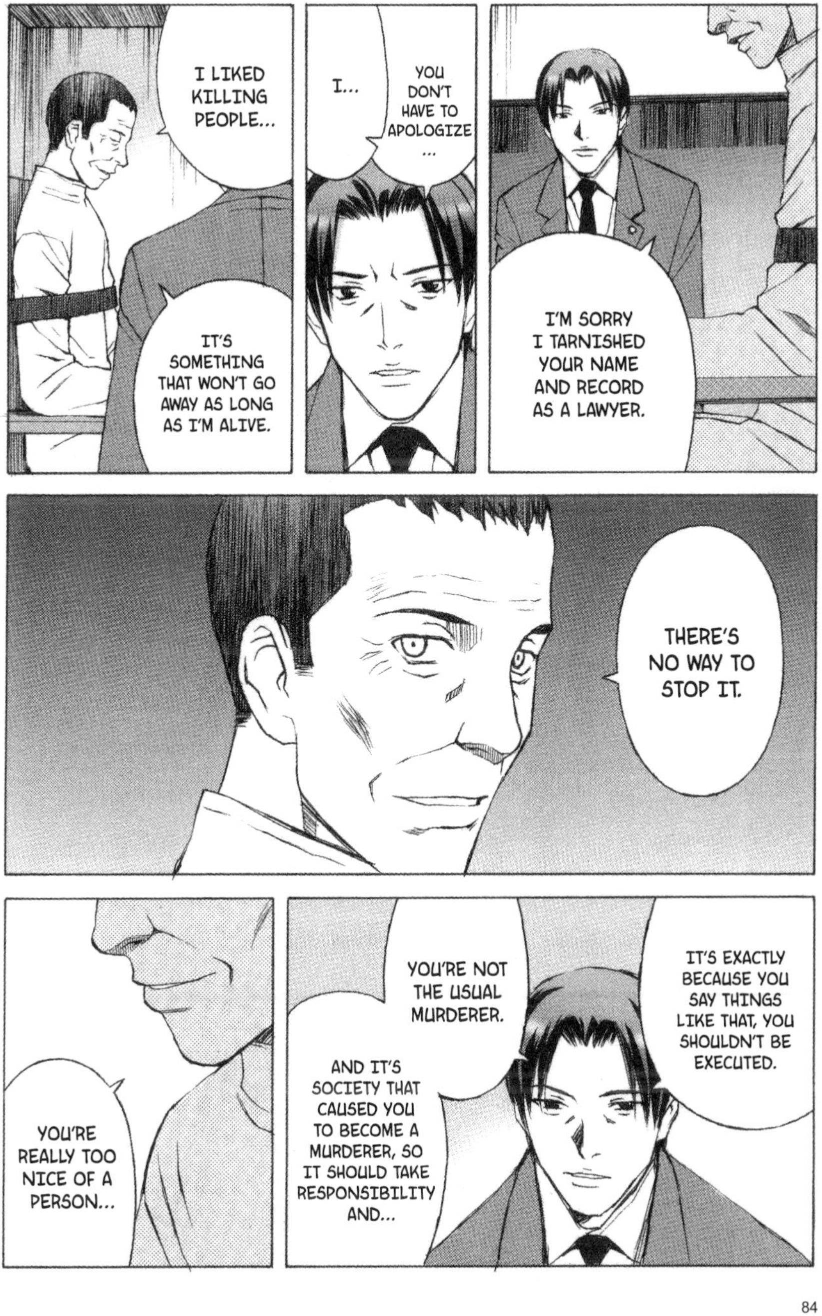
I'M SORRY I TARNISHED YOUR NAME AND RECORD AS A LAWYER.
YOU DON'T HAVE TO APOLOGIZE...
I...
I LIKED KILLING PEOPLE...
IT'S SOMETHING THAT WON'T GO AWAY AS LONG AS I'M ALIVE.
THERE'S NO WAY TO STOP IT.
IT'S EXACTLY BECAUSE YOU SAY THINGS LIKE THAT, YOU SHOULDN'T BE EXECUTED.
YOU'RE NOT THE USUAL MURDERER.
AND IT'S SOCIETY THAT CAUSED YOU TO BECOME A MURDERER, SO IT SHOULD TAKE RESPONSIBILITY AND...
YOU'RE REALLY TOO NICE OF A PERSON...

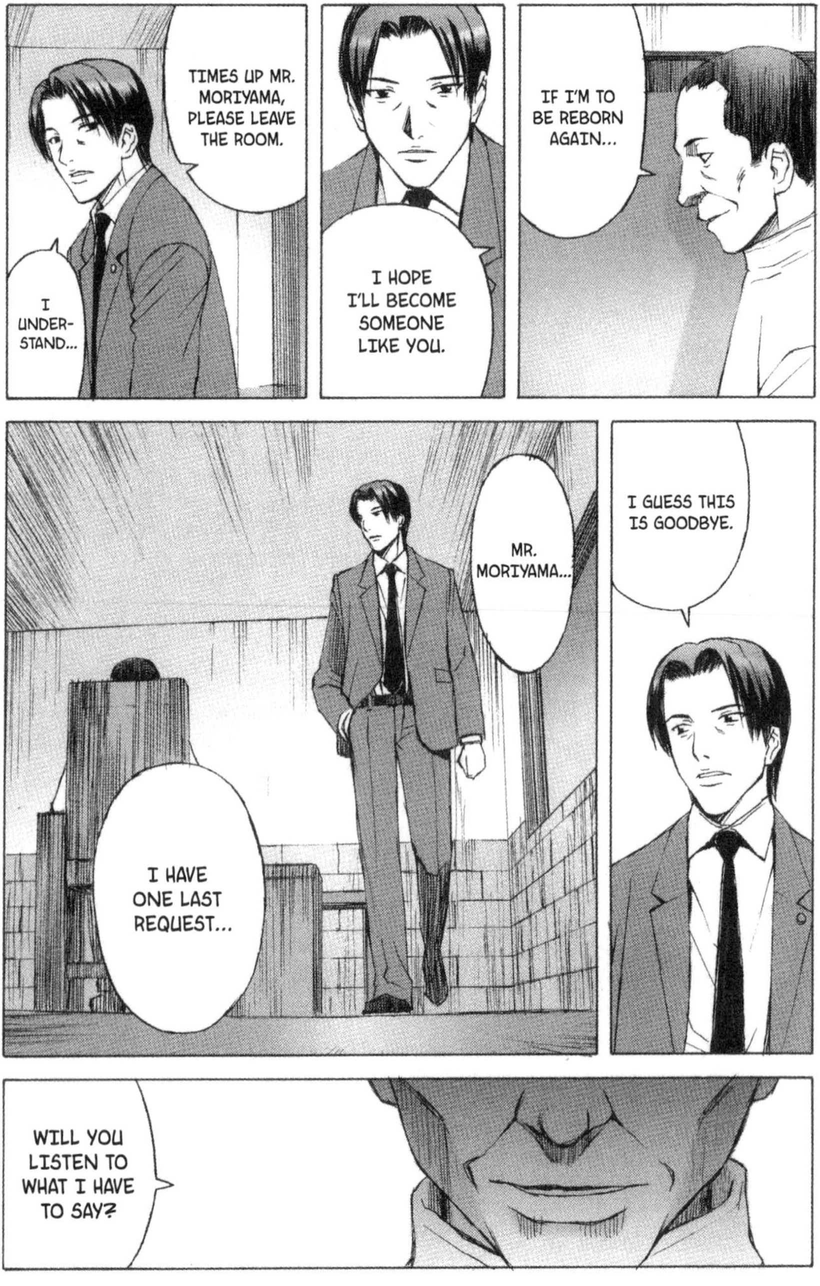
IF I'M TO BE REBORN AGAIN...
I HOPE I'LL BECOME SOMEONE LIKE YOU.
TIMES UP MR. MORIYAMA, PLEASE LEAVE THE ROOM.
I UNDER-STAND...
I GUESS THIS IS GOODBYE.
MR. MORIYAMA...
I HAVE ONE LAST REQUEST...
WILL YOU LISTEN TO WHAT I HAVE TO SAY?

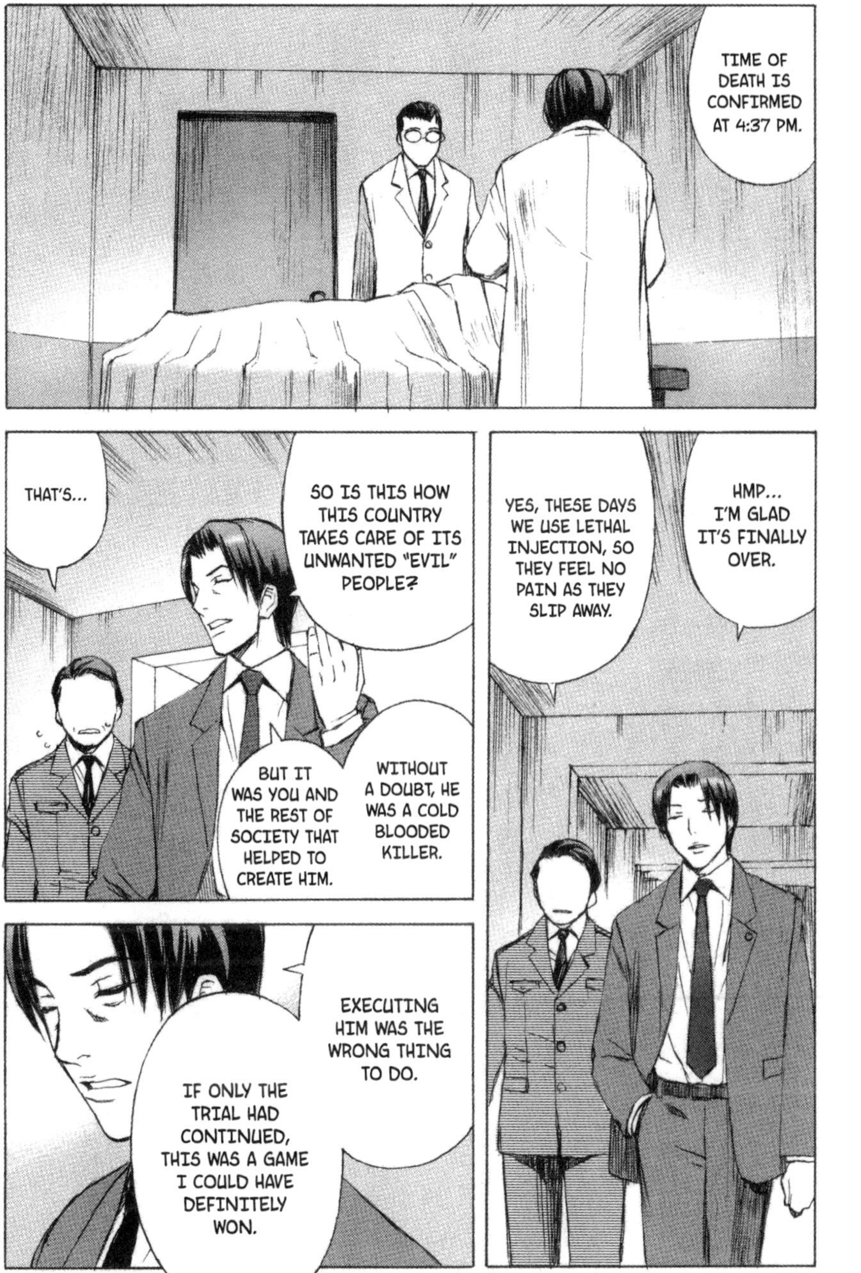
TIME OF DEATH IS CONFIRMED AT 4:37 PM.
HMP... I'M GLAD IT'S FINALLY OVER.
YES, THESE DAYS WE USE LETHAL INJECTION, SO THEY FEEL NO PAIN AS THEY SLIP AWAY.
SO IS THIS HOW THIS COUNTRY TAKES CARE OF ITS UNWANTED "EVIL" PEOPLE?
THAT'S...
WITHOUT A DOUBT, HE WAS A COLD BLOODED KILLER.
BUT IT WAS YOU AND THE REST OF SOCIETY THAT HELPED TO CREATE HIM.
EXECUTING HIM WAS THE WRONG THING TO DO.
IF ONLY THE TRIAL HAD CONTINUED, THIS WAS A GAME I COULD HAVE DEFINITELY WON.

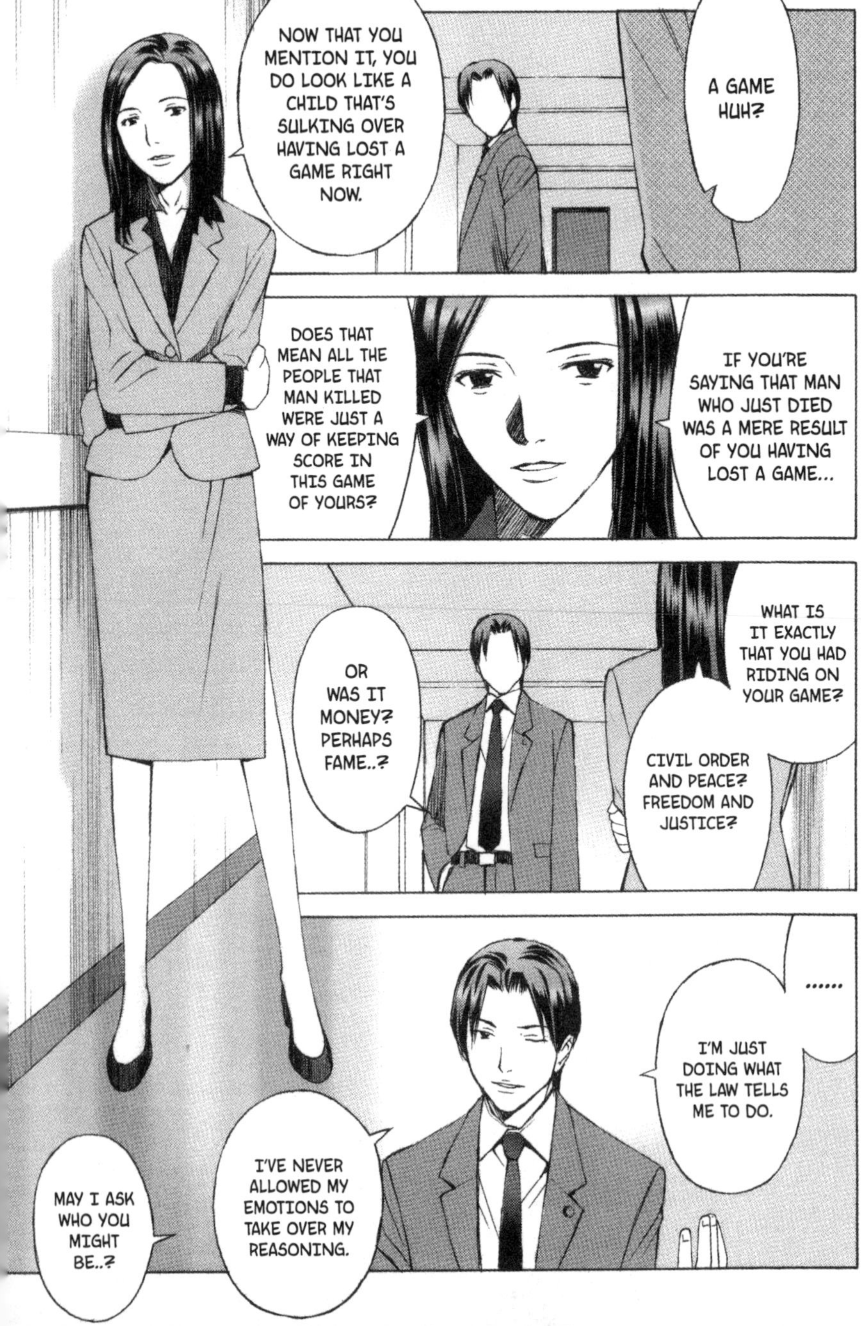
A GAME HUH?
NOW THAT YOU MENTION IT, YOU DO LOOK LIKE A CHILD THAT'S SULKING OVER HAVING LOST A GAME RIGHT NOW.
IF YOU'RE SAYING THAT MAN WHO JUST DIED WAS A MERE RESULT OF YOU HAVING LOST A GAME...
DOES THAT MEAN ALL THE PEOPLE THAT MAN KILLED WERE JUST A WAY OF KEEPING SCORE IN THIS GAME OF YOURS?
WHAT IS IT EXACTLY THAT YOU HAD RIDING ON YOUR GAME?
CIVIL ORDER AND PEACE? FREEDOM AND JUSTICE?
OR WAS IT MONEY? PERHAPS FAME..?
......
I'M JUST DOING WHAT THE LAW TELLS ME TO DO.
I'VE NEVER ALLOWED MY EMOTIONS TO TAKE OVER MY REASONING.
MAY I ASK WHO YOU MIGHT BE..?

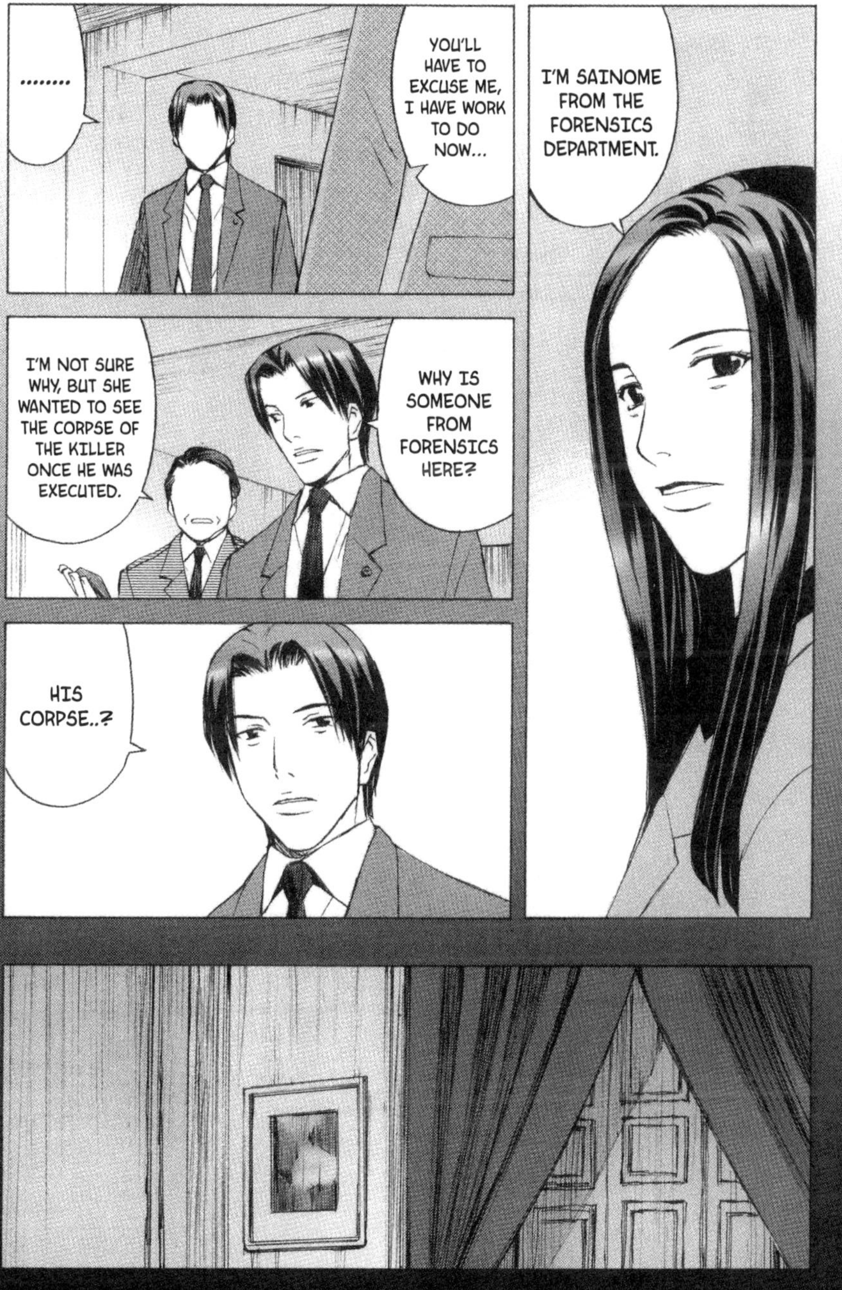
I'M SAINOME FROM THE FORENSICS DEPARTMENT.
YOU'LL HAVE TO EXCUSE ME, I HAVE WORK TO DO NOW...
....
WHY IS SOMEONE FROM FORENSICS HERE?
I'M NOT SURE WHY, BUT SHE WANTED TO SEE THE CORPSE OF THE KILLER ONCE HE WAS EXECUTED.
HIS CORPSE..?

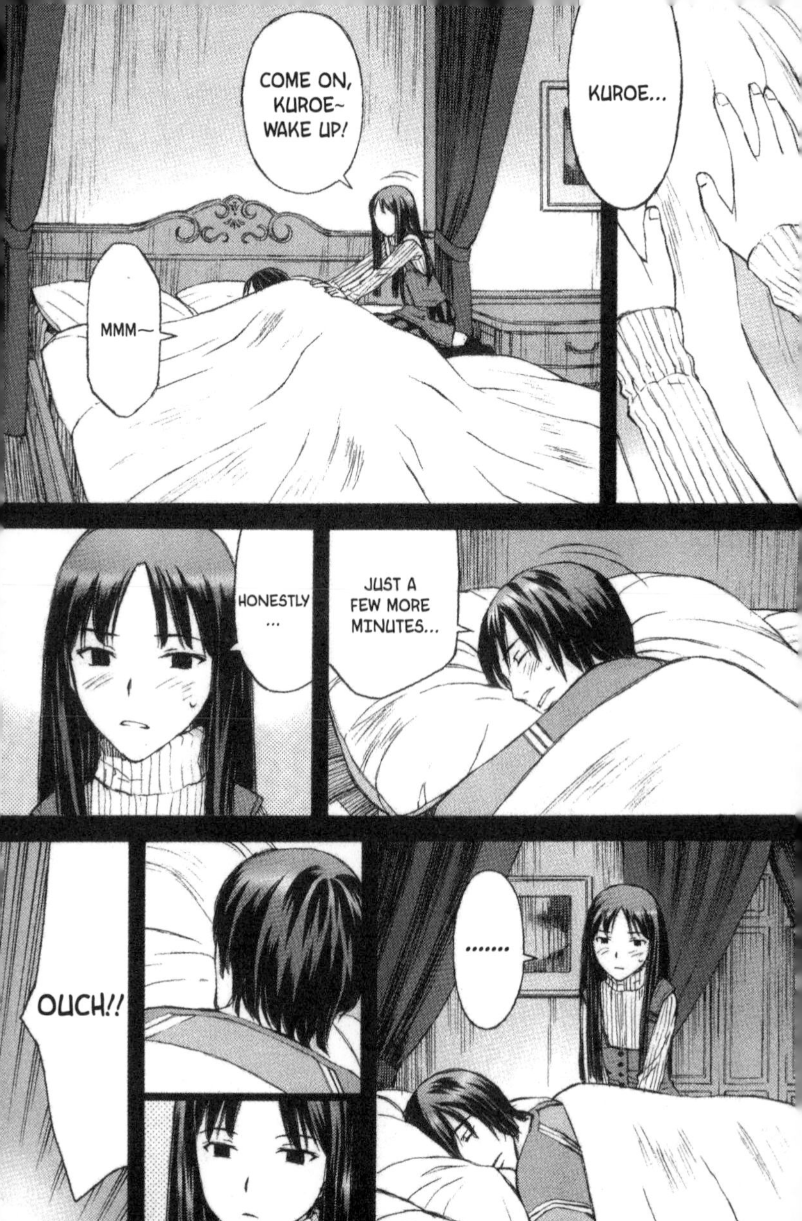
KUROE...
COME ON, KUROE~ WAKE UP!
MMM~
JUST A FEW MORE MINUTES...
HONESTLY ...
....
OUCH!!

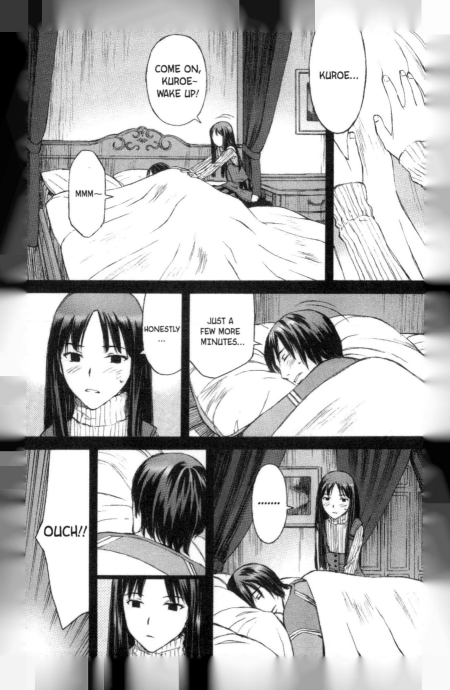

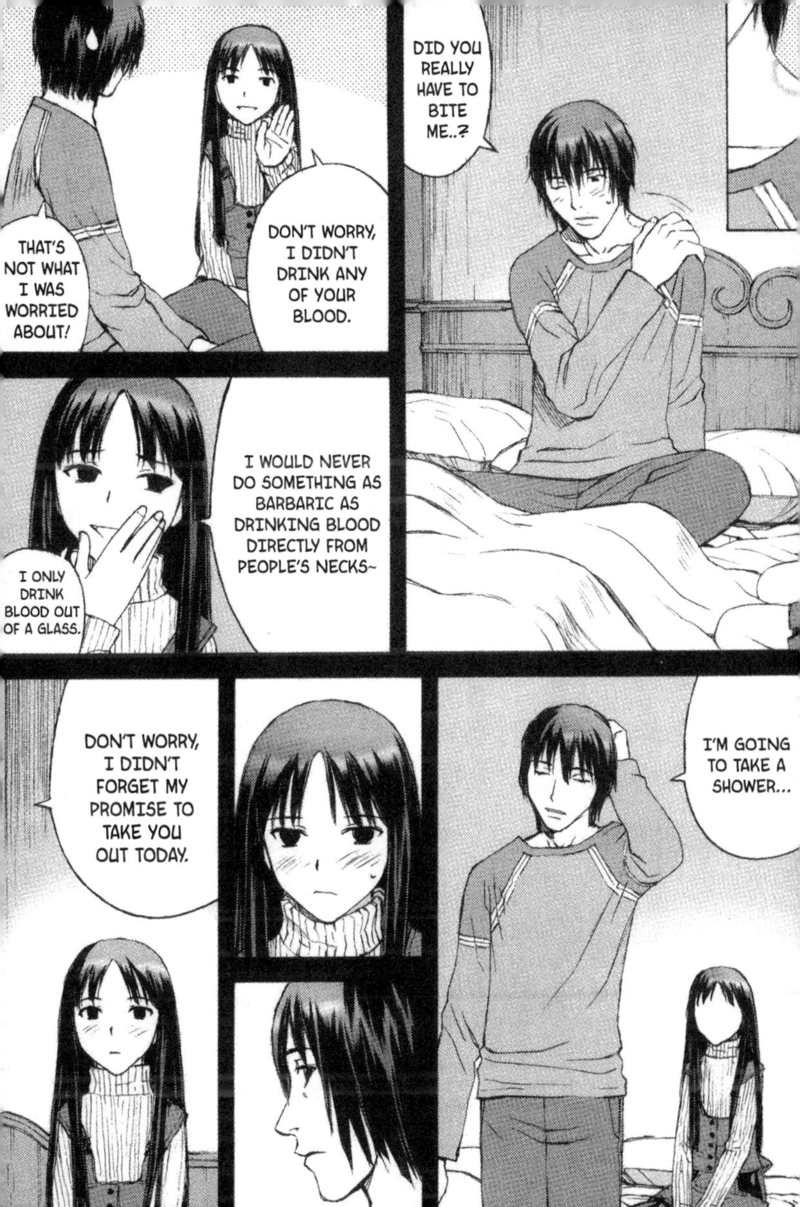
DID YOU REALLY HAVE TO BITE ME..?
DON'T WORRY, I DIDN'T DRINK ANY OF YOUR BLOOD.
THAT'S NOT WHAT I WAS WORRIED ABOUT!
I WOULD NEVER DO SOMETHING AS BARBARIC AS DRINKING BLOOD DIRECTLY FROM PEOPLE'S NECKS~
I ONLY DRINK BLOOD OUT OF A GLASS.
I'M GOING TO TAKE A SHOWER...
DON'T WORRY, I DIDN'T FORGET MY PROMISE TO TAKE YOU OUT TODAY.

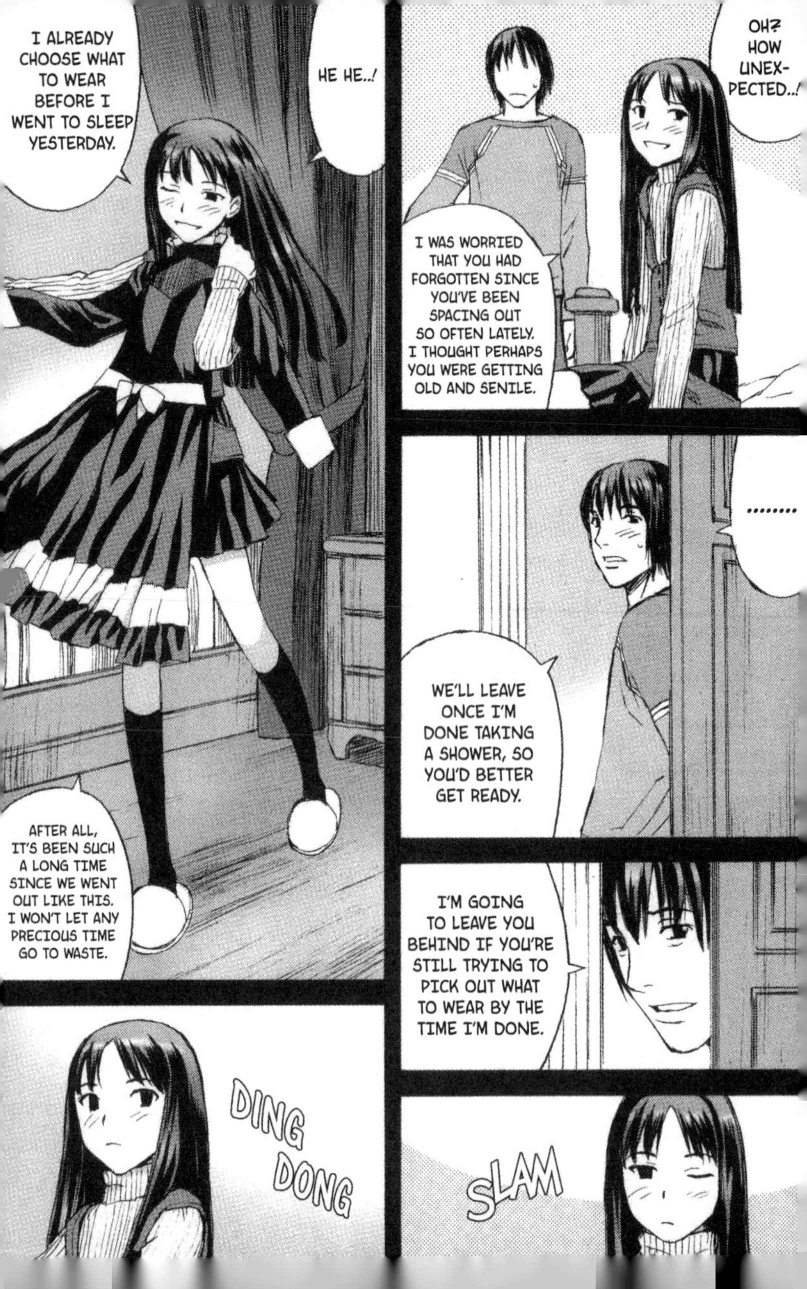
OH? HOW UNEXPECTED..!
I WAS WORRIED THAT YOU HAD FORGOTTEN SINCE YOU'VE BEEN SPACING OUT SO OFTEN LATELY. I THOUGHT PERHAPS YOU WERE GETTING OLD AND SENILE.
HE HE..!
I ALREADY CHOOSE WHAT TO WEAR BEFORE I WENT TO SLEEP YESTERDAY.
AFTER ALL, IT'S BEEN SUCH A LONG TIME SINCE WE WENT OUT LIKE THIS. I WON'T LET ANY PRECIOUS TIME GO TO WASTE.
....
WE'LL LEAVE ONCE I'M DONE TAKING A SHOWER, SO YOU'D BETTER GET READY.
I'M GOING TO LEAVE YOU BEHIND IF YOU'RE STILL TRYING TO PICK OUT WHAT TO WEAR BY THE TIME I'M DONE.
SLAM
DING DONG

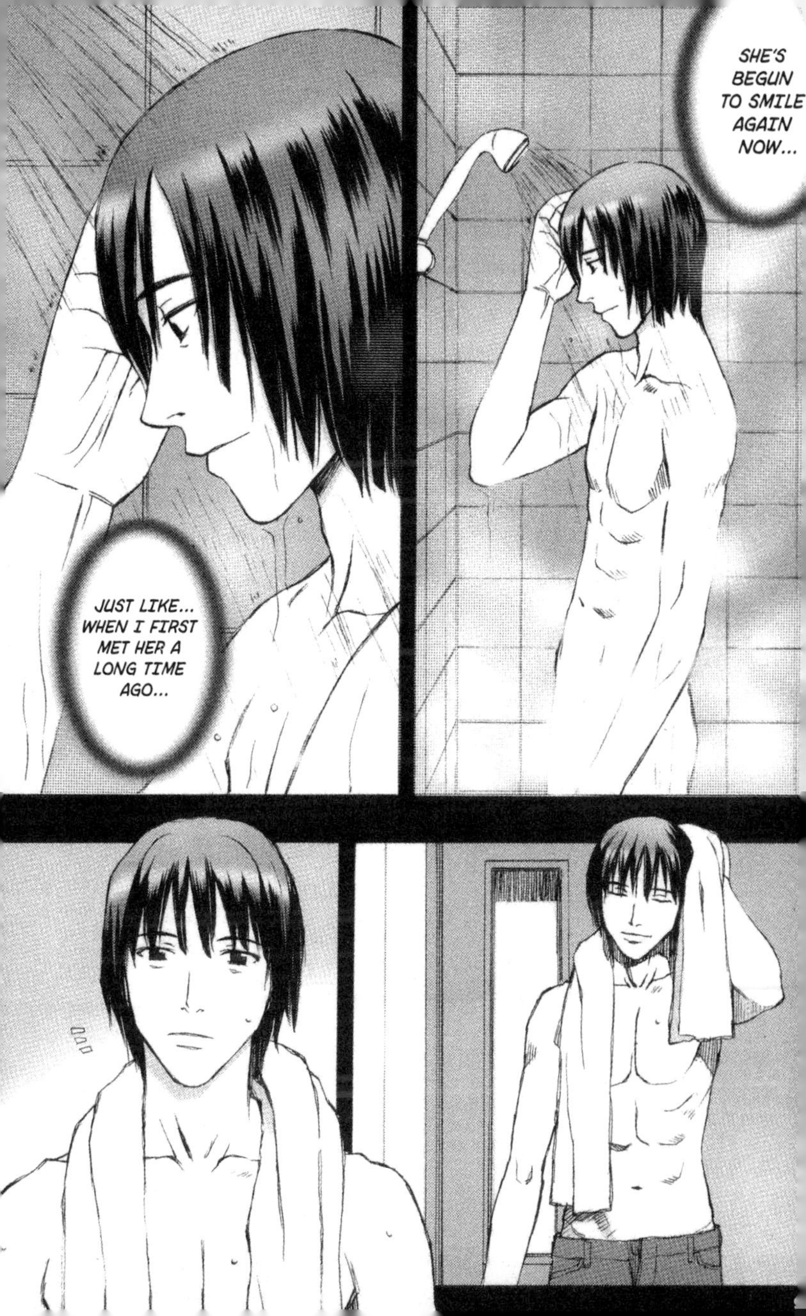
SHE'S BEGUN TO SMILE AGAIN NOW...
JUST LIKE... WHEN I FIRST MET HER A LONG TIME AGO...

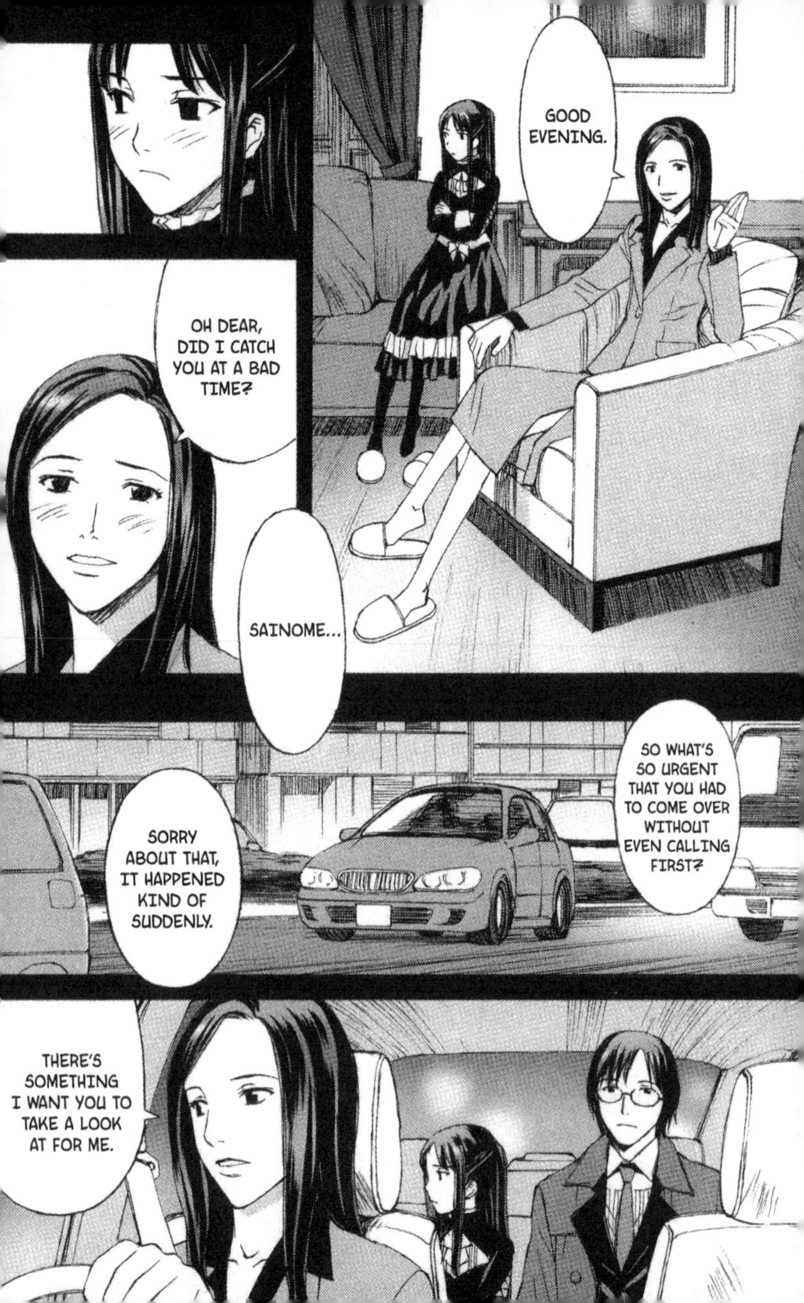
GOOD EVENING.
SAINOME...
OH DEAR, DID I CATCH YOU AT A BAD TIME?
SO WHAT'S SO URGENT THAT YOU HAD TO COME OVER WITHOUT EVEN CALLING FIRST?
SORRY ABOUT THAT, IT HAPPENED KIND OF SUDDENLY.
THERE'S SOMETHING I WANT YOU TO TAKE A LOOK AT FOR ME.

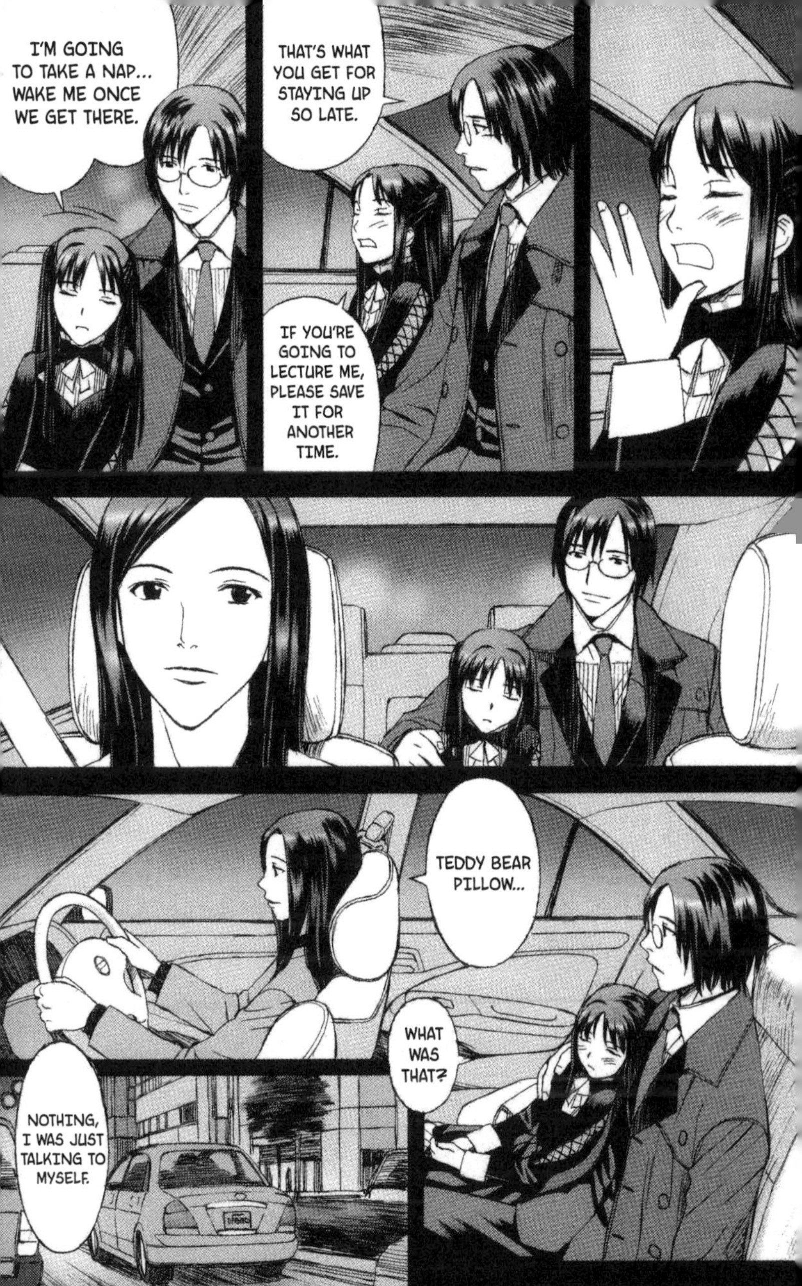
I'M GOING TO TAKE A NAP... WAKE ME ONCE WE GET THERE.
THAT'S WHAT YOU GET FOR STAYING UP SO LATE.
IF YOU'RE GOING TO LECTURE ME, PLEASE SAVE IT FOR ANOTHER TIME.
TEDDY BEAR PILLOW...
WHAT WAS THAT?
NOTHING, I WAS JUST TALKING TO MYSELF.

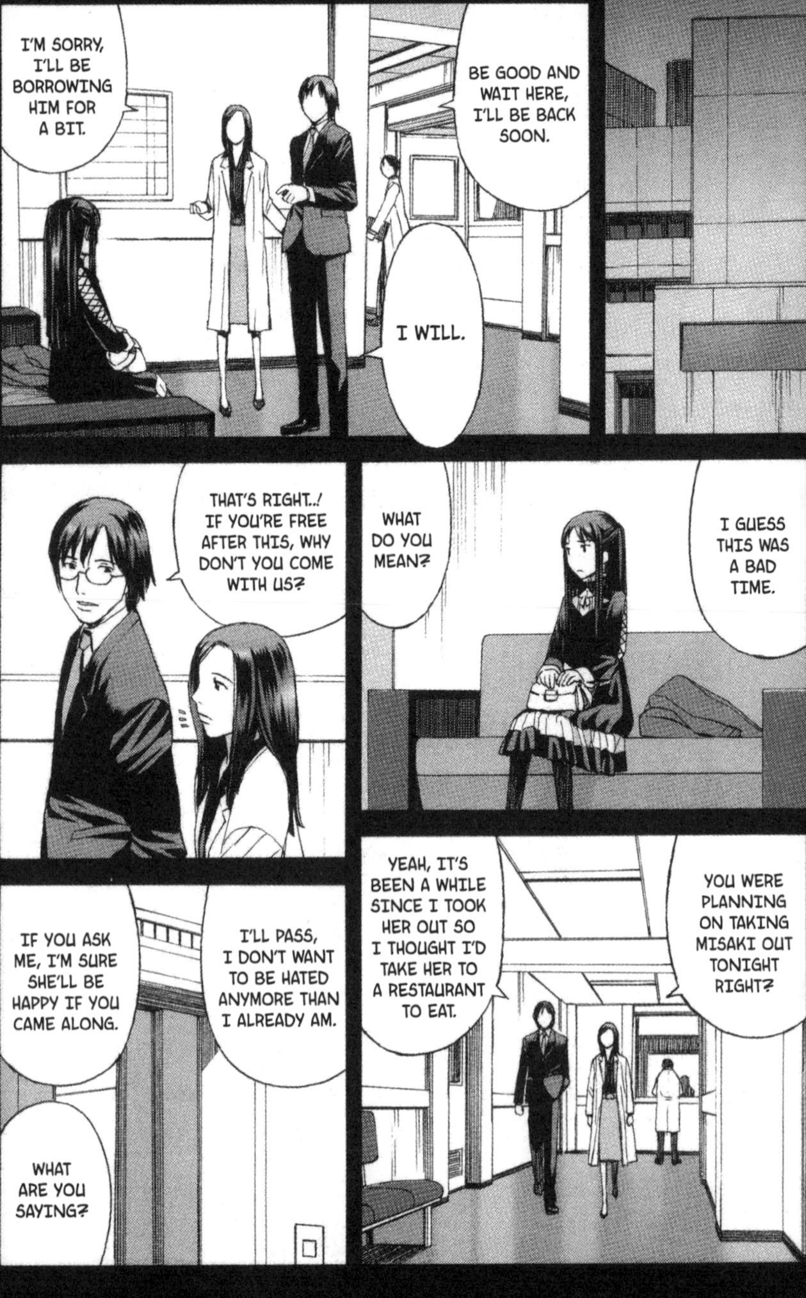
BE GOOD AND WAIT HERE, I'LL BE BACK SOON.
I WILL.
I'M SORRY, I'LL BE BORROWING HIM FOR A BIT.
I GUESS THIS WAS A BAD TIME.
WHAT DO YOU MEAN?
THAT'S RIGHT..! IF YOU'RE FREE AFTER THIS, WHY DON'T YOU COME WITH US?
YOU WERE PLANNING ON TAKING MISAKI OUT TONIGHT RIGHT?
YEAH, IT'S BEEN A WHILE SINCE I TOOK HER OUT SO I THOUGHT I'D TAKE HER TO A RESTAURANT TO EAT.
I'LL PASS, I DON'T WANT TO BE HATED ANYMORE THAN I ALREADY AM.
IF YOU ASK ME, I'M SURE SHE'LL BE HAPPY IF YOU CAME ALONG.
WHAT ARE YOU SAYING?

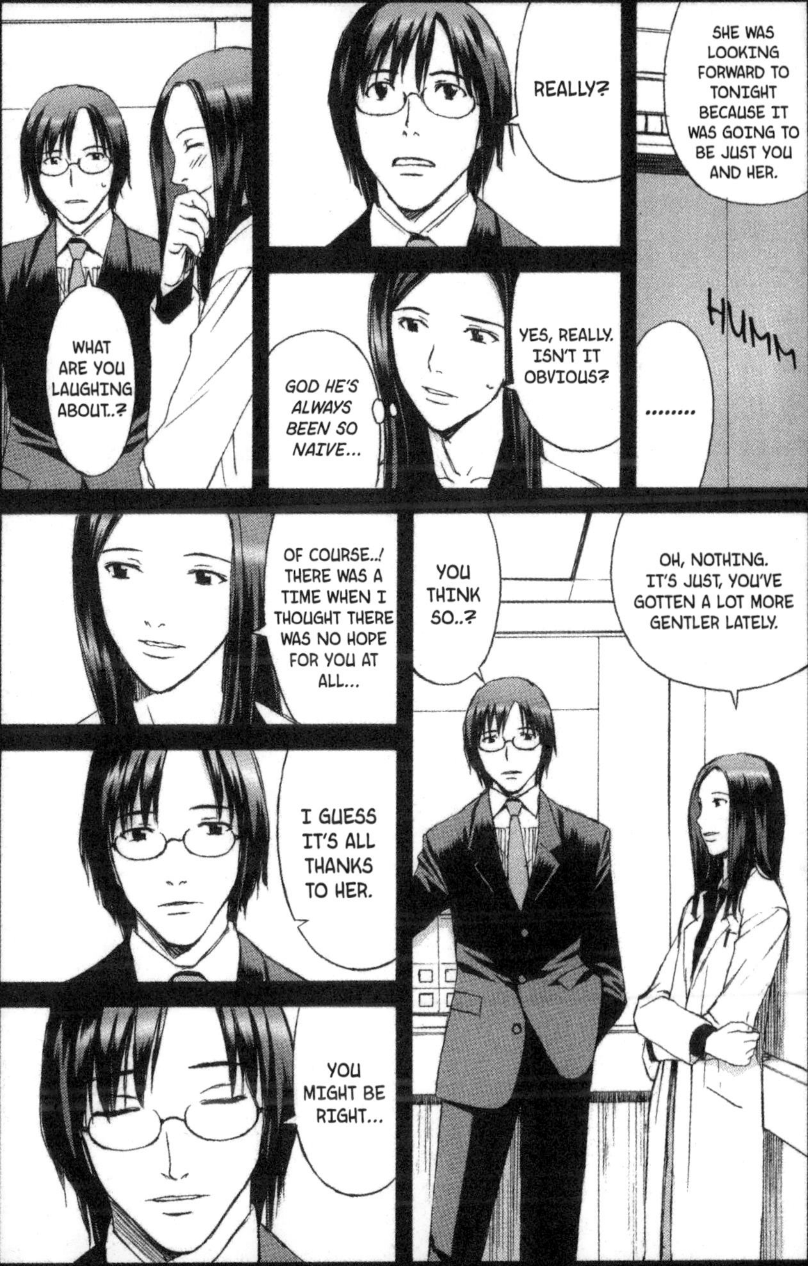

SHE WAS LOOKING FORWARD TO TONIGHT BECAUSE IT WAS GOING TO BE JUST YOU AND HER.
HUMM
....
REALLY?
YES, REALLY. ISN'T IT OBVIOUS?
GOD HE'S ALWAYS BEEN SO NAIVE...
WHAT ARE YOU LAUGHING ABOUT..?
OH, NOTHING. IT'S JUST, YOU'VE GOTTEN A LOT MORE GENTLER LATELY.
YOU THINK SO..?
OF COURSE..! THERE WAS A TIME WHEN I THOUGHT THERE WAS NO HOPE FOR YOU AT ALL...
I GUESS IT'S ALL THANKS TO HER.
YOU MIGHT BE RIGHT...

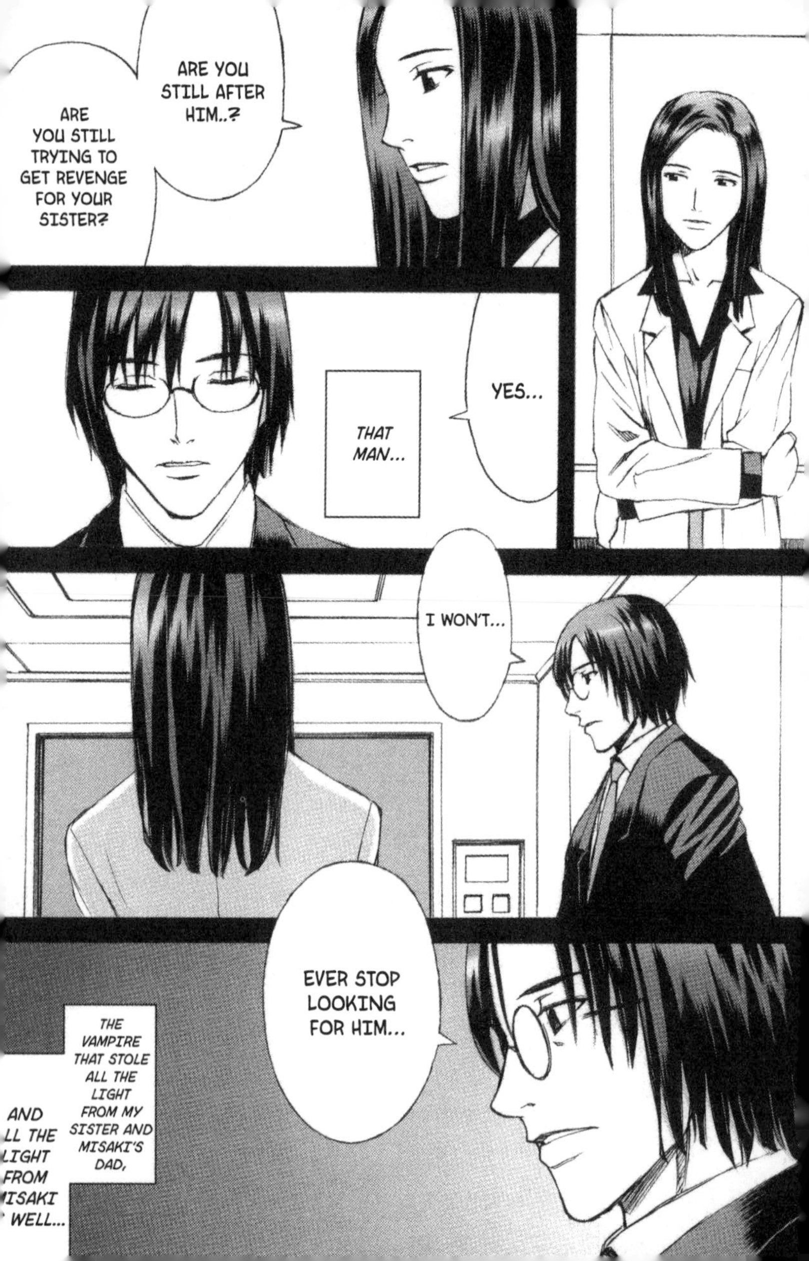
ARE YOU STILL AFTER HIM..?
ARE YOU STILL TRYING TO GET REVENGE FOR YOUR SISTER?
YES...
THAT MAN...
I WON'T...
EVER STOP LOOKING FOR HIM...
THE VAMPIRE THAT STOLE ALL THE LIGHT FROM MY SISTER AND MISAKI'S DAD,
AND LL THE LIGHT FROM ISAKI WELL...

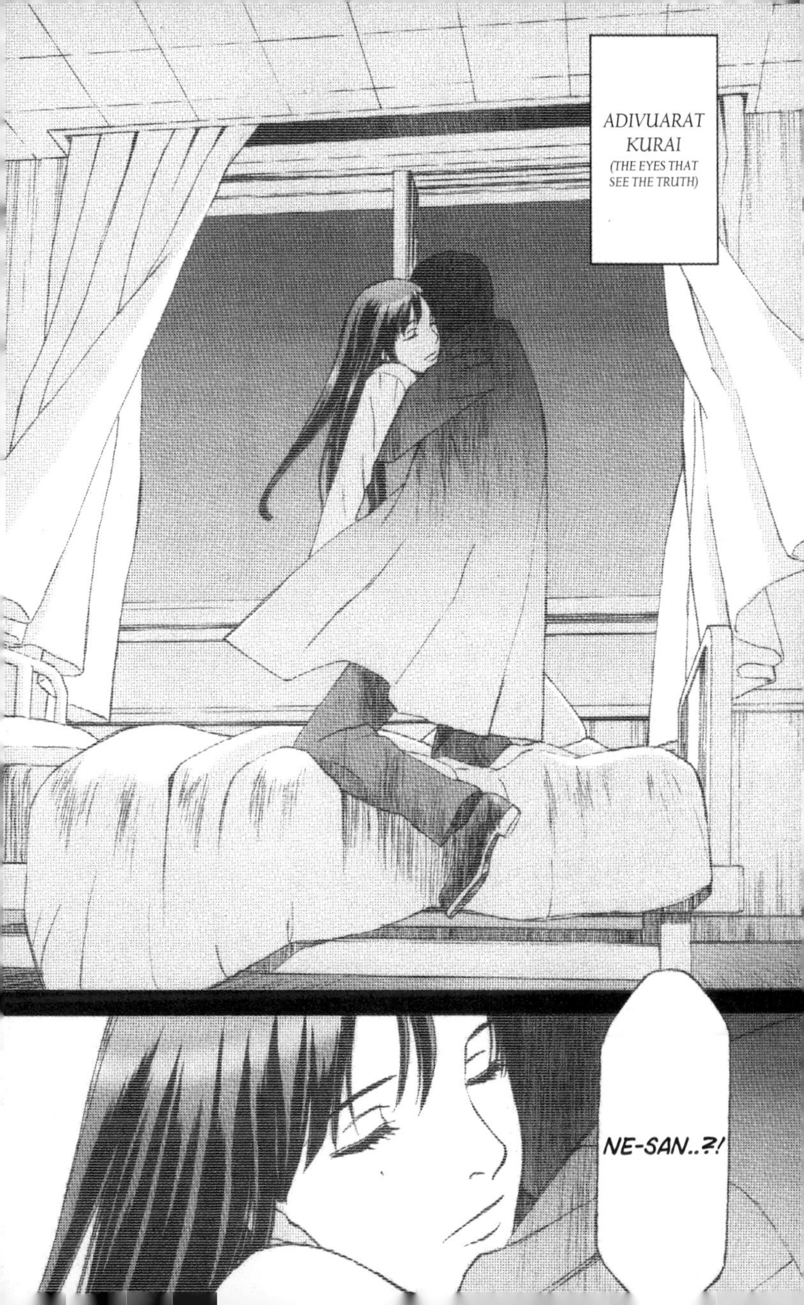
ADIVUARAT KURAI
(THE EYES THAT SEE THE TRUTH)
NE-SAN..?!

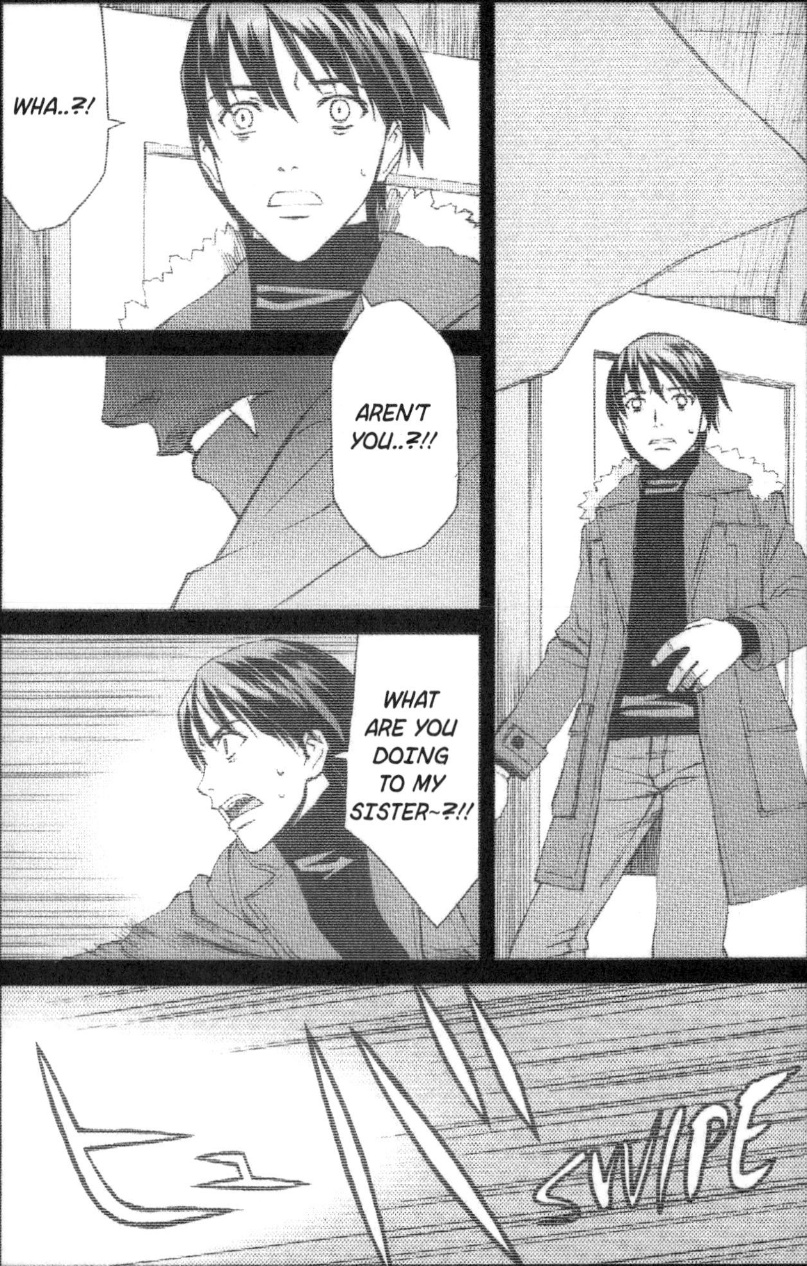
WHA..?!
AREN'T YOU..?!!
WHAT ARE YOU DOING TO MY SISTER~?!!
SWIPE

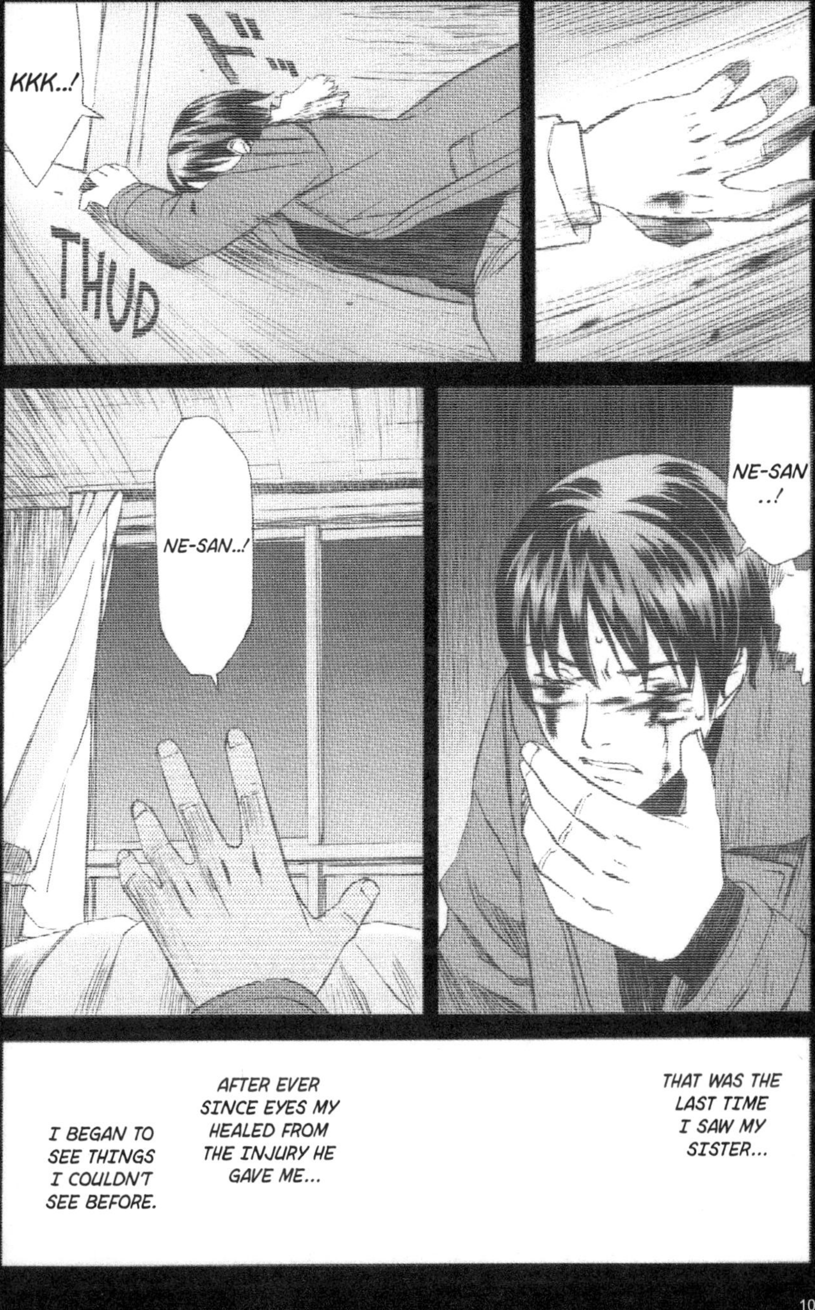
KKK..!
THUD
NE-SAN ..!
NE-SAN..!
THAT WAS THE LAST TIME I SAW MY SISTER...
AFTER EVER SINCE EYES MY HEALED FROM THE INJURY HE GAVE ME...
I BEGAN TO SEE THINGS I COULDN'T SEE BEFORE.

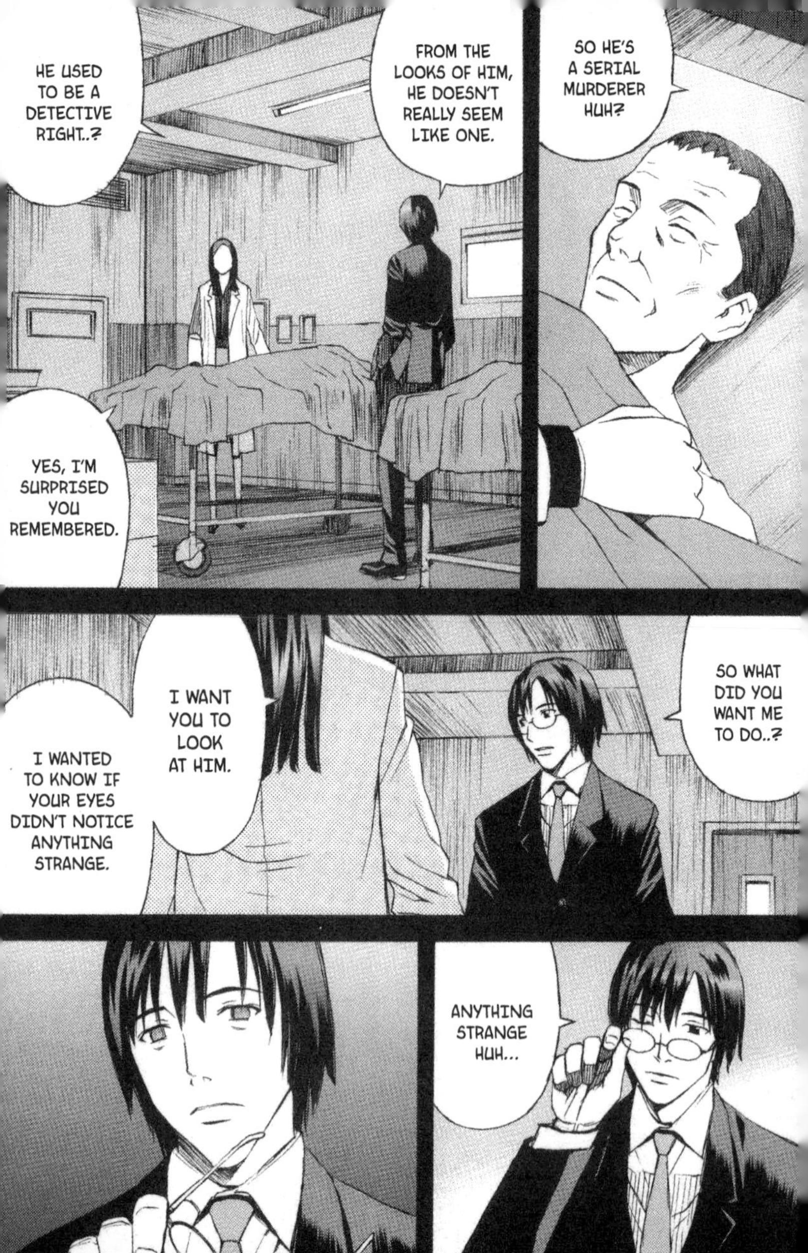
SO HE'S A SERIAL MURDERER HUH?
FROM THE LOOKS OF HIM, HE DOESN'T REALLY SEEM LIKE ONE.
HE USED TO BE A DETECTIVE RIGHT..?
YES, I'M SURPRISED YOU REMEMBERED.
SO WHAT DID YOU WANT ME TO DO..?
I WANT YOU TO LOOK AT HIM.
I WANTED TO KNOW IF YOUR EYES DIDN'T NOTICE ANYTHING STRANGE.
ANYTHING STRANGE HUH...

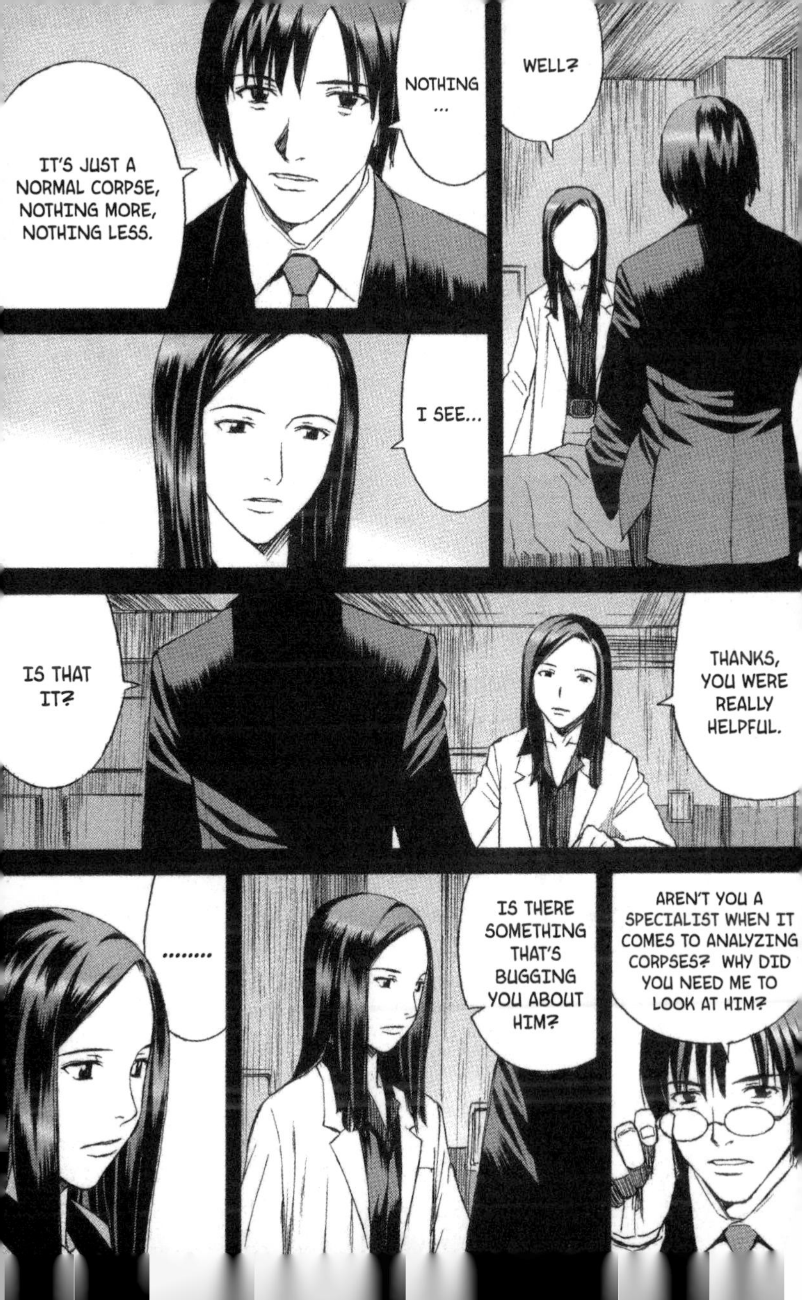
WELL?
NOTHING ...
IT'S JUST A NORMAL CORPSE, NOTHING MORE, NOTHING LESS.
I SEE...
THANKS, YOU WERE REALLY HELPFUL.
IS THAT IT?
AREN'T YOU A SPECIALIST WHEN IT COMES TO ANALYZING CORPSES? WHY DID YOU NEED ME TO LOOK AT HIM?
IS THERE SOMETHING THAT'S BUGGING YOU ABOUT HIM?
....

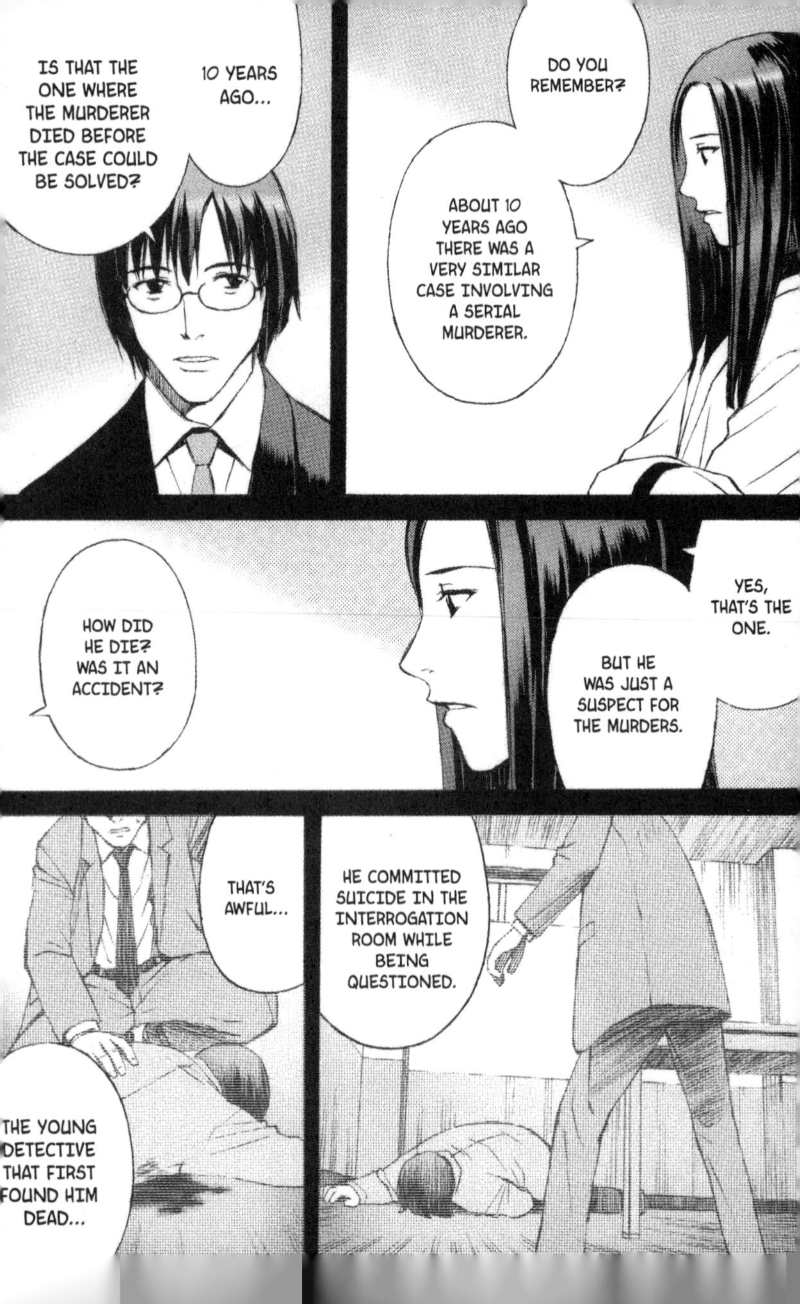
DO YOU REMEMBER?
ABOUT 10 YEARS AGO THERE WAS A VERY SIMILAR CASE INVOLVING A SERIAL MURDERER.
10 YEARS AGO...
IS THAT THE ONE WHERE THE MURDERER DIED BEFORE THE CASE COULD BE SOLVED?
YES, THAT'S THE ONE.
BUT HE WAS JUST A SUSPECT FOR THE MURDERS.
HOW DID HE DIE? WAS IT AN ACCIDENT?
HE COMMITTED SUICIDE IN THE INTERROGATION ROOM WHILE BEING QUESTIONED.
THAT'S AWFUL...
THE YOUNG DETECTIVE THAT FIRST FOUND HIM DEAD...

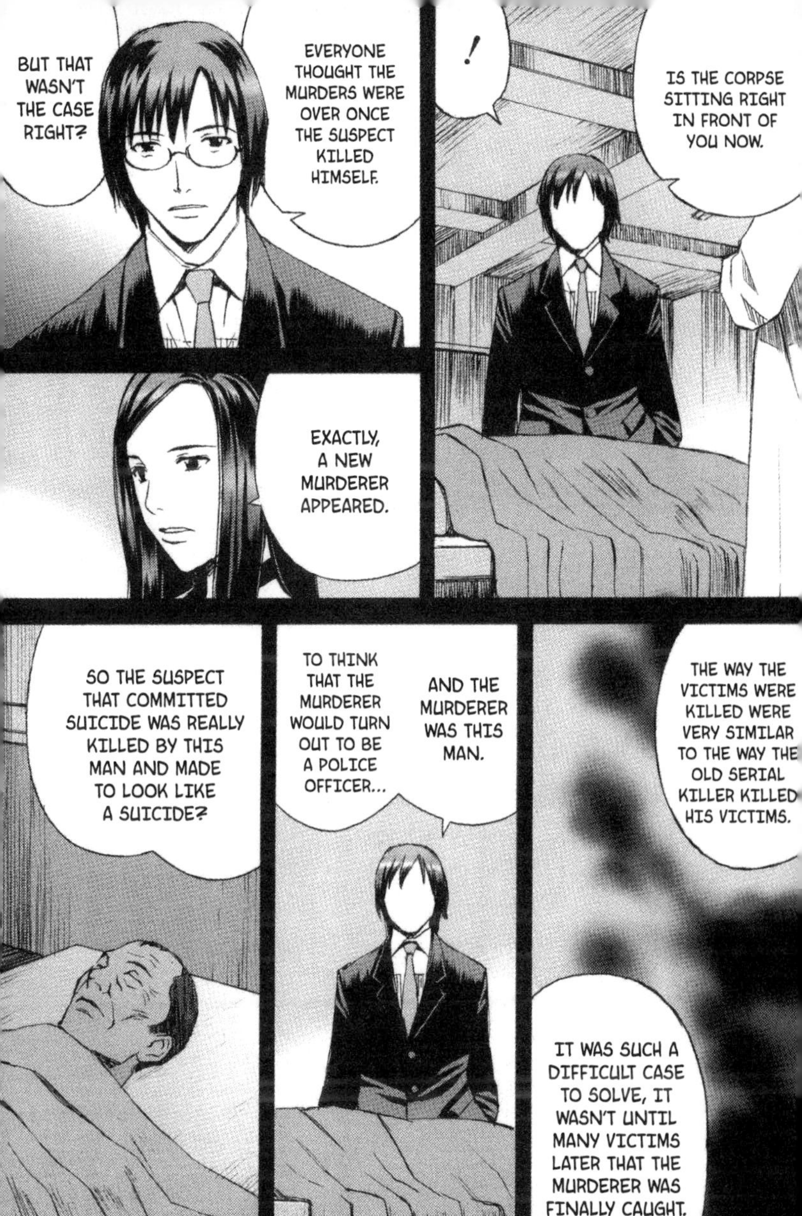
IS THE CORPSE SITTING RIGHT IN FRONT OF YOU NOW.
!
EVERYONE THOUGHT THE MURDERERS WERE OVER ONCE THE SUSPECT KILLED HIMSELF.
BUT THAT WASN'T THE CASE RIGHT?
EXACTLY, A NEW MURDERER APPEARED.
THE WAY THE VICTIMS WERE KILLED WERE VERY SIMILAR TO THE WAY THE OLD SERIAL KILLER KILLED HIS VICTIMS.
IT WAS SUCH A DIFFICULT CASE TO SOLVE, IT WASN'T UNTIL MANY VICTIMS LATER THAT THE MURDERER WAS FINALLY CAUGHT.
AND THE MURDERER WAS THIS MAN.
TO THINK THAT THE MURDERER WOULD TURN OUT TO BE A POLICE OFFICER...
SO THE SUSPECT THAT COMMITTED SUICIDE WAS REALLY KILLED BY THIS MAN AND MADE TO LOOK LIKE A SUICIDE?

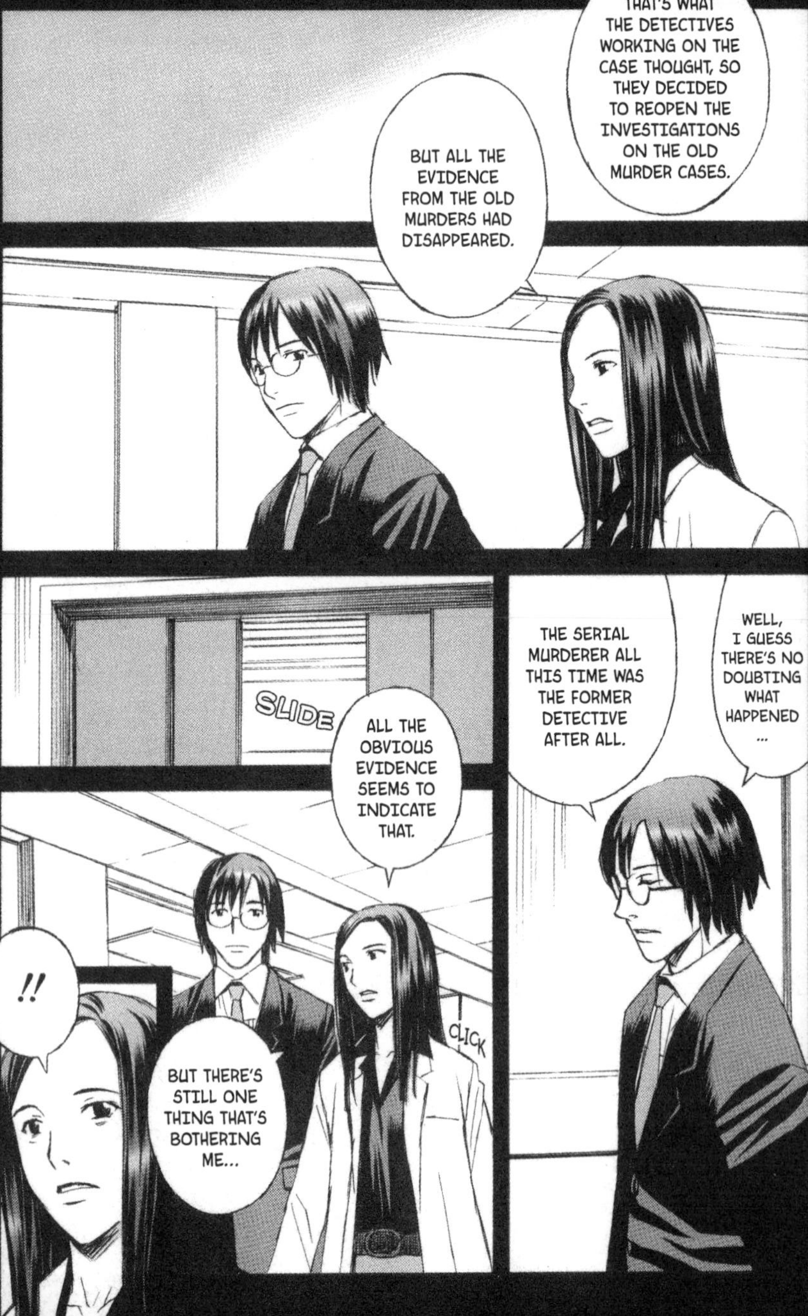
THAT'S WHAT THE DETECTIVES WORKING ON THE CASE THOUGHT, SO THEY DECIDED TO REOPEN THE INVESTIGATIONS ON THE OLD MURDER CASES.
BUT ALL THE EVIDENCE FROM THE OLD MURDERS HAD DISAPPEARED.
WELL, I GUESS THERE'S NO DOUBTING WHAT HAPPENED ...
THE SERIAL MURDERER ALL THIS TIME WAS THE FORMER DETECTIVE AFTER ALL.
SLIDE
ALL THE OBVIOUS EVIDENCE SEEMS TO INDICATE THAT.
CLICK
!!
BUT THERE'S STILL ONE THING THAT'S BOTHERING ME...

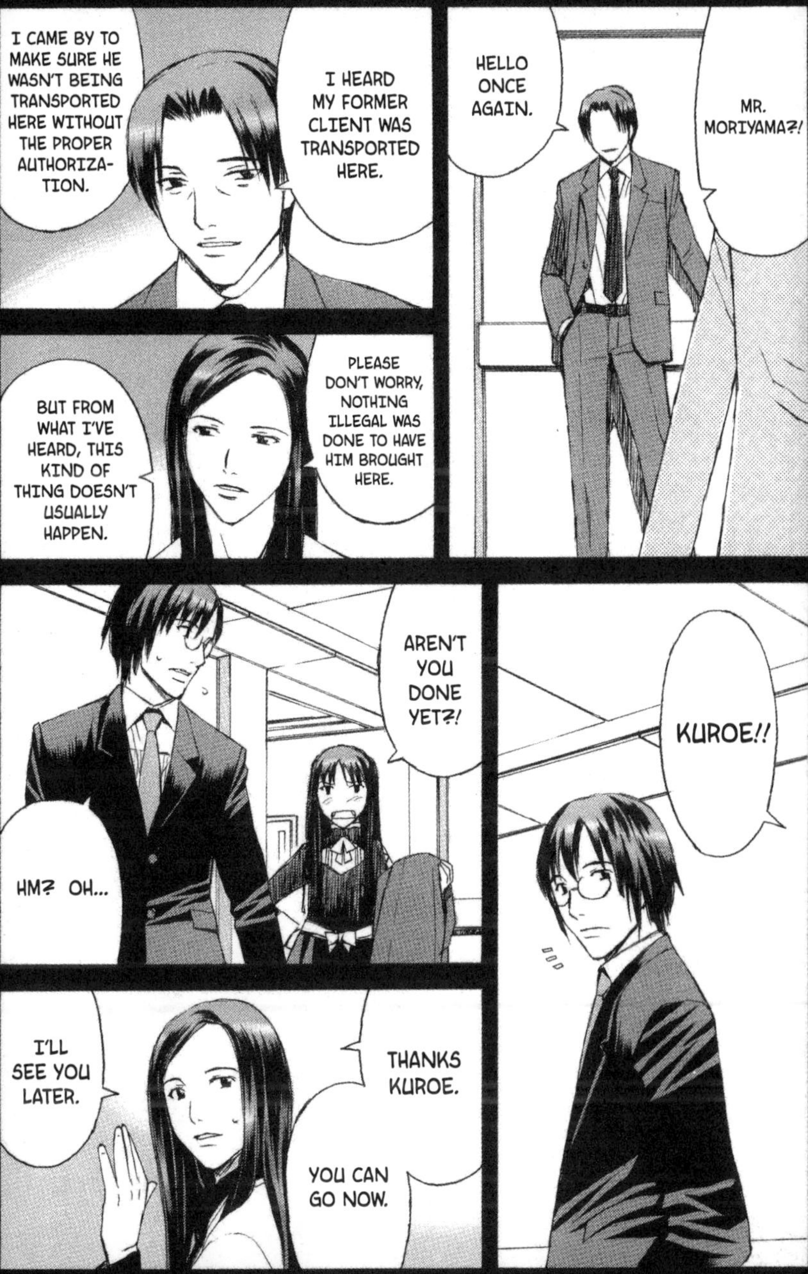
MR. MORIYAMA?!
HELLO ONCE AGAIN.
I HEARD MY FORMER CLIENT WAS TRANSPORTED HERE.
I CAME BY TO MAKE SURE HE WASN'T BEING TRANSPORTED HERE WITHOUT THE PROPER AUTHORIZA-TION.
PLEASE DON'T WORRY, NOTHING ILLEGAL WAS DONE TO HAVE HIM BROUGHT HERE.
BUT FROM WHAT I'VE HEARD, THIS KIND OF THING DOESN'T USUALLY HAPPEN.
KUROE!!
AREN'T YOU DONE YET?!
HM? OH...
THANKS KUROE.
YOU CAN GO NOW.
I'LL SEE YOU LATER.

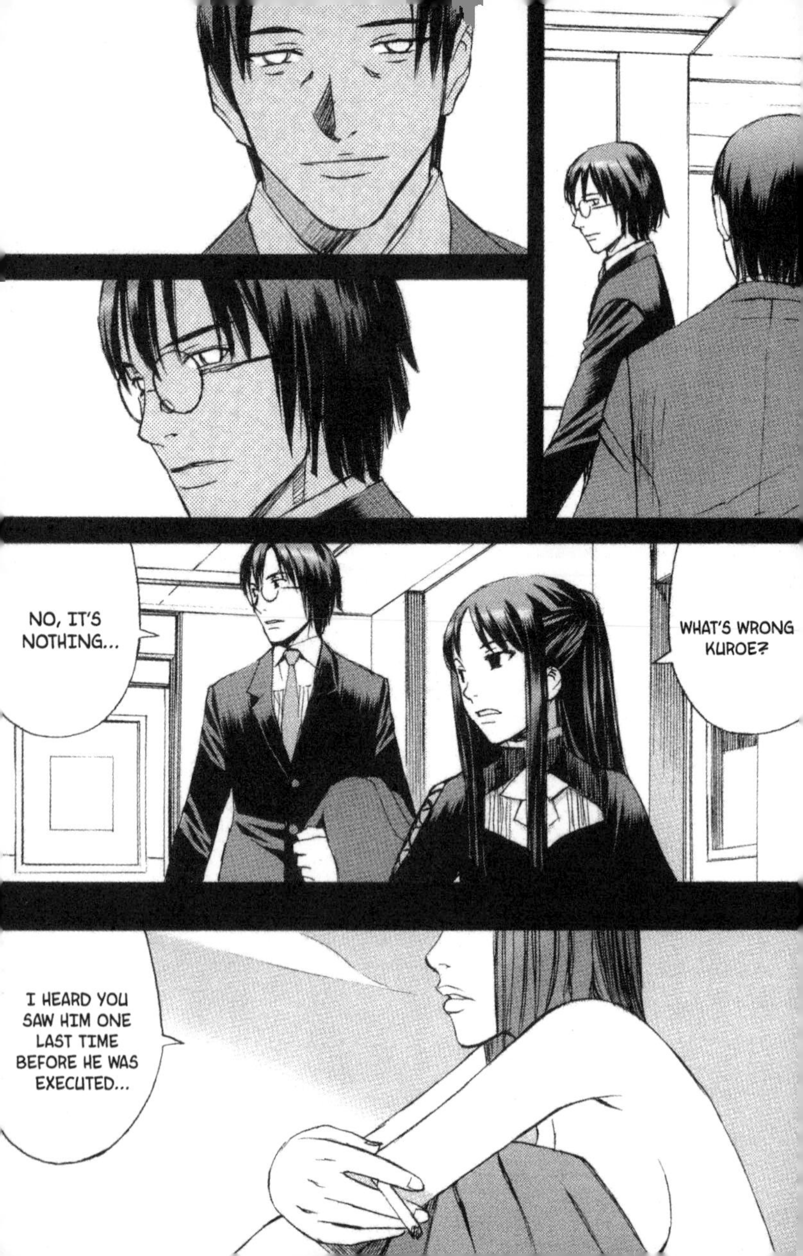
WHAT'S WRONG KUROE?
NO, IT'S NOTHING...
I HEARD YOU SAW HIM ONE LAST TIME BEFORE HE WAS EXECUTED...

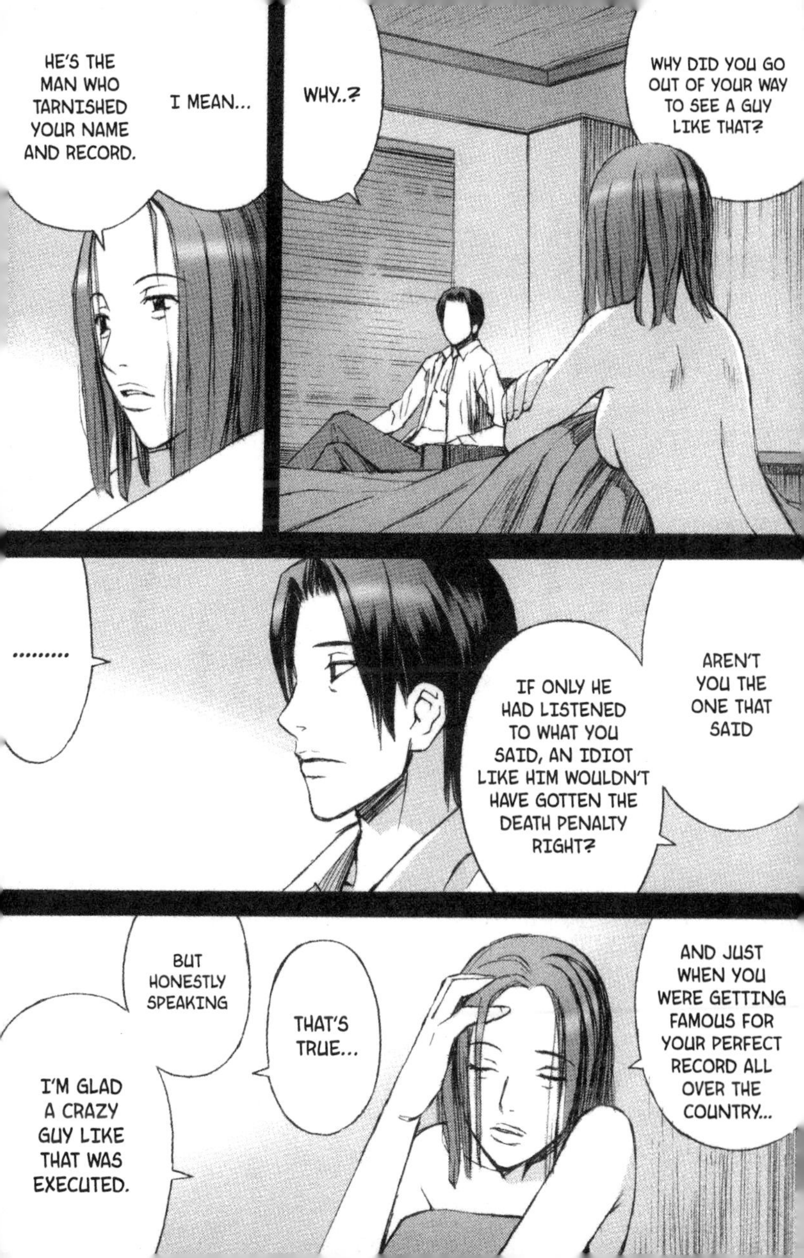
WHY DID YOU GO OUT OF YOUR WAY TO SEE A GUY LIKE THAT?
WHY..?
I MEAN...
HE'S THE MAN WHO TARNISHED YOUR NAME AND RECORD.
AREN'T YOU THE ONE THAT SAID
IF ONLY HE HAD LISTENED TO WHAT YOU SAID, AN IDIOT LIKE HIM WOULDN'T HAVE GOTTEN THE DEATH PENALTY RIGHT?
....
AND JUST WHEN YOU WERE GETTING FAMOUS FOR YOUR PERFECT RECORD ALL OVER THE COUNTRY...
THAT'S TRUE...
BUT HONESTLY SPEAKING
I'M GLAD A CRAZY GUY LIKE THAT WAS EXECUTED.

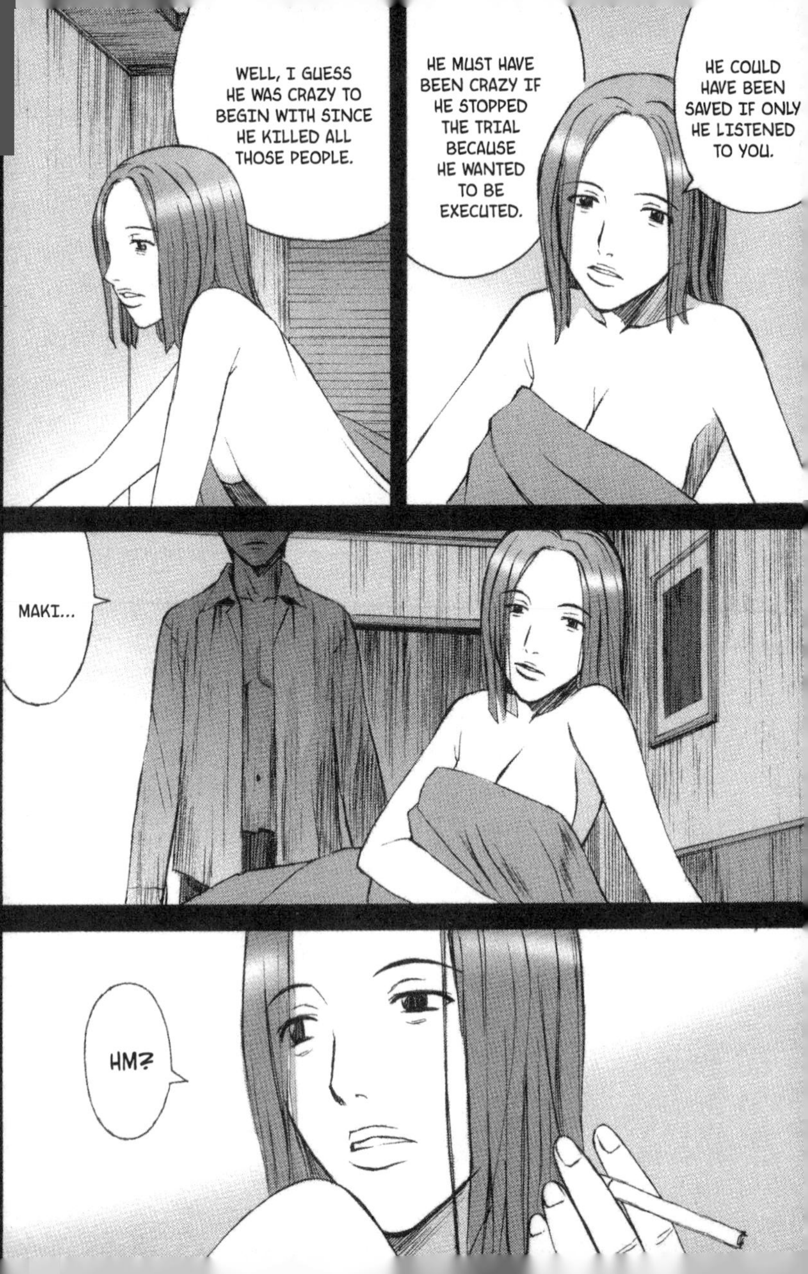
HE COULD HAVE BEEN SAVED IF ONLY HE LISTENED TO YOU.
HE MUST HAVE BEEN CRAZY IF HE STOPPED THE TRIAL BECAUSE HE WANTED TO BE EXECUTED.
WELL, I GUESS HE WAS CRAZY TO BEGIN WITH SINCE HE KILLED ALL THOSE PEOPLE.
MAKI...
HM?

Episode 4

SOUL SLAVE part 2

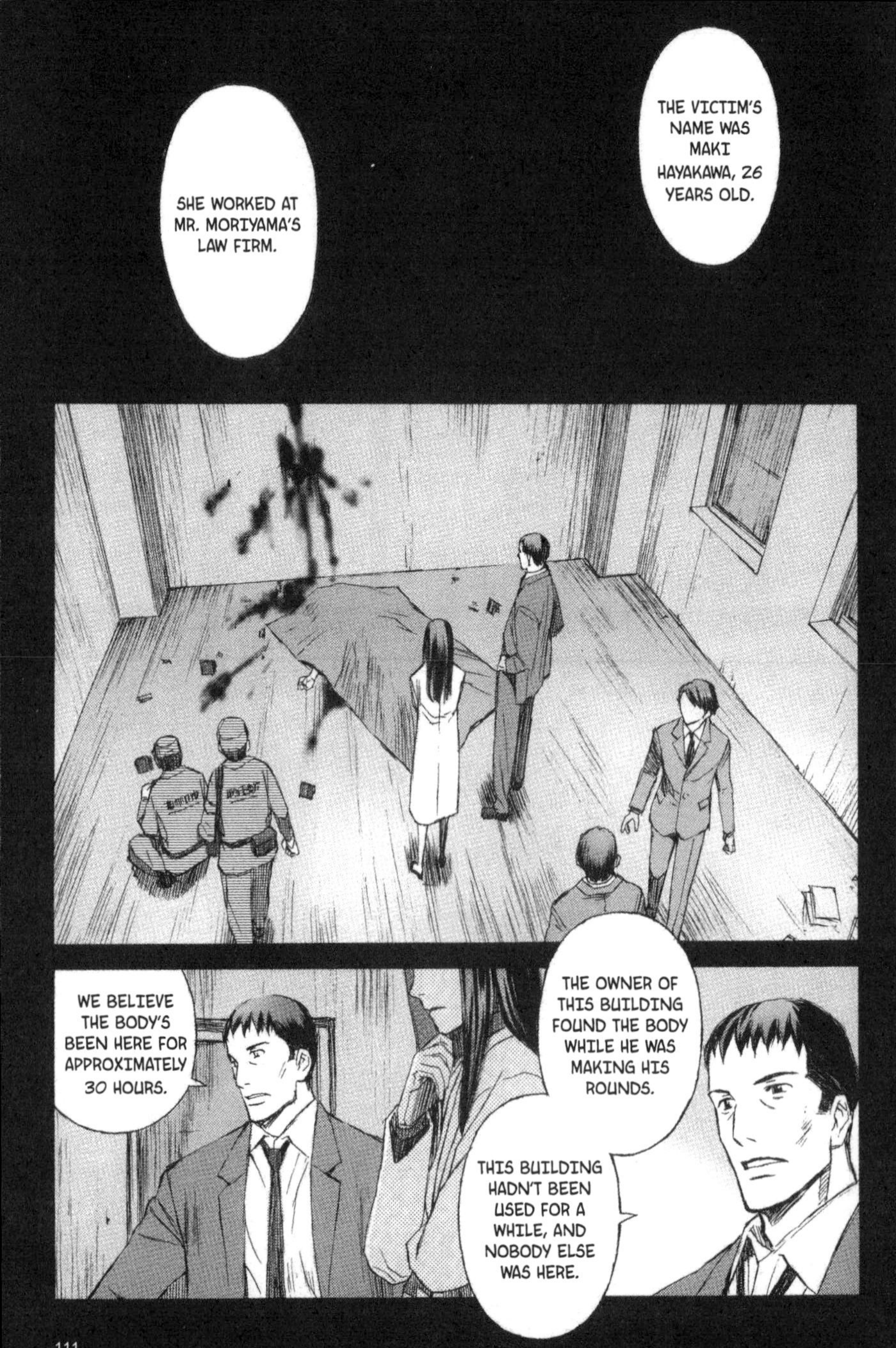
THE VICTIM'S NAME WAS MAKI HAYAKAWA, 26 YEARS OLD.
SHE WORKED AT MR. MORIYAMA'S LAW FIRM.
THE OWNER OF THIS BUILDING FOUND THE BODY WHILE HE WAS MAKING HIS ROUNDS.
WE BELIEVE THE BODY'S BEEN HERE FOR APPROXIMATELY 30 HOURS.
THIS BUILDING HADN'T BEEN USED FOR A WHILE, AND NOBODY ELSE WAS HERE.

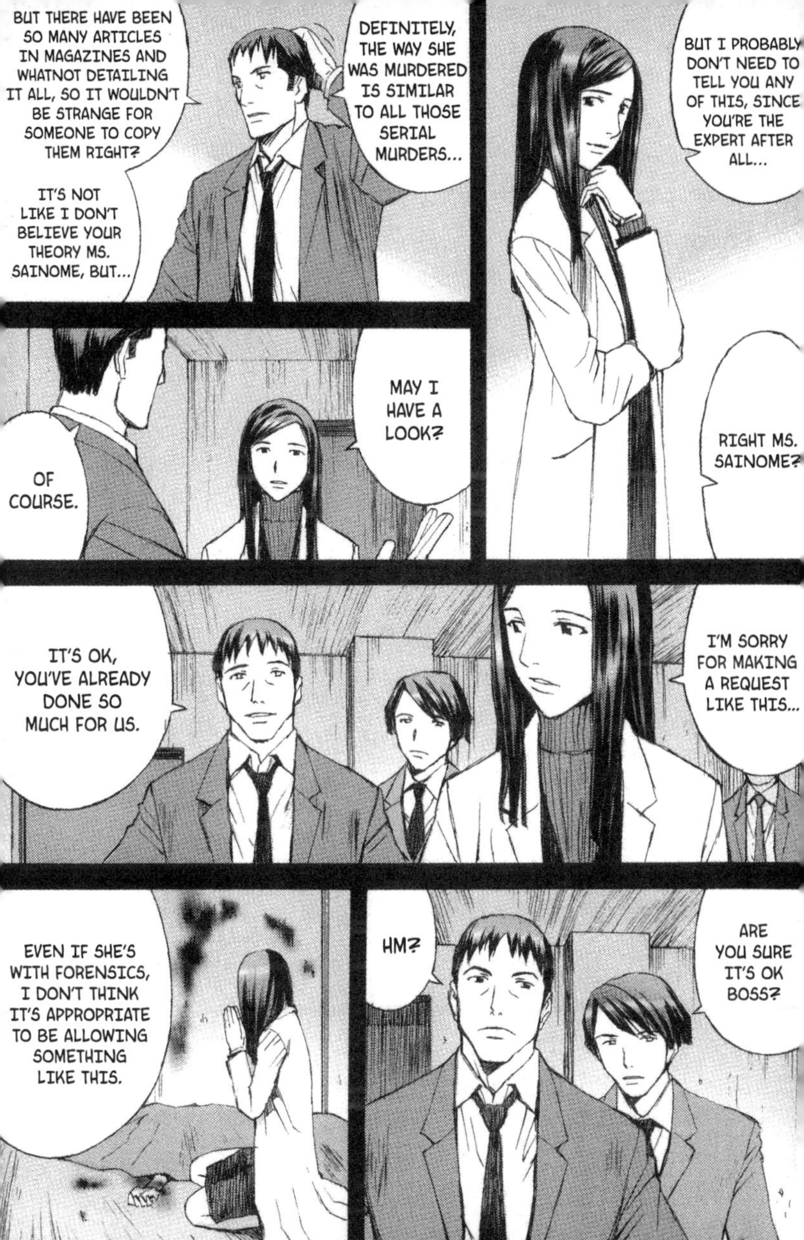
BUT I PROBABLY DON'T NEED TO TELL YOU ANY OF THIS, SINCE YOU'RE THE EXPERT AFTER ALL...
RIGHT MS. SAINOME?
DEFINITELY, THE WAY SHE WAS MURDERED IS SIMILAR TO ALL THOSE SERIAL MURDERS...
BUT THERE HAVE BEEN SO MANY ARTICLES IN MAGAZINES AND WHATNOT DETAILING IT ALL, SO IT WOULDN'T BE STRANGE FOR SOMEONE TO COPY THEM RIGHT?
IT'S NOT LIKE I DON'T BELIEVE YOUR THEORY MS. SAINOME, BUT...
MAY I HAVE A LOOK?
OF COURSE.
I'M SORRY FOR MAKING A REQUEST LIKE THIS...
IT'S OK, YOU'VE ALREADY DONE SO MUCH FOR US.
ARE YOU SURE IT'S OK BOSS?
HM?
EVEN IF SHE'S WITH FORENSICS, I DON'T THINK IT'S APPROPRIATE TO BE ALLOWING SOMETHING LIKE THIS.

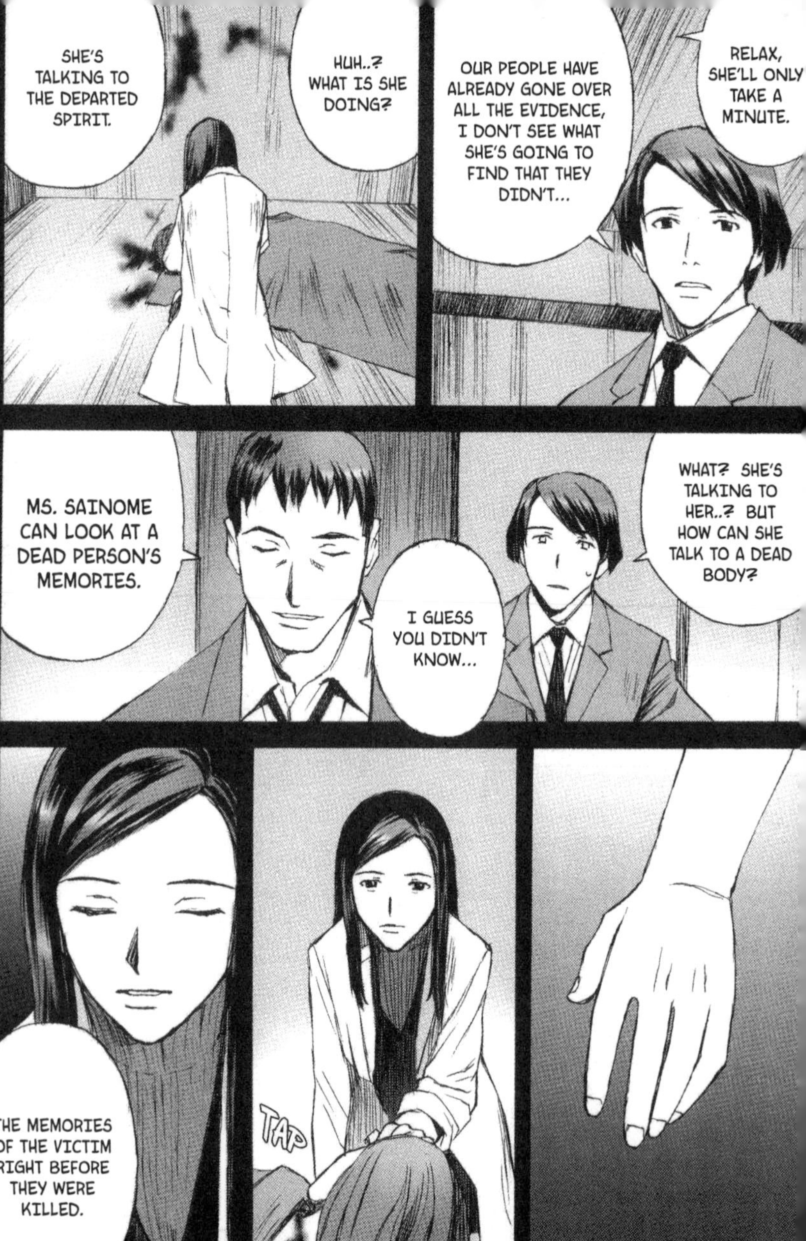
RELAX, SHE'LL ONLY TAKE A MINUTE.
OUR PEOPLE HAVE ALREADY GONE OVER ALL THE EVIDENCE, I DON'T SEE WHAT SHE'S GOING TO FIND THAT THEY DIDN'T...
HUH..? WHAT IS SHE DOING?
SHE'S TALKING TO THE DEPARTED SPIRIT.
WHAT? SHE'S TALKING TO HER..? BUT HOW CAN SHE TALK TO A DEAD BODY?
I GUESS YOU DIDN'T KNOW...
MS. SAINOME CAN LOOK AT A DEAD PERSON'S MEMORIES.
TAP
THE MEMORIES OF THE VICTIM RIGHT BEFORE THEY WERE KILLED.

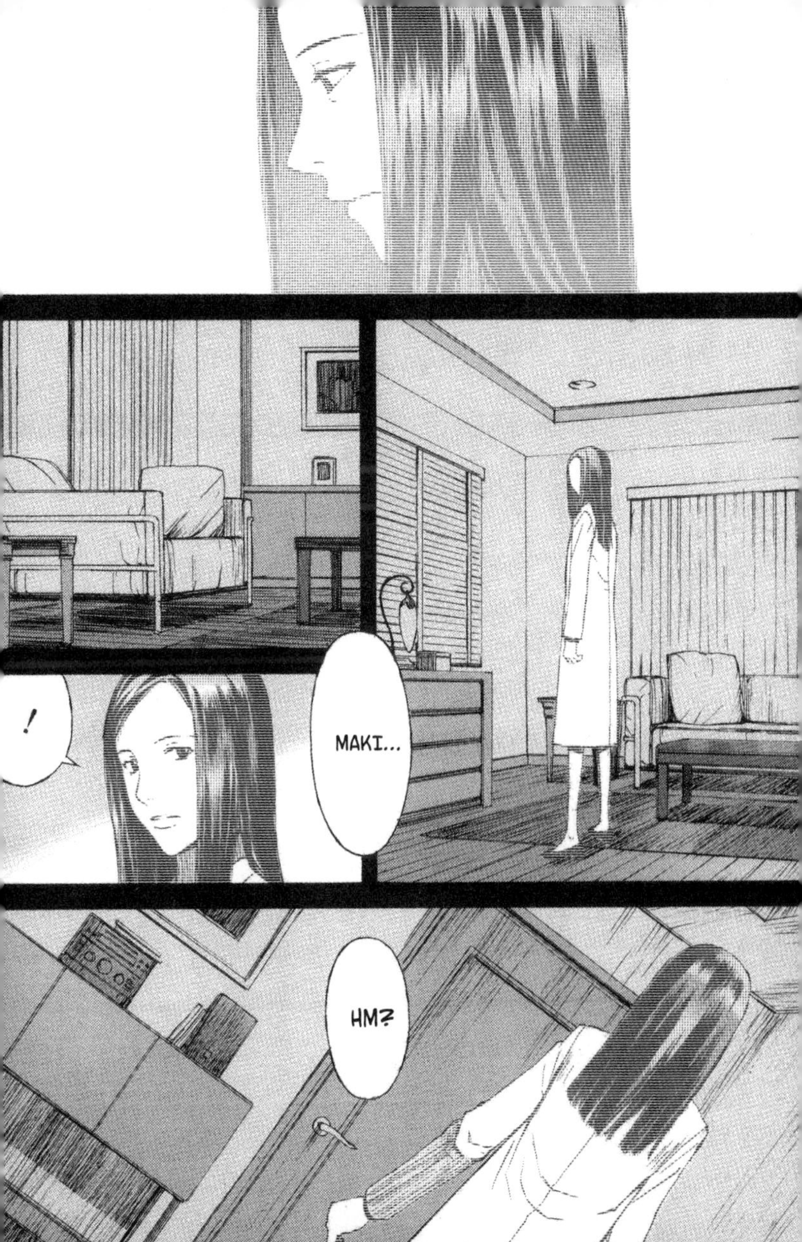
MAKI...
!
HM?

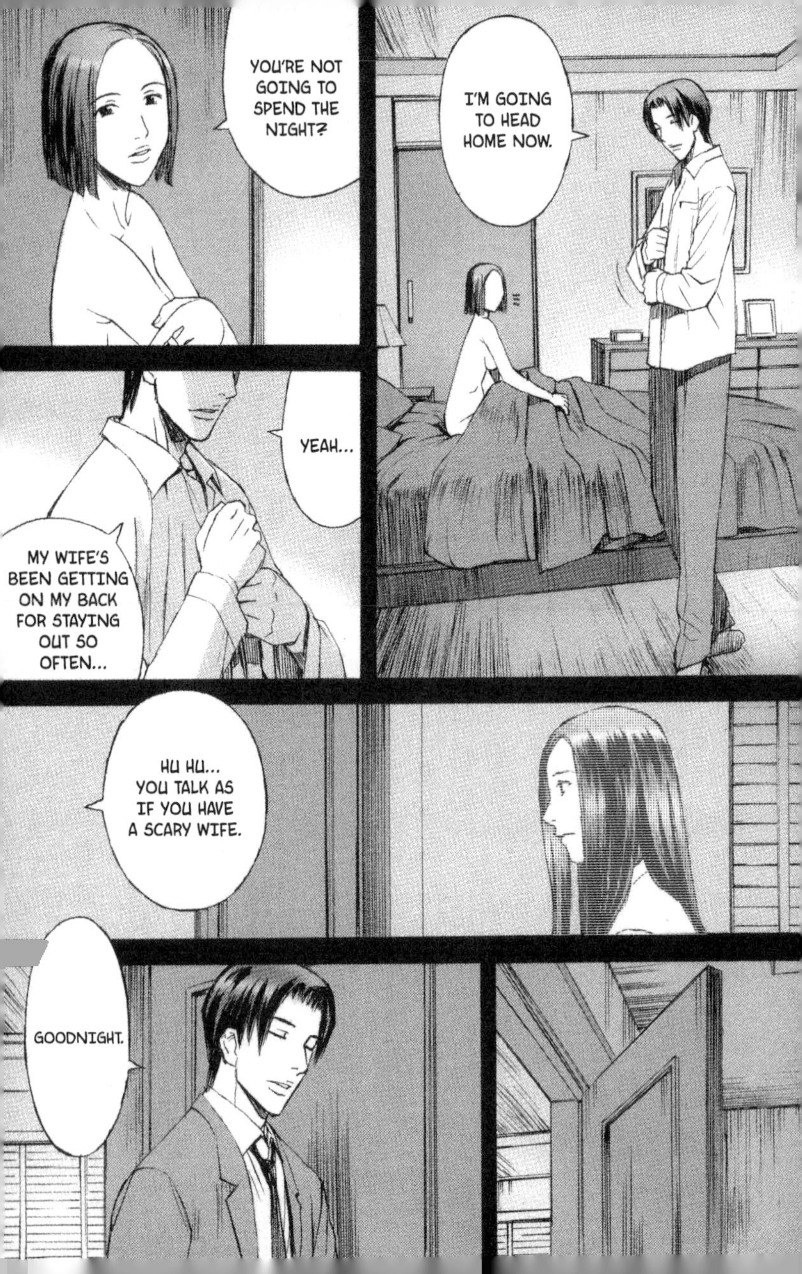
I'M GOING TO HEAD HOME NOW.
YOU'RE NOT GOING TO SPEND THE NIGHT?
YEAH...
MY WIFE'S BEEN GETTING ON MY BACK FOR STAYING OUT SO OFTEN...
HU HU... YOU TALK AS IF YOU HAVE A SCARY WIFE.
GOODNIGHT.

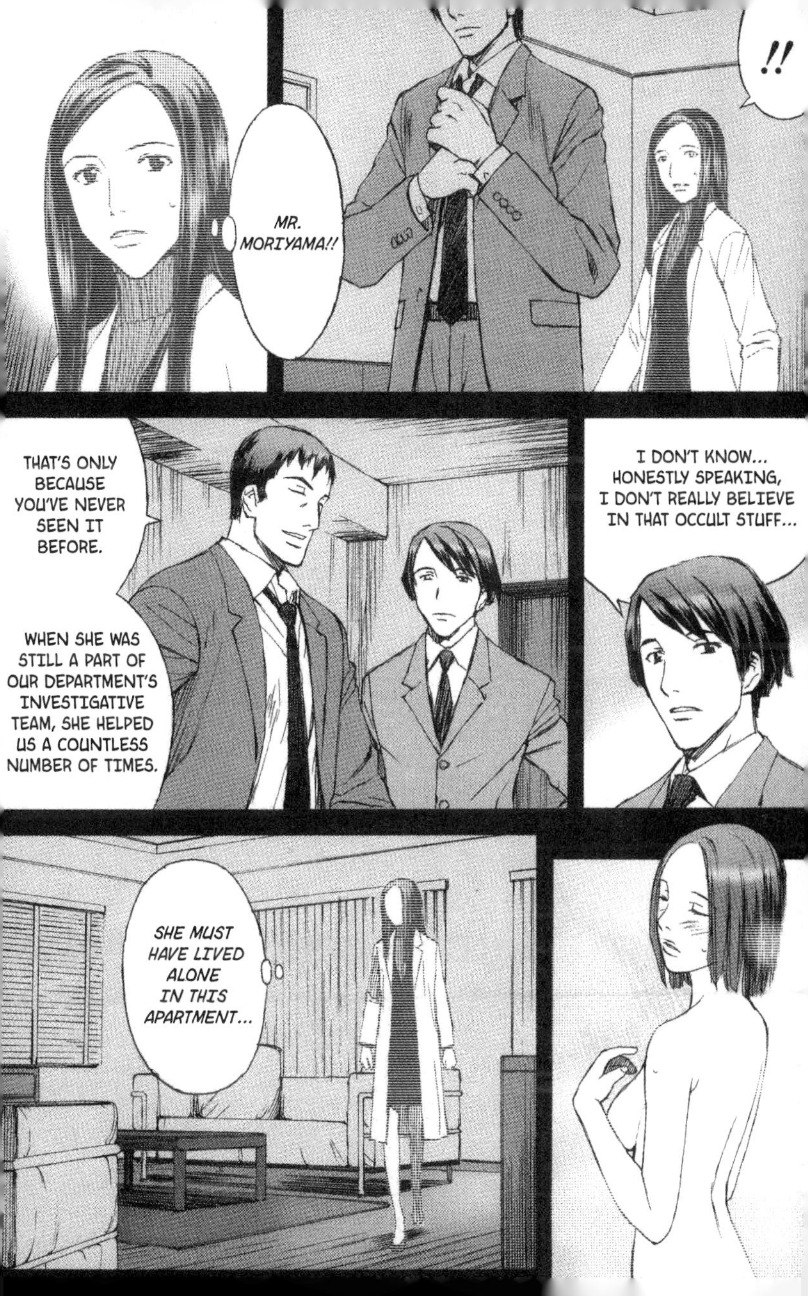
!!
MR. MORIYAMA!!
I DON'T KNOW... HONESTLY SPEAKING, I DON'T REALLY BELIEVE IN THAT OCCULT STUFF...
THAT'S ONLY BECAUSE YOU'VE NEVER SEEN IT BEFORE.
WHEN SHE WAS STILL A PART OF OUR DEPARTMENT'S INVESTIGATIVE TEAM, SHE HELPED US A COUNTLESS NUMBER OF TIMES.
SHE MUST HAVE LIVED ALONE IN THIS APARTMENT...

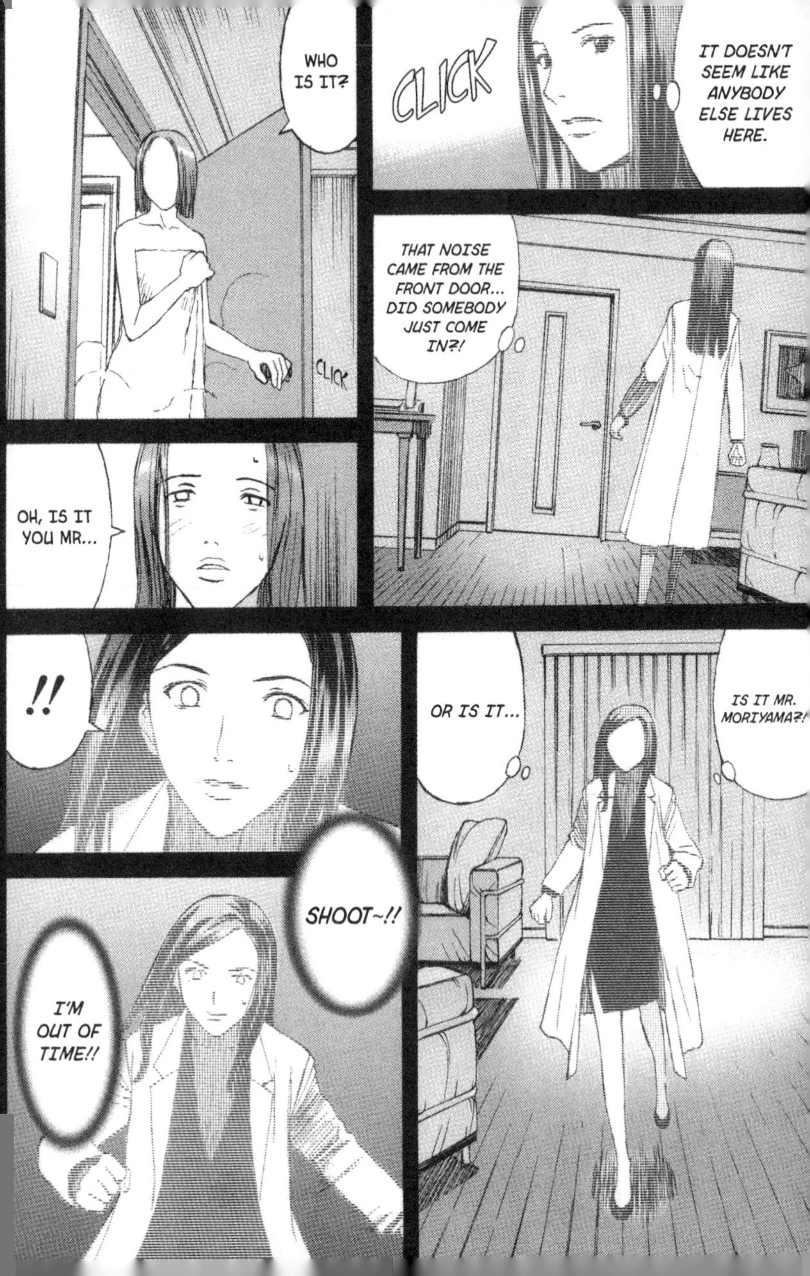
CLICK
IT DOESN'T SEEM LIKE ANYBODY ELSE LIVES HERE.
THAT NOISE CAME FROM THE FRONT DOOR... DID SOMEBODY JUST COME IN?!
WHO IS IT?
CLICK
OH, IS IT YOU MR...
IS IT MR. MORIYAMA?!
OR IS IT...
!!
SHOOT~!!
I'M OUT OF TIME!!

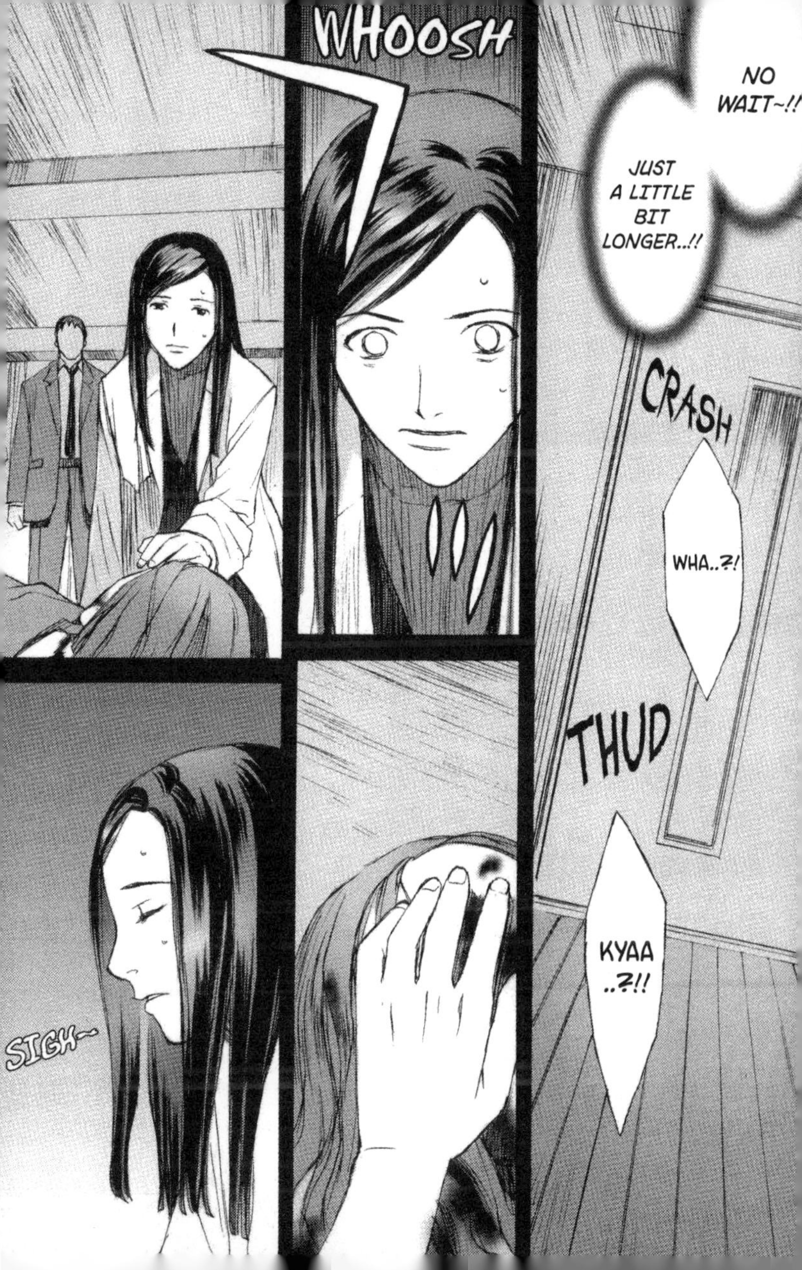
NO WAIT~!!
JUST A LITTLE BIT LONGER..!!
CRASH
WHA..?!
THUD
KYAA ..?!!
WHOOSH
SIGH~

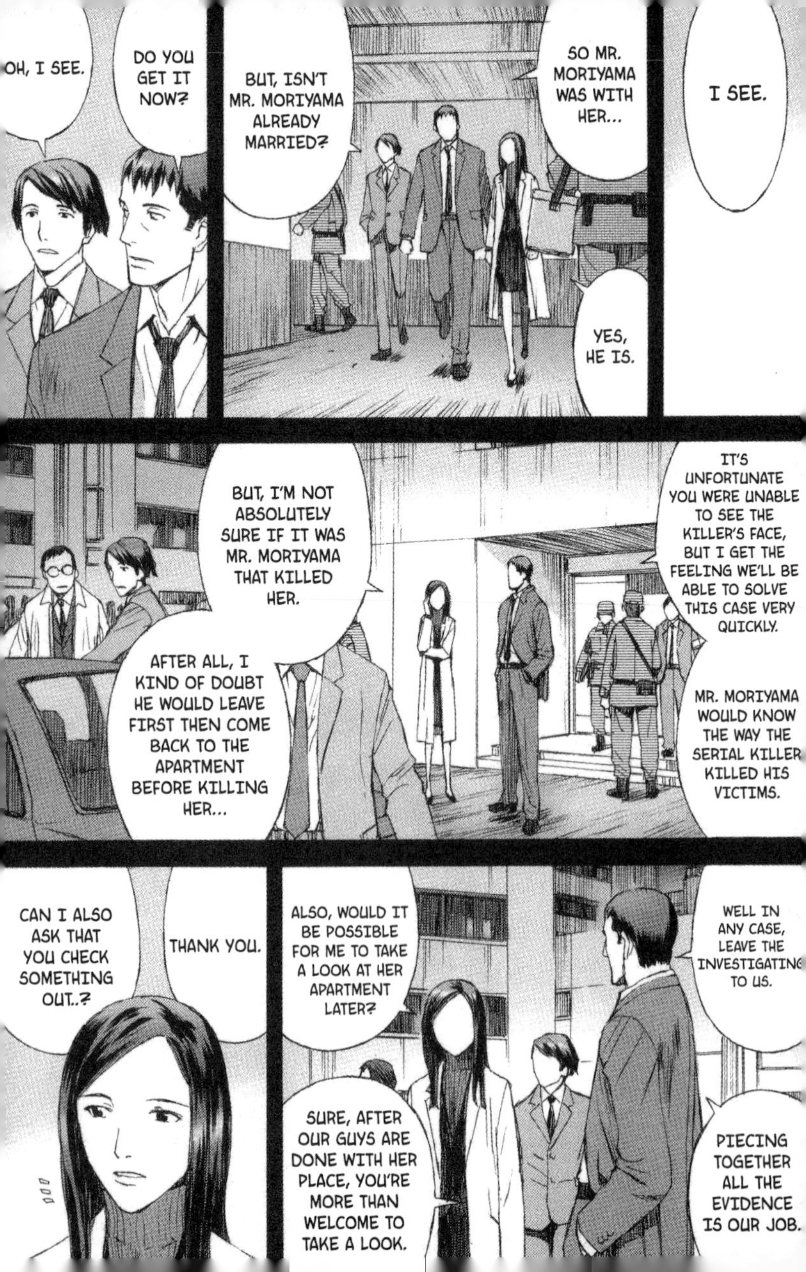
I SEE.
YES, HE IS.
SO MR. MORIYAMA WAS WITH HER...
BUT, ISN'T MR. MORIYAMA ALREADY MARRIED?
DO YOU GET IT NOW?
OH, I SEE.
IT'S UNFORTUNATE YOU WERE UNABLE TO SEE THE KILLER'S FACE, BUT I GET THE FEELING WE'LL BE ABLE TO SOLVE THIS CASE VERY QUICKLY.
MR. MORIYAMA WOULD KNOW THE WAY THE SERIAL KILLER KILLED HIS VICTIMS.
BUT, I'M NOT ABSOLUTELY SURE IF IT WAS MR. MORIYAMA THAT KILLED HER.
AFTER ALL, I KIND OF DOUBT HE WOULD LEAVE FIRST THEN COME BACK TO THE APARTMENT BEFORE KILLING HER...
WELL IN ANY CASE, LEAVE THE INVESTIGATING TO US.
PIECING TOGETHER ALL THE EVIDENCE IS OUR JOB.
ALSO, WOULD IT BE POSSIBLE FOR ME TO TAKE A LOOK AT HER APARTMENT LATER?
SURE, AFTER OUR GUYS ARE DONE WITH HER PLACE, YOU'RE MORE THAN WELCOME TO TAKE A LOOK.
THANK YOU.
CAN I ALSO ASK THAT YOU CHECK SOMETHING OUT..?

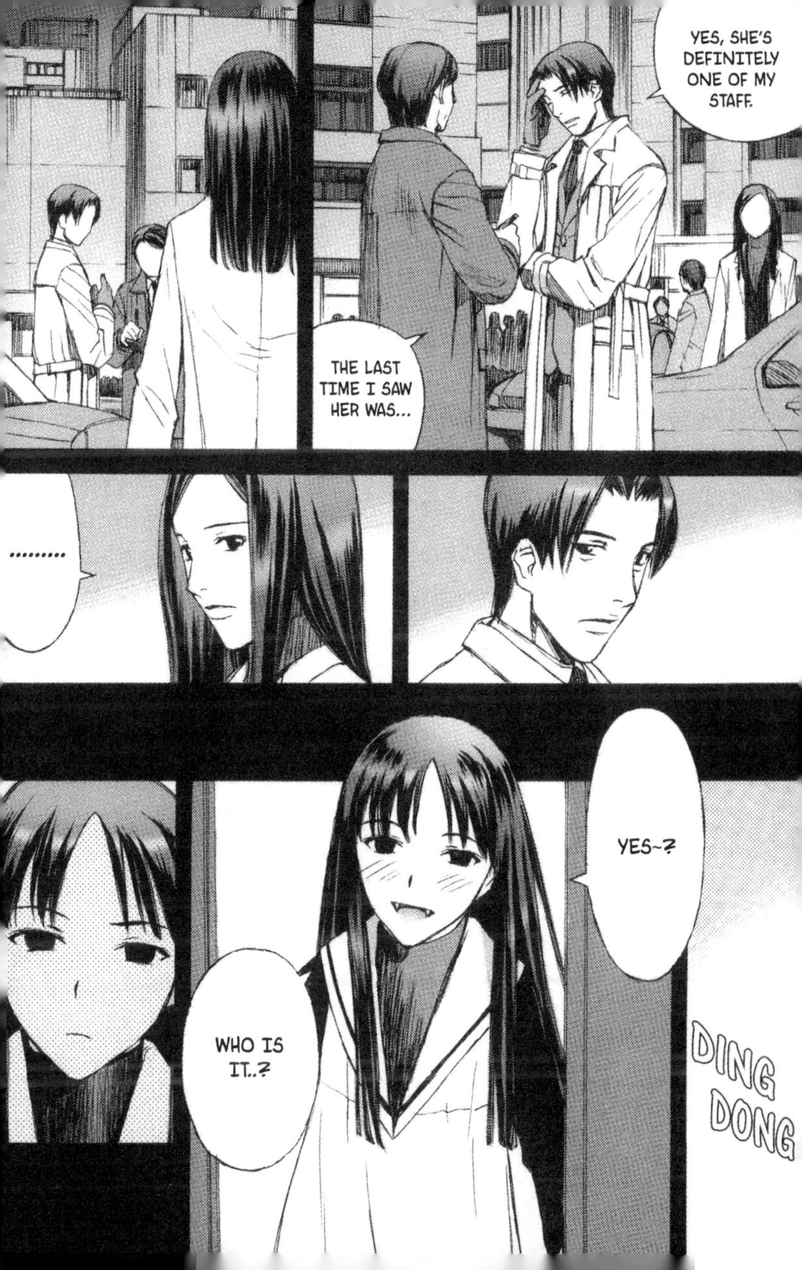
YES, SHE'S DEFINITELY ONE OF MY STAFF.
THE LAST TIME I SAW HER WAS...
....
DING DONG
YES~?
WHO IS IT..?

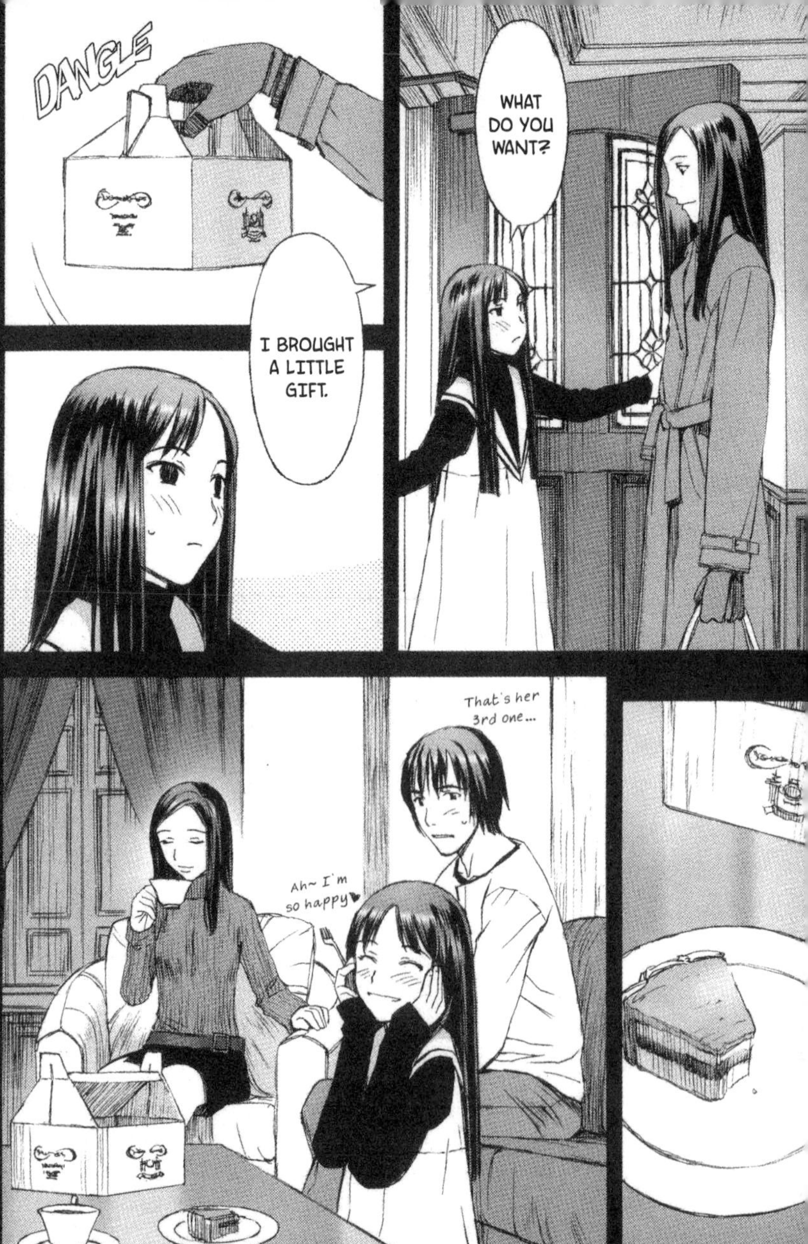
WHAT DO YOU WANT?
DANGLE
I BROUGHT A LITTLE GIFT.
That's her 3rd one...
Ah~ I'm so happy

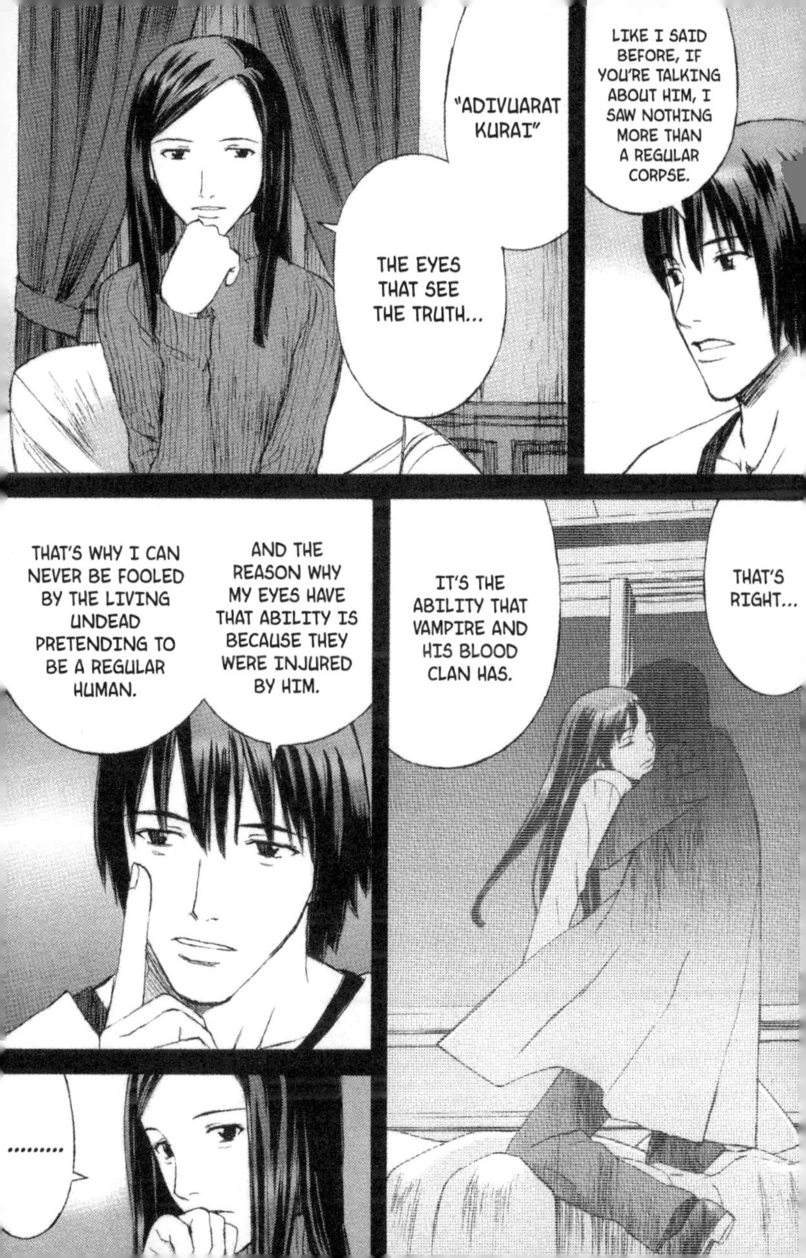
LIKE I SAID BEFORE, IF YOU'RE TALKING ABOUT HIM, I SAW NOTHING MORE THAN A REGULAR CORPSE.
"ADIVUARAT KURAI"
THE EYES THAT SEE THE TRUTH...
THAT'S RIGHT...
IT'S THE ABILITY THAT VAMPIRE AND HIS BLOOD CLAN HAS.
AND THE REASON WHY MY EYES HAVE THAT ABILITY IS BECAUSE THEY WERE INJURED BY HIM.
THAT'S WHY I CAN NEVER BE FOOLED BY THE LIVING UNDEAD PRETENDING TO BE A REGULAR HUMAN.
....

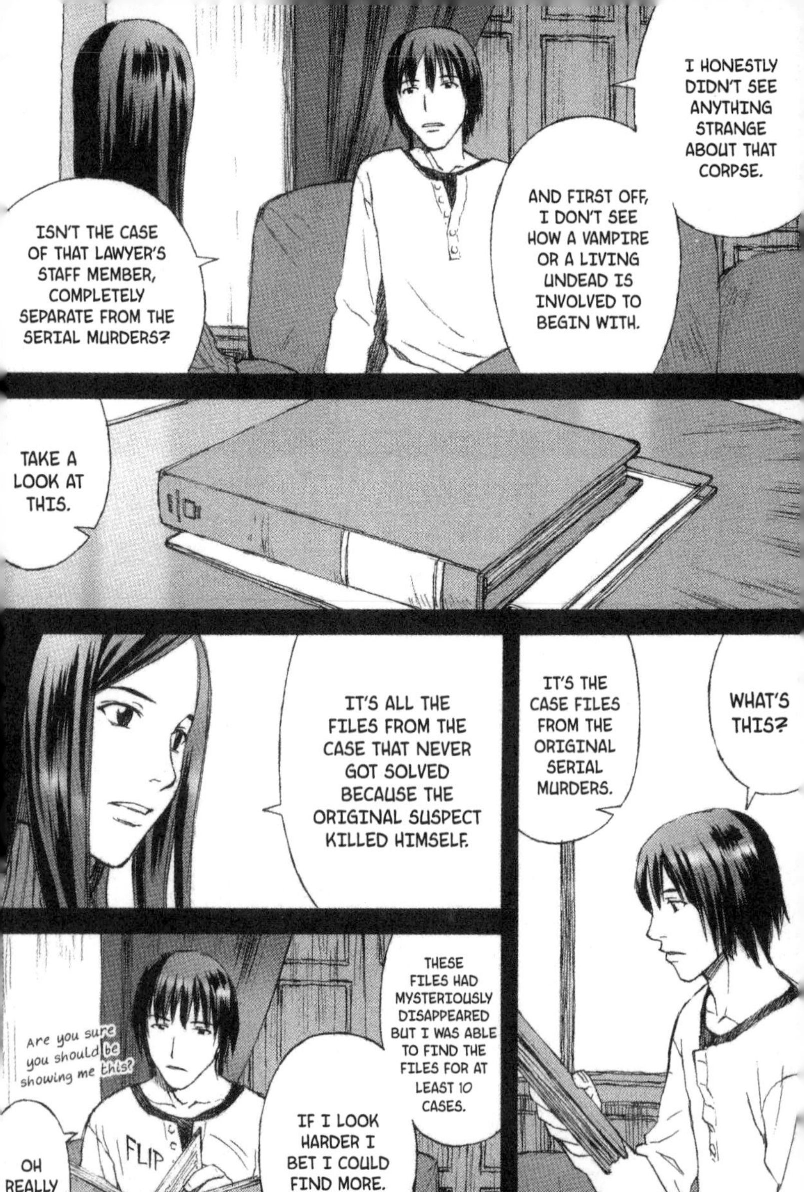
I HONESTLY DIDN'T SEE ANYTHING STRANGE ABOUT THAT CORPSE.
AND FIRST OFF, I DON'T SEE HOW A VAMPIRE OR A LIVING UNDEAD IS INVOLVED TO BEGIN WITH.
ISN'T THE CASE OF THAT LAWYER'S STAFF MEMBER, COMPLETELY SEPARATE FROM THE SERIAL MURDERS?
TAKE A LOOK AT THIS.
WHAT'S THIS?
IT'S THE CASE FILES FROM THE ORIGINAL SERIAL MURDERS.
IT'S ALL THE FILES FROM THE CASE THAT NEVER GOT SOLVED BECAUSE THE ORIGINAL SUSPECT KILLED HIMSELF.
THESE FILES HAD MYSTERIOUSLY DISAPPEARED BUT I WAS ABLE TO FIND THE FILES FOR AT LEAST 10 CASES.
IF I LOOK HARDER I BET I COULD FIND MORE.
Are you sure you should be showing me this?
FLIP
OH REALLY ...

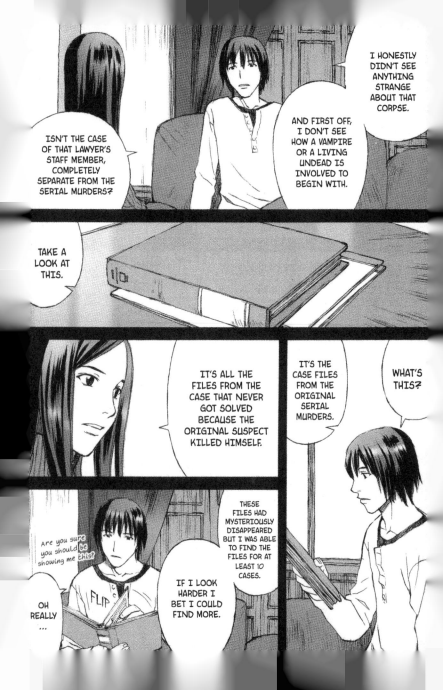

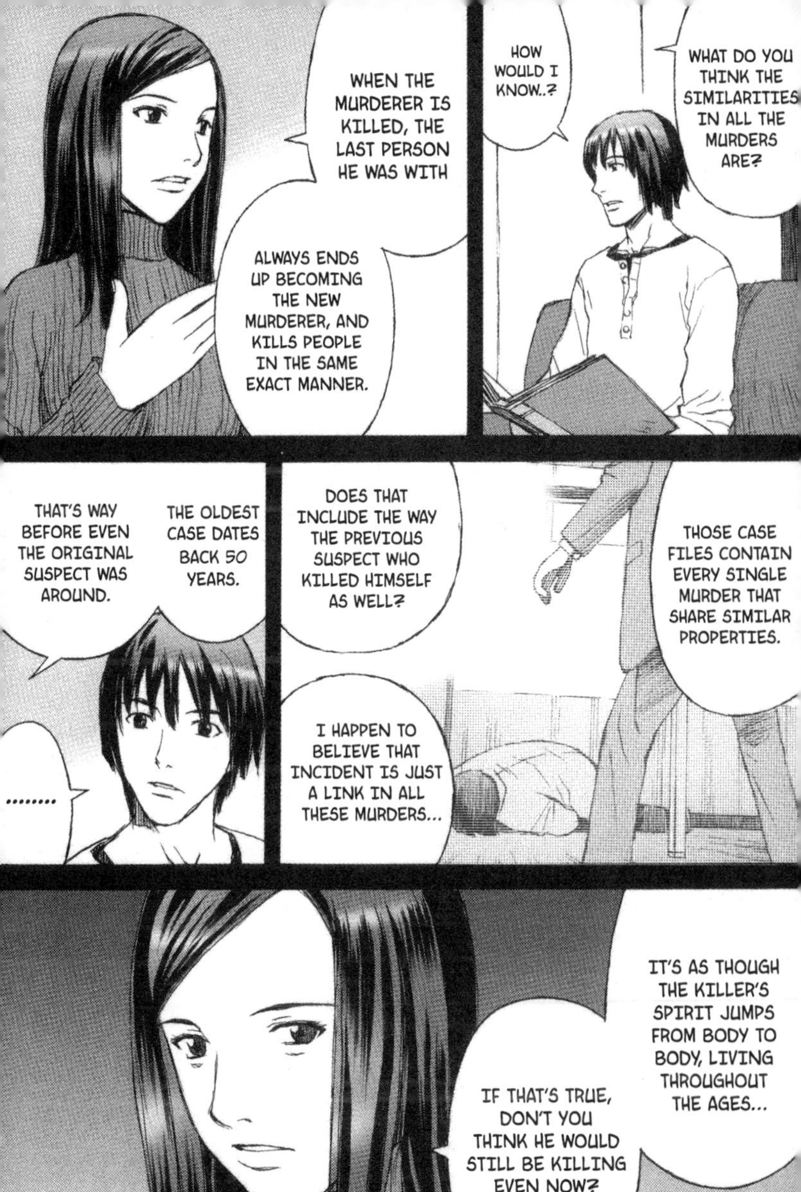
WHAT DO YOU THINK THE SIMILARITIES IN ALL THE MURDERS ARE?
HOW WOULD I KNOW..?
WHEN THE MURDERER IS KILLED, THE LAST PERSON HE WAS WITH
ALWAYS ENDS UP BECOMING THE NEW MURDERER, AND KILLS PEOPLE IN THE SAME EXACT MANNER.
THOSE CASE FILES CONTAIN EVERY SINGLE MURDER THAT SHARE SIMILAR PROPERTIES.
DOES THAT INCLUDE THE WAY THE PREVIOUS SUSPECT WHO KILLED HIMSELF AS WELL?
I HAPPEN TO BELIEVE THAT INCIDENT IS JUST A LINK IN ALL THESE MURDERS...
THE OLDEST CASE DATES BACK 50 YEARS.
THAT'S WAY BEFORE EVEN THE ORIGINAL SUSPECT WAS AROUND.
....
IT'S AS THOUGH THE KILLER'S SPIRIT JUMPS FROM BODY TO BODY, LIVING THROUGHOUT THE AGES...
IF THAT'S TRUE, DON'T YOU THINK HE WOULD STILL BE KILLING EVEN NOW?

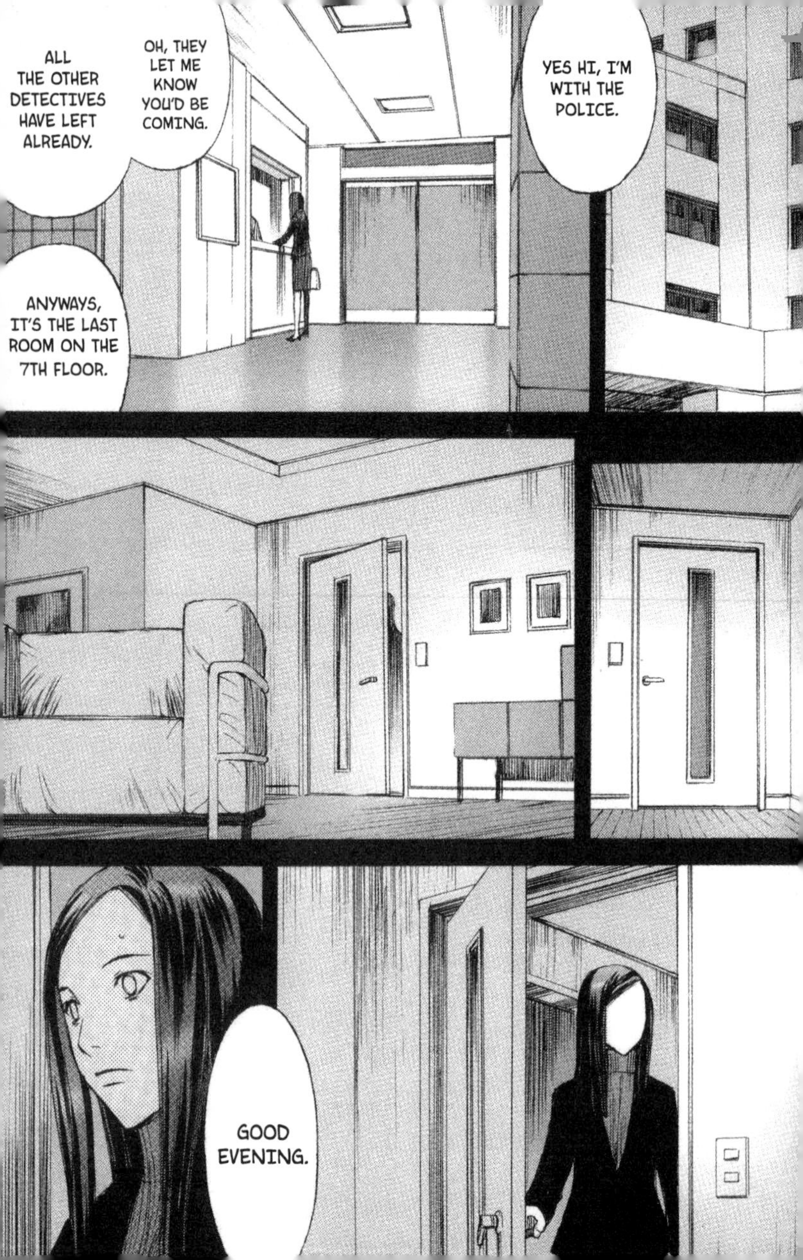
YES HI, I'M WITH THE POLICE.
OH, THEY LET ME KNOW YOU'D BE COMING.
ALL THE OTHER DETECTIVES HAVE LEFT ALREADY.
ANYWAYS, IT'S THE LAST ROOM ON THE 7TH FLOOR.
GOOD EVENING.

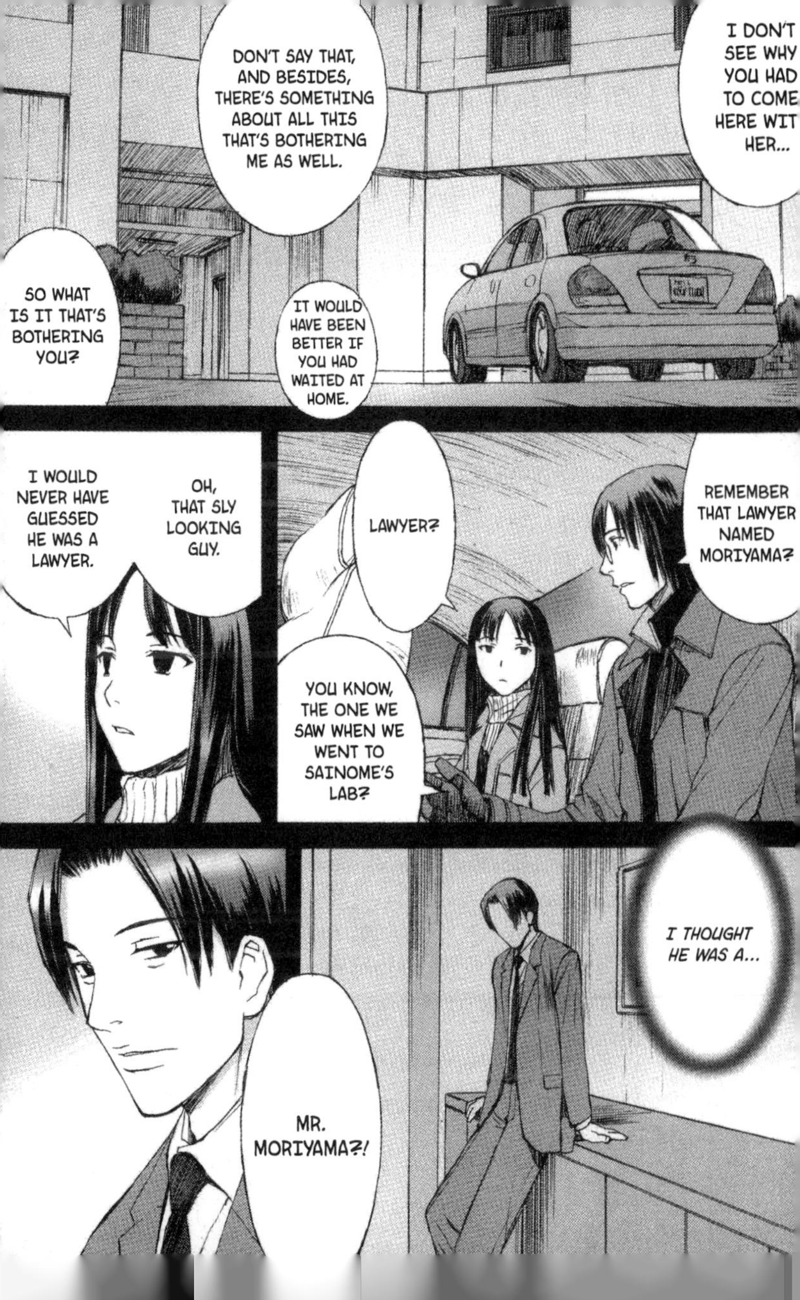
I DON'T SEE WHY YOU HAD TO COME HERE WIT HER...
DON'T SAY THAT, AND BESIDES, THERE'S SOMETHING ABOUT ALL THIS THAT'S BOTHERING ME AS WELL.
IT WOULD HAVE BEEN BETTER IF YOU HAD WAITED AT HOME.
SO WHAT IS IT THAT'S BOTHERING YOU?
REMEMBER THAT LAWYER NAMED MORIYAMA?
LAWYER?
YOU KNOW, THE ONE WE SAW WHEN WE WENT TO SAINOME'S LAB?
OH, THAT SLY LOOKING GUY.
I WOULD NEVER HAVE GUESSED HE WAS A LAWYER.
I THOUGHT HE WAS A...
MR. MORIYAMA?!

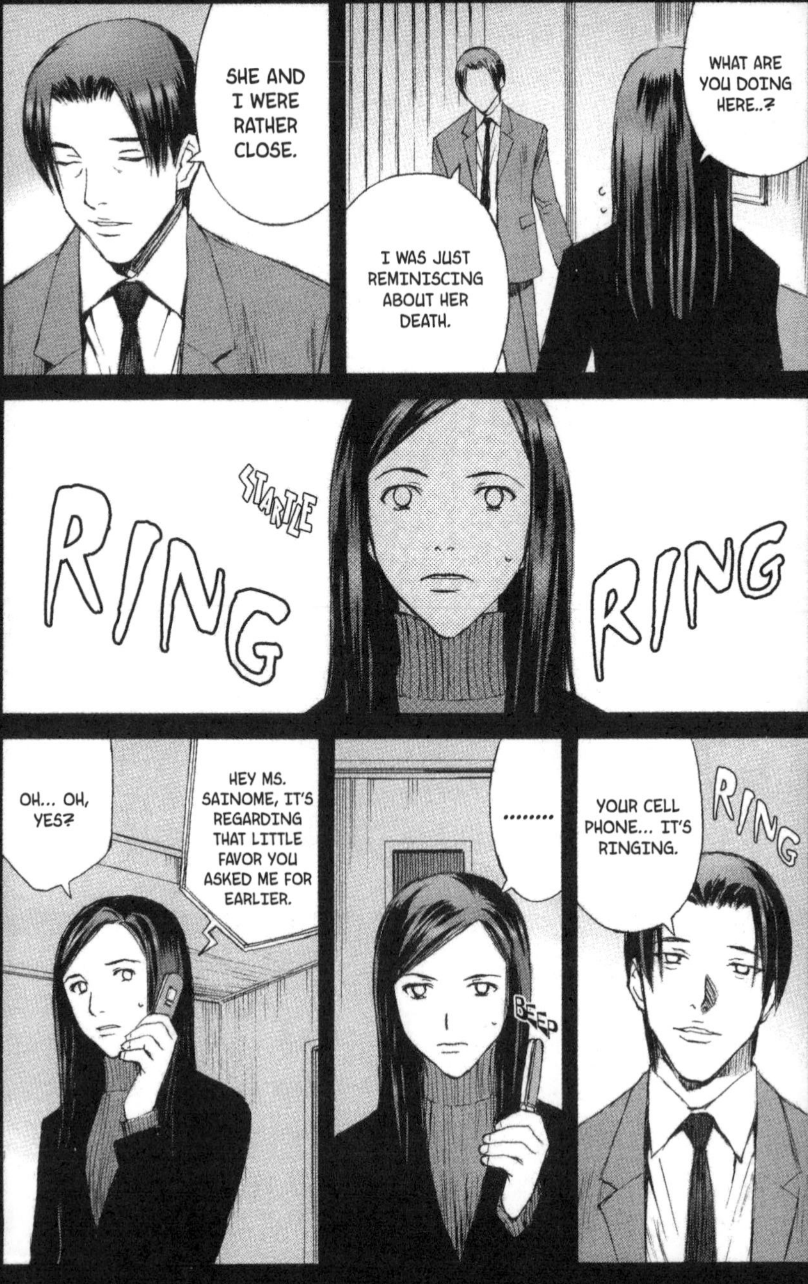

WHAT ARE YOU DOING HERE..?
I WAS JUST REMINISCING ABOUT HER DEATH.
SHE AND I WERE RATHER CLOSE.
RING
STARTLE
RING
RING
YOUR CELL PHONE... IT'S RINGING.
....
BEEP
HEY MS. SAINOME, IT'S REGARDING THAT LITTLE FAVOR YOU ASKED ME FOR EARLIER.
OH... OH, YES?

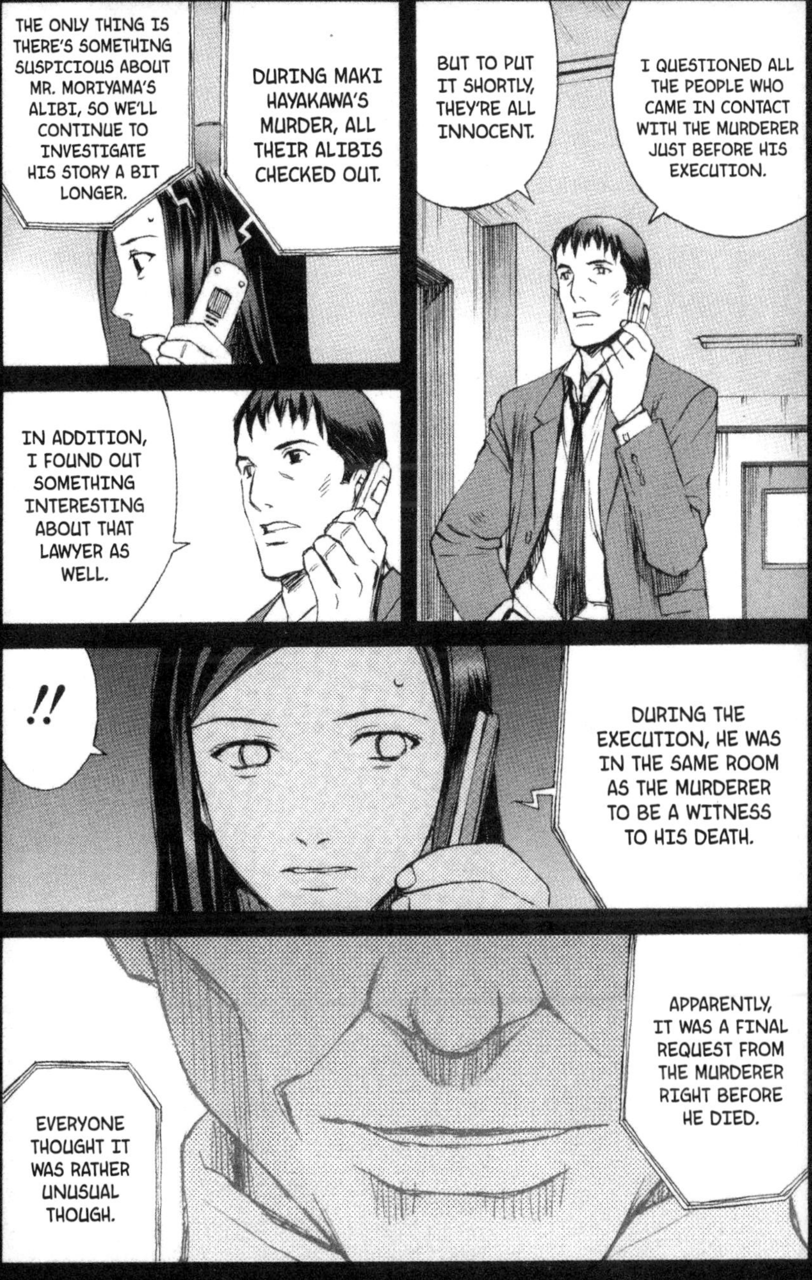
I QUESTIONED ALL THE PEOPLE WHO CAME IN CONTACT WITH THE MURDERER JUST BEFORE HIS EXECUTION.
BUT TO PUT IT SHORTLY, THEY'RE ALL INNOCENT.
DURING MAKI HAYAKAWA'S MURDER, ALL THEIR ALIBIS CHECKED OUT.
THE ONLY THING IS THERE'S SOMETHING SUSPICIOUS ABOUT MR. MORIYAMA'S ALIBI, SO WE'LL CONTINUE TO INVESTIGATE HIS STORY A BIT LONGER.
IN ADDITION, I FOUND OUT SOMETHING INTERESTING ABOUT THAT LAWYER AS WELL.
DURING THE EXECUTION, HE WAS IN THE SAME ROOM AS THE MURDERER TO BE A WITNESS TO HIS DEATH.
!!
APPARENTLY, IT WAS A FINAL REQUEST FROM THE MURDERER RIGHT BEFORE HE DIED.
EVERYONE THOUGHT IT WAS RATHER UNUSUAL THOUGH.

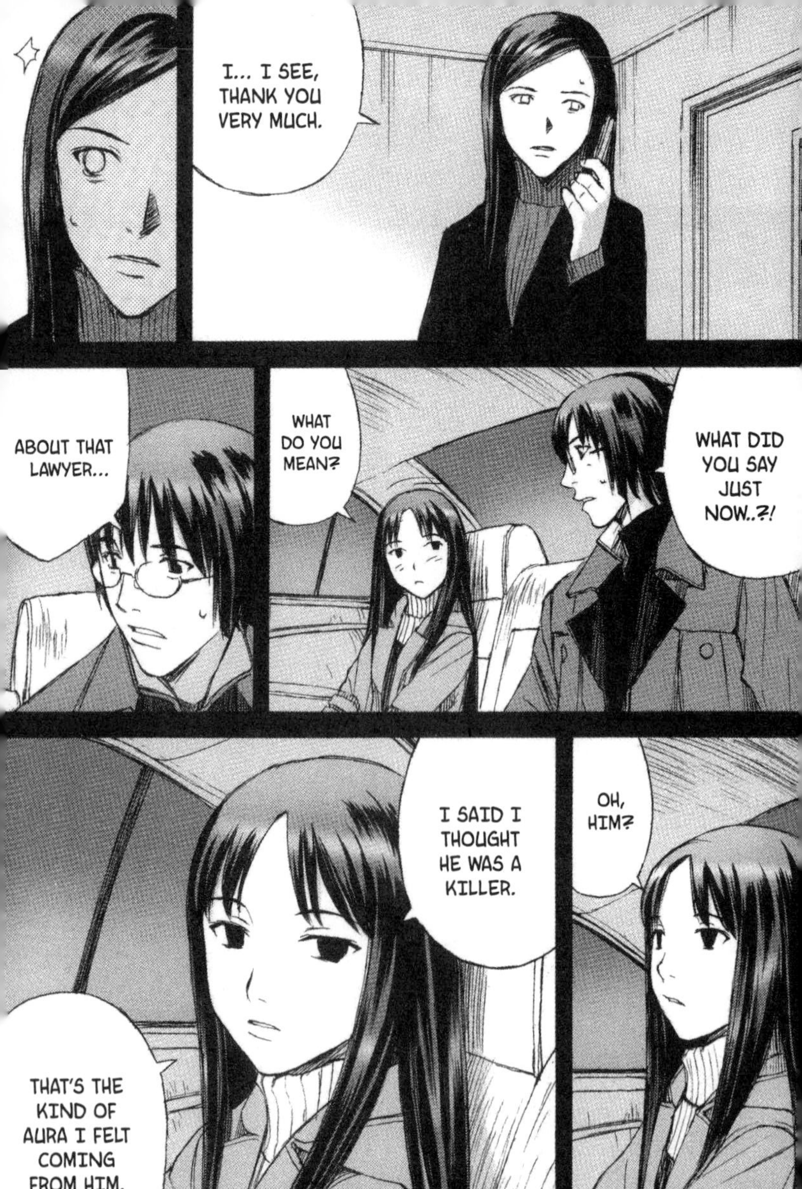
I... I SEE, THANK YOU VERY MUCH.
WHAT DID YOU SAY JUST NOW..?!
WHAT DO YOU MEAN?
ABOUT THAT LAWYER...
OH, HIM?
I SAID I THOUGHT HE WAS A KILLER.
THAT'S THE KIND OF AURA I FELT COMING FROM HIM.

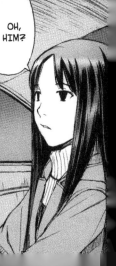

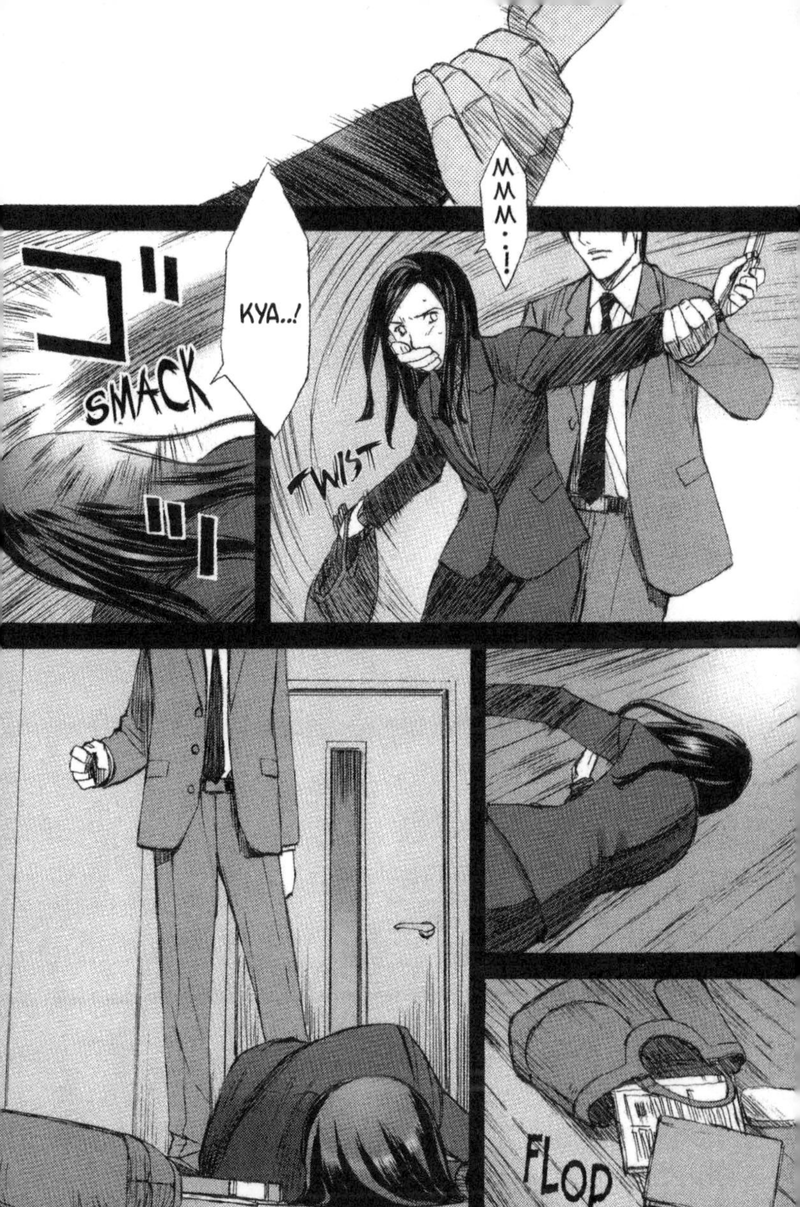
MMM...!
TWIST
KYA..!
ゴッ
SMACK
FLOP

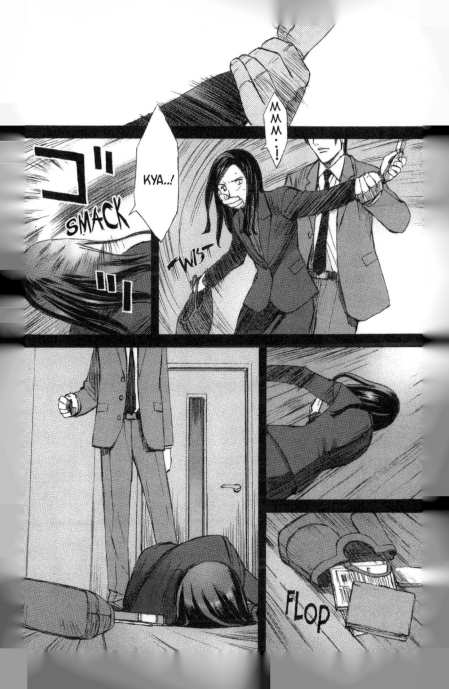

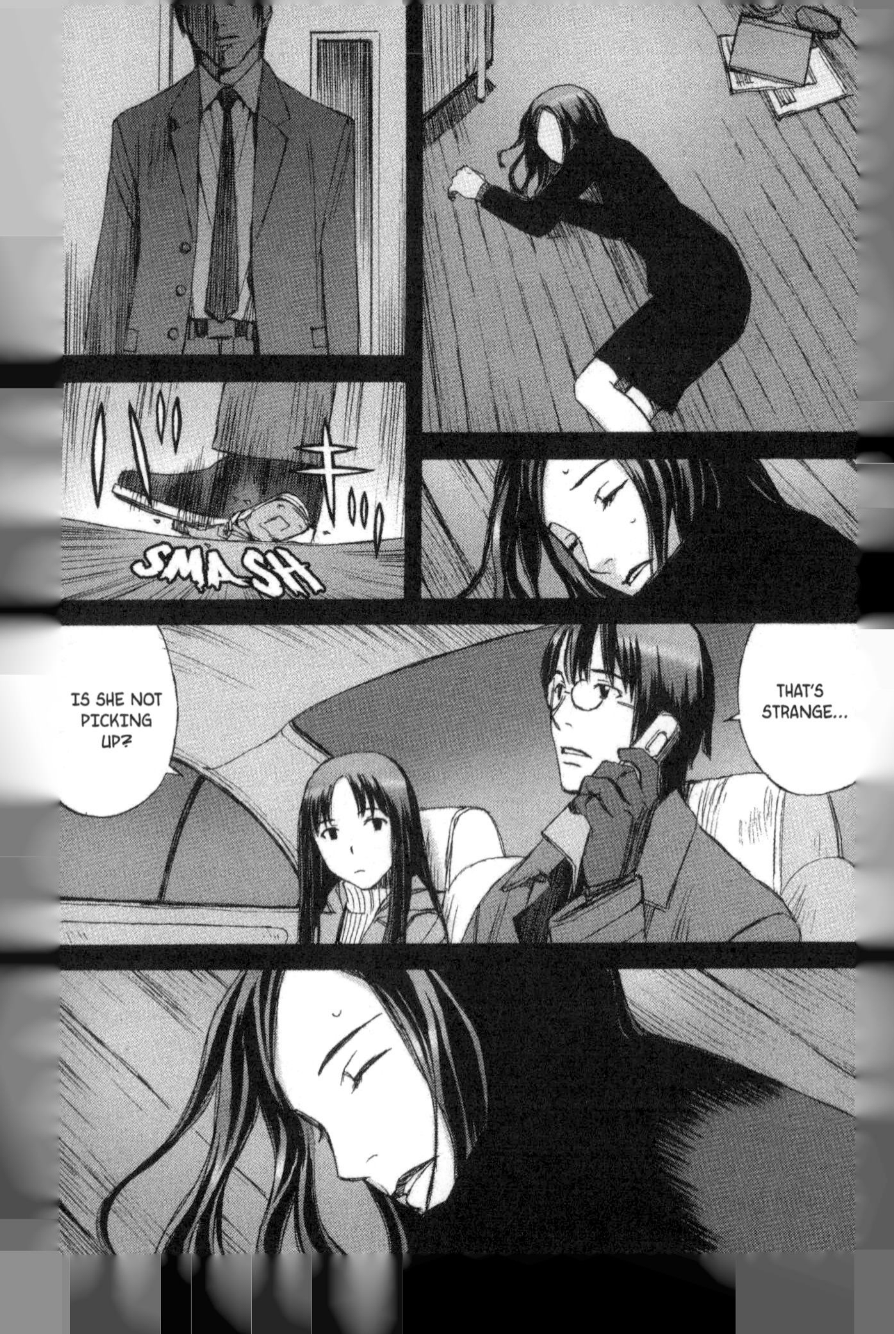
SMASH
THAT'S STRANGE...
IS SHE NOT PICKING UP?

Episode 5

SOUL SLAVE part 3

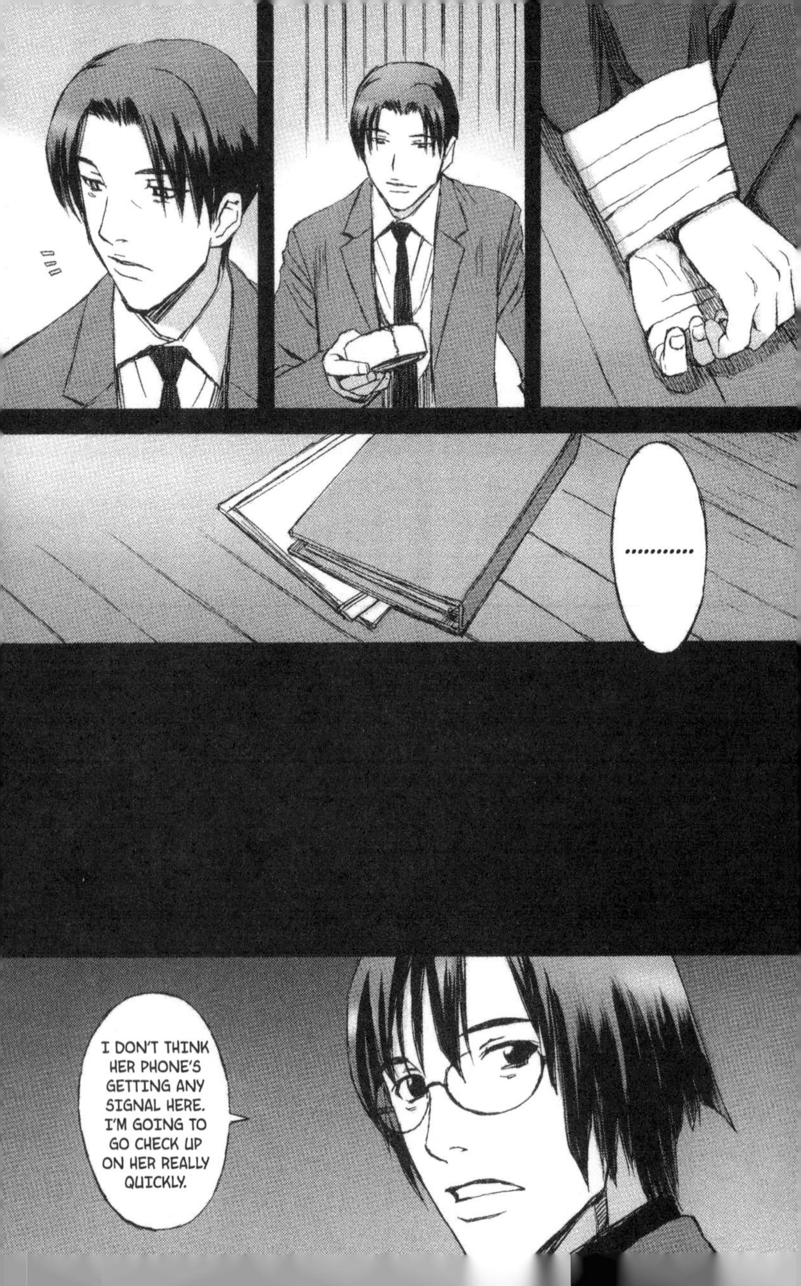
....
I DON'T THINK HER PHONE'S GETTING ANY SIGNAL HERE. I'M GOING TO GO CHECK UP ON HER REALLY QUICKLY.

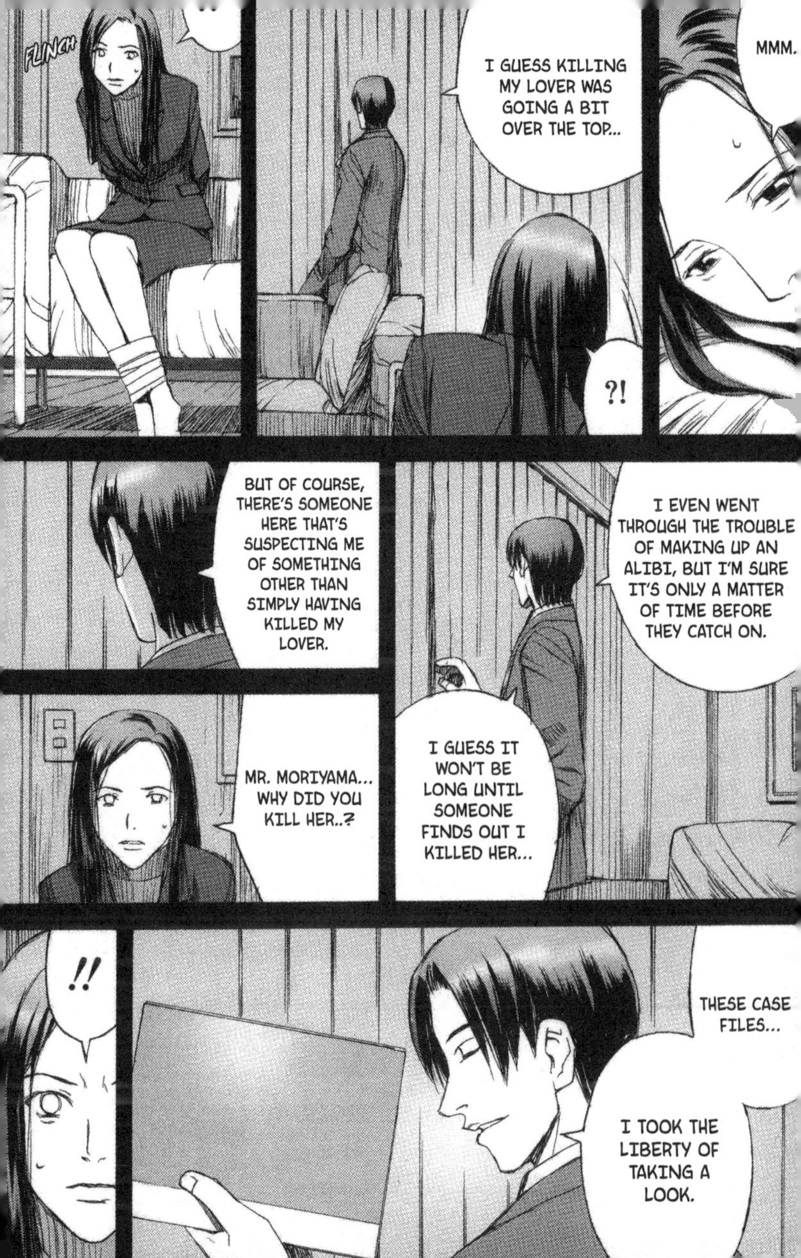
MMM.
I GUESS KILLING MY LOVER WAS GOING A BIT OVER THE TOP...
?!
FLINCH
I EVEN WENT THROUGH THE TROUBLE OF MAKING UP AN ALIBI, BUT I'M SURE IT'S ONLY A MATTER OF TIME BEFORE THEY CATCH ON.
I GUESS IT WON'T BE LONG UNTIL SOMEONE FINDS OUT I KILLED HER...
BUT OF COURSE, THERE'S SOMEONE HERE THAT'S SUSPECTING ME OF SOMETHING OTHER THAN SIMPLY HAVING KILLED MY LOVER.
MR. MORIYAMA... WHY DID YOU KILL HER..?
THESE CASE FILES...
I TOOK THE LIBERTY OF TAKING A LOOK.
!!

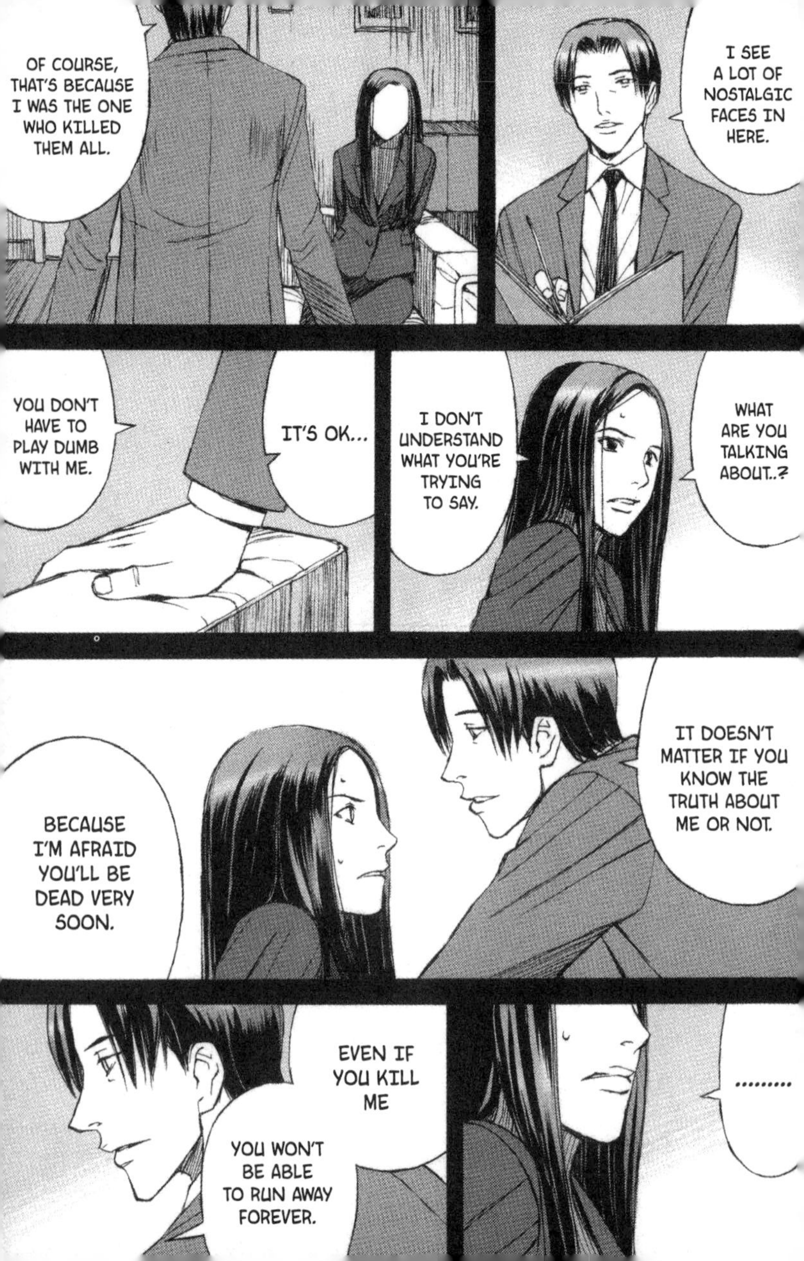
I SEE A LOT OF NOSTALGIC FACES IN HERE.
OF COURSE, THAT'S BECAUSE I WAS THE ONE WHO KILLED THEM ALL.
WHAT ARE YOU TALKING ABOUT..?
I DON'T UNDERSTAND WHAT YOU'RE TRYING TO SAY.
IT'S OK...
YOU DON'T HAVE TO PLAY DUMB WITH ME.
IT DOESN'T MATTER IF YOU KNOW THE TRUTH ABOUT ME OR NOT.
BECAUSE I'M AFRAID YOU'LL BE DEAD VERY SOON.
....
EVEN IF YOU KILL ME
YOU WON'T BE ABLE TO RUN AWAY FOREVER.

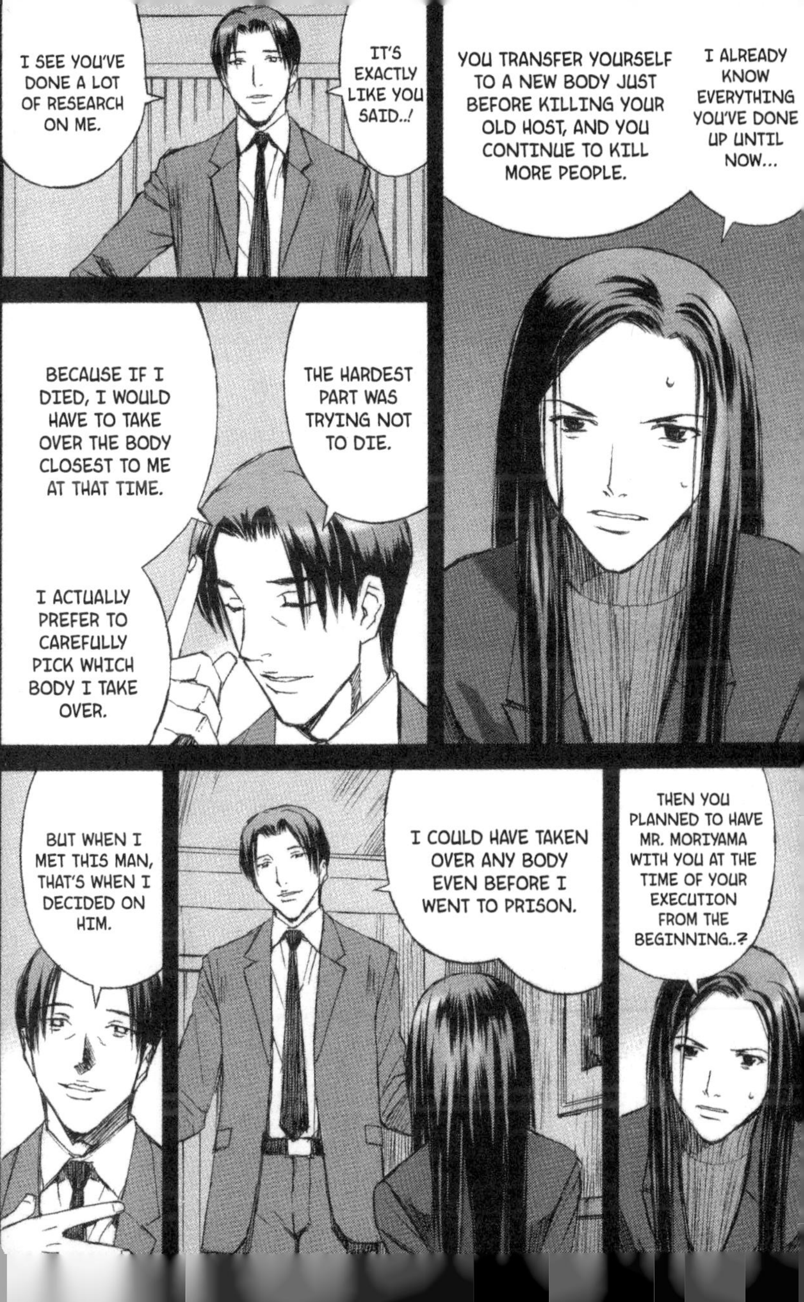
I ALREADY KNOW EVERYTHING YOU'VE DONE UP UNTIL NOW...
YOU TRANSFER YOURSELF TO A NEW BODY JUST BEFORE KILLING YOUR OLD HOST, AND YOU CONTINUE TO KILL MORE PEOPLE.
IT'S EXACTLY LIKE YOU SAID..!
I SEE YOU'VE DONE A LOT OF RESEARCH ON ME.
THE HARDEST PART WAS TRYING NOT TO DIE.
BECAUSE IF I DIED, I WOULD HAVE TO TAKE OVER THE BODY CLOSEST TO ME AT THAT TIME.
I ACTUALLY PREFER TO CAREFULLY PICK WHICH BODY I TAKE OVER.
THEN YOU PLANNED TO HAVE MR. MORIYAMA WITH YOU AT THE TIME OF YOUR EXECUTION FROM THE BEGINNING..?
I COULD HAVE TAKEN OVER ANY BODY EVEN BEFORE I WENT TO PRISON.
BUT WHEN I MET THIS MAN, THAT'S WHEN I DECIDED ON HIM.

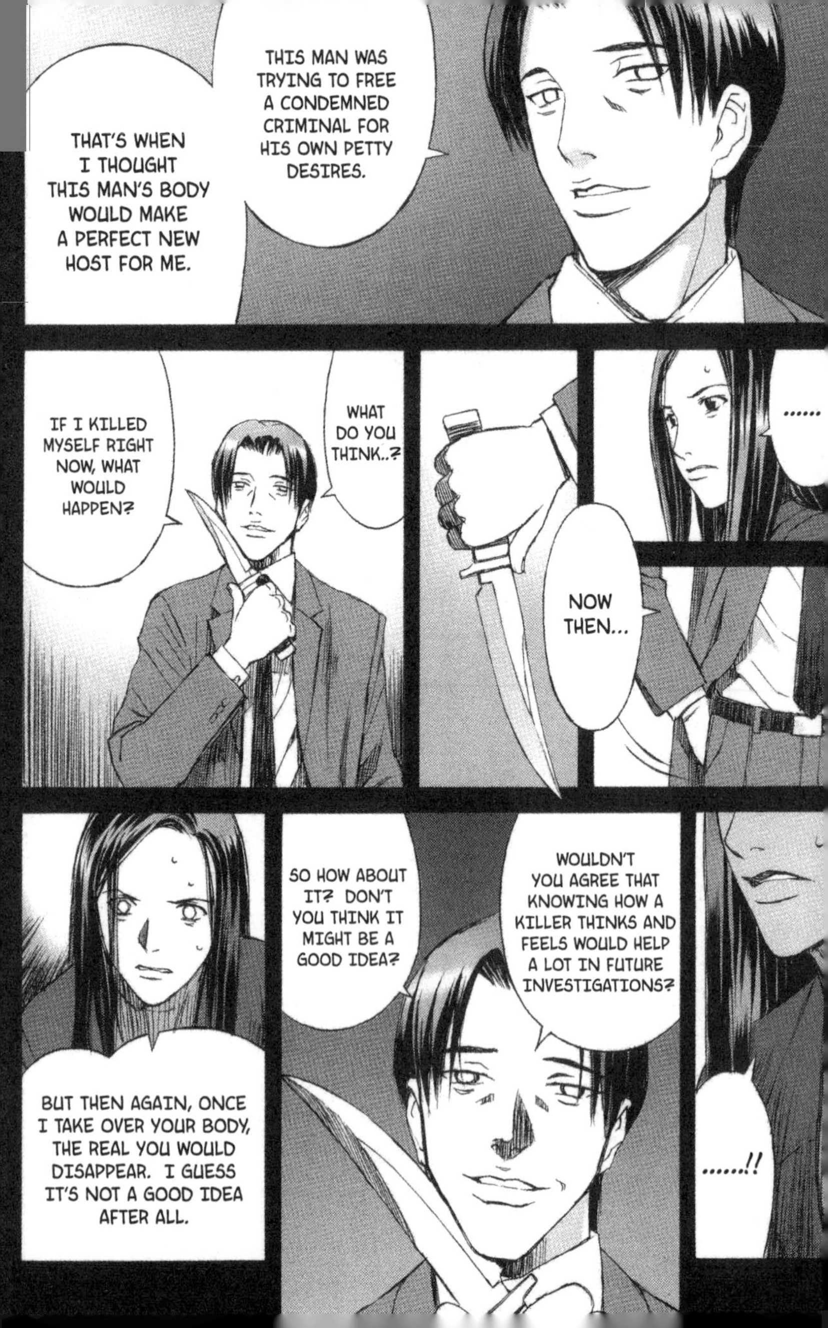
THIS MAN WAS TRYING TO FREE A CONDEMNED CRIMINAL FOR HIS OWN PETTY DESIRES.
THAT'S WHEN I THOUGHT THIS MAN'S BODY WOULD MAKE A PERFECT NEW HOST FOR ME.
......
NOW THEN...
WHAT DO YOU THINK..?
IF I KILLED MYSELF RIGHT NOW, WHAT WOULD HAPPEN?
......!!
WOULDN'T YOU AGREE THAT KNOWING HOW A KILLER THINKS AND FEELS WOULD HELP A LOT IN FUTURE INVESTIGATIONS?
SO HOW ABOUT IT? DON'T YOU THINK IT MIGHT BE A GOOD IDEA?
BUT THEN AGAIN, ONCE I TAKE OVER YOUR BODY, THE REAL YOU WOULD DISAPPEAR. I GUESS IT'S NOT A GOOD IDEA AFTER ALL.

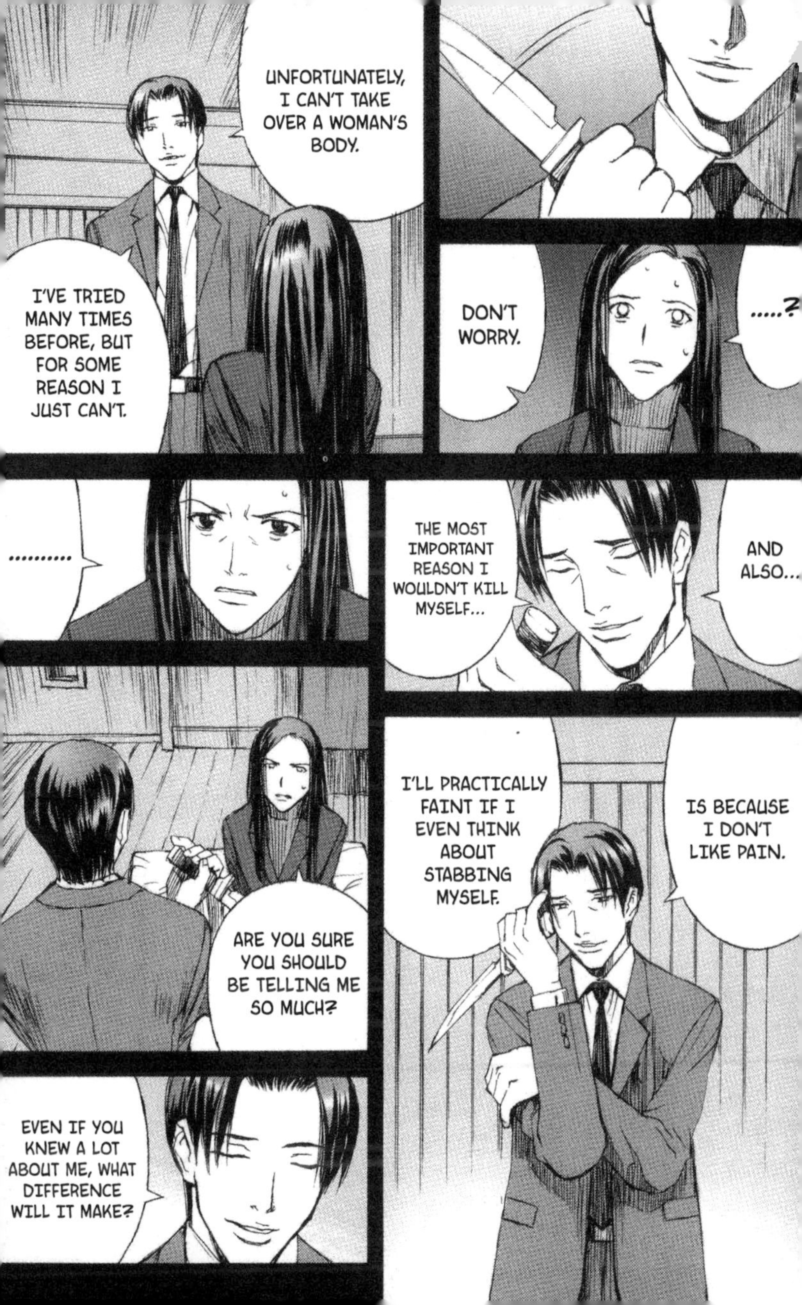

.....?
DON'T WORRY.
UNFORTUNATELY, I CAN'T TAKE OVER A WOMAN'S BODY.
I'VE TRIED MANY TIMES BEFORE, BUT FOR SOME REASON I JUST CAN'T.
AND ALSO...
THE MOST IMPORTANT REASON I WOULDN'T KILL MYSELF...
IS BECAUSE I DON'T LIKE PAIN.
I'LL PRACTICALLY FAINT IF I EVEN THINK ABOUT STABBING MYSELF.
....
ARE YOU SURE YOU SHOULD BE TELLING ME SO MUCH?
EVEN IF YOU KNEW A LOT ABOUT ME, WHAT DIFFERENCE WILL IT MAKE?

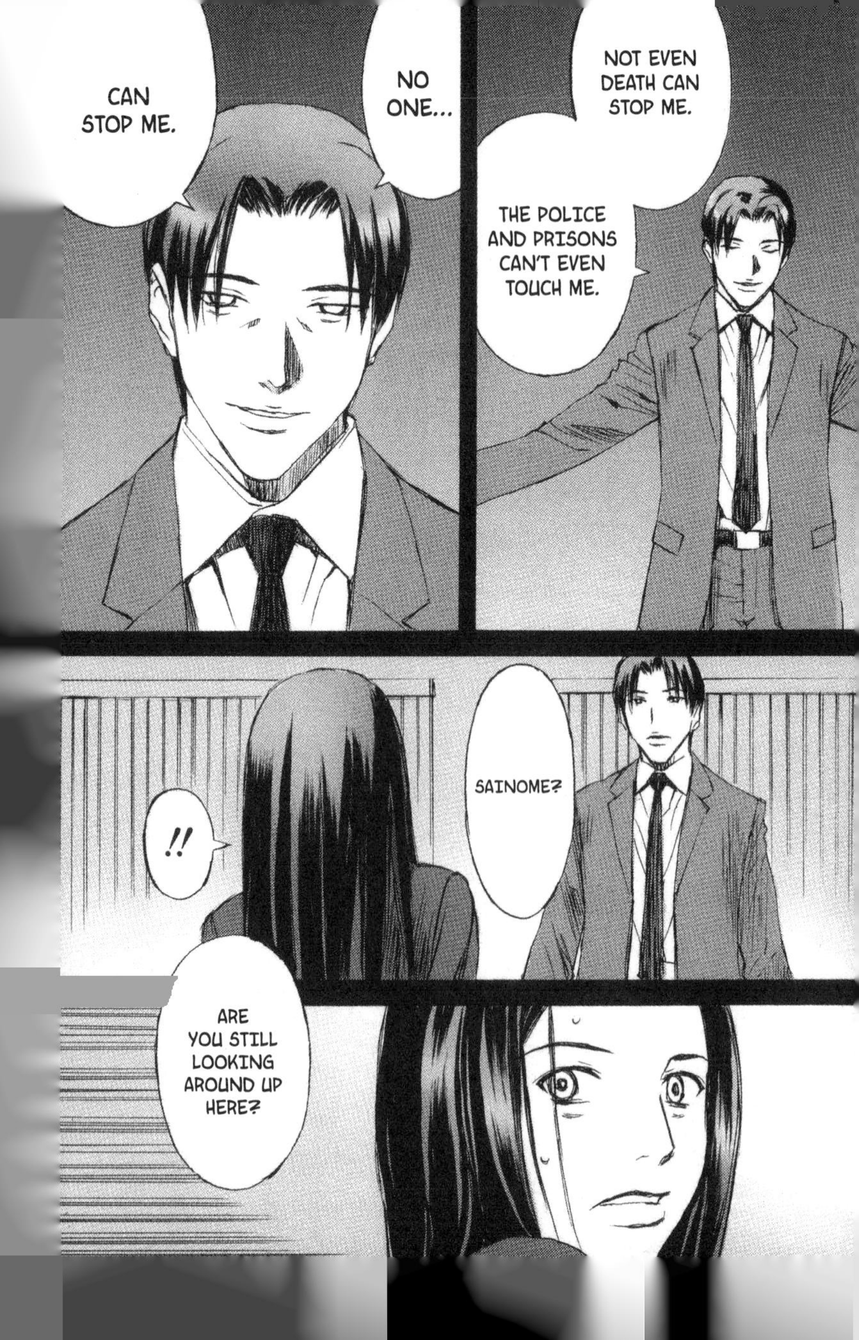
NOT EVEN DEATH CAN STOP ME.
THE POLICE AND PRISONS CAN'T EVEN TOUCH ME.
NO ONE...
CAN STOP ME.
SAINOME?
!!
ARE YOU STILL LOOKING AROUND UP HERE?

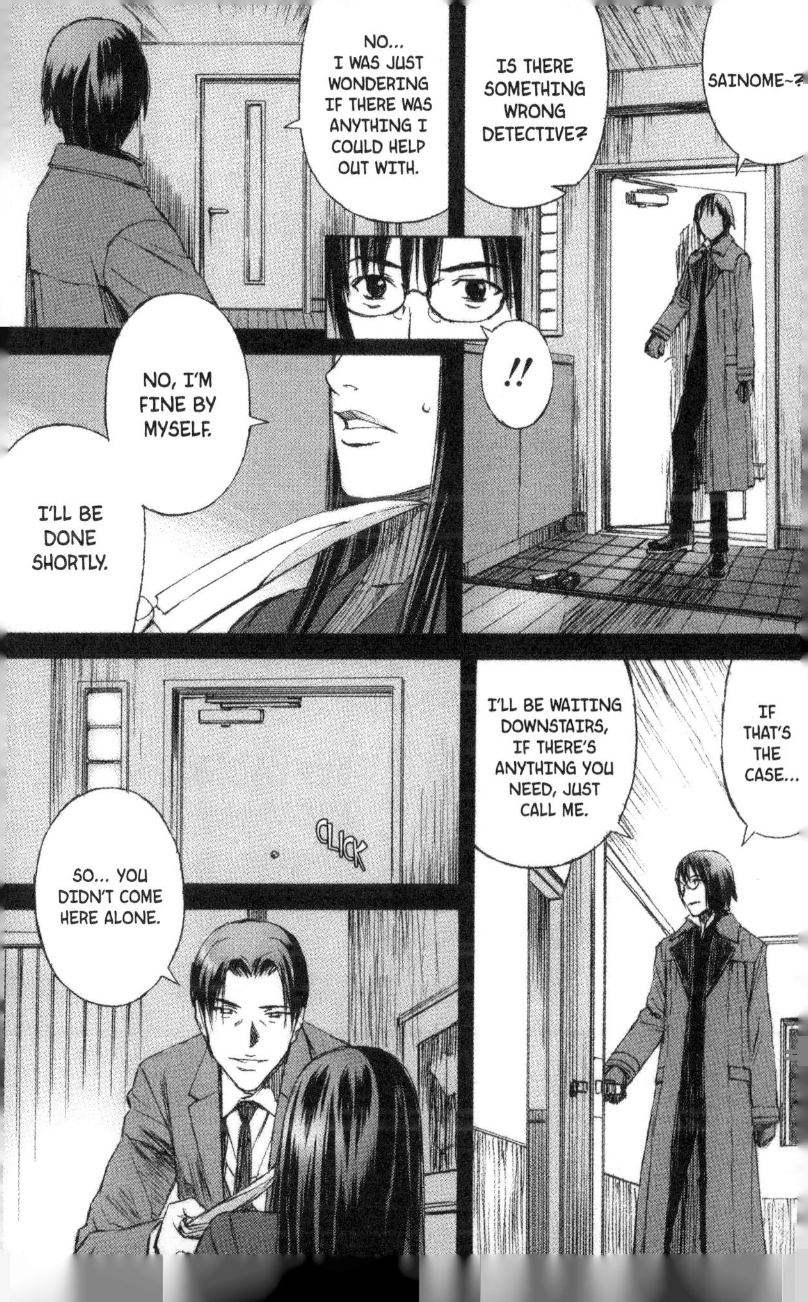
SAINOME~?
IS THERE SOMETHING WRONG DETECTIVE?
NO... I WAS JUST WONDERING IF THERE WAS ANYTHING I COULD HELP OUT WITH.
!!
NO, I'M FINE BY MYSELF.
I'LL BE DONE SHORTLY.
IF THAT'S THE CASE...
I'LL BE WAITING DOWNSTAIRS, IF THERE'S ANYTHING YOU NEED, JUST CALL ME.
CLICK
SO... YOU DIDN'T COME HERE ALONE.

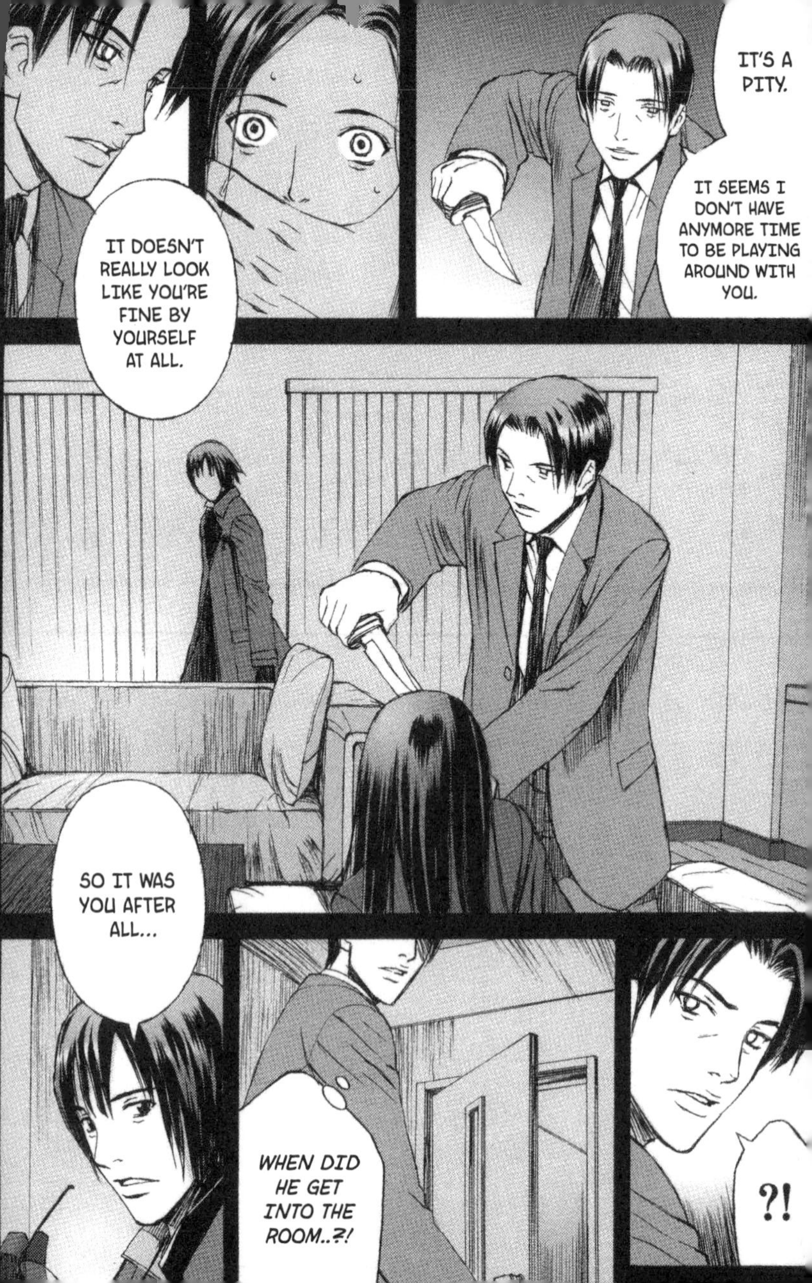
IT'S A PITY.
IT SEEMS I DON'T HAVE ANYMORE TIME TO BE PLAYING AROUND WITH YOU.
IT DOESN'T REALLY LOOK LIKE YOU'RE FINE BY YOURSELF AT ALL.
?!
WHEN DID HE GET INTO THE ROOM..?!
SO IT WAS YOU AFTER ALL...

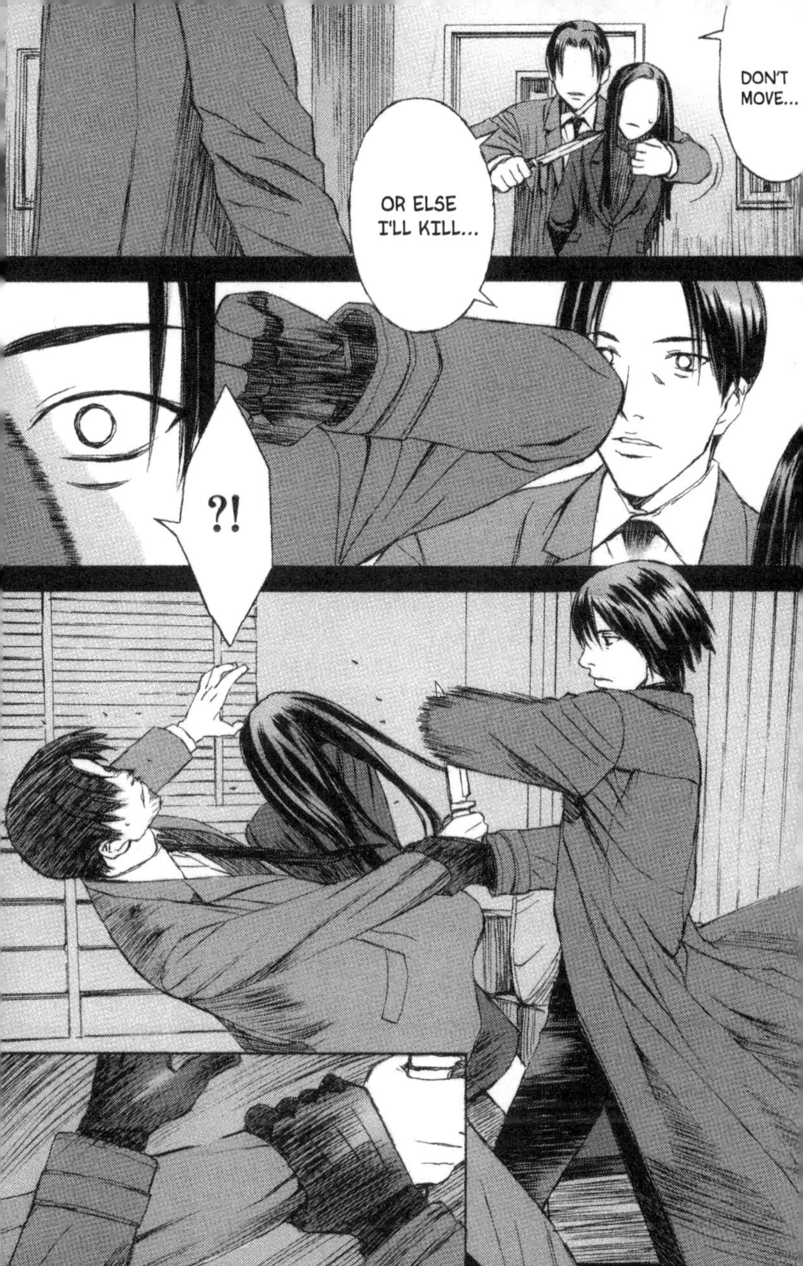
DON'T MOVE...
OR ELSE I'LL KILL...
?!

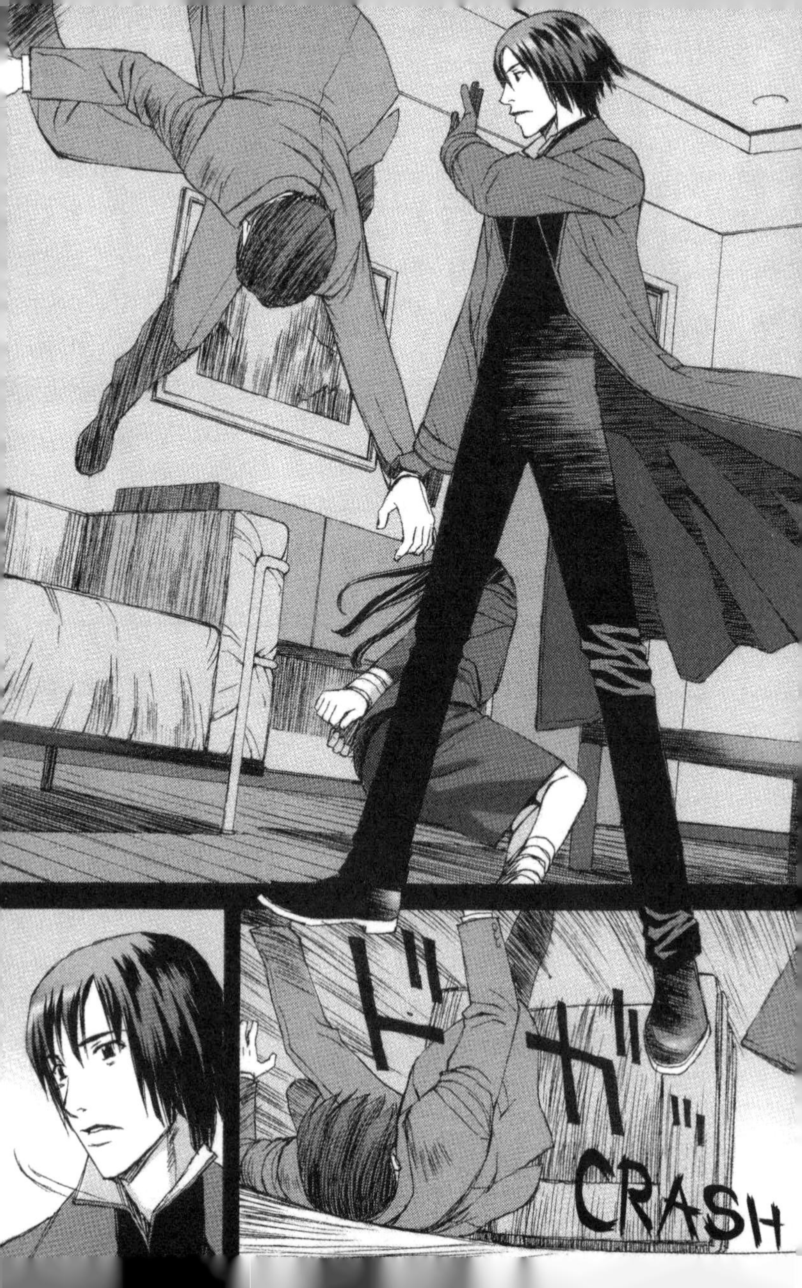
ドガッ
CRASH

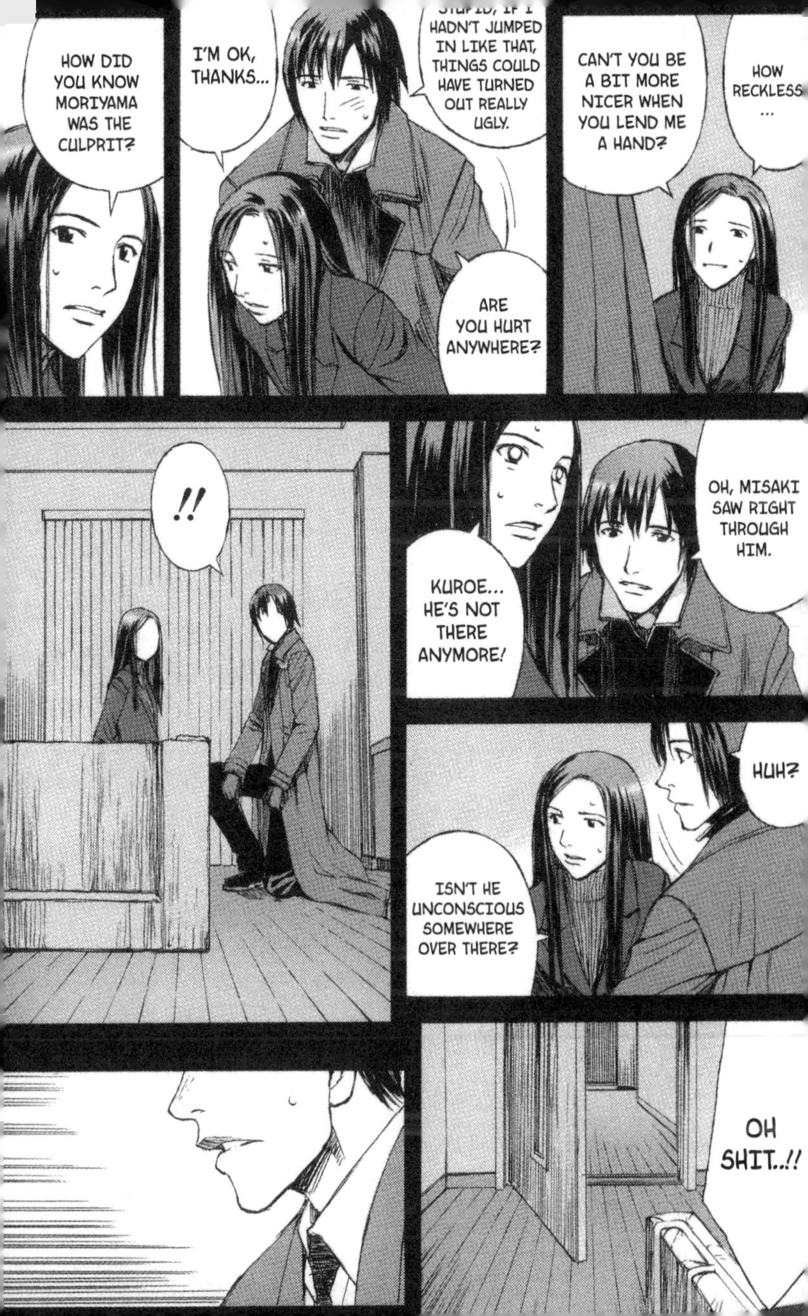
HOW RECKLESS ...
CAN'T YOU BE A BIT MORE NICER WHEN YOU LEND ME A HAND?
HADN'T JUMPED IN LIKE THAT, THINGS COULD HAVE TURNED OUT REALLY UGLY.
ARE YOU HURT ANYWHERE?
I'M OK, THANKS...
HOW DID YOU KNOW MORIYAMA WAS THE CULPRIT?
OH, MISAKI SAW RIGHT THROUGH HIM.
KUROE... HE'S NOT THERE ANYMORE!
HUH?
ISN'T HE UNCONSCIOUS SOMEWHERE OVER THERE?
!!
OH SHIT..!!

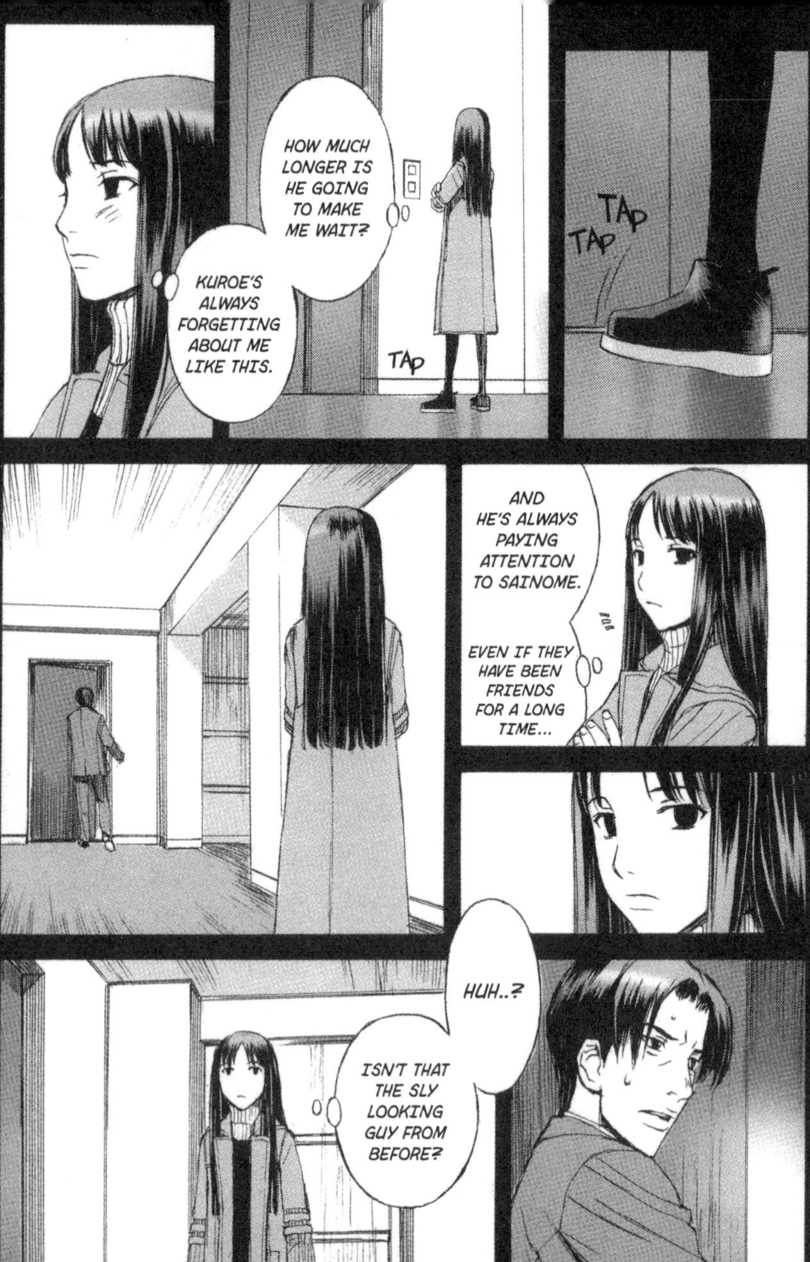
TAP TAP
HOW MUCH LONGER IS HE GOING TO MAKE ME WAIT?
TAP
KUROE'S ALWAYS FORGETTING ABOUT ME LIKE THIS.
AND HE'S ALWAYS PAYING ATTENTION TO SAINOME.
EVEN IF THEY HAVE BEEN FRIENDS FOR A LONG TIME...
HUH..?
ISN'T THAT THE SLY LOOKING GUY FROM BEFORE?

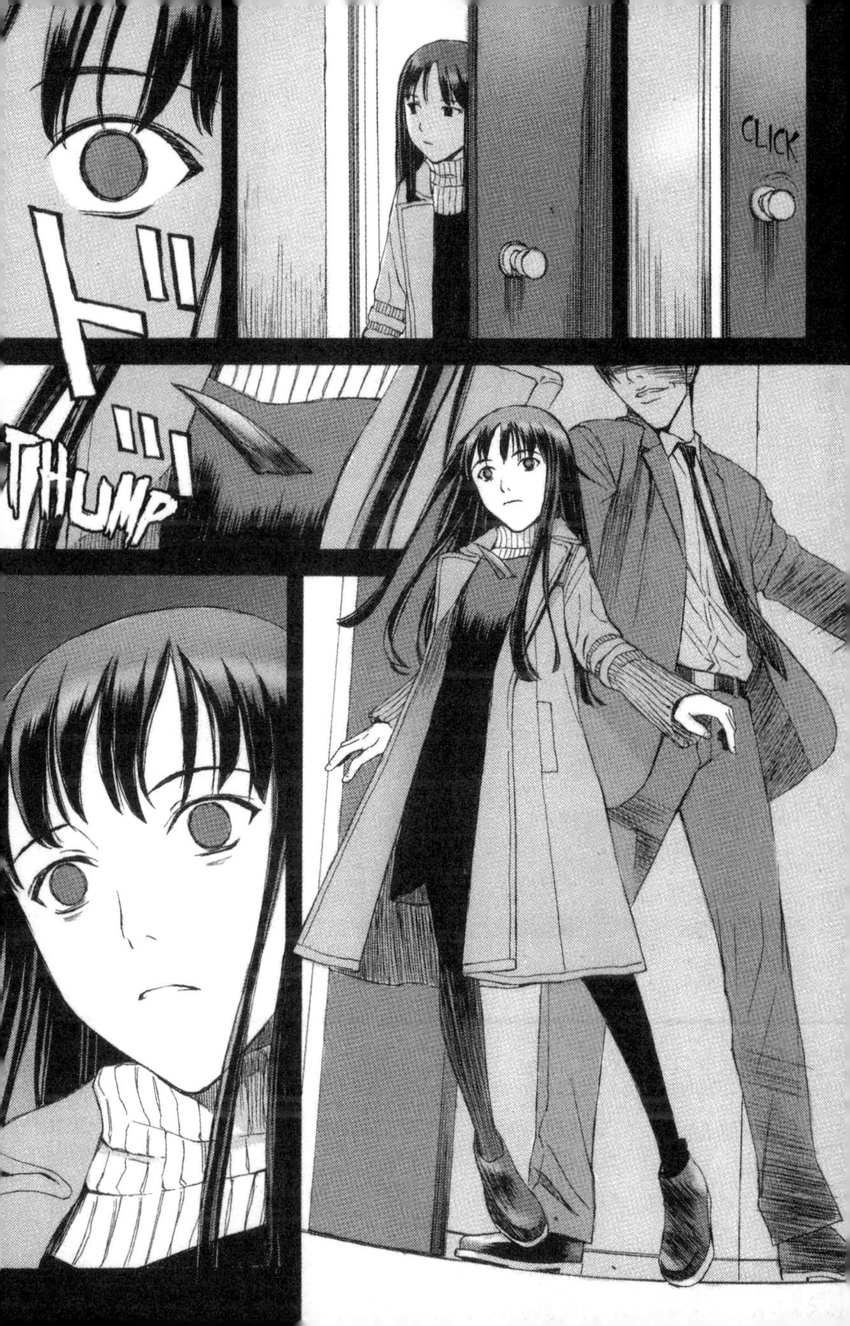
CLICK
ドッ
THUMP

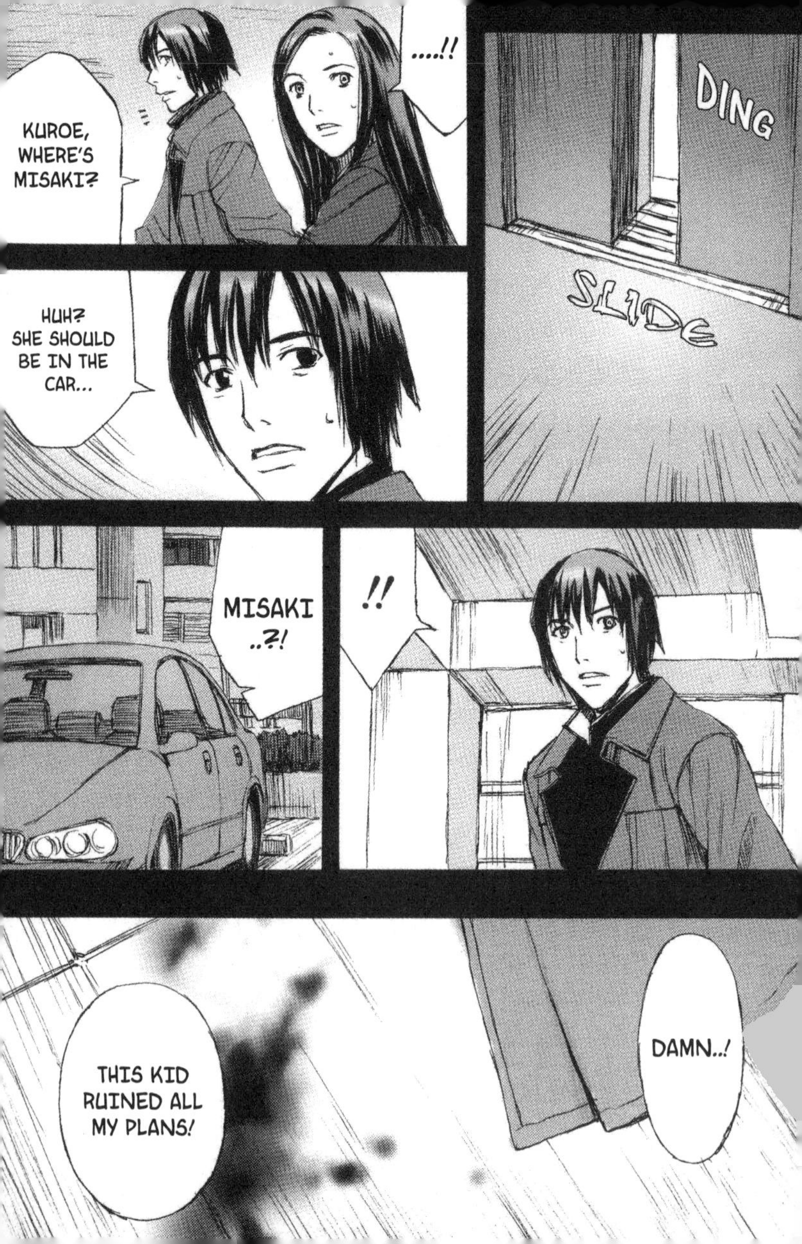
DING
SLIDE
....!!
KUROE, WHERE'S MISAKI?
HUH? SHE SHOULD BE IN THE CAR...
!!
MISAKI ..?!
DAMN..!
THIS KID RUINED ALL MY PLANS!

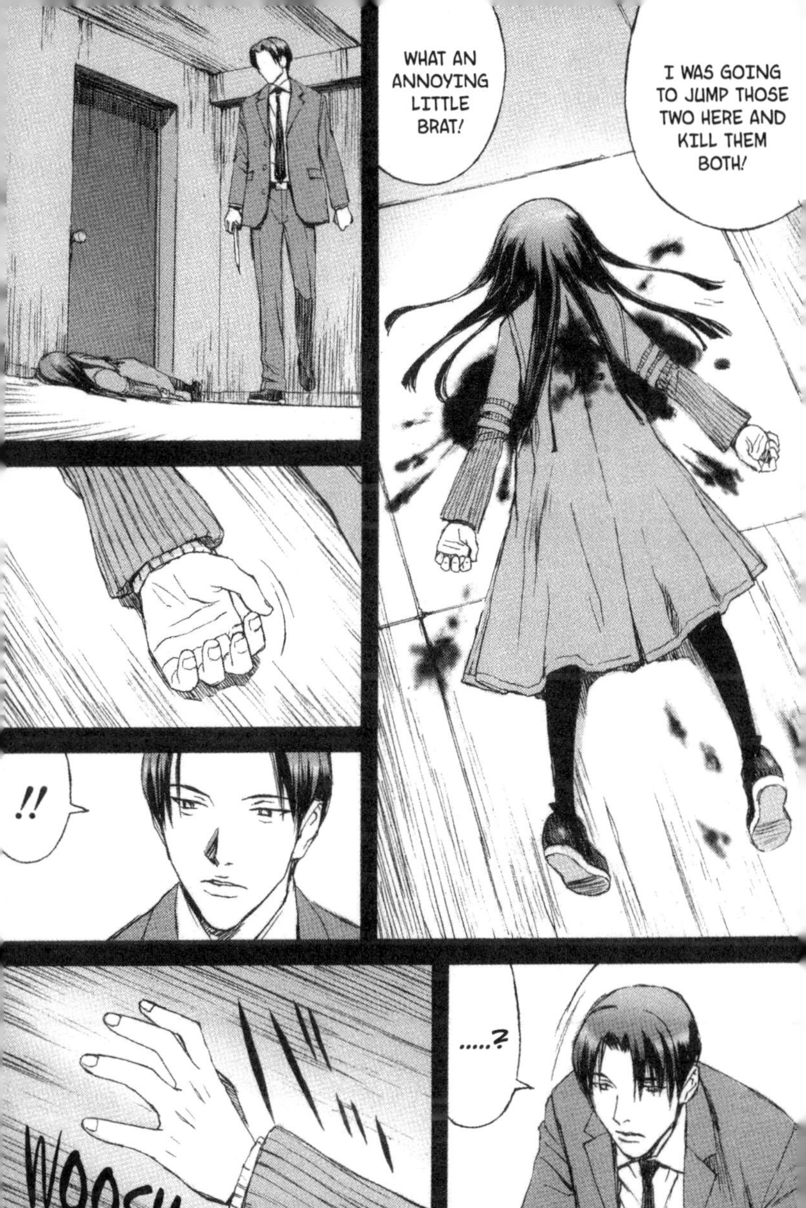
I WAS GOING TO JUMP THOSE TWO HERE AND KILL THEM BOTH!
WHAT AN ANNOYING LITTLE BRAT!
!!
.....?
WOOSH

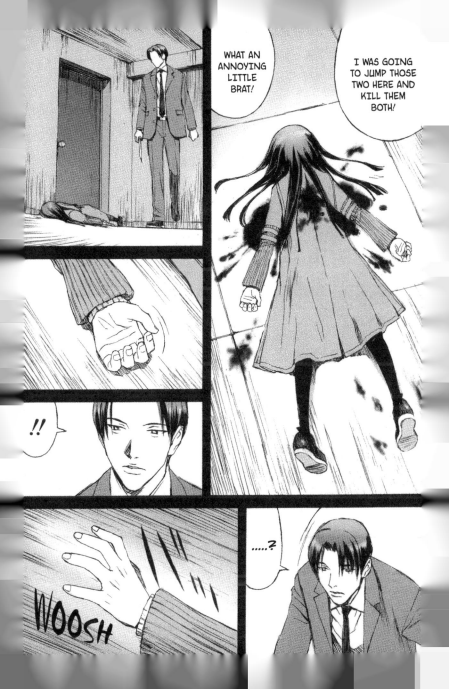

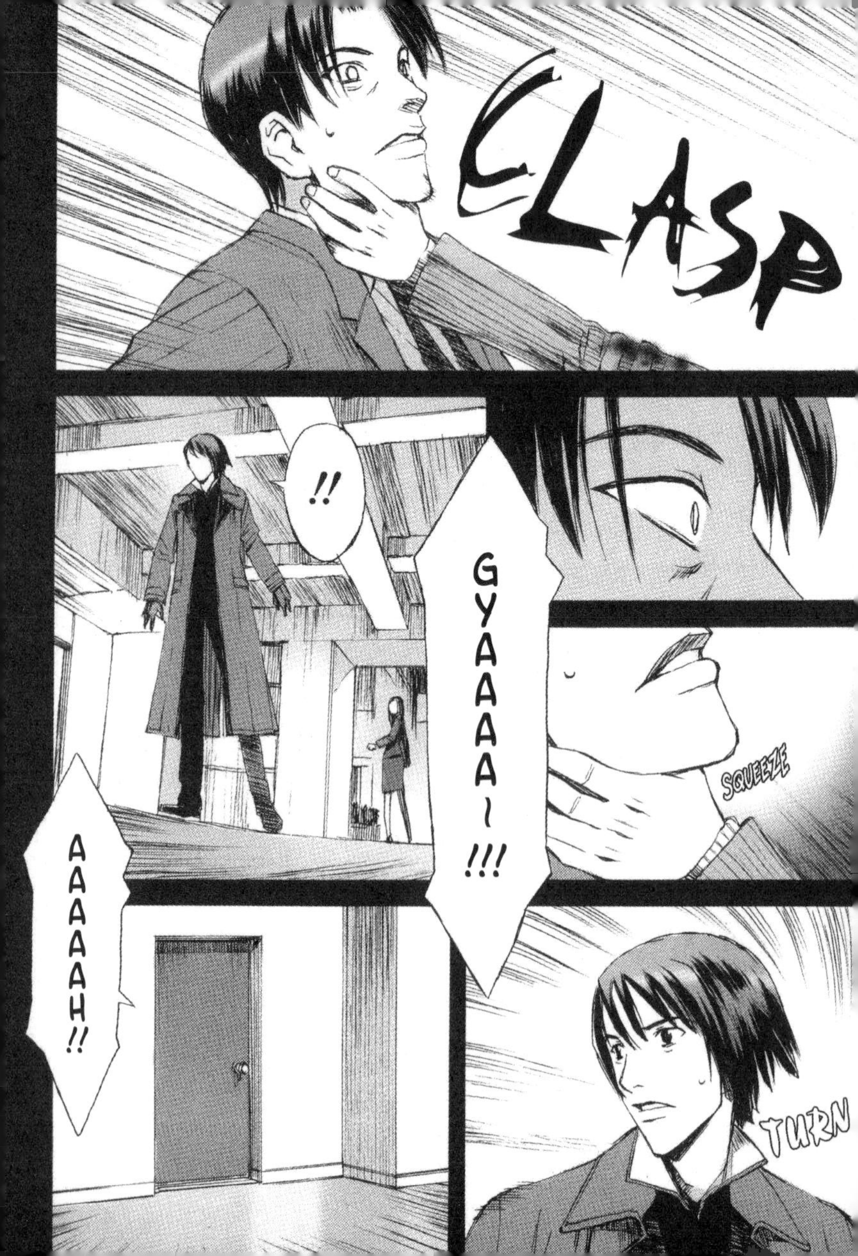
CLASP
GYAAAAA~!!!
SQUEEZE
!!
TURN
AAAAAAH!!

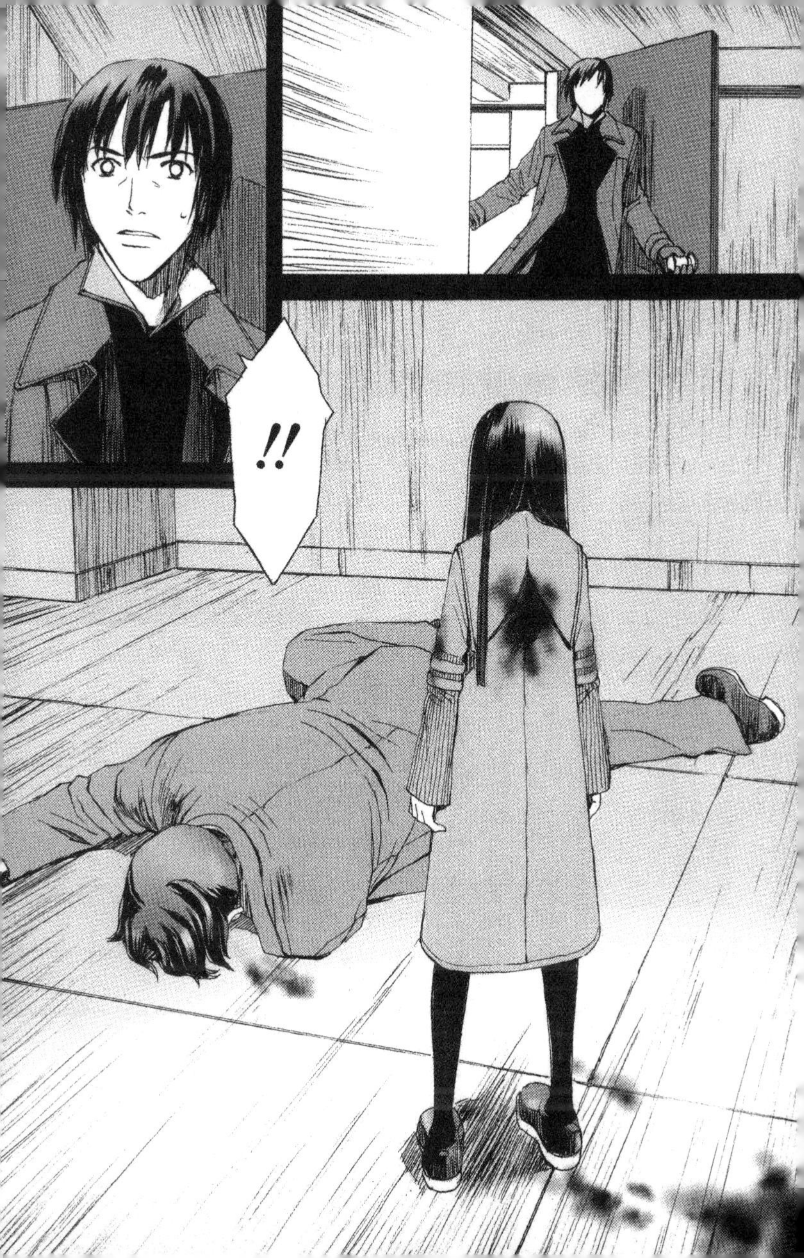
!!

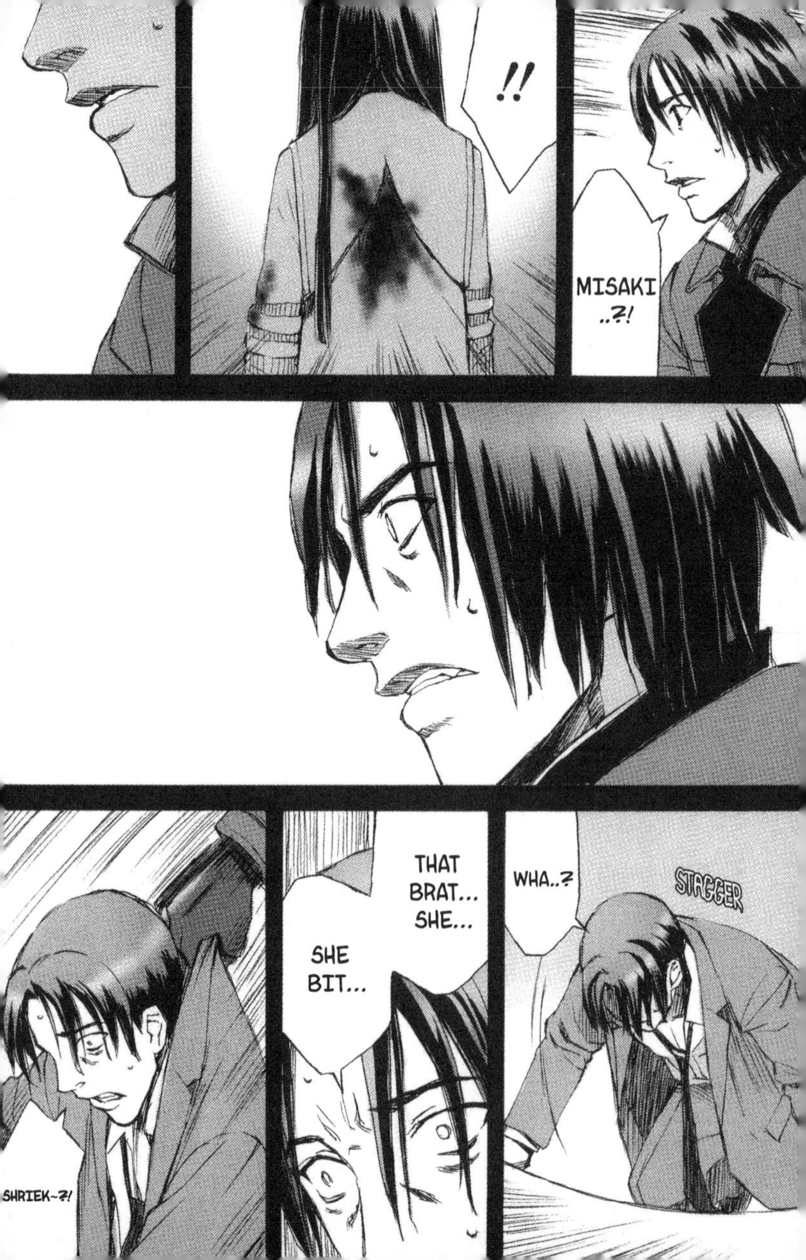
MISAKI ..?!
!!
STAGGER
WHA..?
THAT BRAT... SHE...
SHE BIT...
SHRIEK~?!

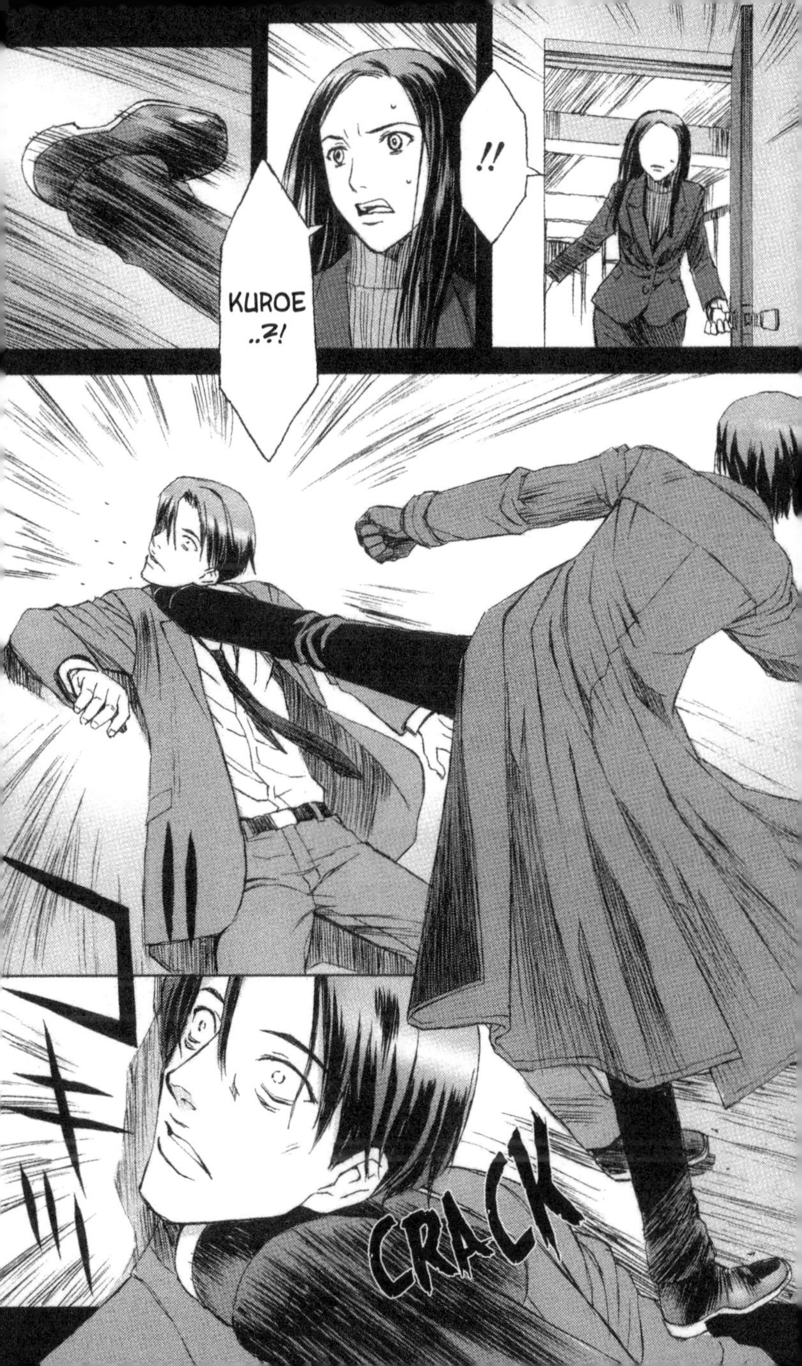
!!
KUROE ..?!
CRACK

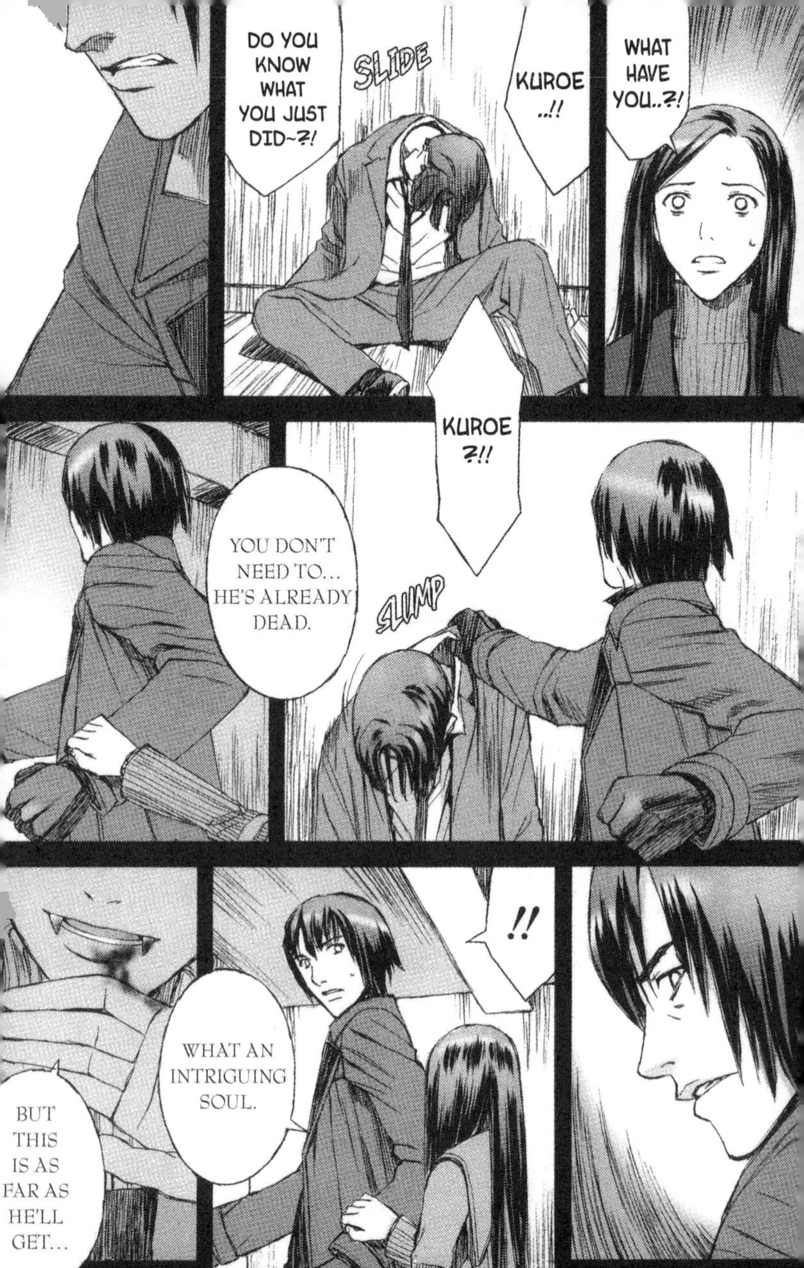
WHAT HAVE YOU..?!
KUROE ..!!
SLIDE
DO YOU KNOW WHAT YOU JUST DID~?!
KUROE ?!!
SLUMP
YOU DON'T NEED TO… HE'S ALREADY DEAD.
!!
WHAT AN INTRIGUING SOUL.
BUT THIS IS AS FAR AS HE'LL GET…

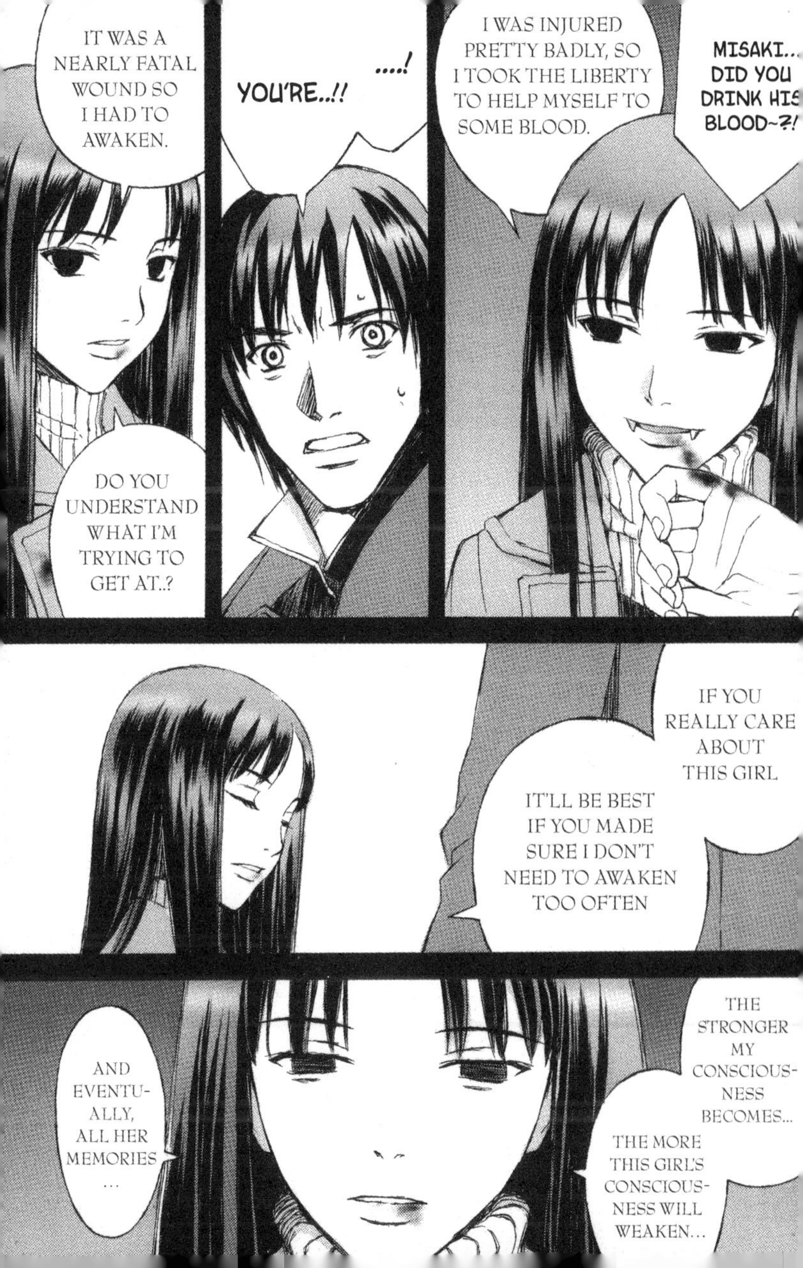
MISAKI... DID YOU DRINK HIS BLOOD~?!
I WAS INJURED PRETTY BADLY, SO I TOOK THE LIBERTY TO HELP MYSELF TO SOME BLOOD.
....!
YOU'RE..!!
IT WAS A NEARLY FATAL WOUND SO I HAD TO AWAKEN.
DO YOU UNDERSTAND WHAT I'M TRYING TO GET AT..?
IF YOU REALLY CARE ABOUT THIS GIRL
IT'LL BE BEST IF YOU MADE SURE I DON'T NEED TO AWAKEN TOO OFTEN
THE STRONGER MY CONSCIOUS-NESS BECOMES...
THE MORE THIS GIRL'S CONSCIOUS-NESS WILL WEAKEN...
AND EVENTU-ALLY, ALL HER MEMORIES ...

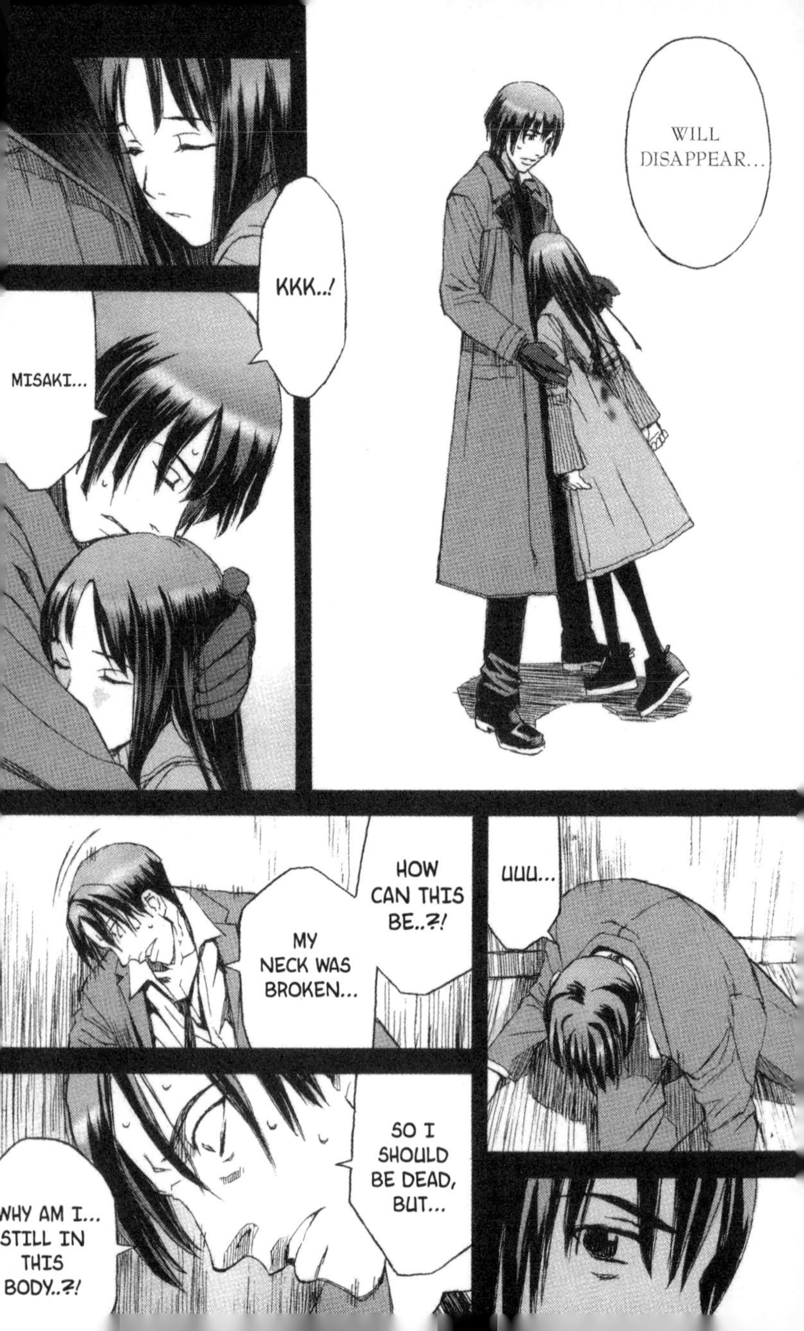
WILL DISAPPEAR...
KKK..!
MISAKI...
UUU...
HOW CAN THIS BE..?!
MY NECK WAS BROKEN...
SO I SHOULD BE DEAD, BUT...
WHY AM I... STILL IN THIS BODY..?!

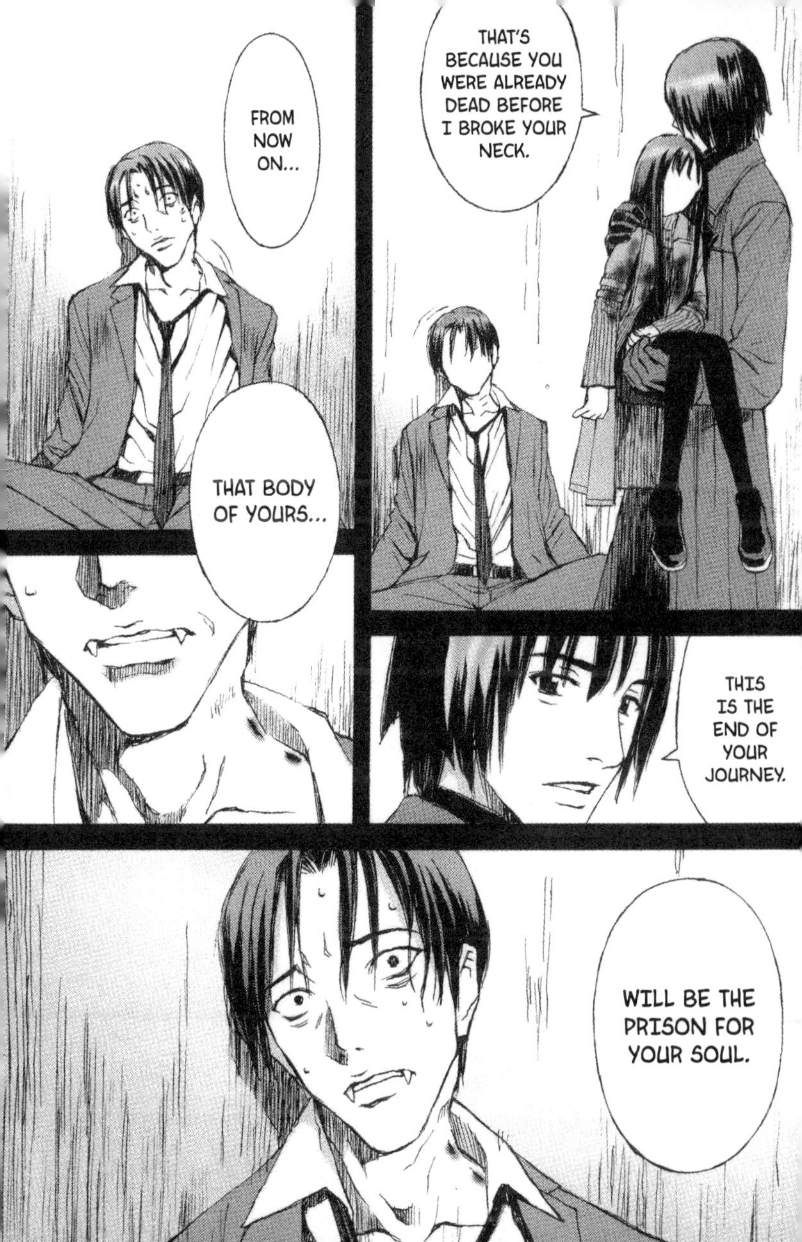
THAT'S BECAUSE YOU WERE ALREADY DEAD BEFORE I BROKE YOUR NECK.
FROM NOW ON...
THAT BODY OF YOURS...
THIS IS THE END OF YOUR JOURNEY.
WILL BE THE PRISON FOR YOUR SOUL.

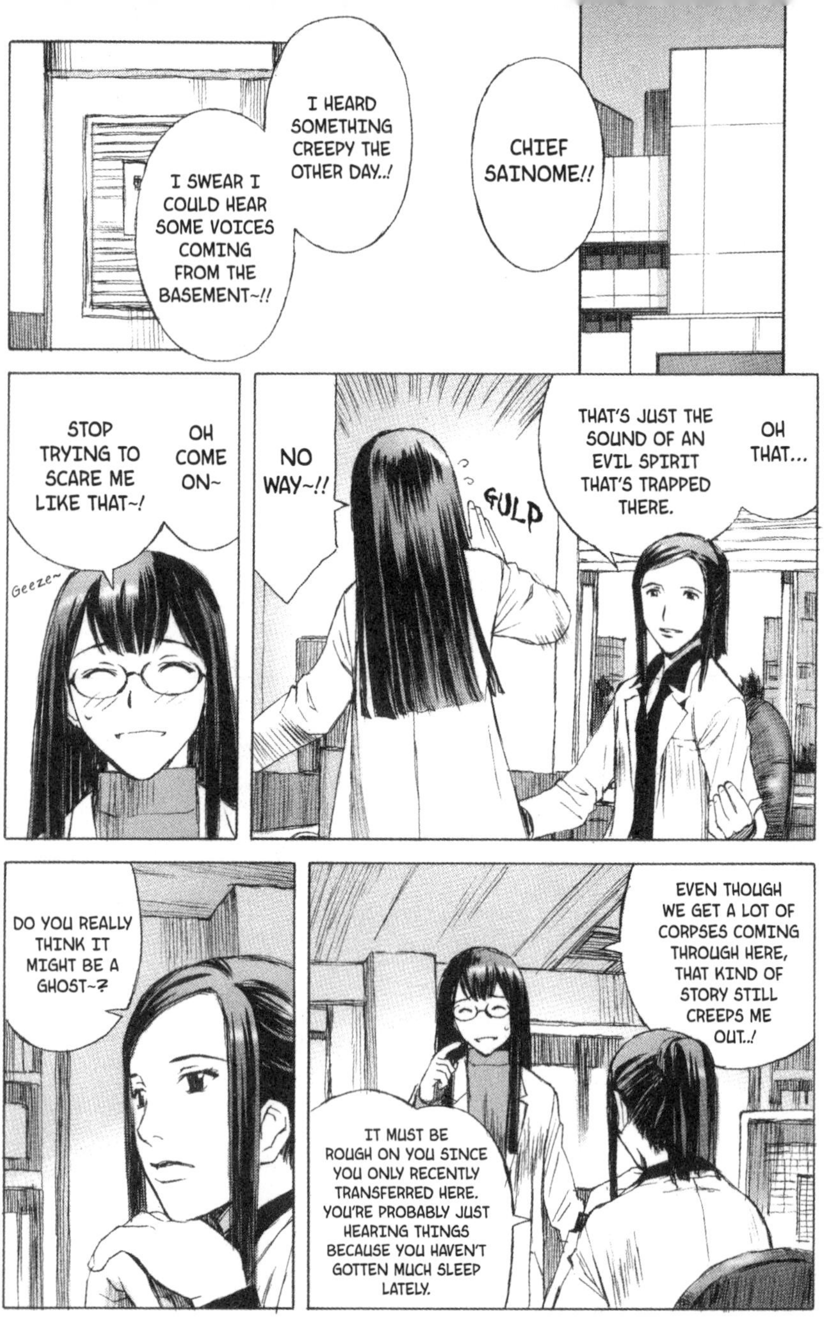
CHIEF SAINOME!!
I HEARD SOMETHING CREEPY THE OTHER DAY..!
I SWEAR I COULD HEAR SOME VOICES COMING FROM THE BASEMENT~!!
OH THAT...
THAT'S JUST THE SOUND OF AN EVIL SPIRIT THAT'S TRAPPED THERE.
GULP
NO WAY~!!
OH COME ON~
STOP TRYING TO SCARE ME LIKE THAT~!
Geeze~
EVEN THOUGH WE GET A LOT OF CORPSES COMING THROUGH HERE, THAT KIND OF STORY STILL CREEPS ME OUT..!
IT MUST BE ROUGH ON YOU SINCE YOU ONLY RECENTLY TRANSFERRED HERE. YOU'RE PROBABLY JUST HEARING THINGS BECAUSE YOU HAVEN'T GOTTEN MUCH SLEEP LATELY.
DO YOU REALLY THINK IT MIGHT BE A GHOST~?

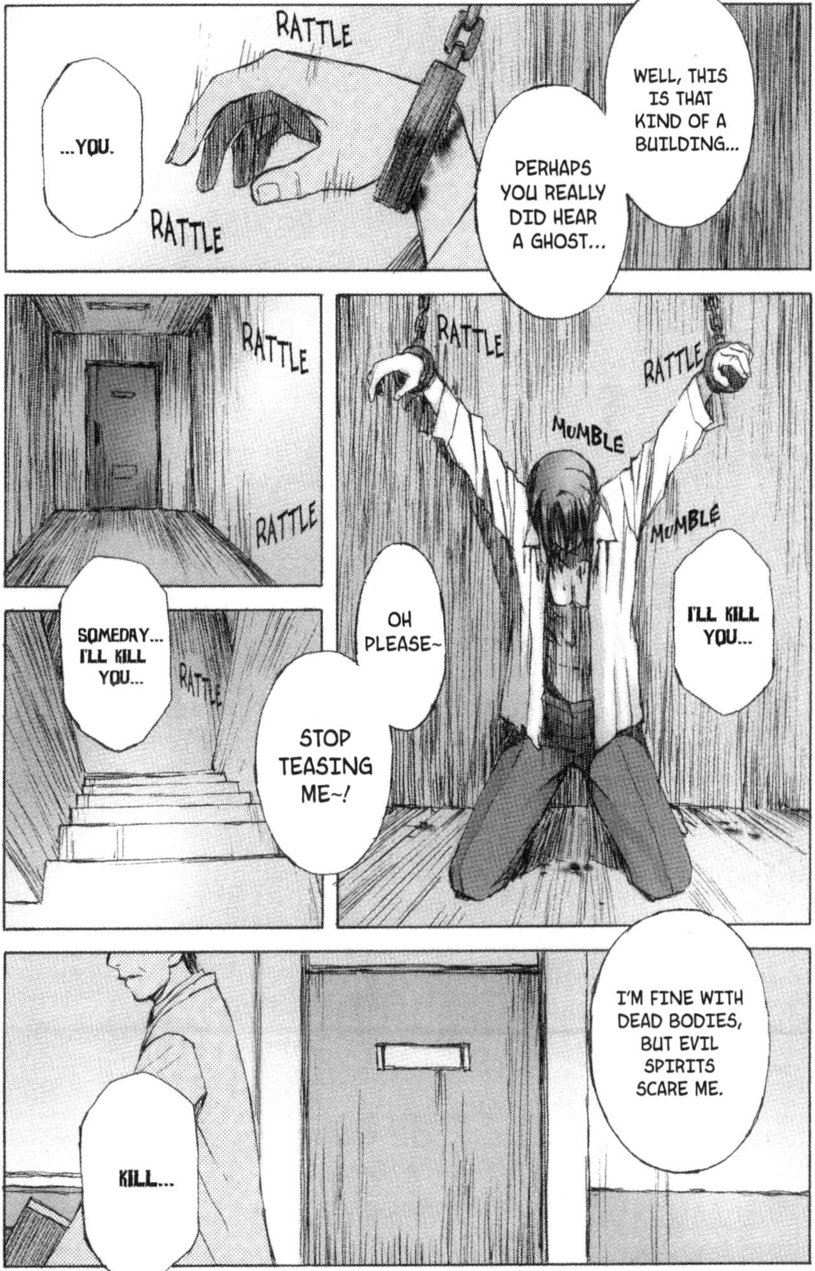
WELL, THIS IS THAT KIND OF A BUILDING...
PERHAPS YOU REALLY DID HEAR A GHOST...
RATTLE
...YOU.
RATTLE
RATTLE
RATTLE
MUMBLE
MUMBLE
I'LL KILL YOU...
OH PLEASE~
STOP TEASING ME~!
RATTLE
RATTLE
SOMEDAY... I'LL KILL YOU...
RATTLE
I'M FINE WITH DEAD BODIES, BUT EVIL SPIRITS SCARE ME.
KILL...

Episode 6
CLASP YOUR HAND
あなたが目を覚ますまで – Until the Moment You Wake Up

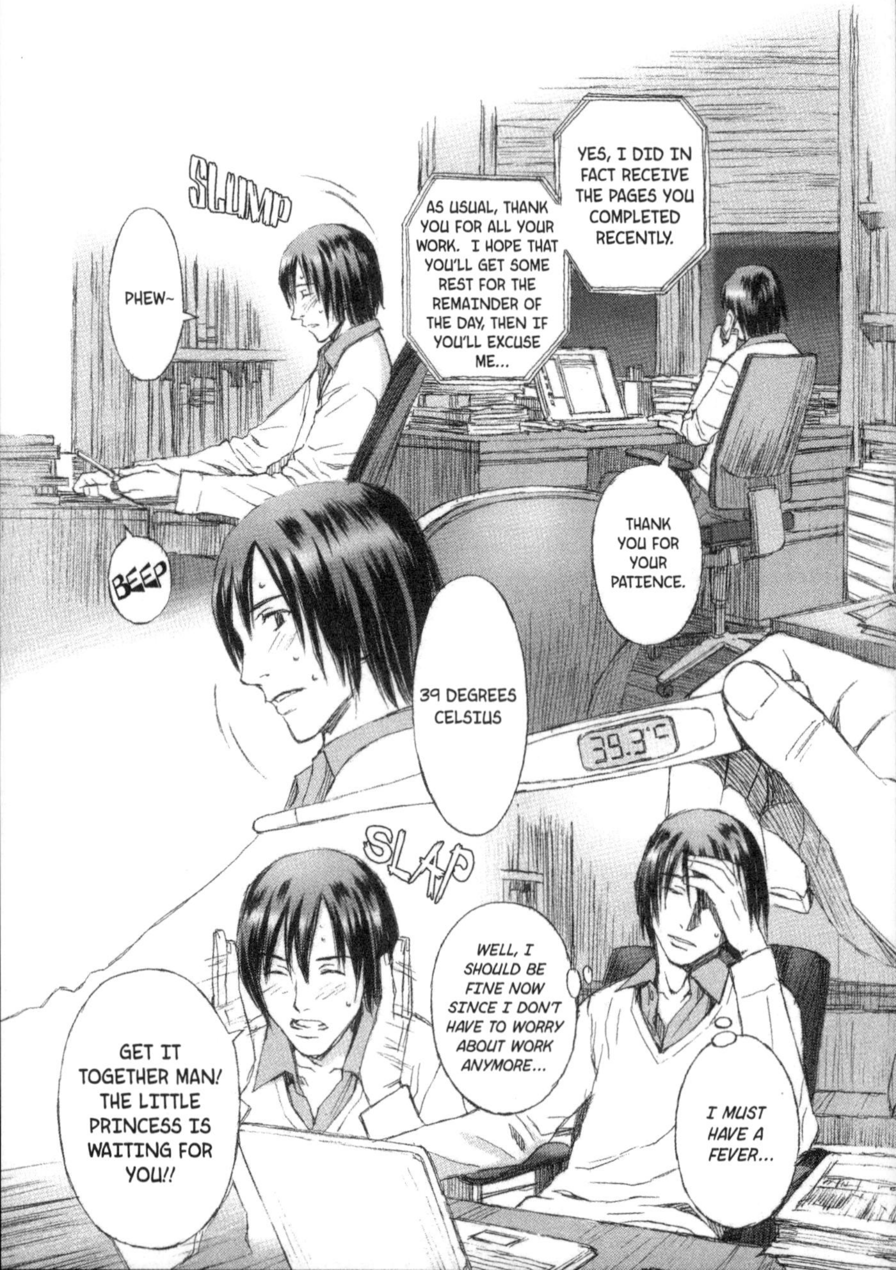
YES, I DID IN FACT RECEIVE THE PAGES YOU COMPLETED RECENTLY.
AS USUAL, THANK YOU FOR ALL YOUR WORK. I HOPE THAT YOU'LL GET SOME REST FOR THE REMAINDER OF THE DAY, THEN IF YOU'LL EXCUSE ME...
THANK YOU FOR YOUR PATIENCE.
SLUMP
PHEW~
39.3°C
39 DEGREES CELSIUS
BEEP
I MUST HAVE A FEVER...
WELL, I SHOULD BE FINE NOW SINCE I DON'T HAVE TO WORRY ABOUT WORK ANYMORE...
SLAP
GET IT TOGETHER MAN! THE LITTLE PRINCESS IS WAITING FOR YOU!!

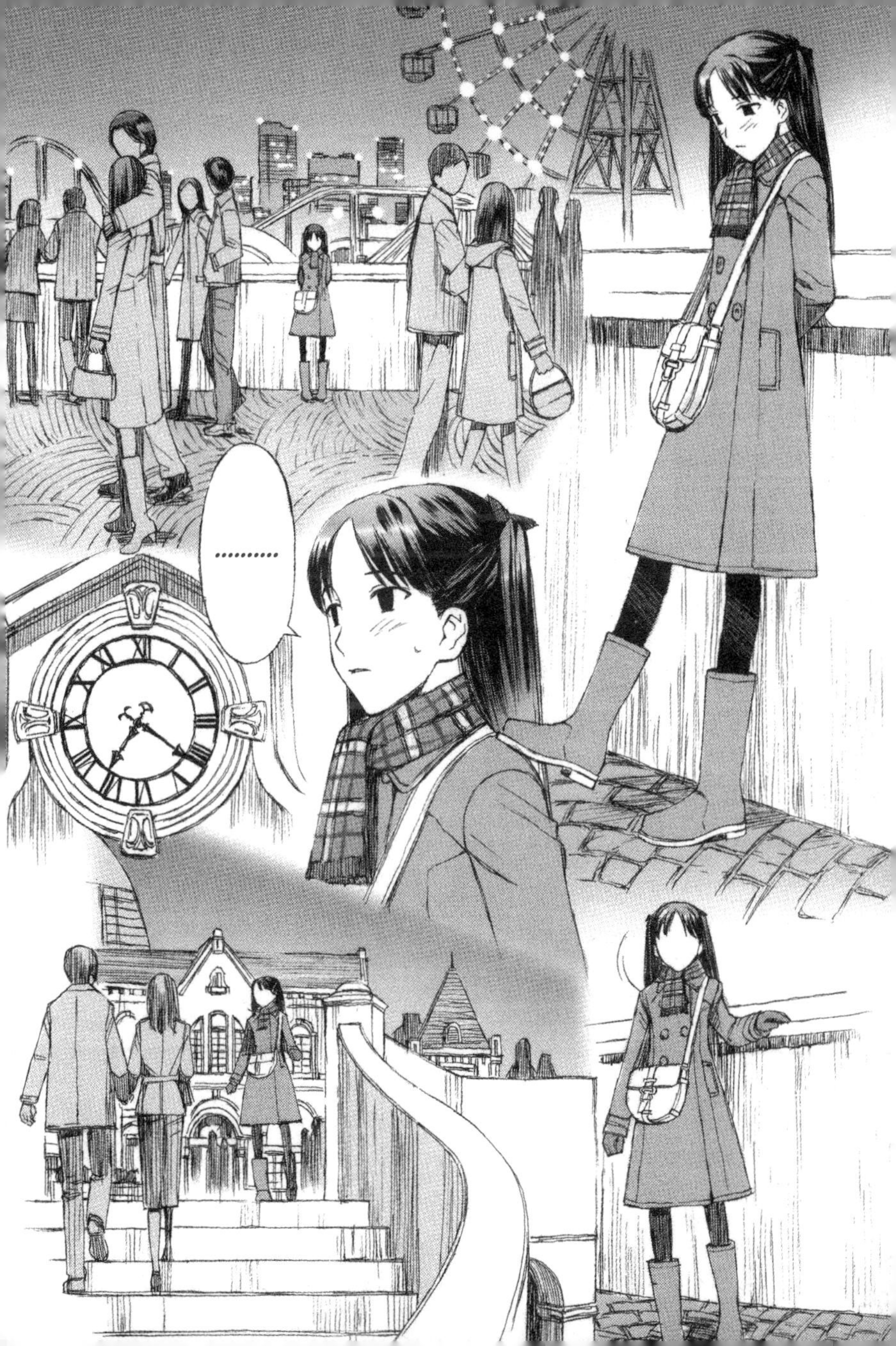
....

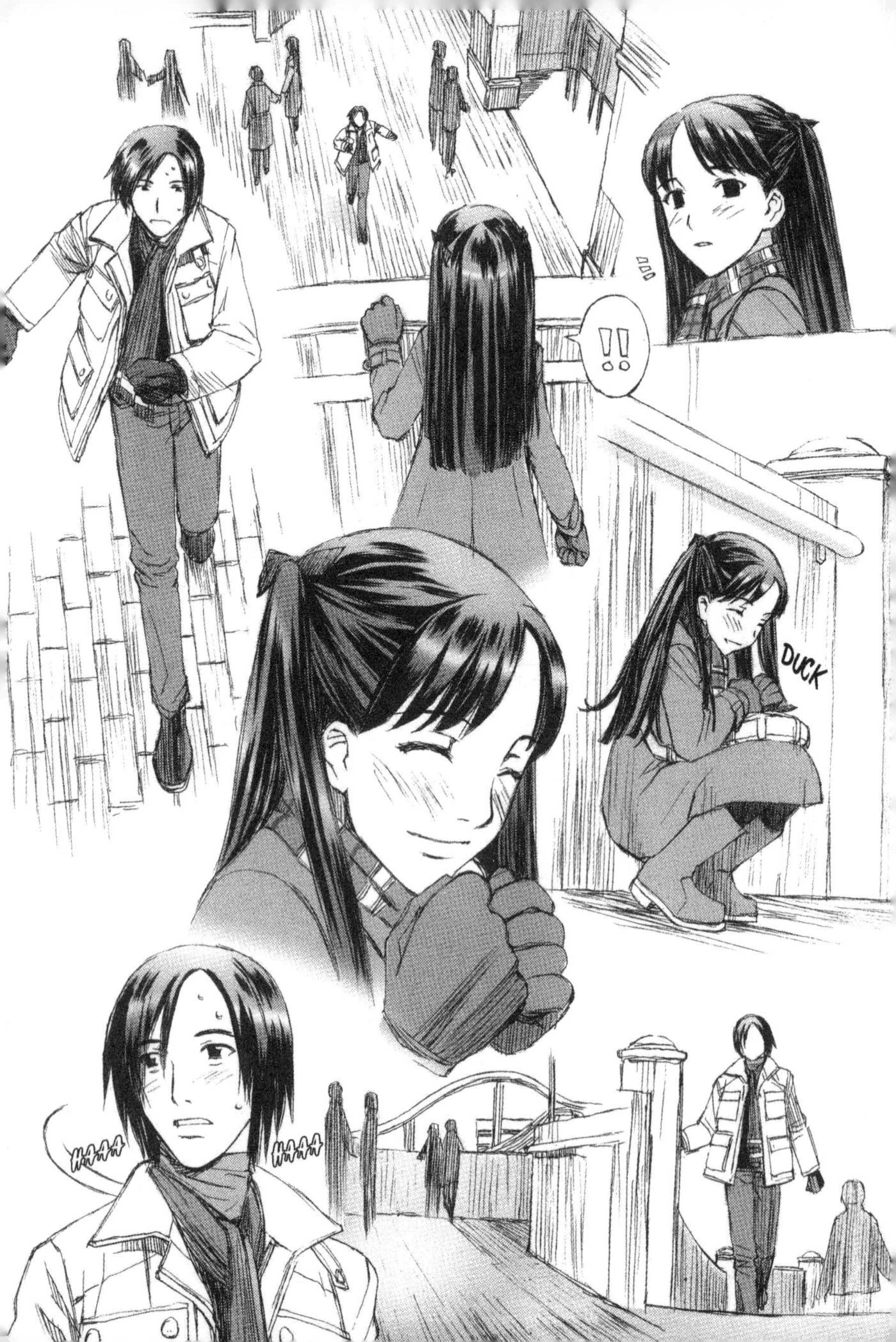
!!
DUCK
HAAA
HAAA

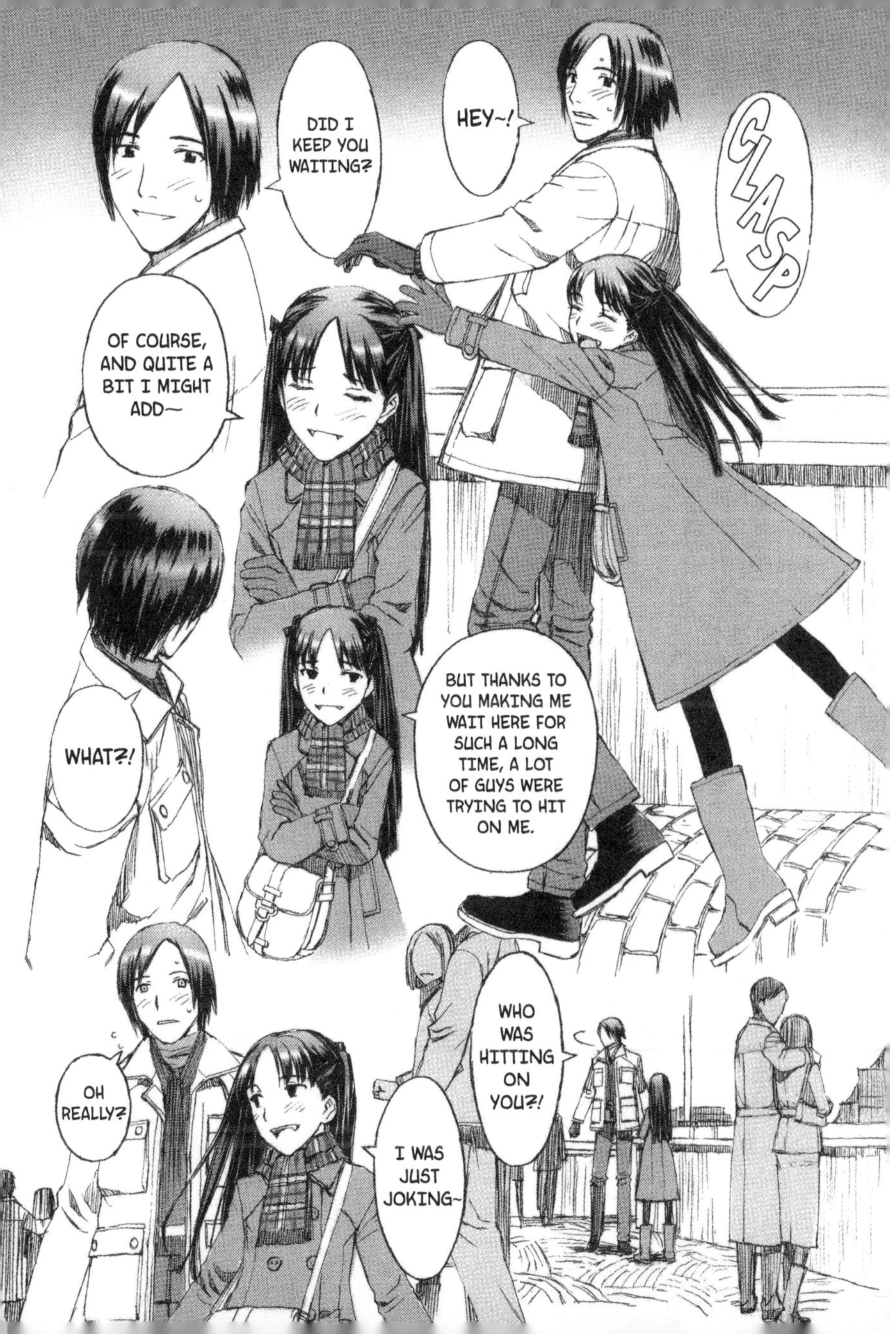
CLASP
HEY~!
DID I KEEP YOU WAITING?
OF COURSE, AND QUITE A BIT I MIGHT ADD~
BUT THANKS TO YOU MAKING ME WAIT HERE FOR SUCH A LONG TIME, A LOT OF GUYS WERE TRYING TO HIT ON ME.
WHAT?!
WHO WAS HITTING ON YOU?!
I WAS JUST JOKING~
OH REALLY?

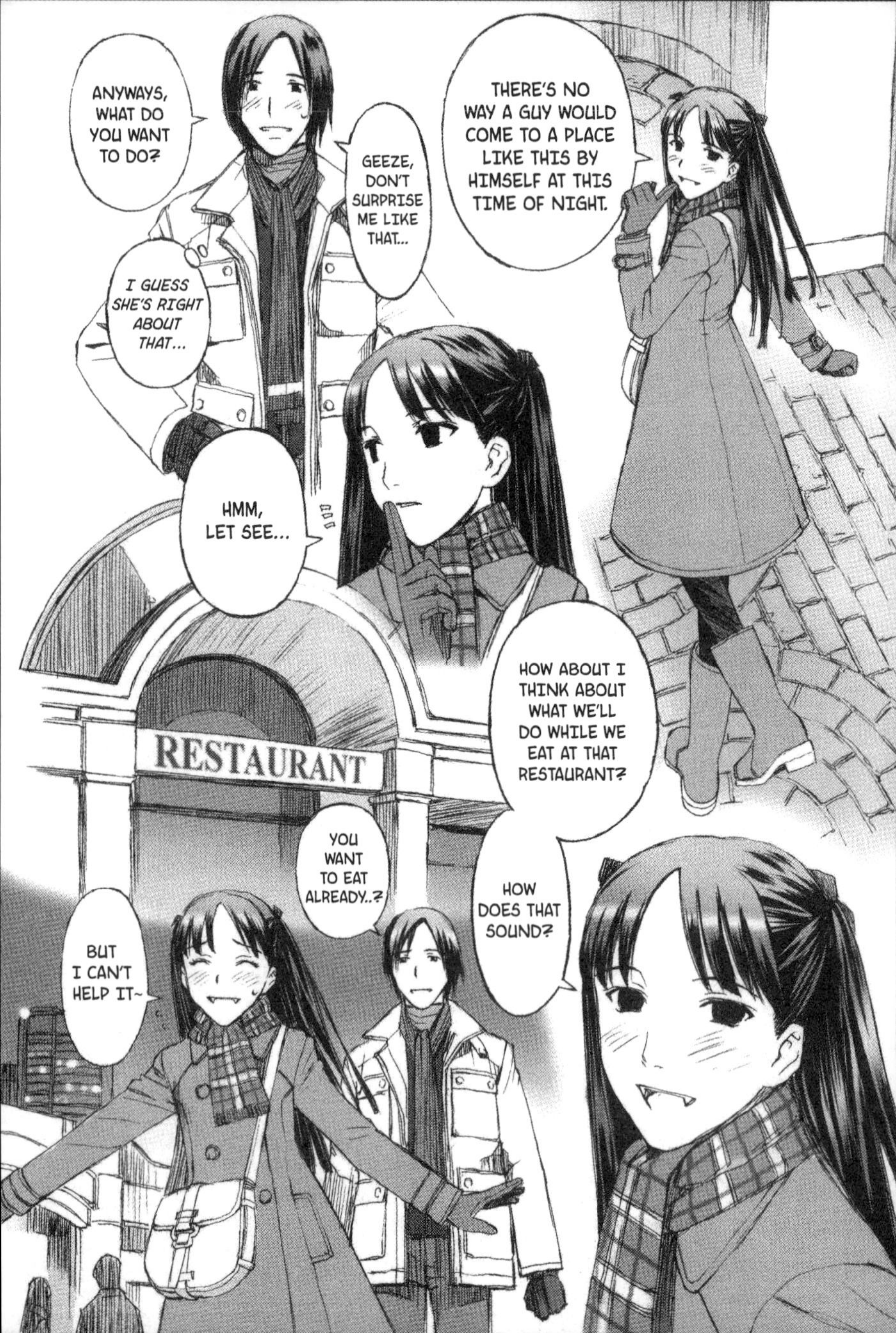
THERE'S NO WAY A GUY WOULD COME TO A PLACE LIKE THIS BY HIMSELF AT THIS TIME OF NIGHT.
GEEZE, DON'T SURPRISE ME LIKE THAT...
ANYWAYS, WHAT DO YOU WANT TO DO?
I GUESS SHE'S RIGHT ABOUT THAT...
HMM, LET SEE...
RESTAURANT
HOW ABOUT I THINK ABOUT WHAT WE'LL DO WHILE WE EAT AT THAT RESTAURANT?
HOW DOES THAT SOUND?
YOU WANT TO EAT ALREADY..?
BUT I CAN'T HELP IT~

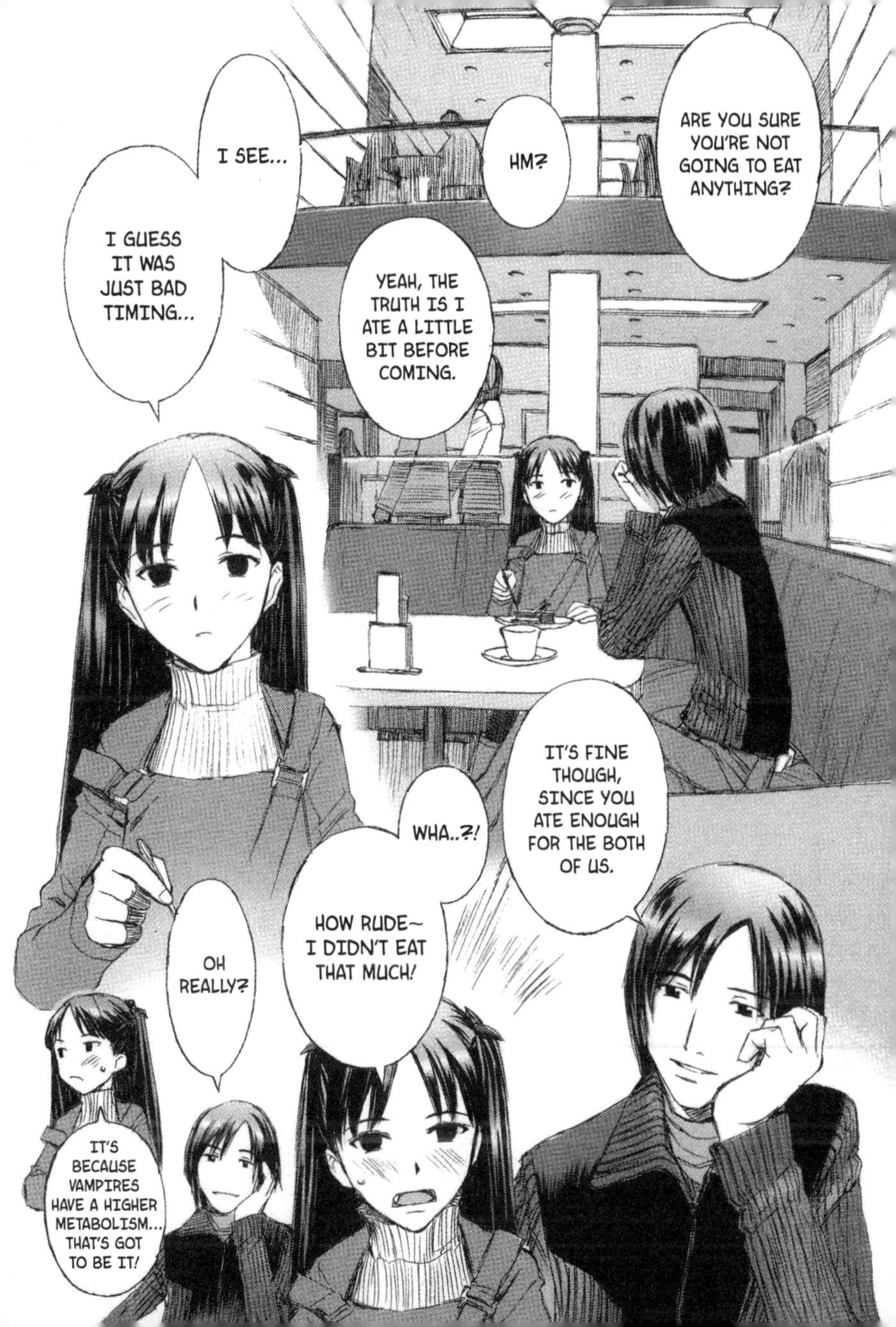
ARE YOU SURE YOU'RE NOT GOING TO EAT ANYTHING?
HM?
YEAH, THE TRUTH IS I ATE A LITTLE BIT BEFORE COMING.
I SEE...
I GUESS IT WAS JUST BAD TIMING...
IT'S FINE THOUGH, SINCE YOU ATE ENOUGH FOR THE BOTH OF US.
WHA..?!
HOW RUDE~ I DIDN'T EAT THAT MUCH!
OH REALLY?
IT'S BECAUSE VAMPIRES HAVE A HIGHER METABOLISM... THAT'S GOT TO BE IT!

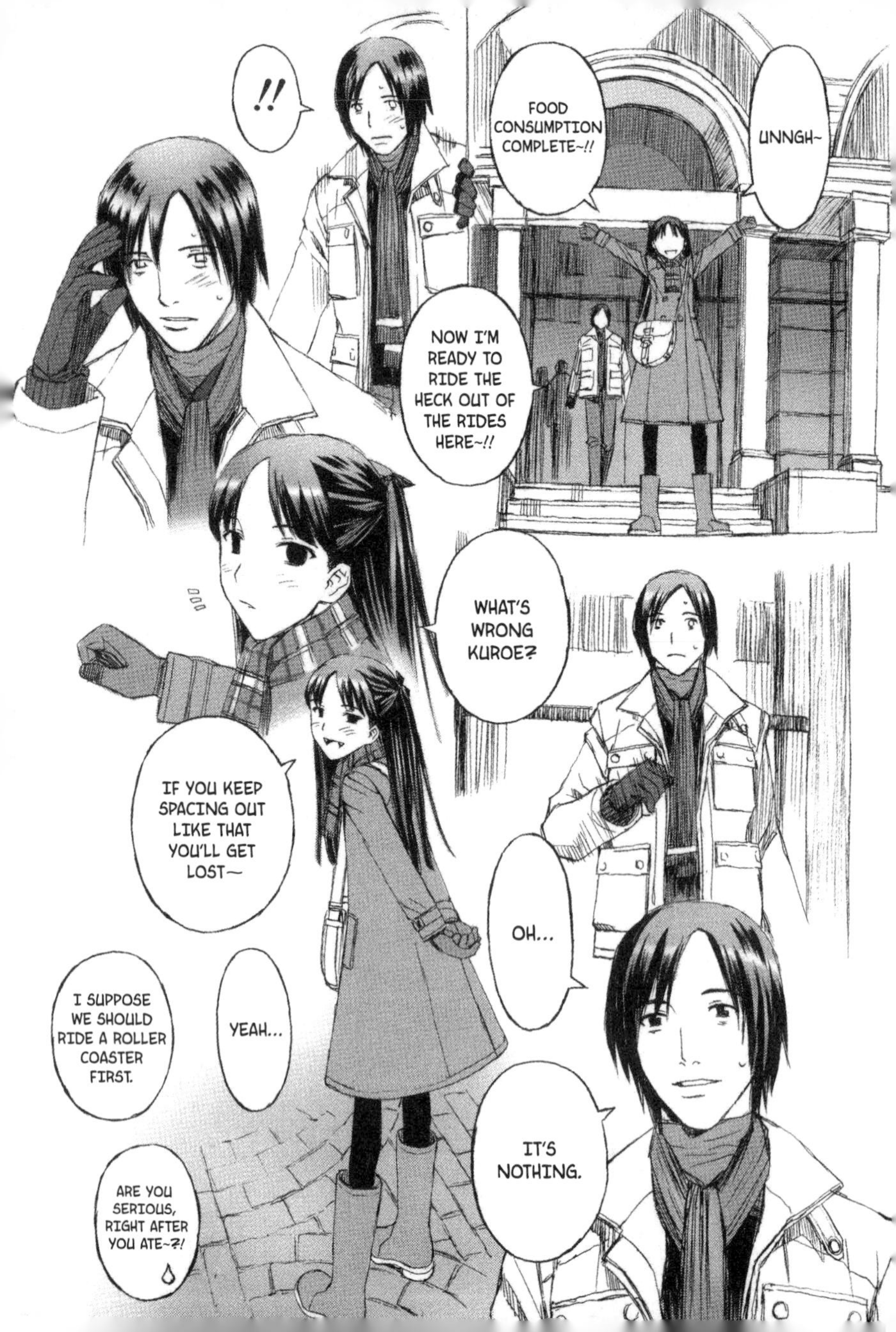
UNNGH~
FOOD CONSUMPTION COMPLETE~!!
NOW I'M READY TO RIDE THE HECK OUT OF THE RIDES HERE~!!
!!
WHAT'S WRONG KUROE?
OH...
IT'S NOTHING.
IF YOU KEEP SPACING OUT LIKE THAT YOU'LL GET LOST~
YEAH...
I SUPPOSE WE SHOULD RIDE A ROLLER COASTER FIRST.
ARE YOU SERIOUS, RIGHT AFTER YOU ATE~?!

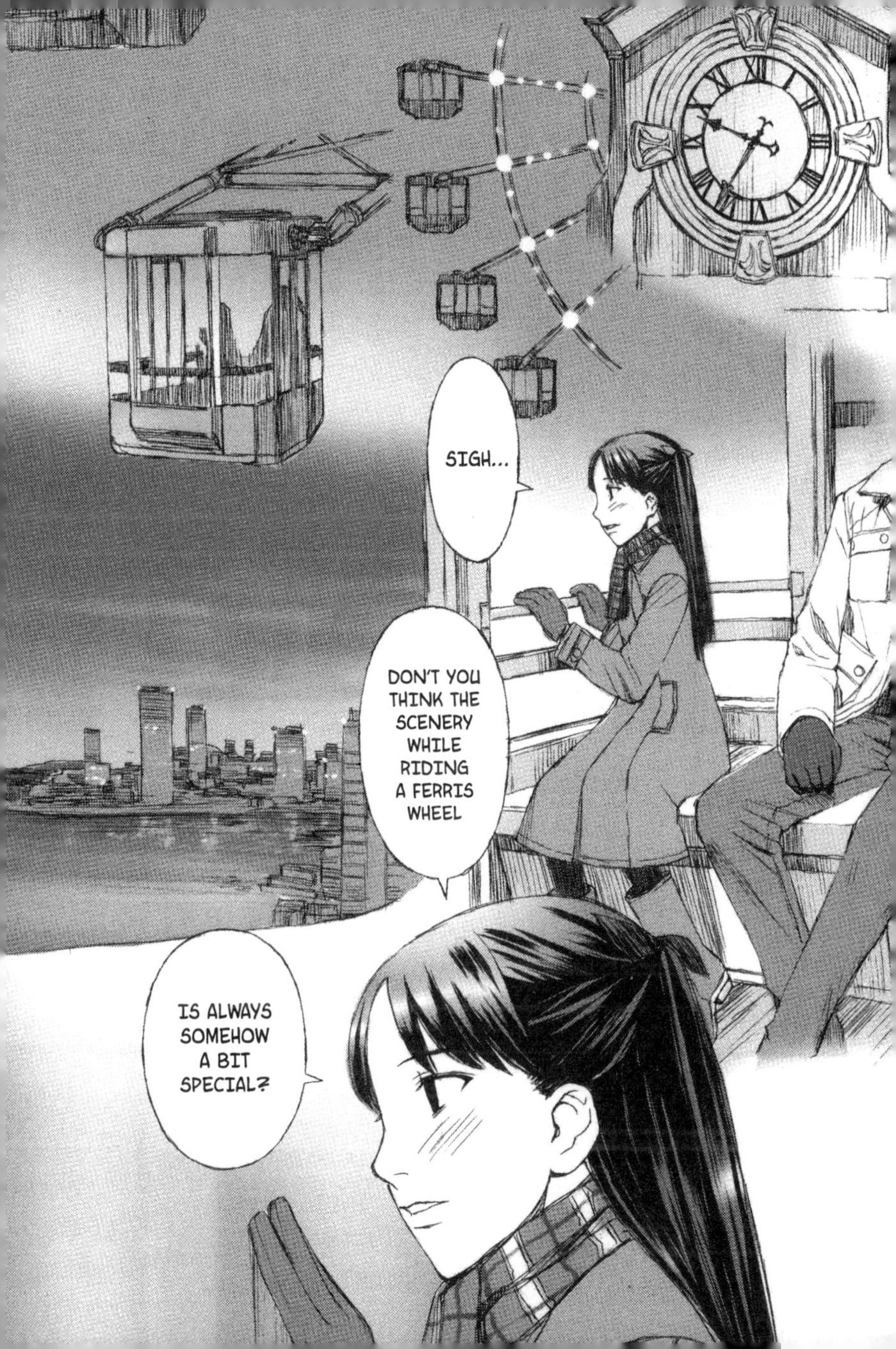
SIGH...
DON'T YOU THINK THE SCENERY WHILE RIDING A FERRIS WHEEL
IS ALWAYS SOMEHOW A BIT SPECIAL?

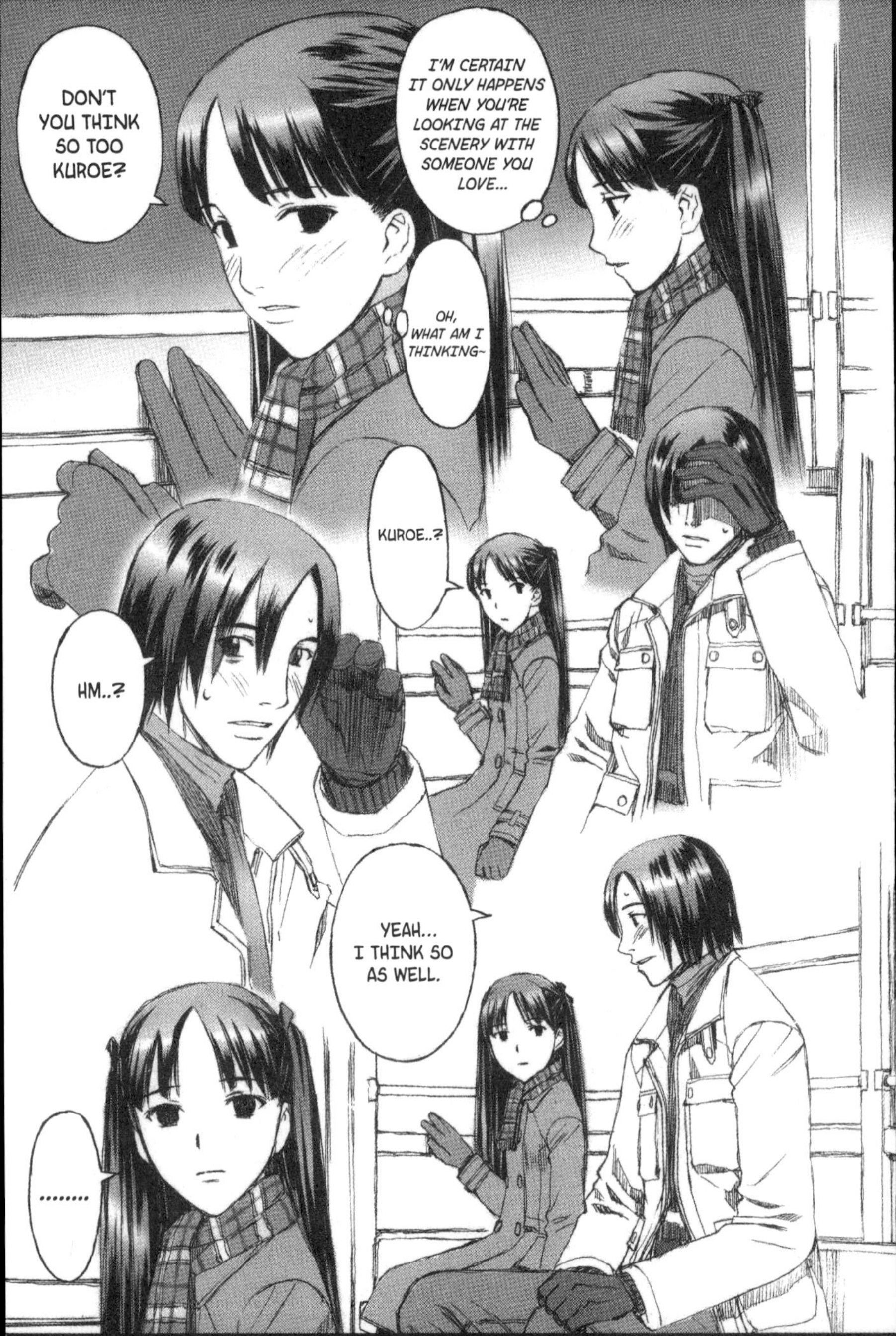
I'M CERTAIN IT ONLY HAPPENS WHEN YOU'RE LOOKING AT THE SCENERY WITH SOMEONE YOU LOVE...
OH, WHAT AM I THINKING~
DON'T YOU THINK SO TOO KUROE?
KUROE..?
HM..?
YEAH... I THINK SO AS WELL.
....

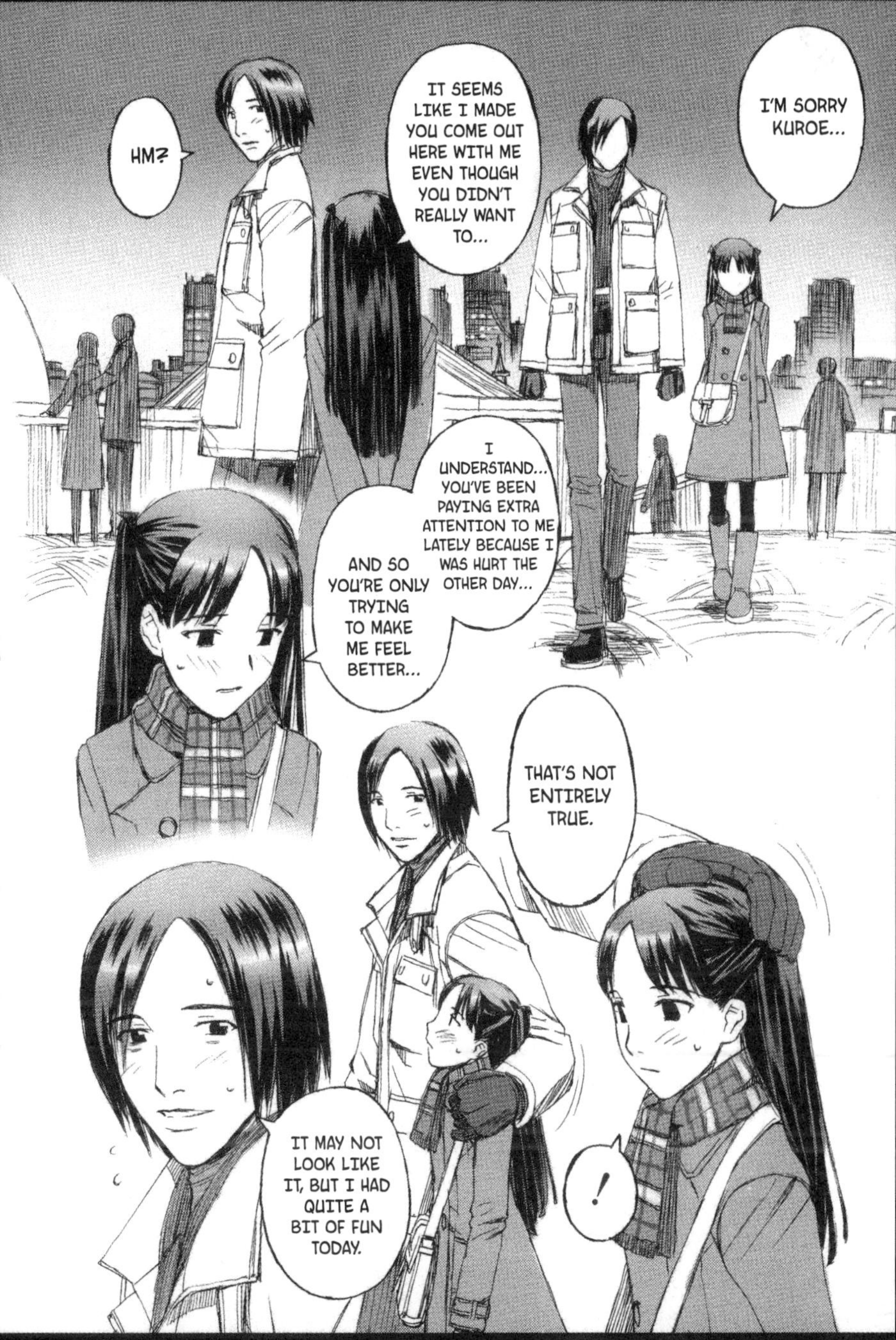
I'M SORRY KUROE...
IT SEEMS LIKE I MADE YOU COME OUT HERE WITH ME EVEN THOUGH YOU DIDN'T REALLY WANT TO...
HM?
I UNDERSTAND... YOU'VE BEEN PAYING EXTRA ATTENTION TO ME LATELY BECAUSE I WAS HURT THE OTHER DAY...
AND SO YOU'RE ONLY TRYING TO MAKE ME FEEL BETTER...
THAT'S NOT ENTIRELY TRUE.
!
IT MAY NOT LOOK LIKE IT, BUT I HAD QUITE A BIT OF FUN TODAY.

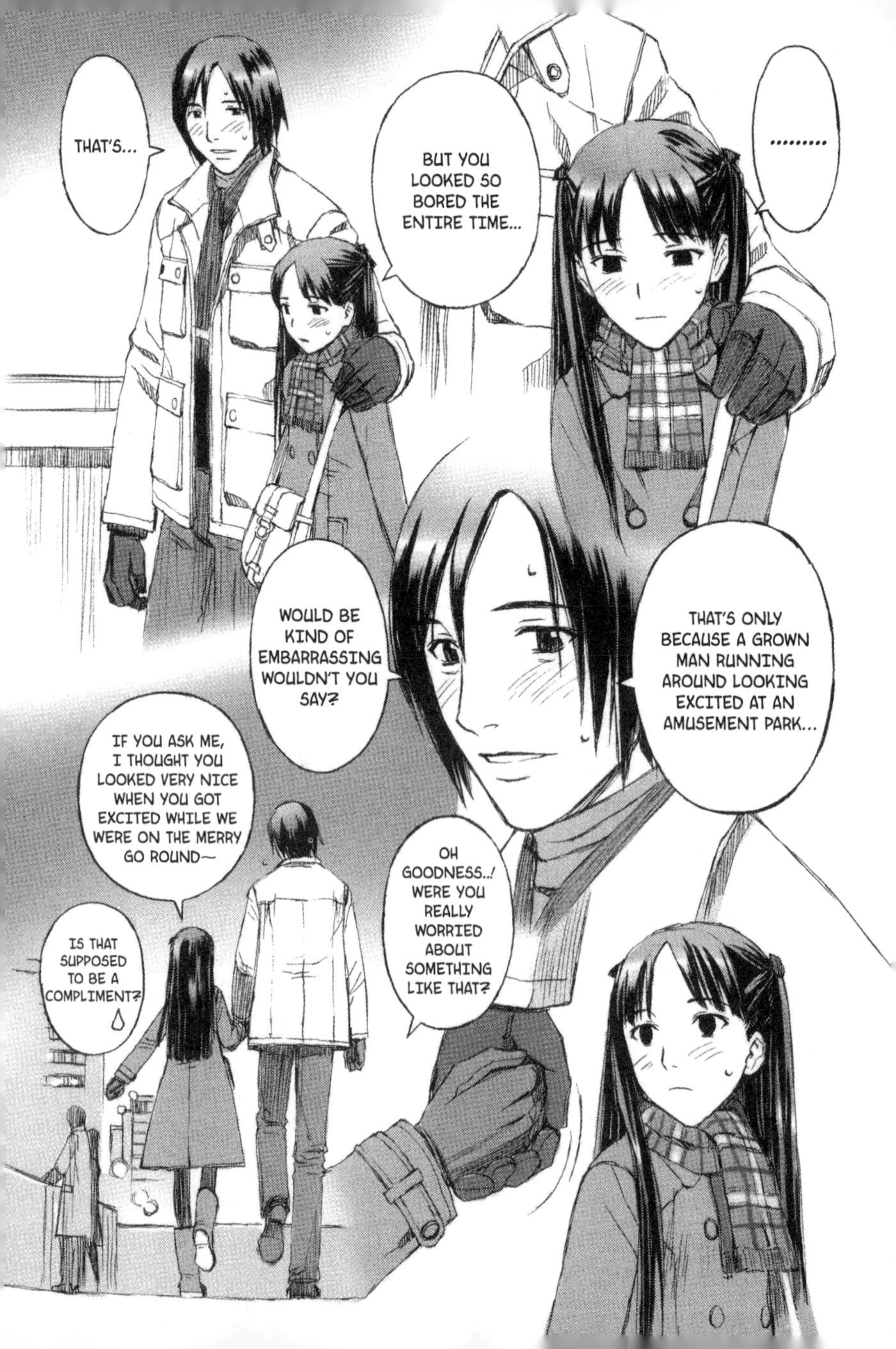
BUT YOU LOOKED SO BORED THE ENTIRE TIME...
THAT'S...
....
THAT'S ONLY BECAUSE A GROWN MAN RUNNING AROUND LOOKING EXCITED AT AN AMUSEMENT PARK...
WOULD BE KIND OF EMBARRASSING WOULDN'T YOU SAY?
OH GOODNESS..! WERE YOU REALLY WORRIED ABOUT SOMETHING LIKE THAT?
IF YOU ASK ME, I THOUGHT YOU LOOKED VERY NICE WHEN YOU GOT EXCITED WHILE WE WERE ON THE MERRY GO ROUND~
IS THAT SUPPOSED TO BE A COMPLIMENT?

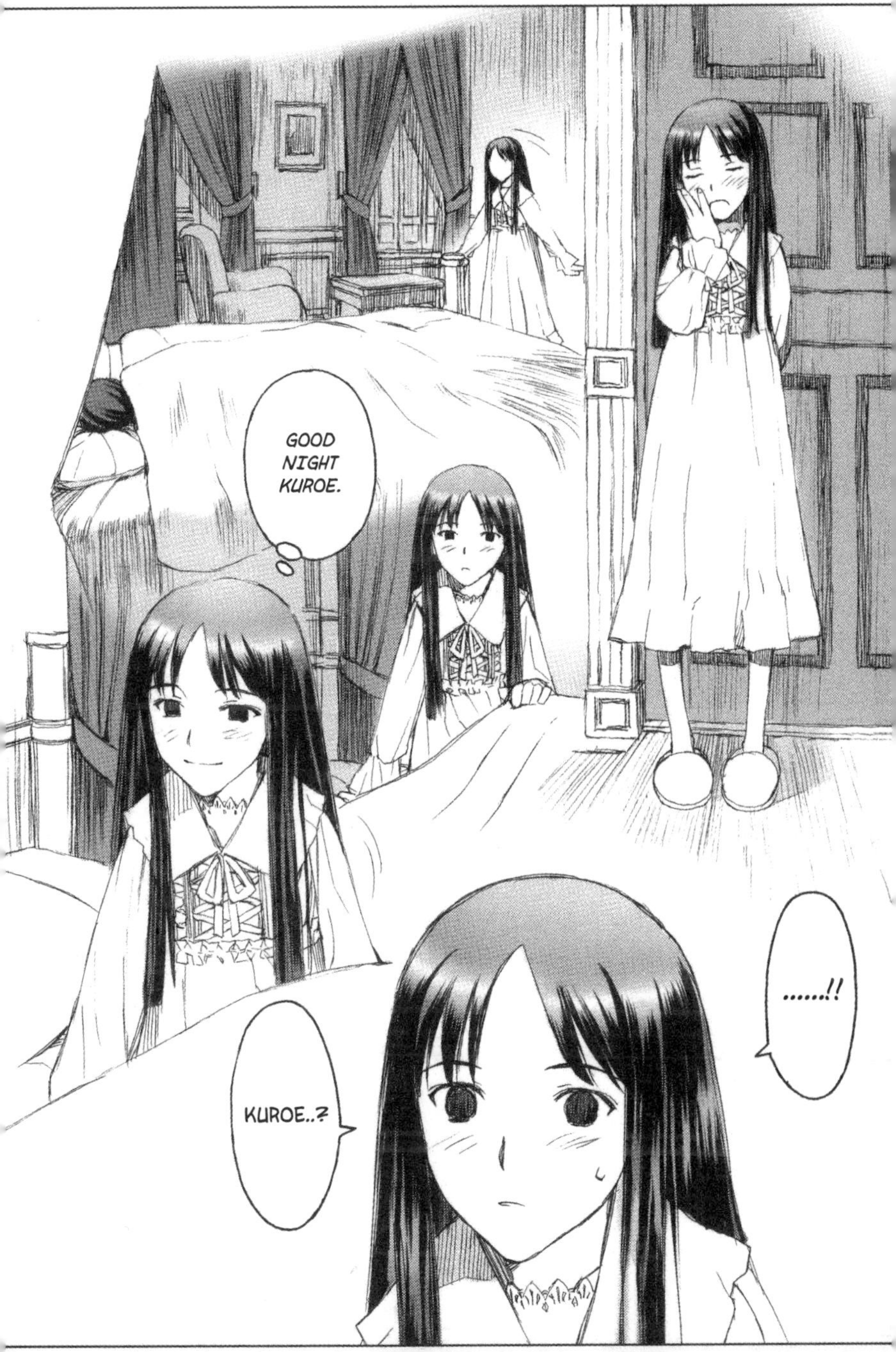
GOOD NIGHT KUROE.
......!!
KUROE..?

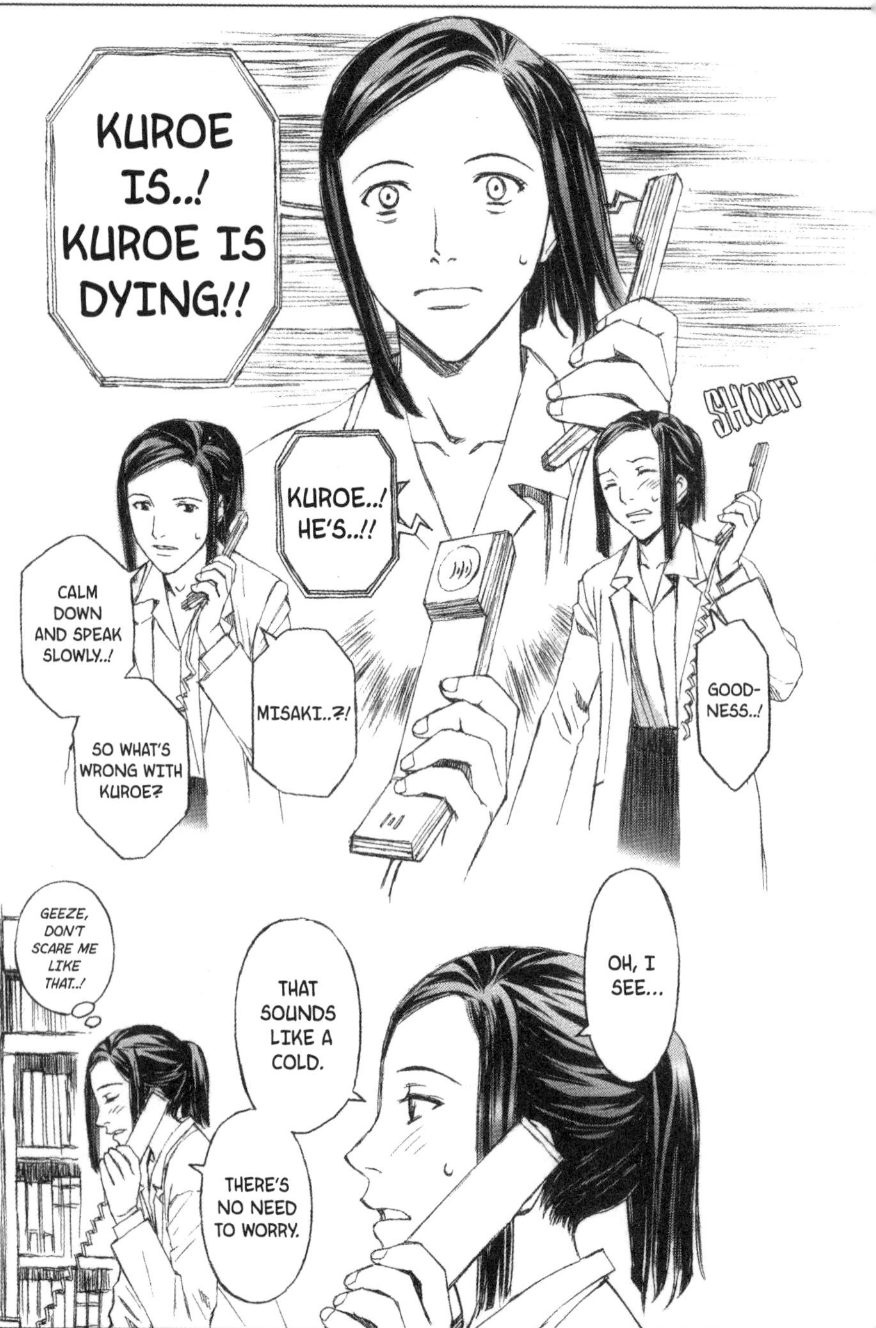
KUROE IS..! KUROE IS DYING!!
SHOUT
GOODNESS..!
KUROE..! HE'S..!!
MISAKI..?!
CALM DOWN AND SPEAK SLOWLY..!
SO WHAT'S WRONG WITH KUROE?
OH, I SEE...
THAT SOUNDS LIKE A COLD.
THERE'S NO NEED TO WORRY.
GEEZE, DON'T SCARE ME LIKE THAT..!

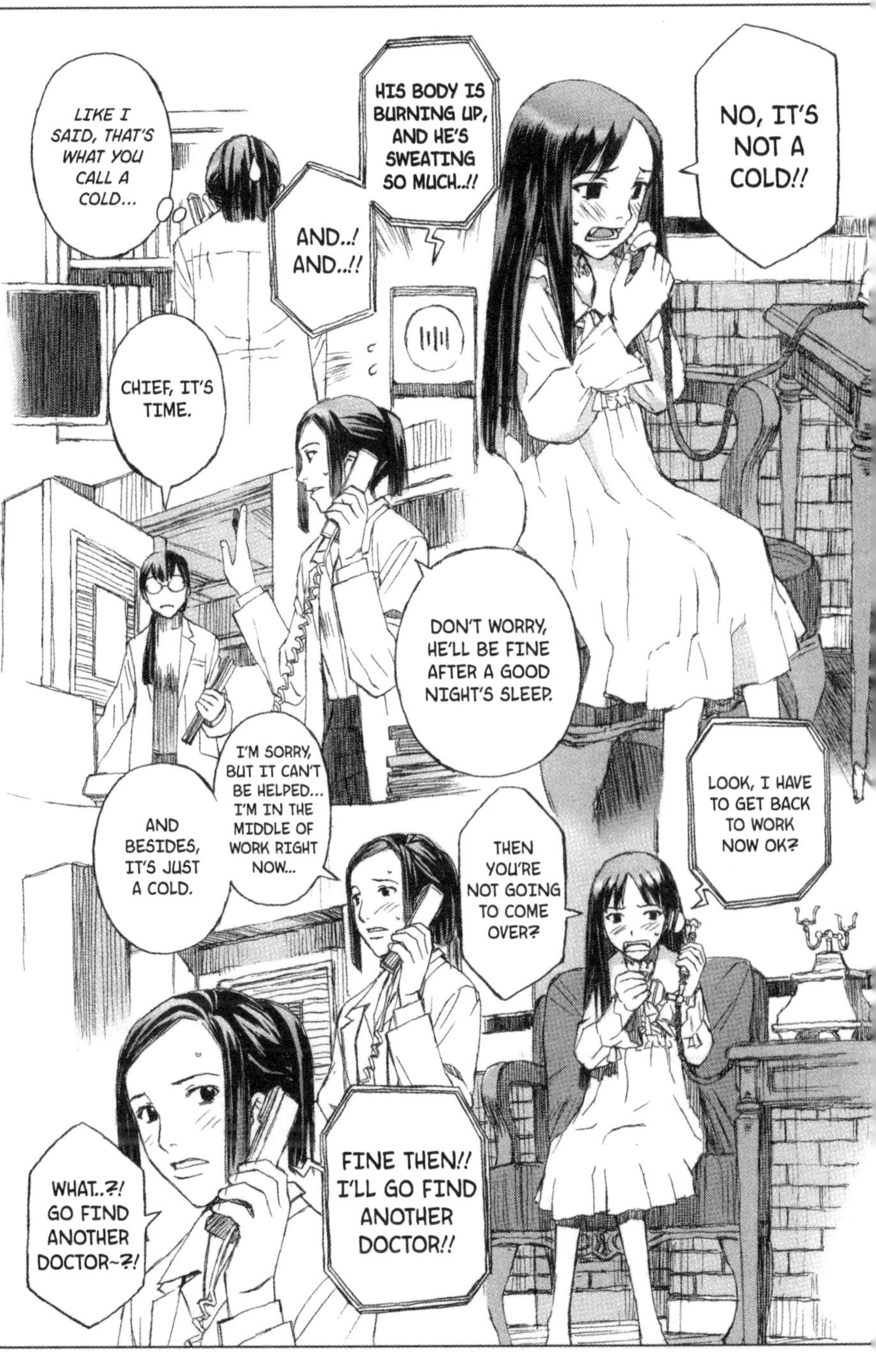

NO, IT'S NOT A COLD!!
HIS BODY IS BURNING UP, AND HE'S SWEATING SO MUCH..!!
AND..! AND..!!
LIKE I SAID, THAT'S WHAT YOU CALL A COLD...
DON'T WORRY, HE'LL BE FINE AFTER A GOOD NIGHT'S SLEEP.
CHIEF, IT'S TIME.
LOOK, I HAVE TO GET BACK TO WORK NOW OK?
THEN YOU'RE NOT GOING TO COME OVER?
I'M SORRY, BUT IT CAN'T BE HELPED... I'M IN THE MIDDLE OF WORK RIGHT NOW...
AND BESIDES, IT'S JUST A COLD.
FINE THEN!! I'LL GO FIND ANOTHER DOCTOR!!
WHAT..?! GO FIND ANOTHER DOCTOR~?!

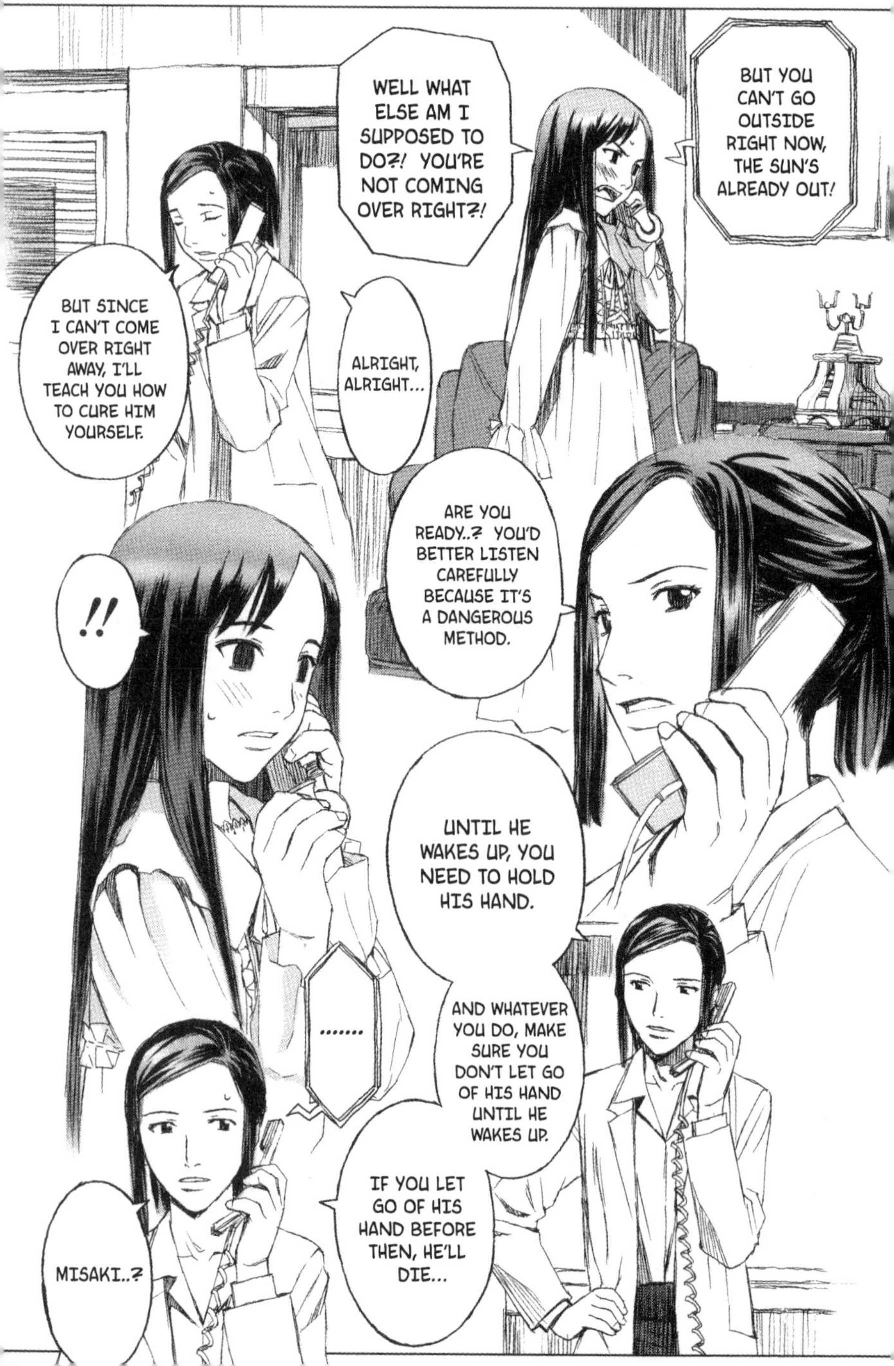

BUT YOU CAN'T GO OUTSIDE RIGHT NOW, THE SUN'S ALREADY OUT!
WELL WHAT ELSE AM I SUPPOSED TO DO?! YOU'RE NOT COMING OVER RIGHT?!
ALRIGHT, ALRIGHT...
BUT SINCE I CAN'T COME OVER RIGHT AWAY, I'LL TEACH YOU HOW TO CURE HIM YOURSELF.
ARE YOU READY..? YOU'D BETTER LISTEN CAREFULLY BECAUSE IT'S A DANGEROUS METHOD.
UNTIL HE WAKES UP, YOU NEED TO HOLD HIS HAND.
!!
AND WHATEVER YOU DO, MAKE SURE YOU DON'T LET GO OF HIS HAND UNTIL HE WAKES UP.
IF YOU LET GO OF HIS HAND BEFORE THEN, HE'LL DIE...
....
MISAKI..?

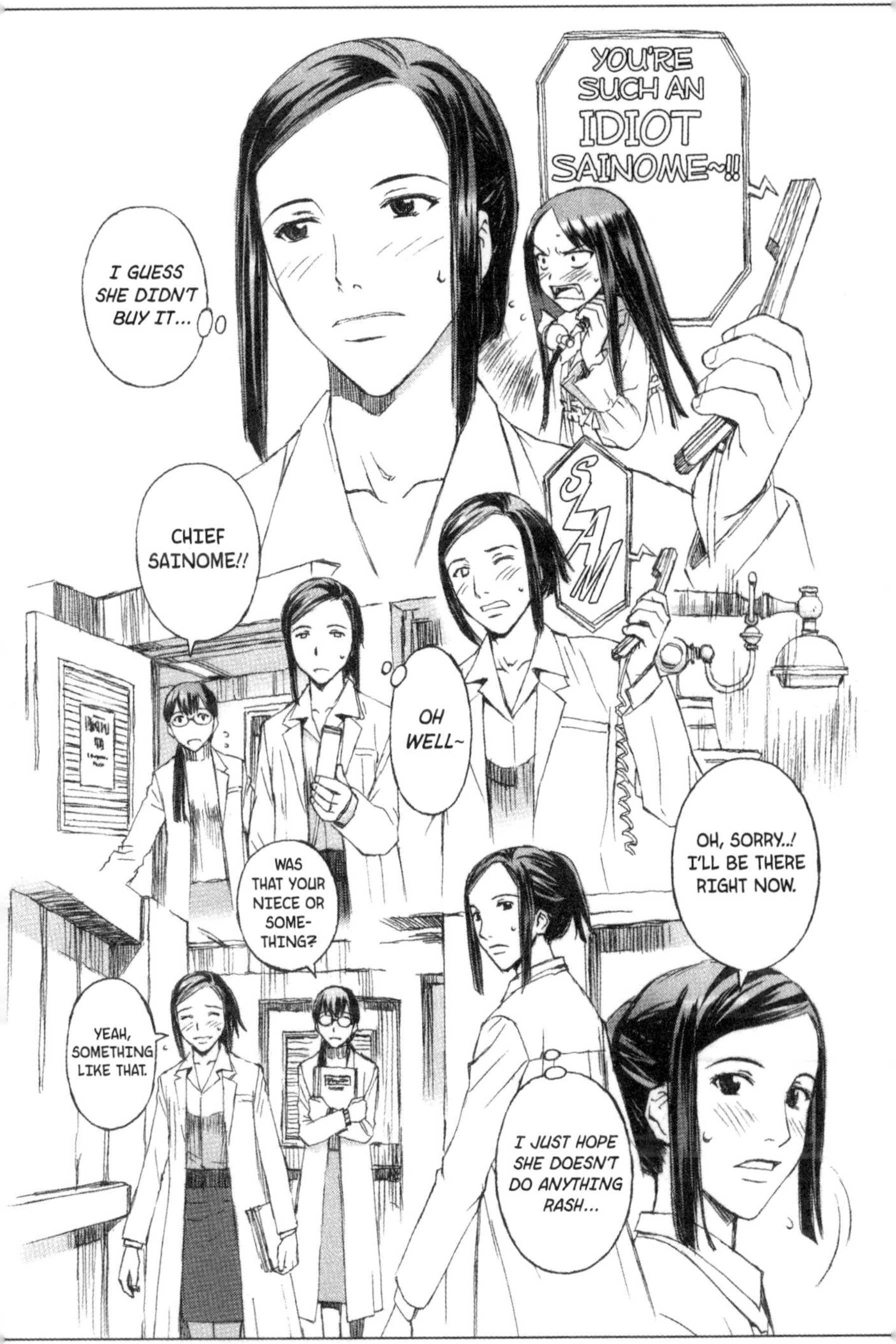
YOU'RE SUCH AN IDIOT SAINOME~!!
I GUESS SHE DIDN'T BUY IT...
SLAM
OH WELL~
CHIEF SAINOME!!
WAS THAT YOUR NIECE OR SOME-THING?
YEAH, SOMETHING LIKE THAT.
OH, SORRY..! I'LL BE THERE RIGHT NOW.
I JUST HOPE SHE DOESN'T DO ANYTHING RASH...

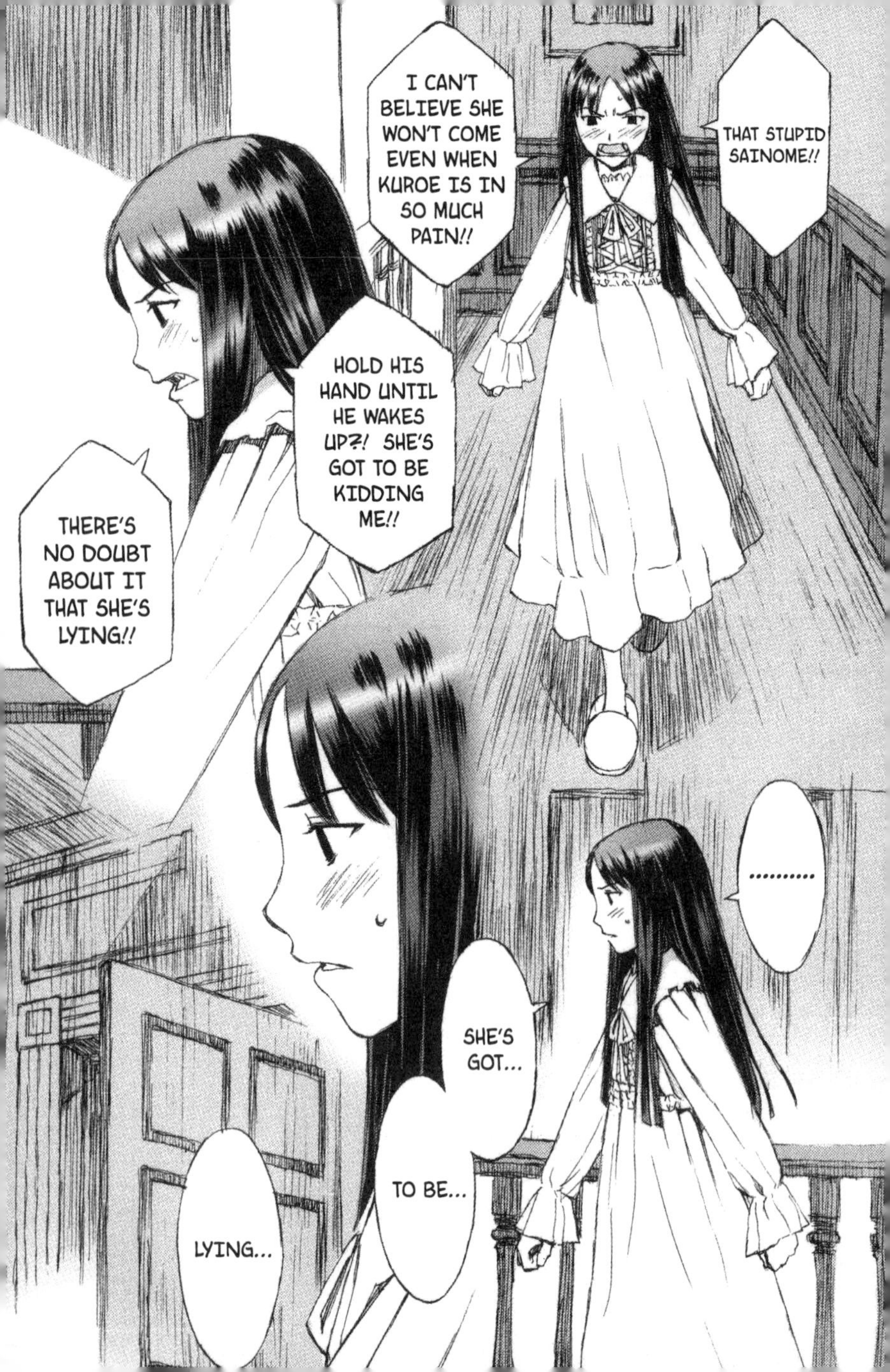
THAT STUPID SAINOME!!
I CAN'T BELIEVE SHE WON'T COME EVEN WHEN KUROE IS IN SO MUCH PAIN!!
HOLD HIS HAND UNTIL HE WAKES UP?! SHE'S GOT TO BE KIDDING ME!!
THERE'S NO DOUBT ABOUT IT THAT SHE'S LYING!!
....
SHE'S GOT...
TO BE...
LYING...

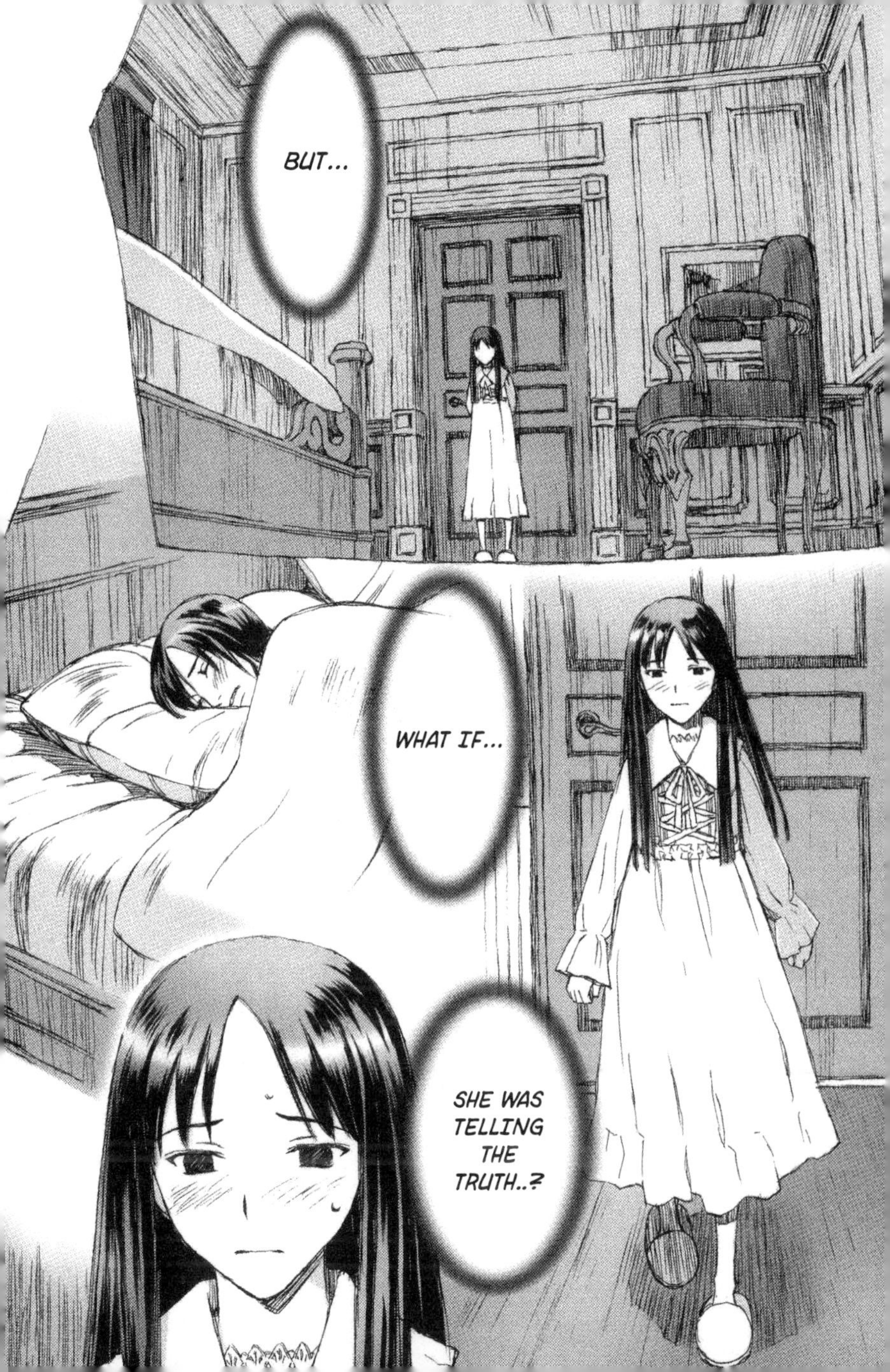
BUT...
WHAT IF...
SHE WAS TELLING THE TRUTH..?

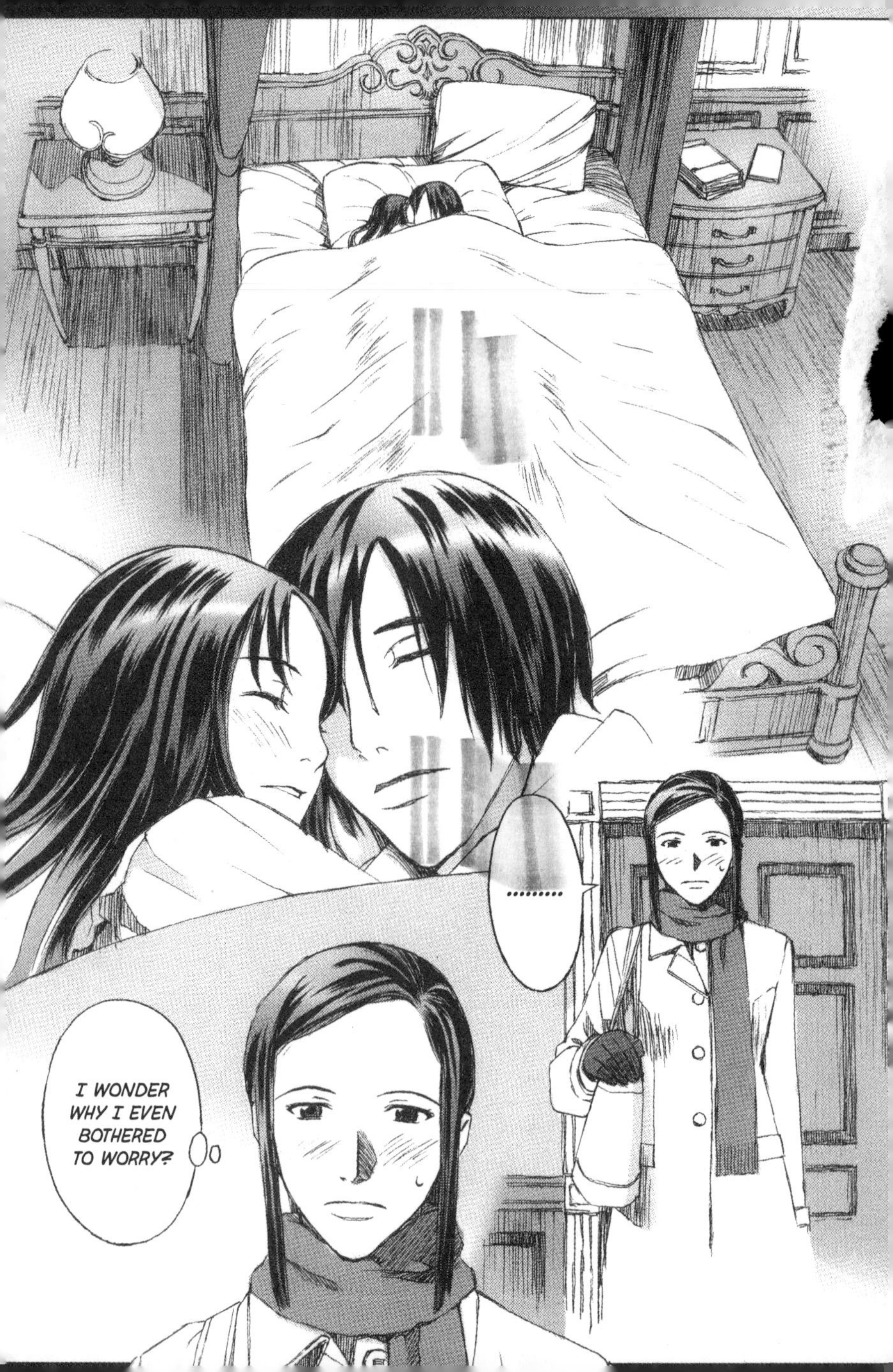
....
I WONDER WHY I EVEN BOTHERED TO WORRY?

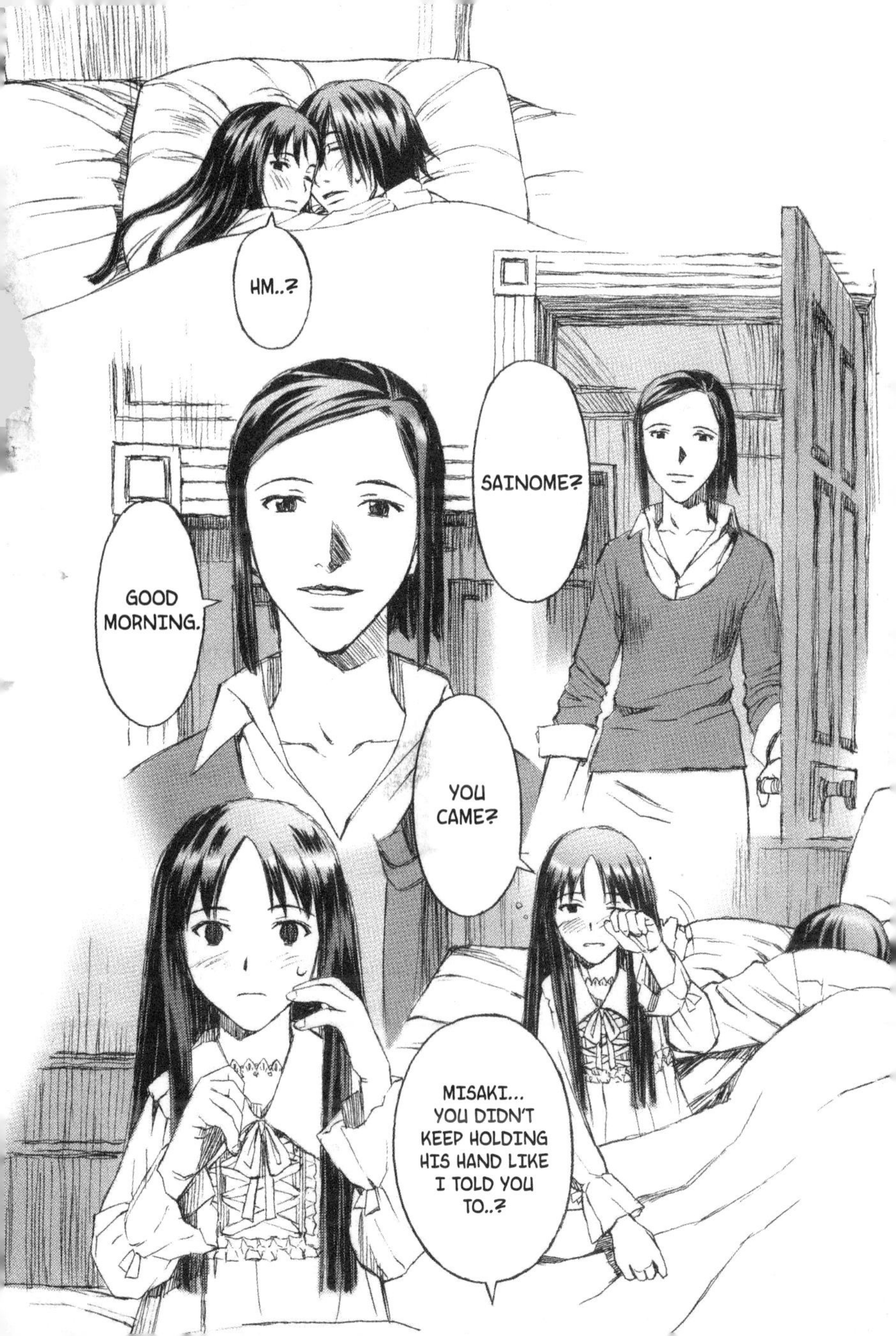
HM..?
SAINOME?
GOOD MORNING.
YOU CAME?
MISAKI... YOU DIDN'T KEEP HOLDING HIS HAND LIKE I TOLD YOU TO..?

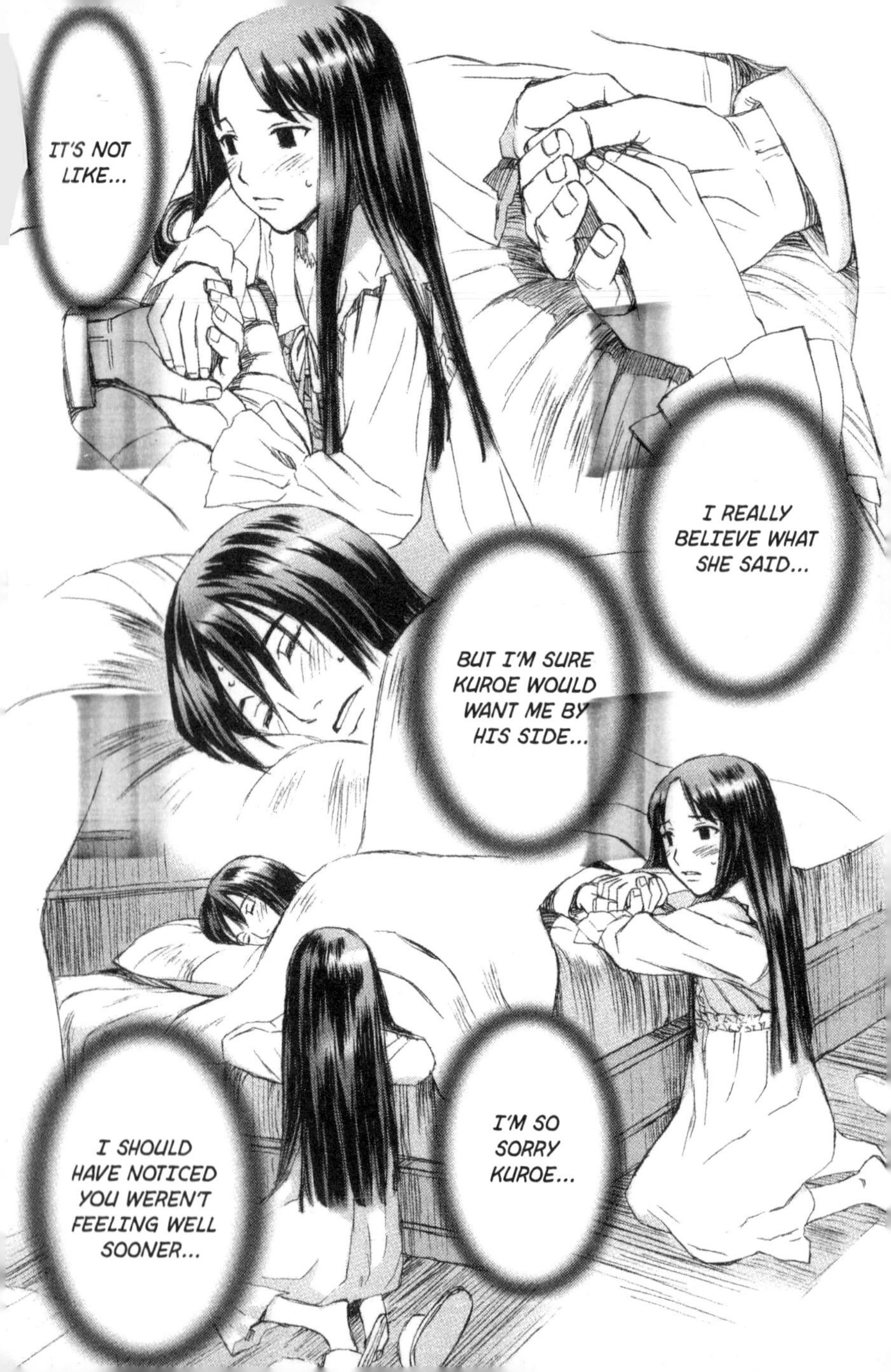
IT'S NOT LIKE...
I REALLY BELIEVE WHAT SHE SAID...
BUT I'M SURE KUROE WOULD WANT ME BY HIS SIDE...
I'M SO SORRY KUROE...
I SHOULD HAVE NOTICED YOU WEREN'T FEELING WELL SOONER...

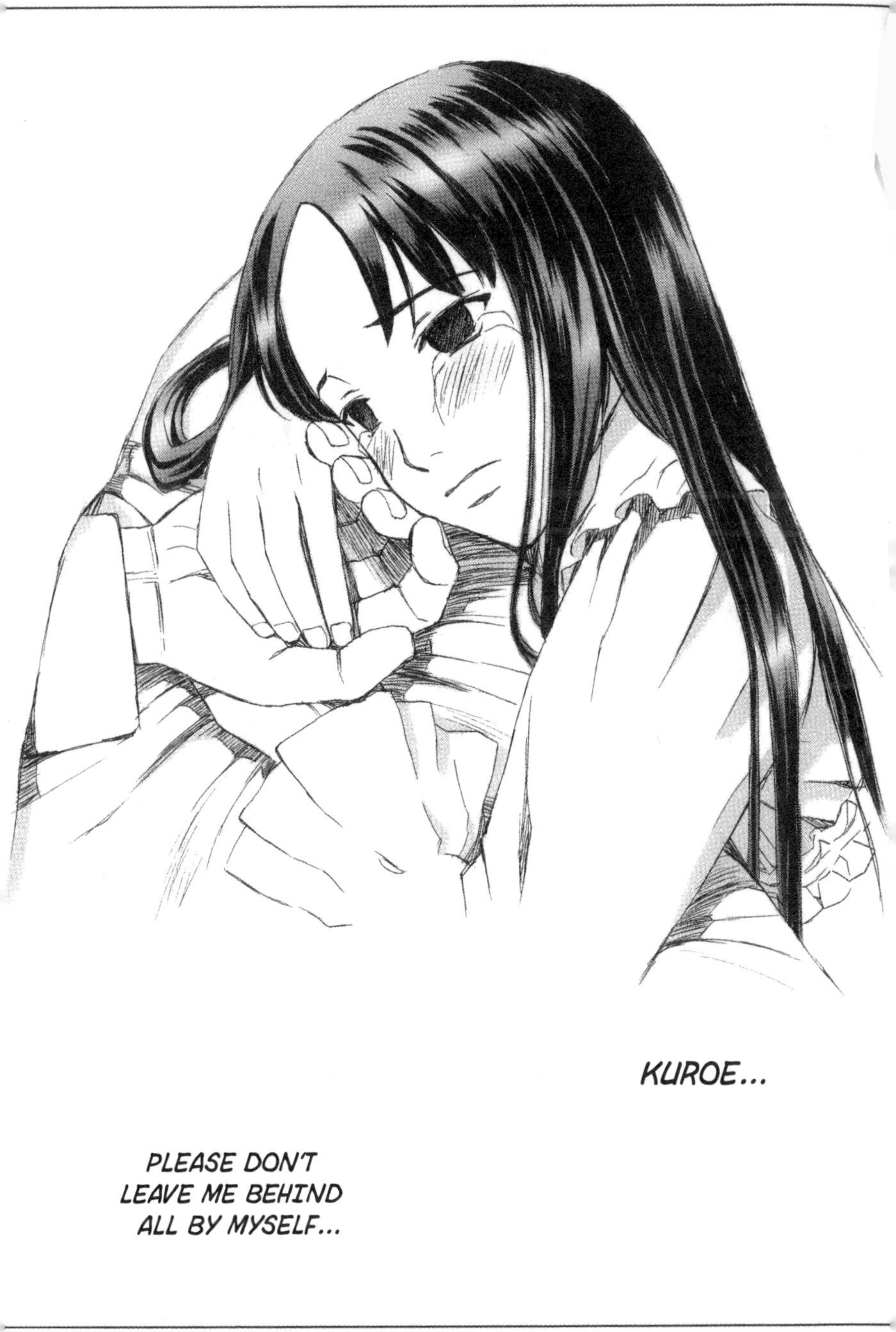
KUROE...
PLEASE DON'T LEAVE ME BEHIND ALL BY MYSELF...

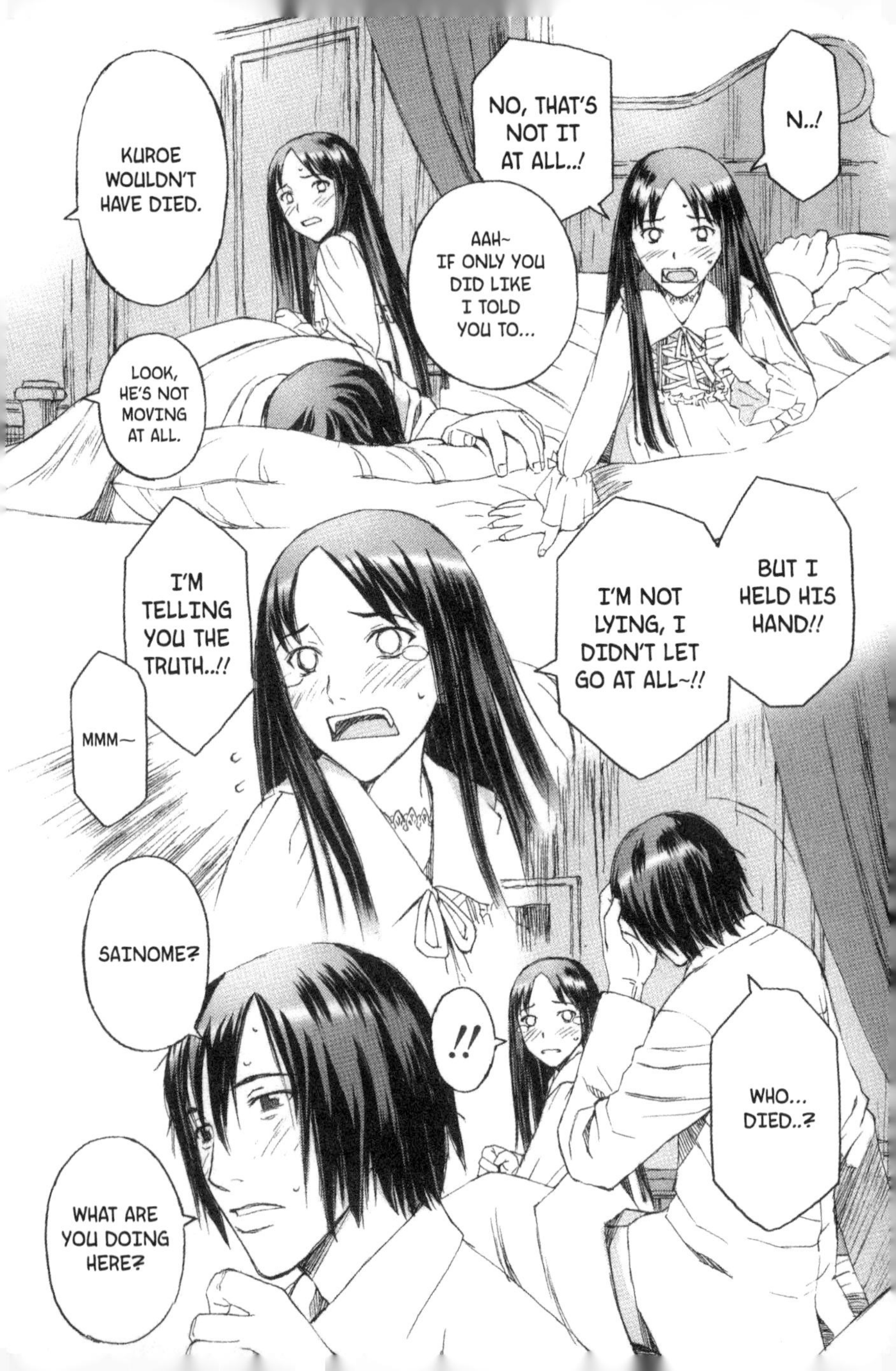
N..!
NO, THAT'S NOT IT AT ALL..!
AAH~ IF ONLY YOU DID LIKE I TOLD YOU TO...
KUROE WOULDN'T HAVE DIED.
LOOK, HE'S NOT MOVING AT ALL.
BUT I HELD HIS HAND!!
I'M NOT LYING, I DIDN'T LET GO AT ALL~!!
I'M TELLING YOU THE TRUTH..!!
MMM~
WHO... DIED..?
!!
SAINOME?
WHAT ARE YOU DOING HERE?

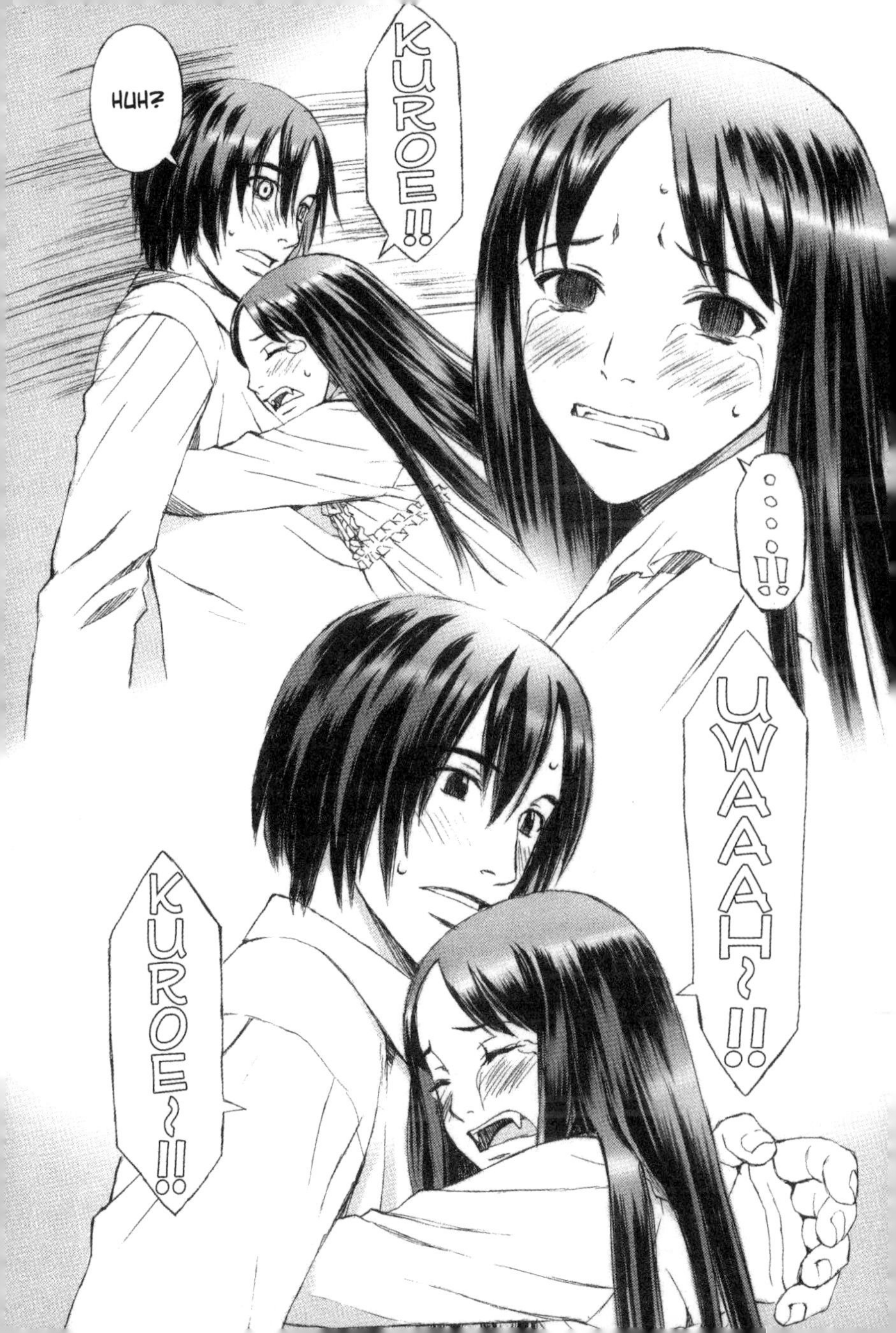
KUROE!!
HUH?
....!!
UWAAAH~!!
KUROE~!!

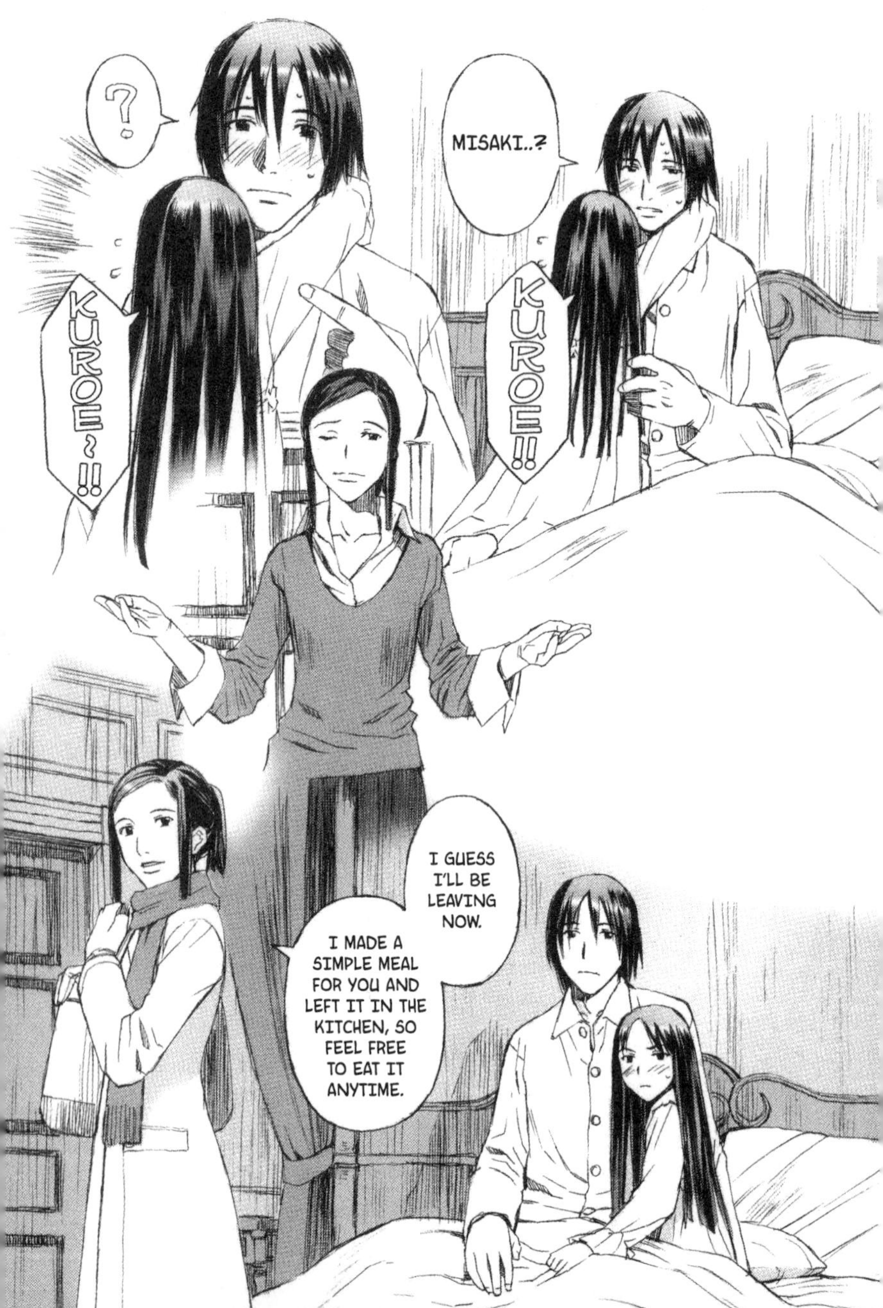
MISAKI..?
KUROE!!
?
KUROE~!!
I GUESS I'LL BE LEAVING NOW.
I MADE A SIMPLE MEAL FOR YOU AND LEFT IT IN THE KITCHEN, SO FEEL FREE TO EAT IT ANYTIME.

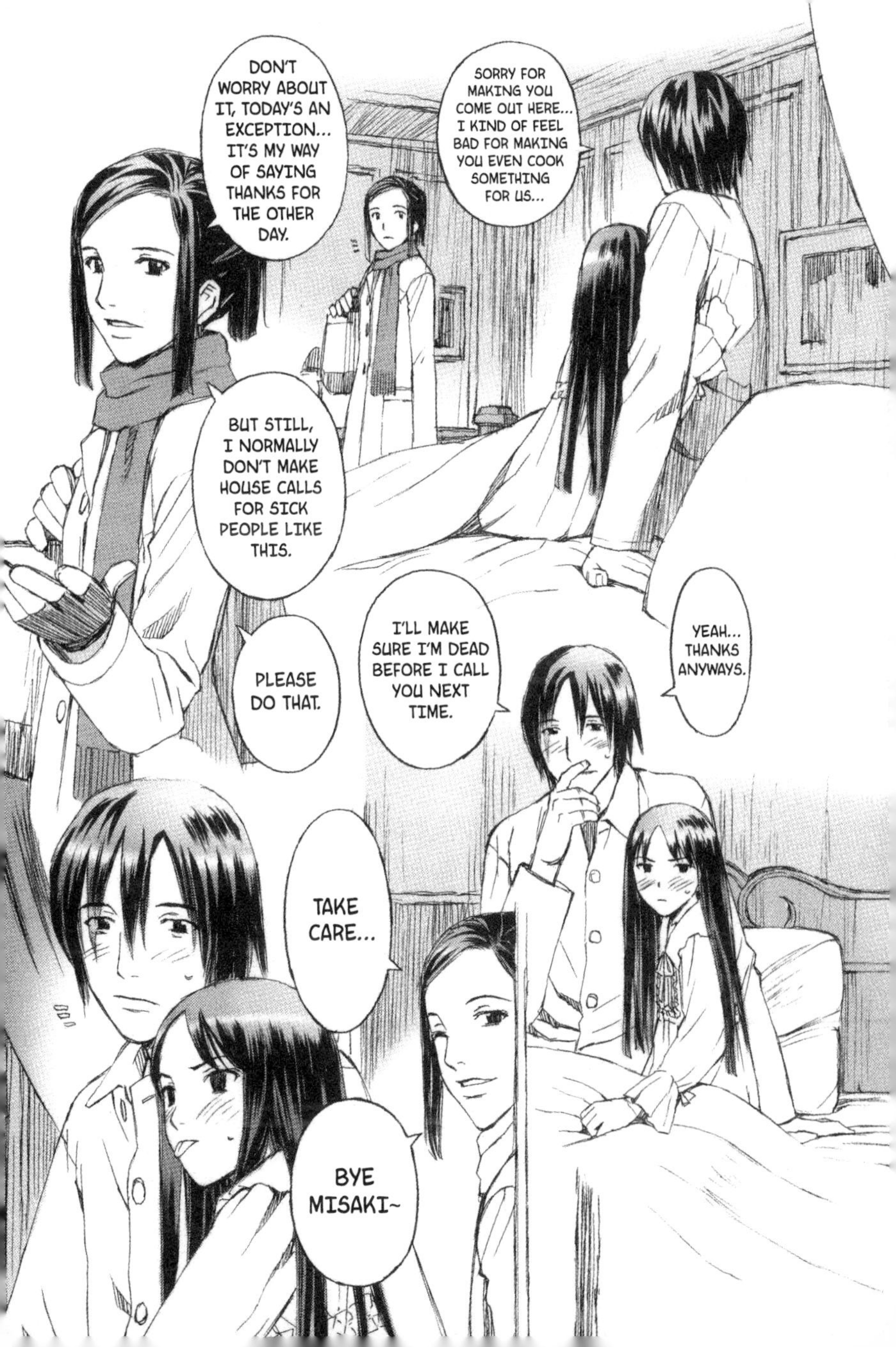
SORRY FOR MAKING YOU COME OUT HERE... I KIND OF FEEL BAD FOR MAKING YOU EVEN COOK SOMETHING FOR US...
DON'T WORRY ABOUT IT, TODAY'S AN EXCEPTION... IT'S MY WAY OF SAYING THANKS FOR THE OTHER DAY.
BUT STILL, I NORMALLY DON'T MAKE HOUSE CALLS FOR SICK PEOPLE LIKE THIS.
YEAH... THANKS ANYWAYS.
I'LL MAKE SURE I'M DEAD BEFORE I CALL YOU NEXT TIME.
PLEASE DO THAT.
TAKE CARE...
BYE MISAKI~

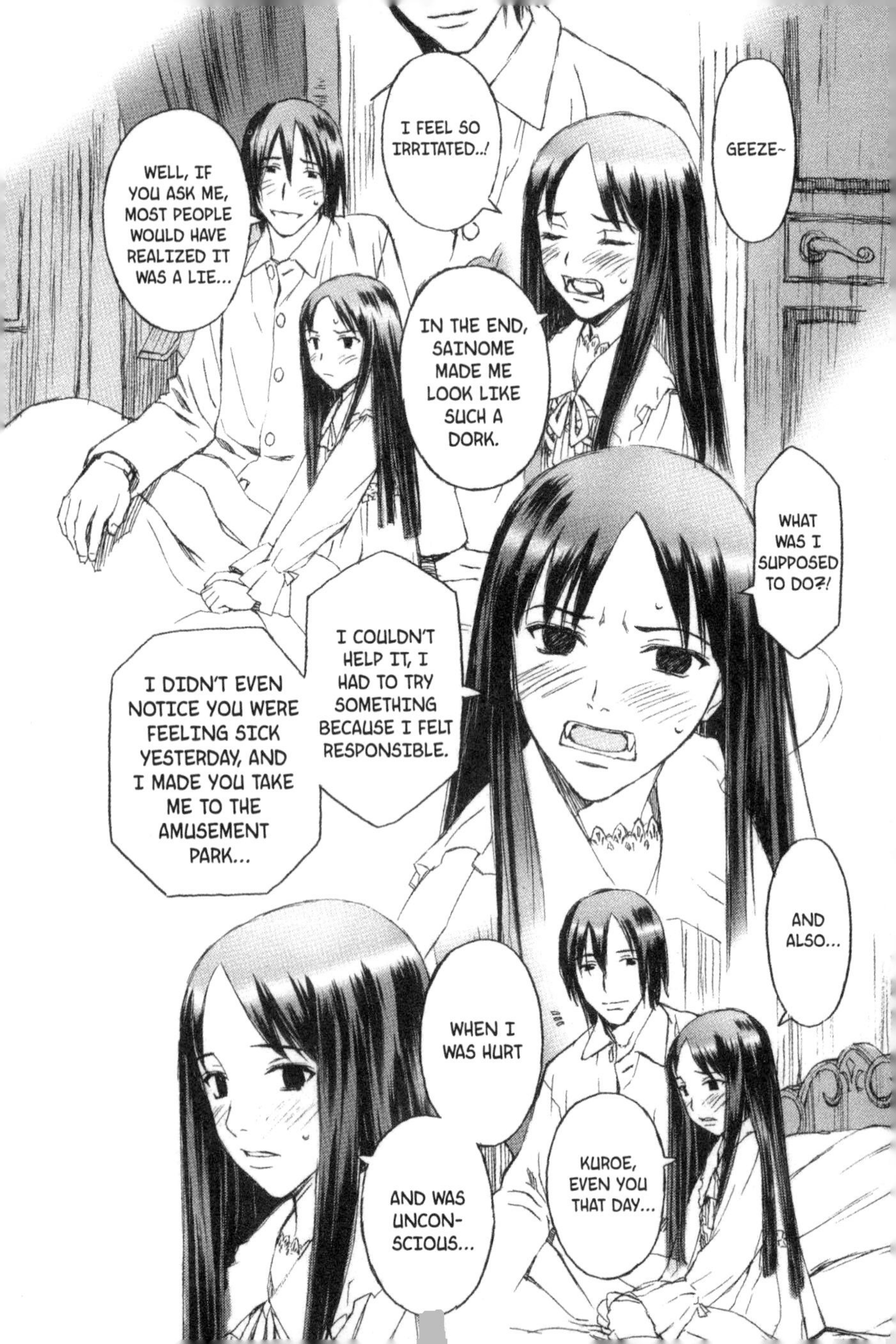
GEEZE~
I FEEL SO IRRITATED..!
IN THE END, SAINOME MADE ME LOOK LIKE SUCH A DORK.
WELL, IF YOU ASK ME, MOST PEOPLE WOULD HAVE REALIZED IT WAS A LIE...
WHAT WAS I SUPPOSED TO DO?!
I COULDN'T HELP IT, I HAD TO TRY SOMETHING BECAUSE I FELT RESPONSIBLE.
I DIDN'T EVEN NOTICE YOU WERE FEELING SICK YESTERDAY, AND I MADE YOU TAKE ME TO THE AMUSEMENT PARK...
AND ALSO...
KUROE, EVEN YOU THAT DAY...
WHEN I WAS HURT
AND WAS UNCON-SCIOUS...

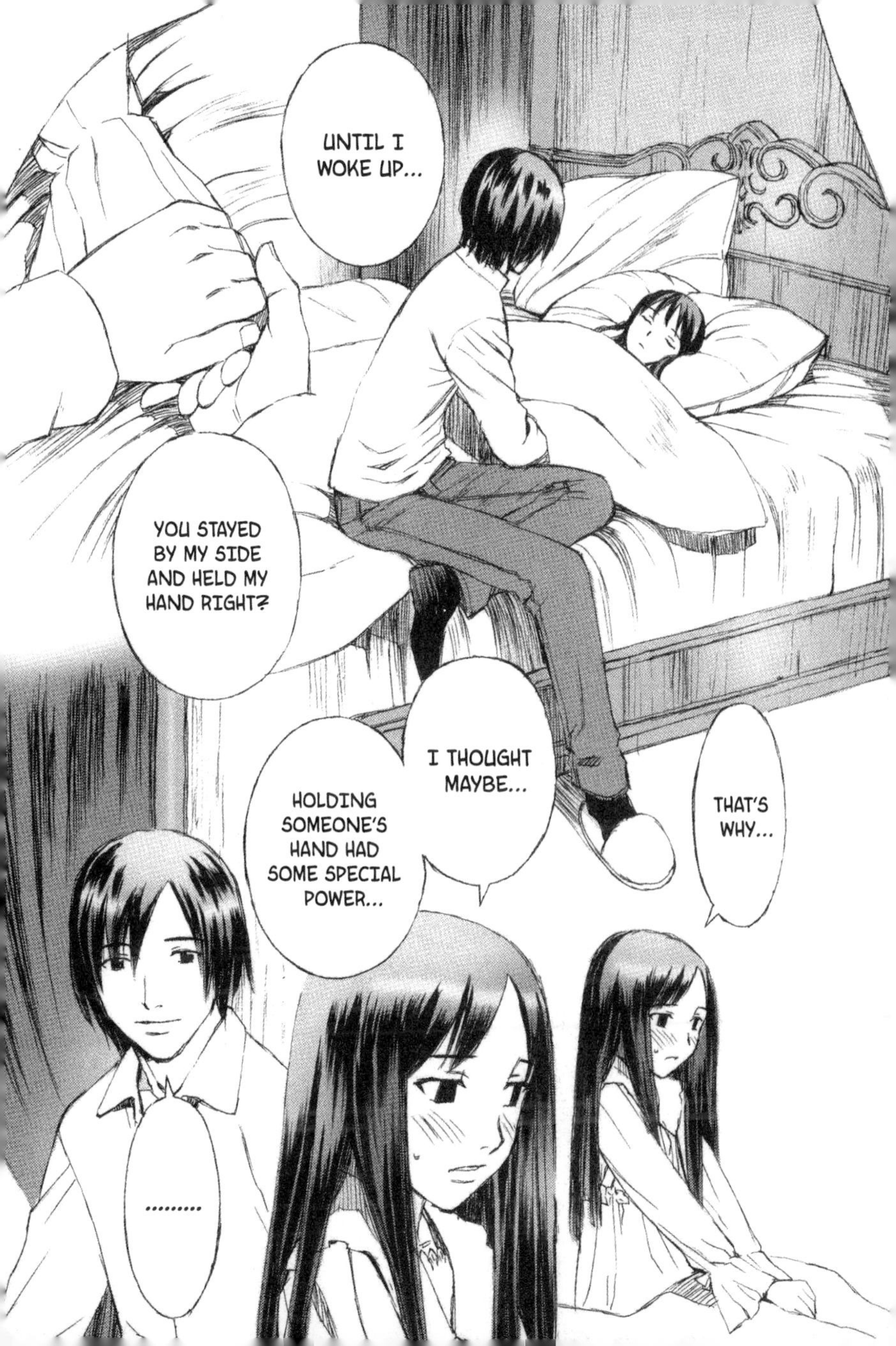
UNTIL I WOKE UP...
YOU STAYED BY MY SIDE AND HELD MY HAND RIGHT?
THAT'S WHY...
I THOUGHT MAYBE...
HOLDING SOMEONE'S HAND HAD SOME SPECIAL POWER...
....

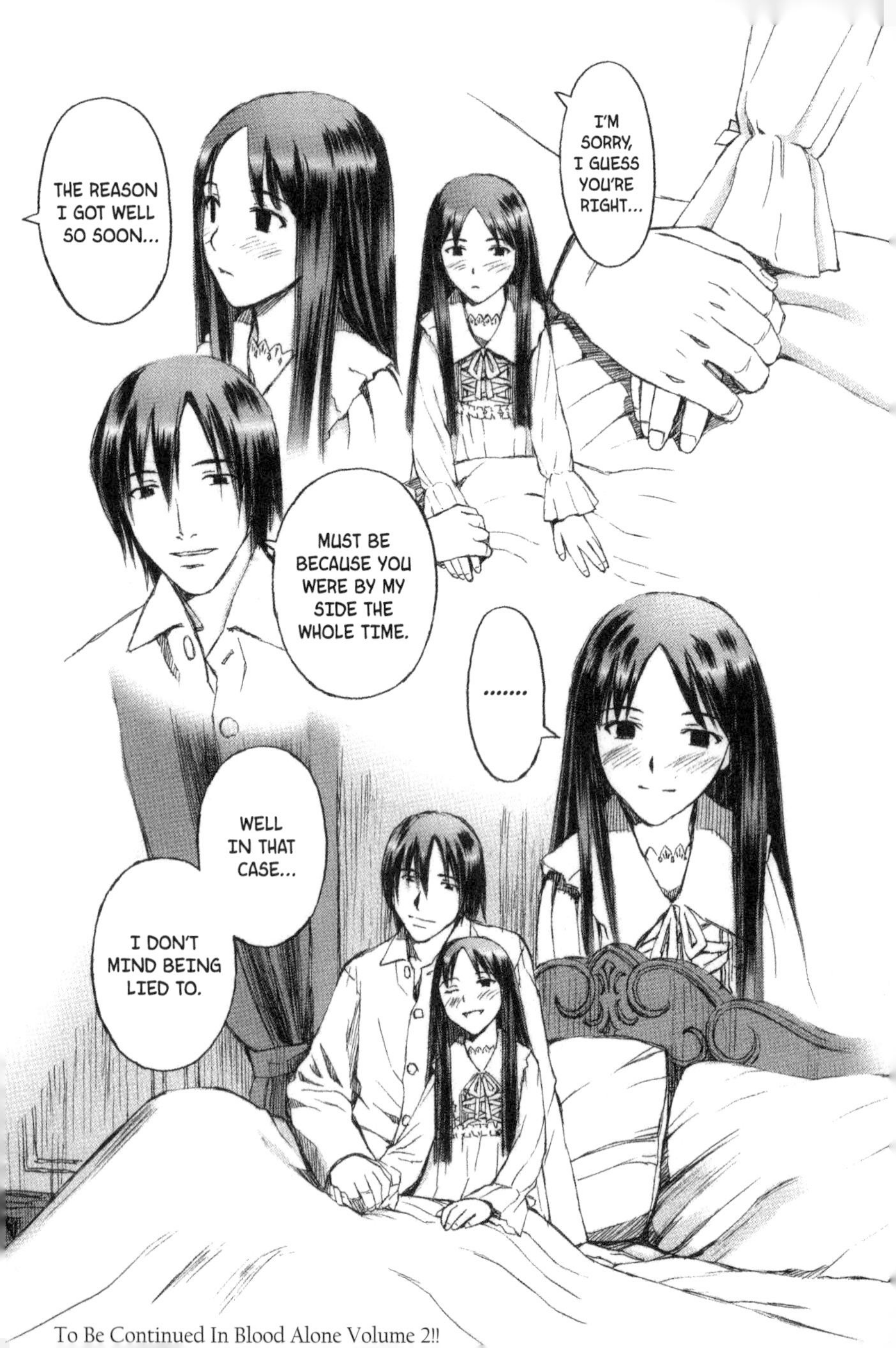
I'M SORRY, I GUESS YOU'RE RIGHT...
THE REASON I GOT WELL SO SOON...
MUST BE BECAUSE YOU WERE BY MY SIDE THE WHOLE TIME.
....
WELL IN THAT CASE...
I DON'T MIND BEING LIED TO.

To Be Continued In Blood Alone Volume 2!!

Appendix

IN MY BED I SCREAM

クロエの朝帰り – Kuroe’s Return in the Morning

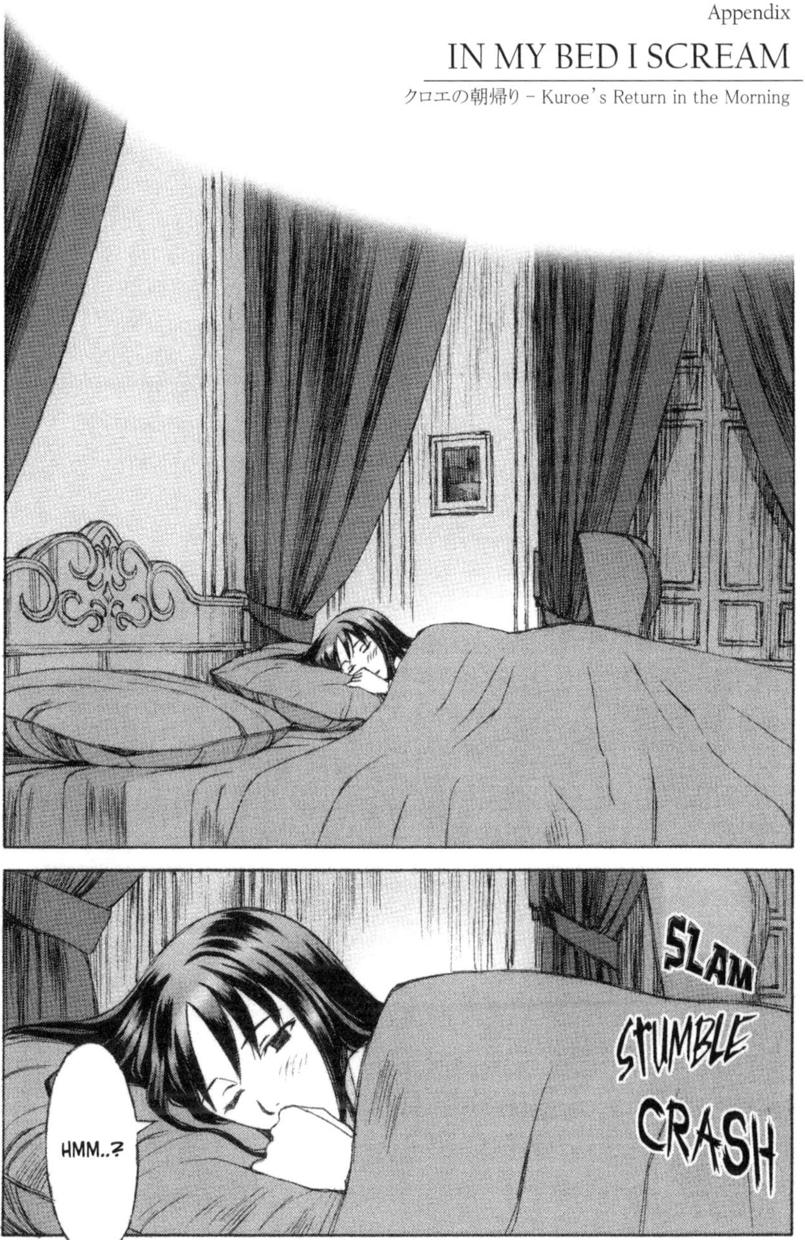
SLAM
STUMBLE
CRASH
HMM..?

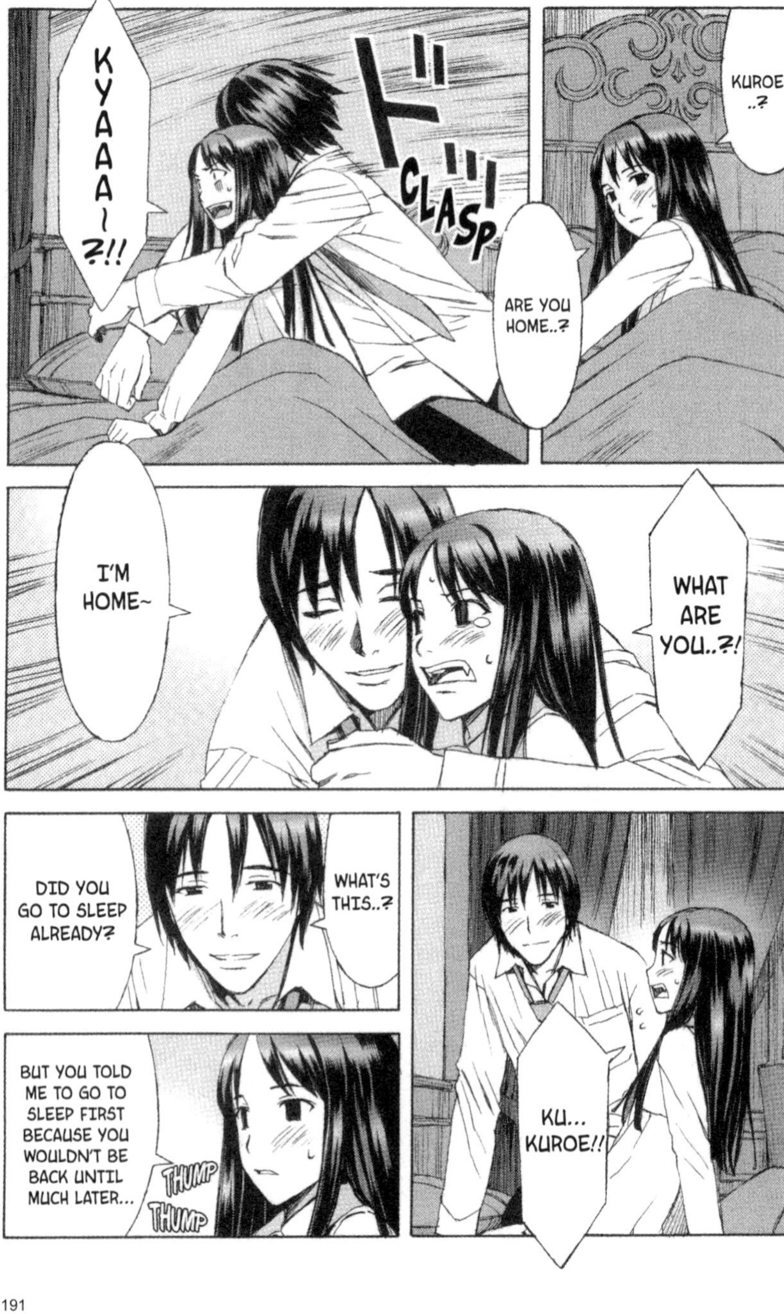
KUROE ..?
ARE YOU HOME..?
ド
CLASP
KYAAAA~ ?!!
WHAT ARE YOU..?!
I'M HOME~
KU... KUROE!!
WHAT'S THIS..?
DID YOU GO TO SLEEP ALREADY?
BUT YOU TOLD ME TO GO TO SLEEP FIRST BECAUSE YOU WOULDN'T BE BACK UNTIL MUCH LATER...
THUMP
THUMP

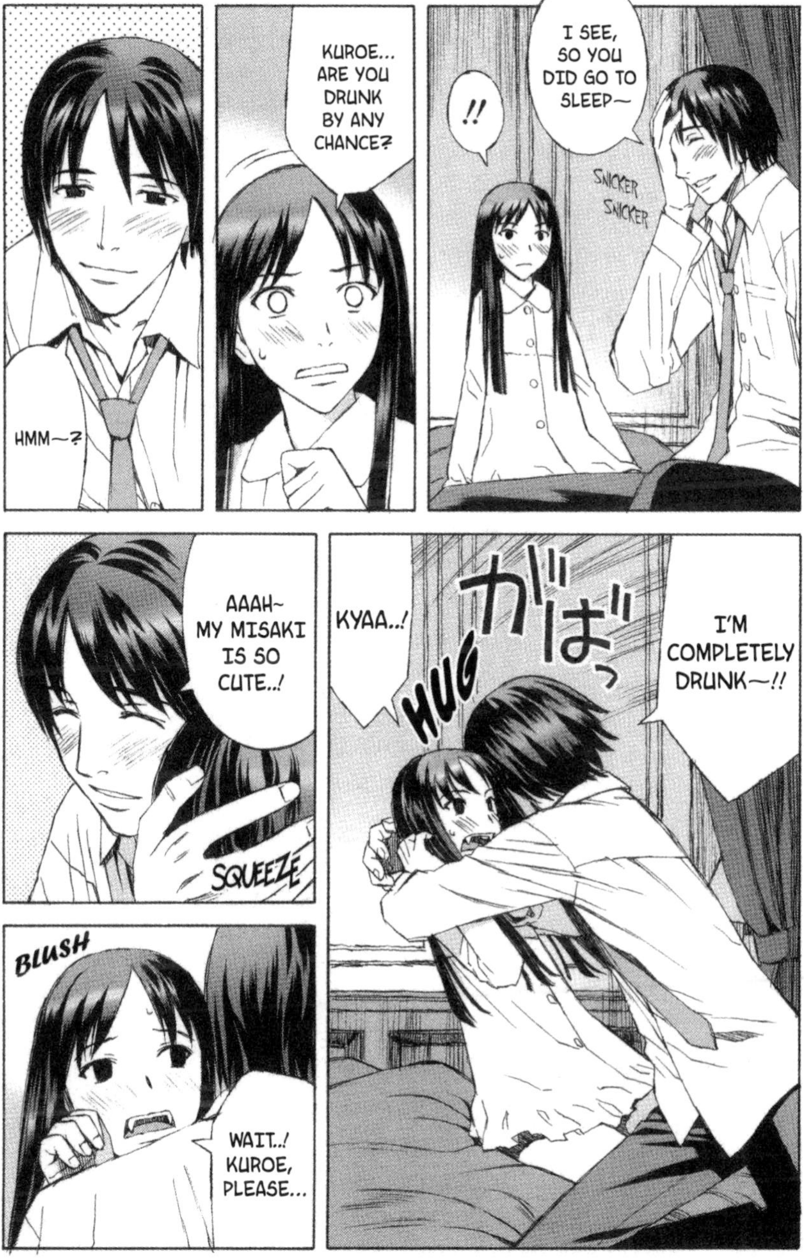
I SEE, SO YOU DID GO TO SLEEP~
!!
SNICKER SNICKER
KUROE... ARE YOU DRUNK BY ANY CHANCE?
HMM~?
I'M COMPLETELY DRUNK~!!
がばっ
HUG
KYAA..!
AAAH~ MY MISAKI IS SO CUTE..!
SQUEEZE
BLUSH
WAIT..! KUROE, PLEASE...

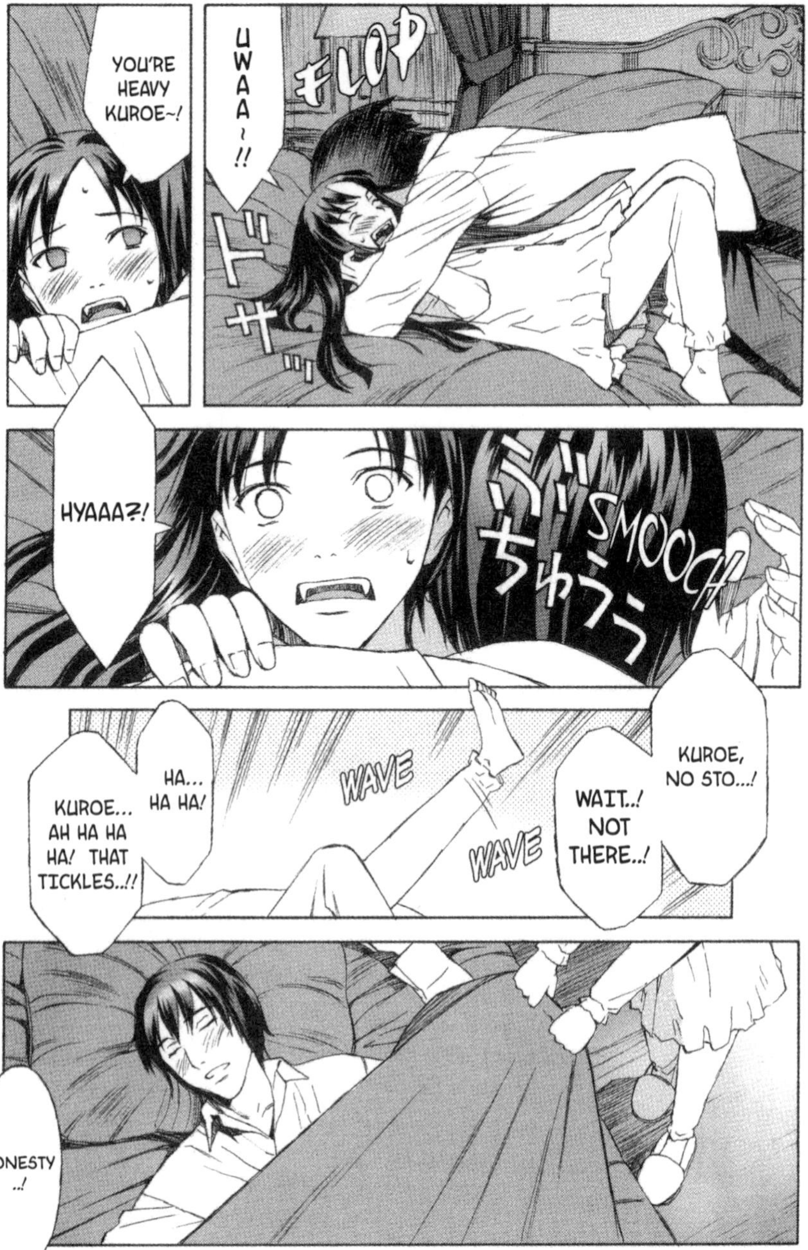
UWAA~!!
FLOP
YOU'RE HEAVY KUROE~!
SMOOCH
HYAAA?!
KUROE, NO STO...!
WAIT..! NOT THERE..!
WAVE
WAVE
HA... HA HA!
KUROE... AH HA HA HA! THAT TICKLES..!!
HONESTY ..!

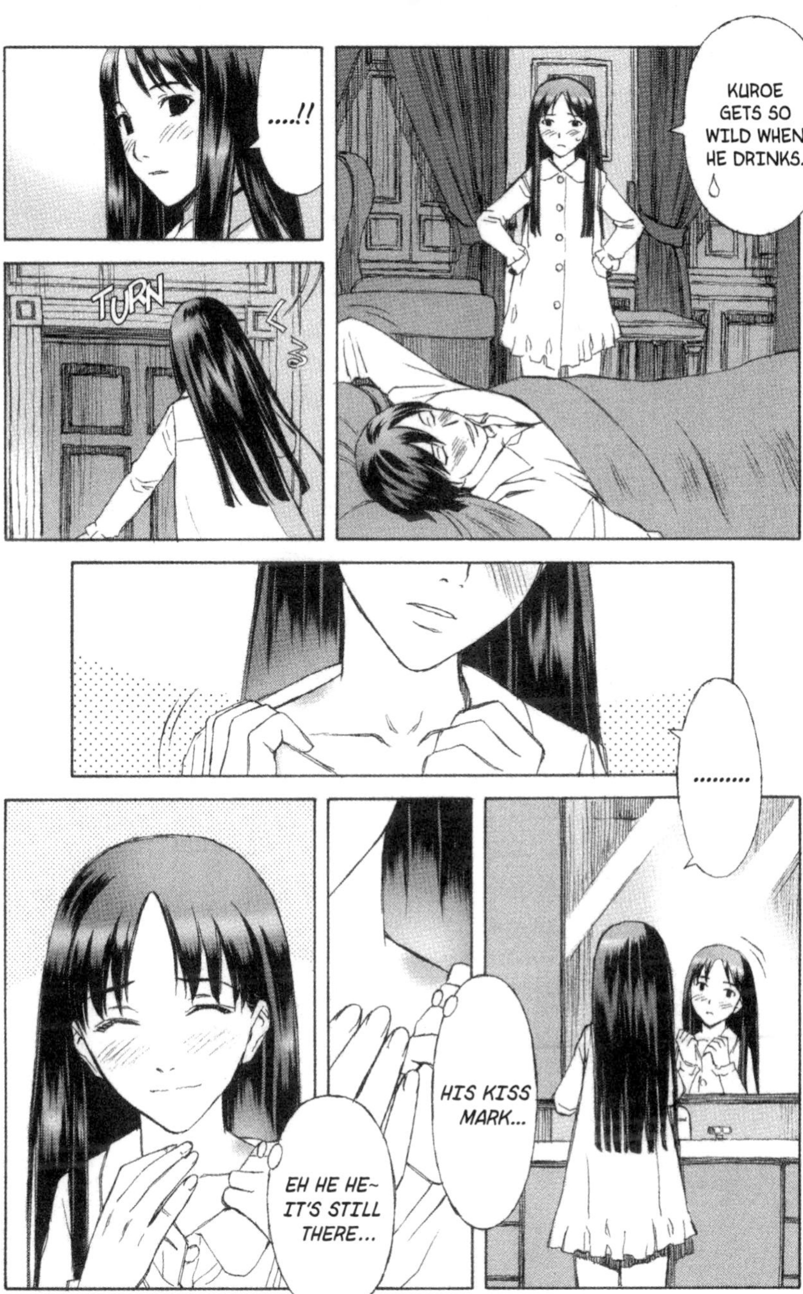
KUROE GETS SO WILD WHEN HE DRINKS.
....!!
TURN
くる
....
HIS KISS MARK...
EH HE HE~ IT'S STILL THERE...

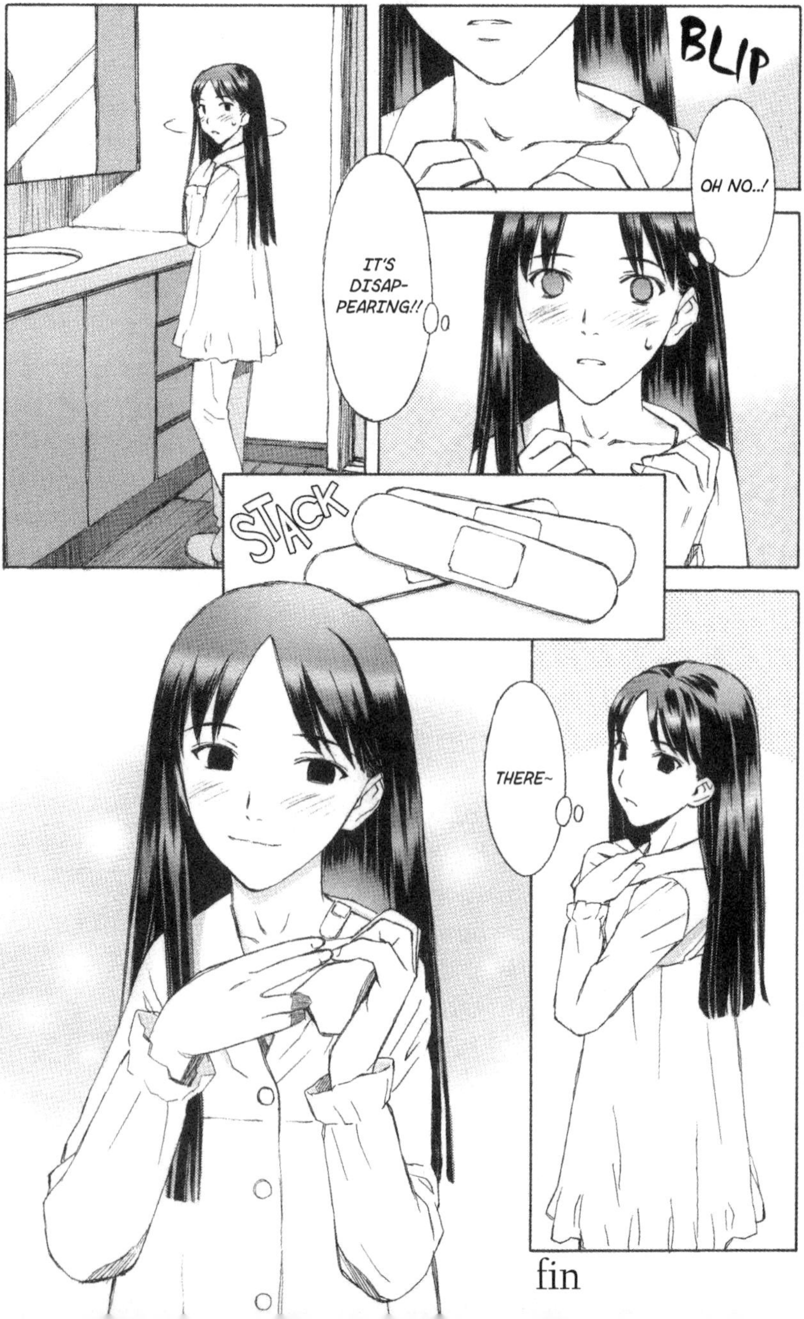
BLIP
OH NO..!
IT'S DISAPPEARING!!
STACK
THERE~

fin

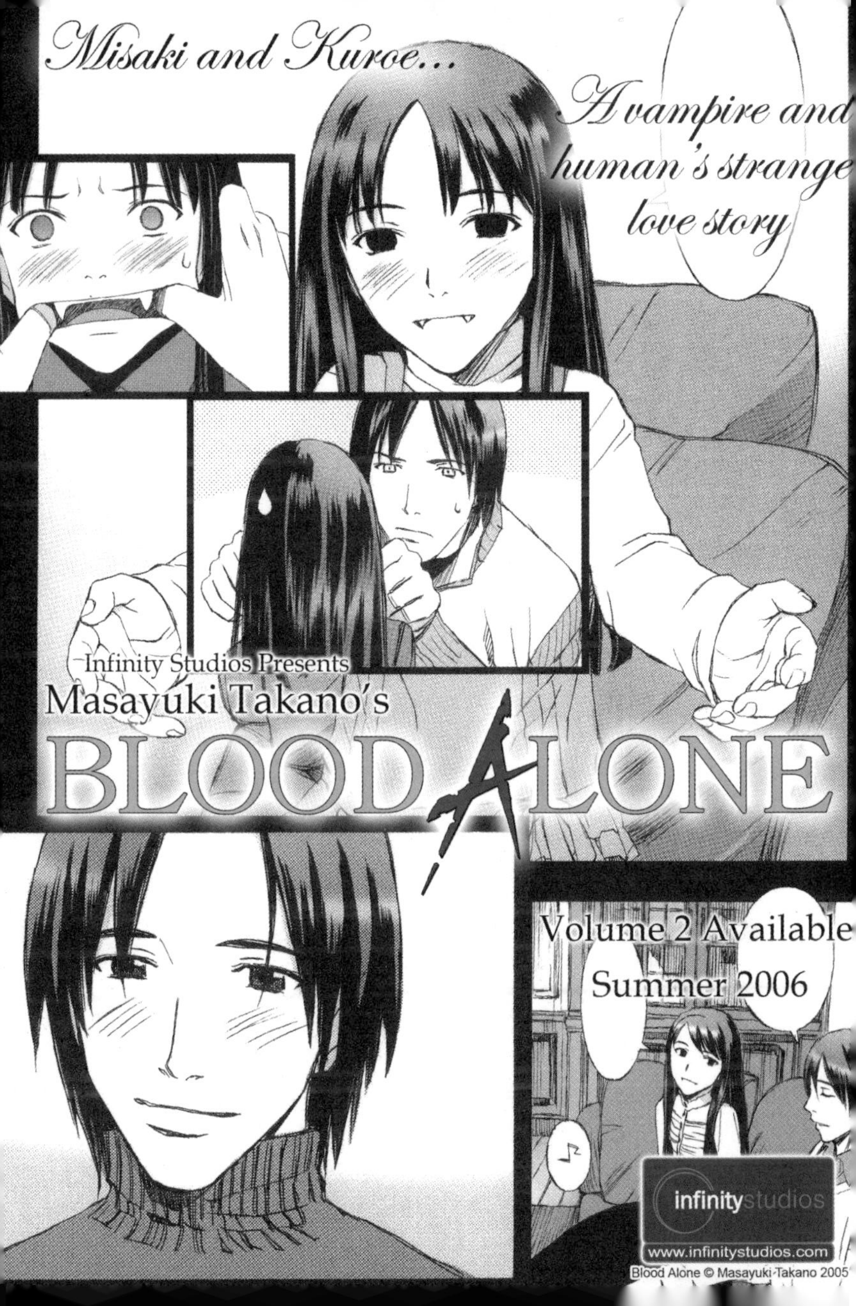

Misaki and Kuroe...
A vampire and human's strange love story
Infinity Studios Presents
Masayuki Takano's
BLOOD ALONE
Volume 2 Available Summer 2006
infinitystudios
www.infinitystudios.com
Blood Alone © Masayuki Takano 2005

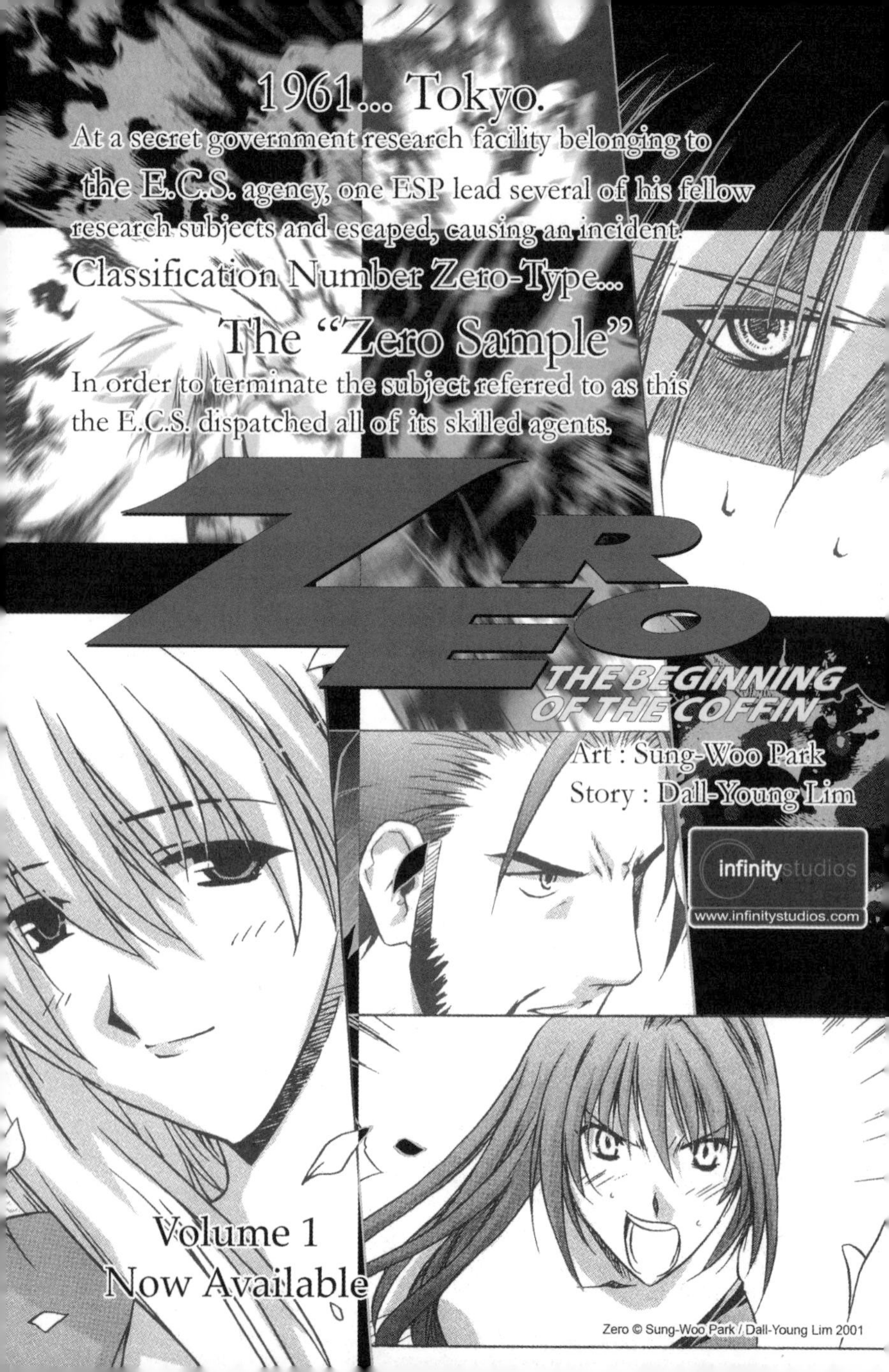
1961... Tokyo.
At a secret government research facility belonging to the E.C.S. agency, one ESP lead several of his fellow research subjects and escaped, causing an incident.
Classification Number Zero-Type...
The "Zero Sample"
In order to terminate the subject referred to as this the E.C.S. dispatched all of its skilled agents.
ZERO
THE BEGINNING OF THE COFFIN
Art : Sung-Woo Park
Story : Dall-Young Lim
infinitystudios
www.infinitystudios.com
Volume 1
Now Available
Zero © Sung-Woo Park / Dall-Young Lim 2001

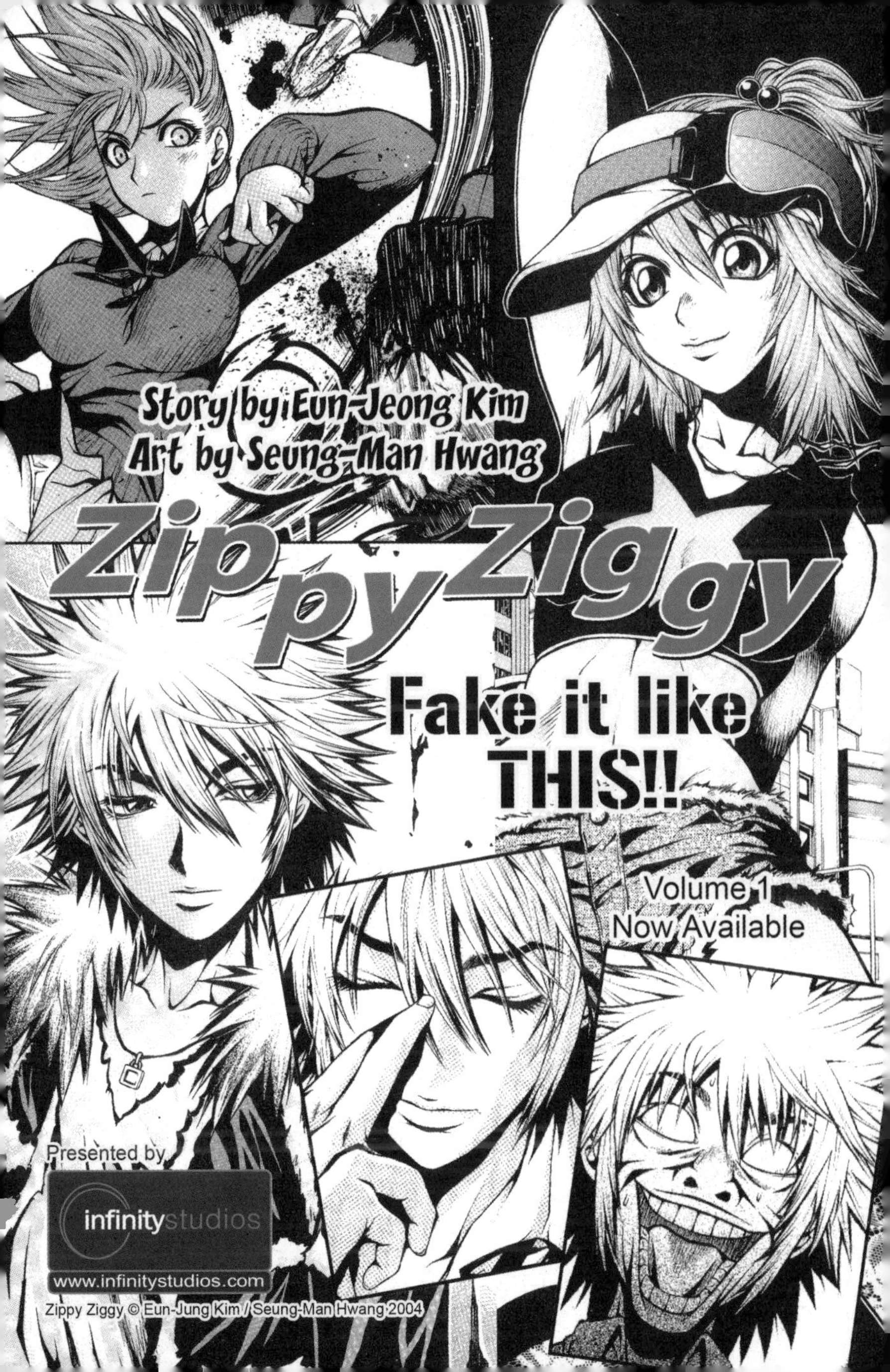

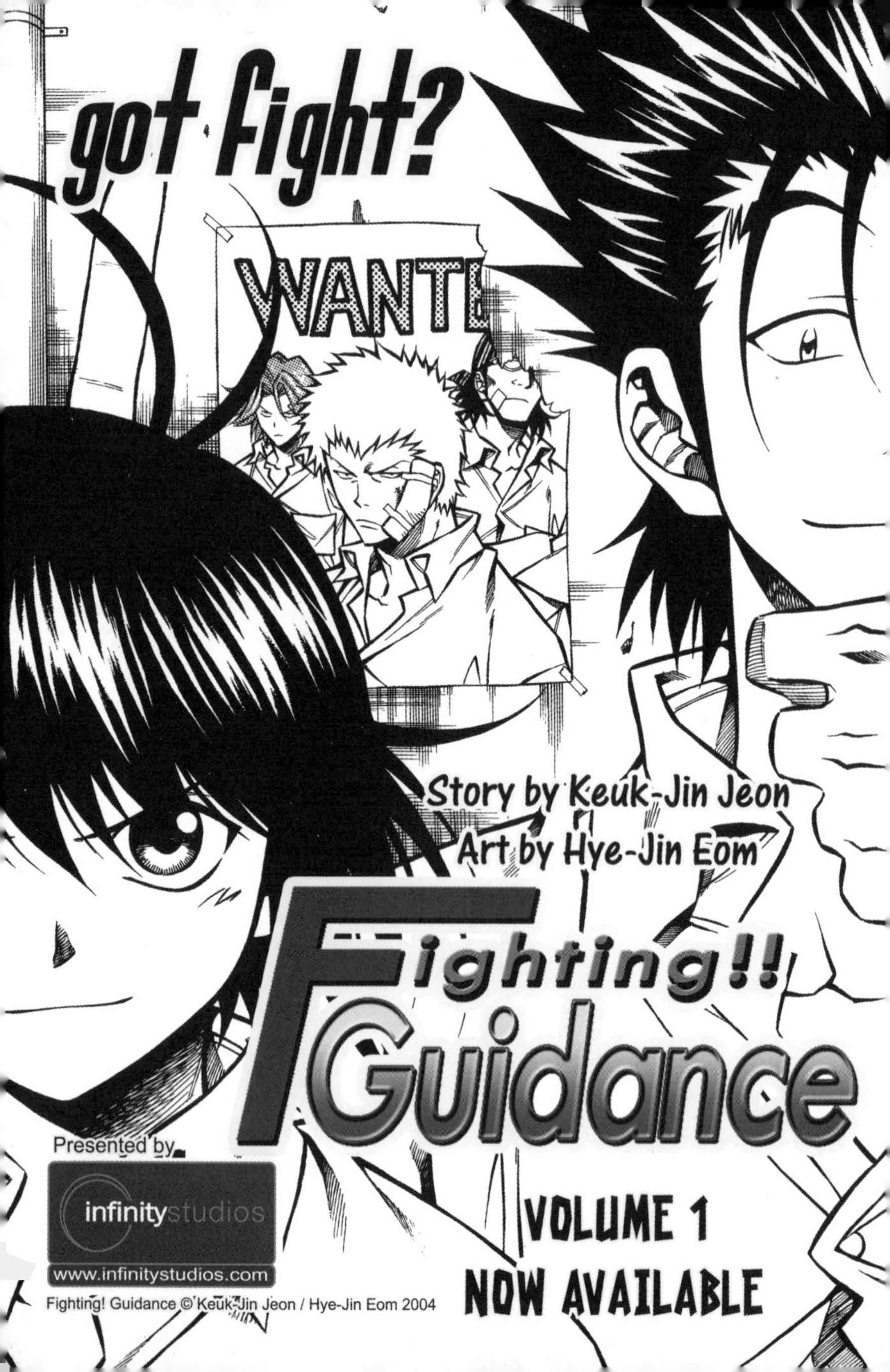
got fight?
WANTE
Story by Keuk-Jin Jeon
Art by Hye-Jin Eom
Fighting!! Guidance
Presented by
infinitystudios
www.infinitystudios.com
Fighting! Guidance © Keuk-Jin Jeon / Hye-Jin Eom 2004
VOLUME 1
NOW AVAILABLE

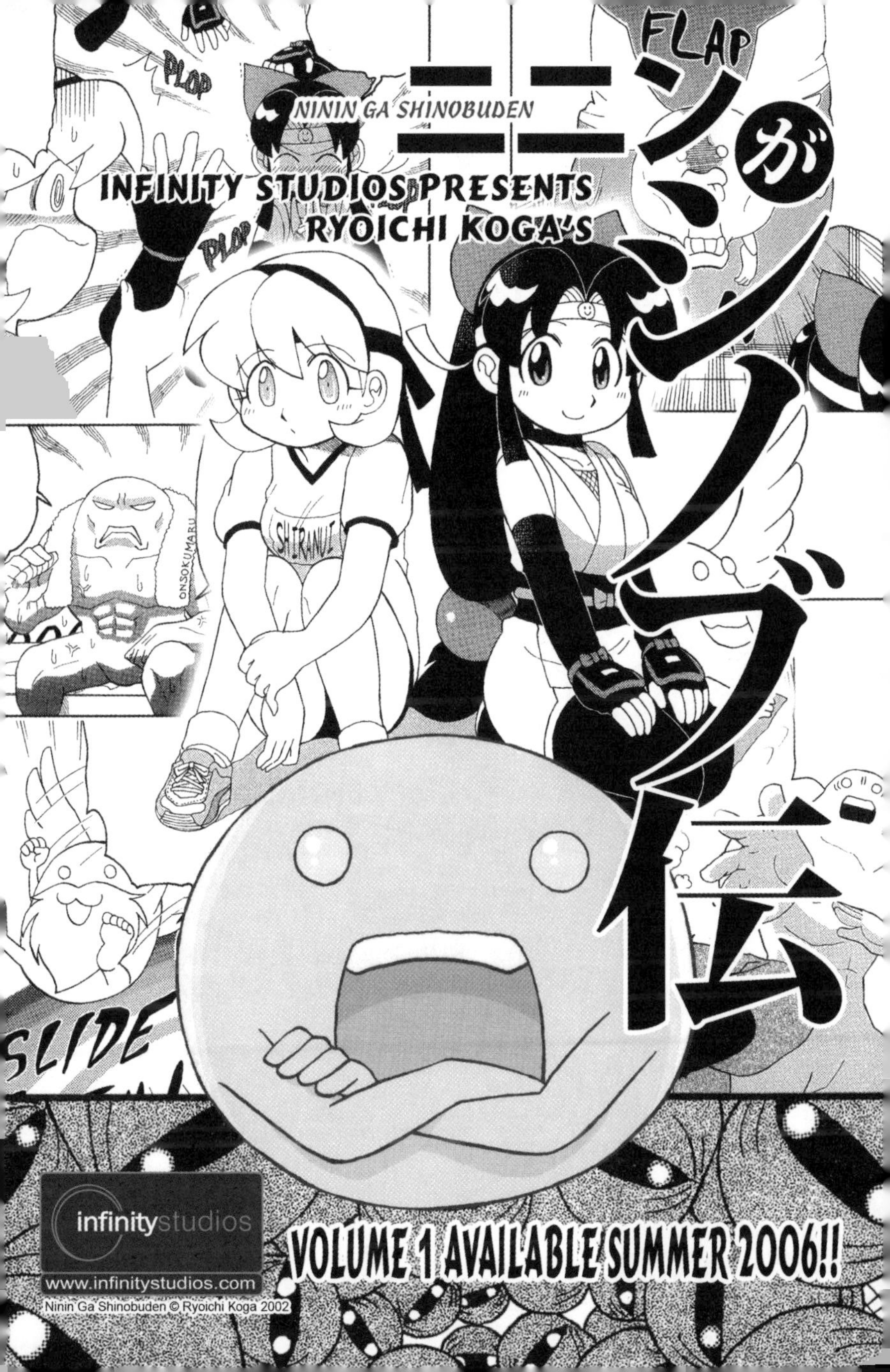

NININ GA SHINOBUDEN
ニニンがシノブ伝
INFINITY STUDIOS PRESENTS
RYOICHI KOGA'S
FLAP
PLOP
PLOP
SHIRANUI
ONSOKUMARU
SLIDE
infinitystudios
www.infinitystudios.com
VOLUME 1 AVAILABLE SUMMER 2006!!
Ninin Ga Shinobuden © Ryoichi Koga 2002

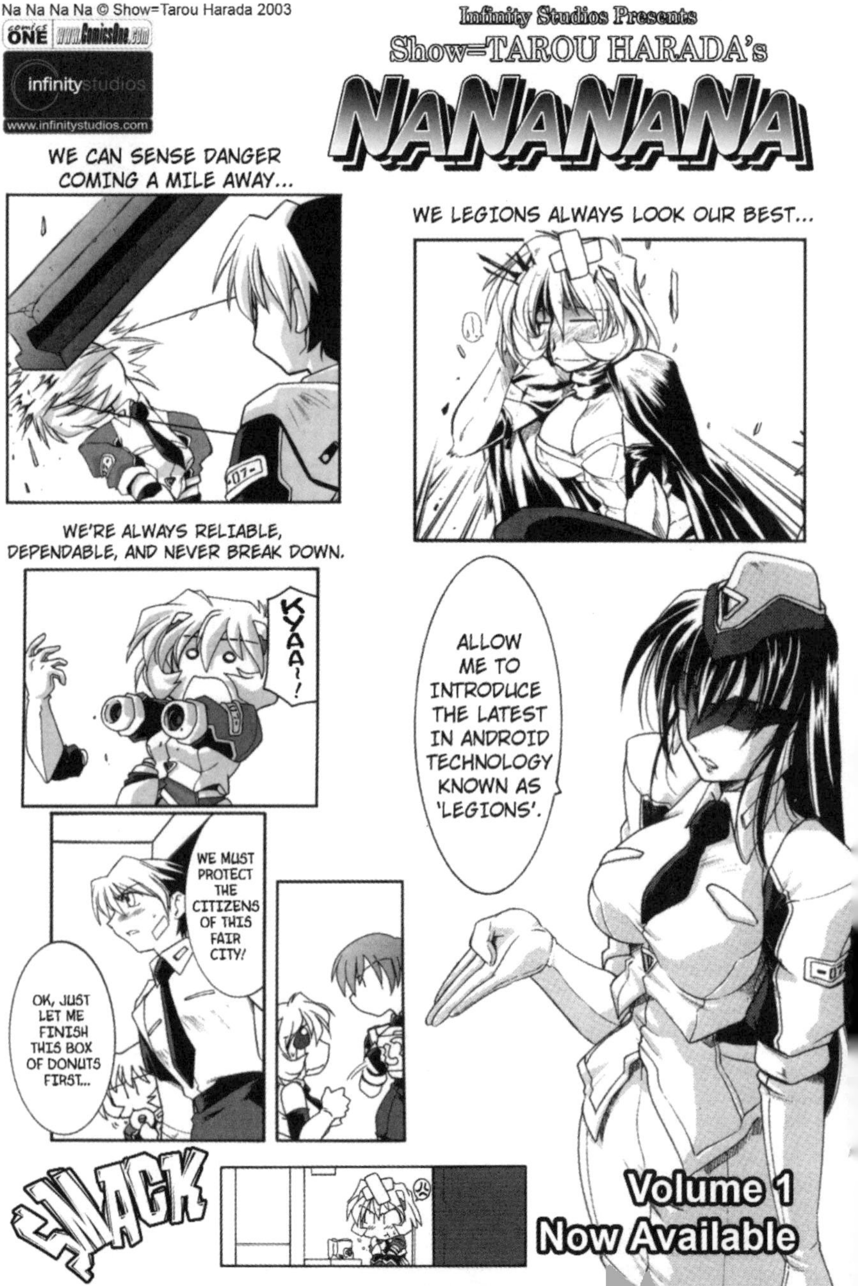

Infinity Studios Presents
Show=TAROU HARADA's
NANANANA
WE LEGIONS ALWAYS LOOK OUR BEST...
WE CAN SENSE DANGER COMING A MILE AWAY...
ALLOW ME TO INTRODUCE THE LATEST IN ANDROID TECHNOLOGY KNOWN AS 'LEGIONS'.
WE'RE ALWAYS RELIABLE, DEPENDABLE, AND NEVER BREAK DOWN.
KYAA~!
WE MUST PROTECT THE CITIZENS OF THIS FAIR CITY!
OK, JUST LET ME FINISH THIS BOX OF DONUTS FIRST...
SMACK
Volume 1
Now Available

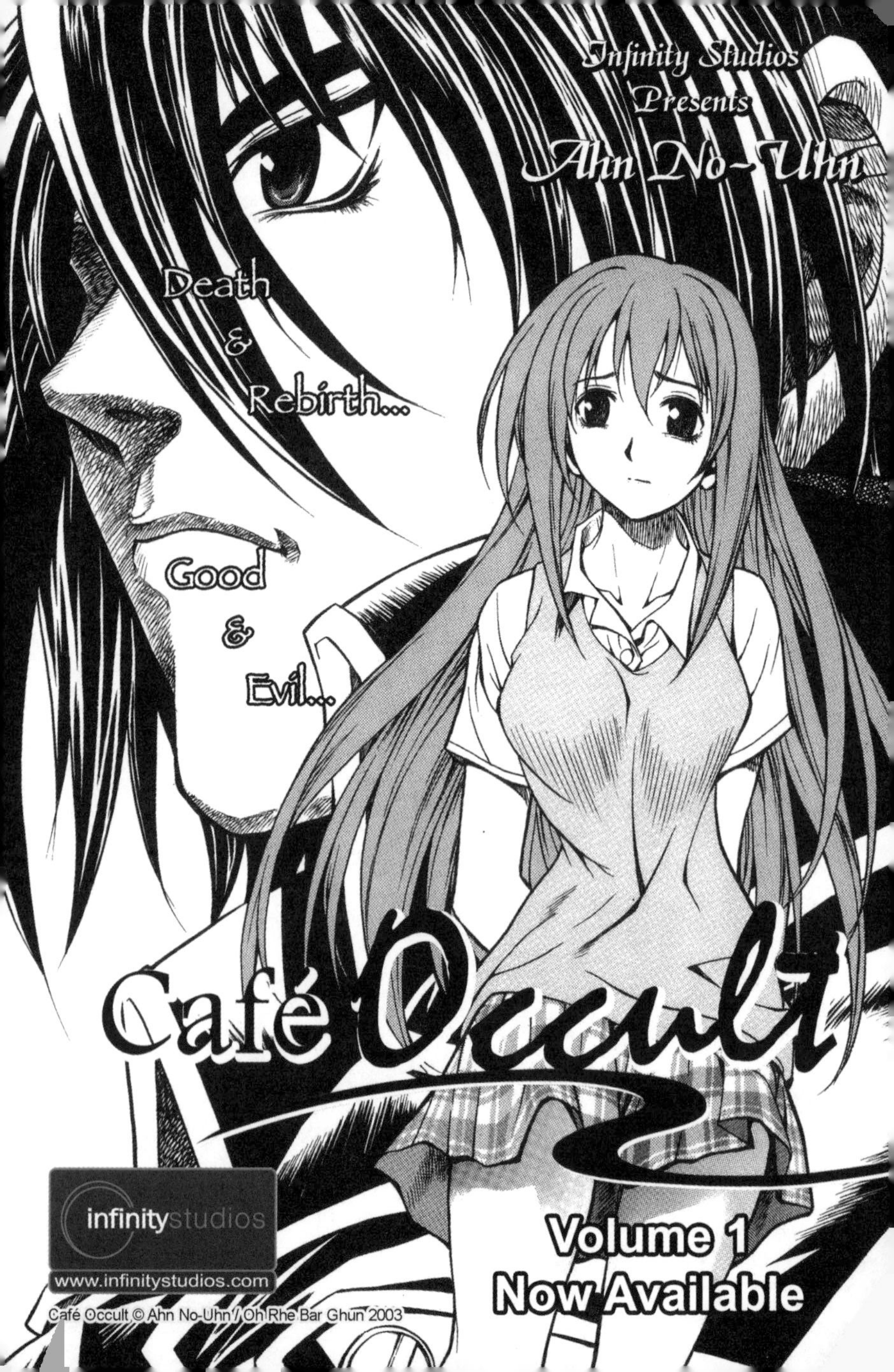
Infinity Studios
Presents
Ahn No-Uhn
Death
&
Rebirth...
Good
&
Evil...
Café Occult
infinitystudios
www.infinitystudios.com
Volume 1
Now Available
Café Occult © Ahn No-Uhn / Oh Rhe Bar Ghun 2003

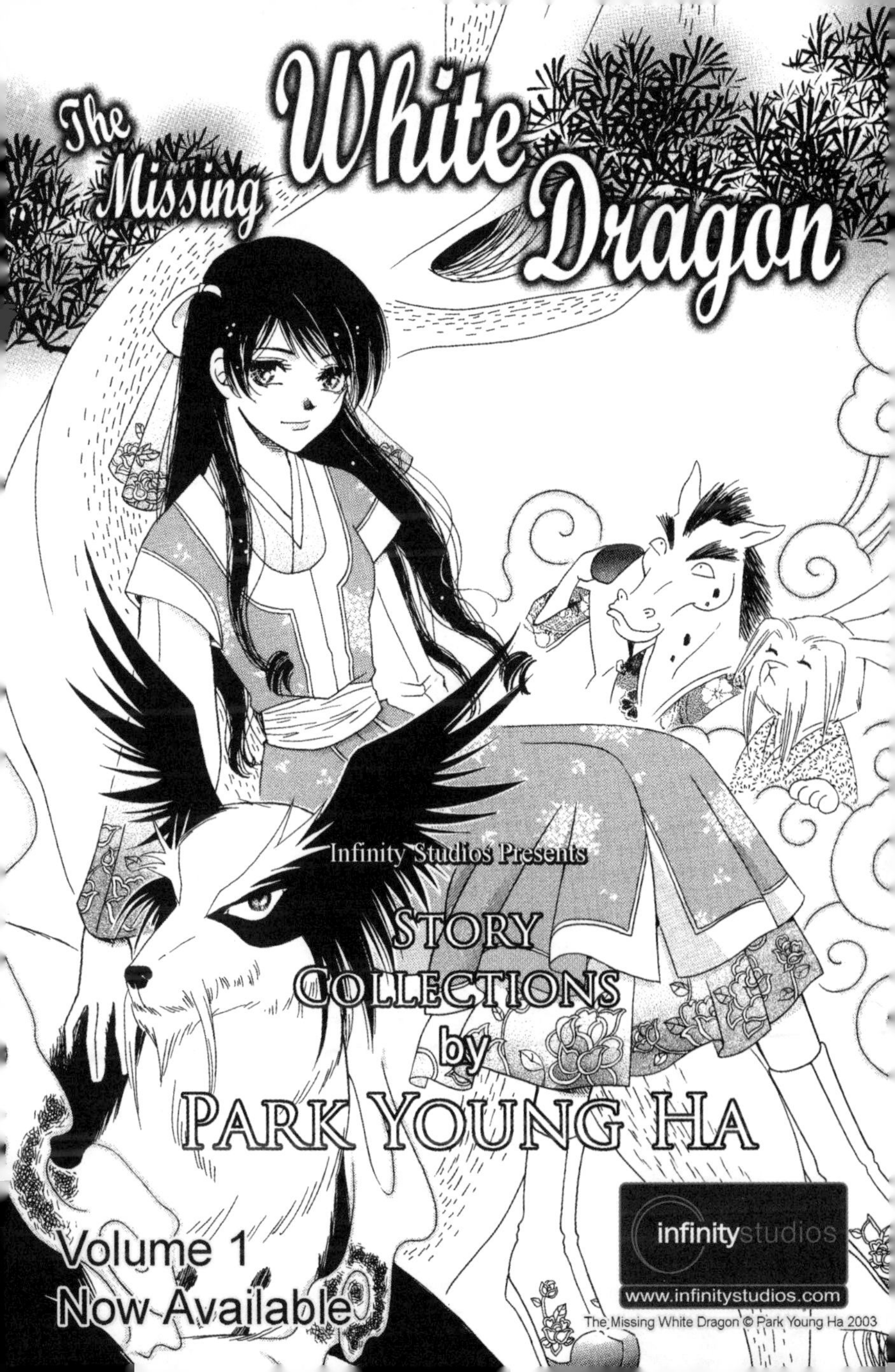
The Missing White Dragon
Infinity Studios Presents
STORY COLLECTIONS by
PARK YOUNG HA
Volume 1
Now Available
infinitystudios
www.infinitystudios.com
The Missing White Dragon © Park Young Ha 2003

Infinity Studios Presents

Witch Class

Story & Art By ✿ Lee Ru

Name : Dorothy
Occupation : Student
Goal : "I want to become
a witch to live out the
romantic dream every girl
wishes for... you know,
like turning the world into a
dark hellish cauldron, making
everyone bow to me, and
summoning cute zombies,
tee hee hee~!

Volume 1 Now Available

It takes a great deal to survive in outer space...

HURRAH! SAILOR

Volume 1
Story by Rintaro Koike
Character Designs by Kouichi Kiga
Comic by Katsuwo Nakane

Now Available

But it takes even more to survive in outer space with this bunch.

BLOOD ALONE

Translator : Kentaro Abe

English Adaptation : Je-Wa Jeong

Editor : Je-Wa Jeong / Miho Koto /
Soung Lee / Kentaro Abe

Layout : Miho Koto

Art Director : Soung Lee

Licensing : Masayoshi Kojima

Vice President : Steve Chung

C.E.O. : Jay Chung

Blood Alone Volume 1 © MASAYUKI TAKANO 2005
First published in 2005 by Media Works Inc., Tokyo, Japan.
English translation rights arranged with Media Works Inc.

Publisher
Infinity Studios, LLC
525 South 31st St.
Richmond, CA 94804
www.infinitystudios.com

First Edition : January 2006
ISBN : 1-59697-251-3

Printed in China

BLOOD ALONE

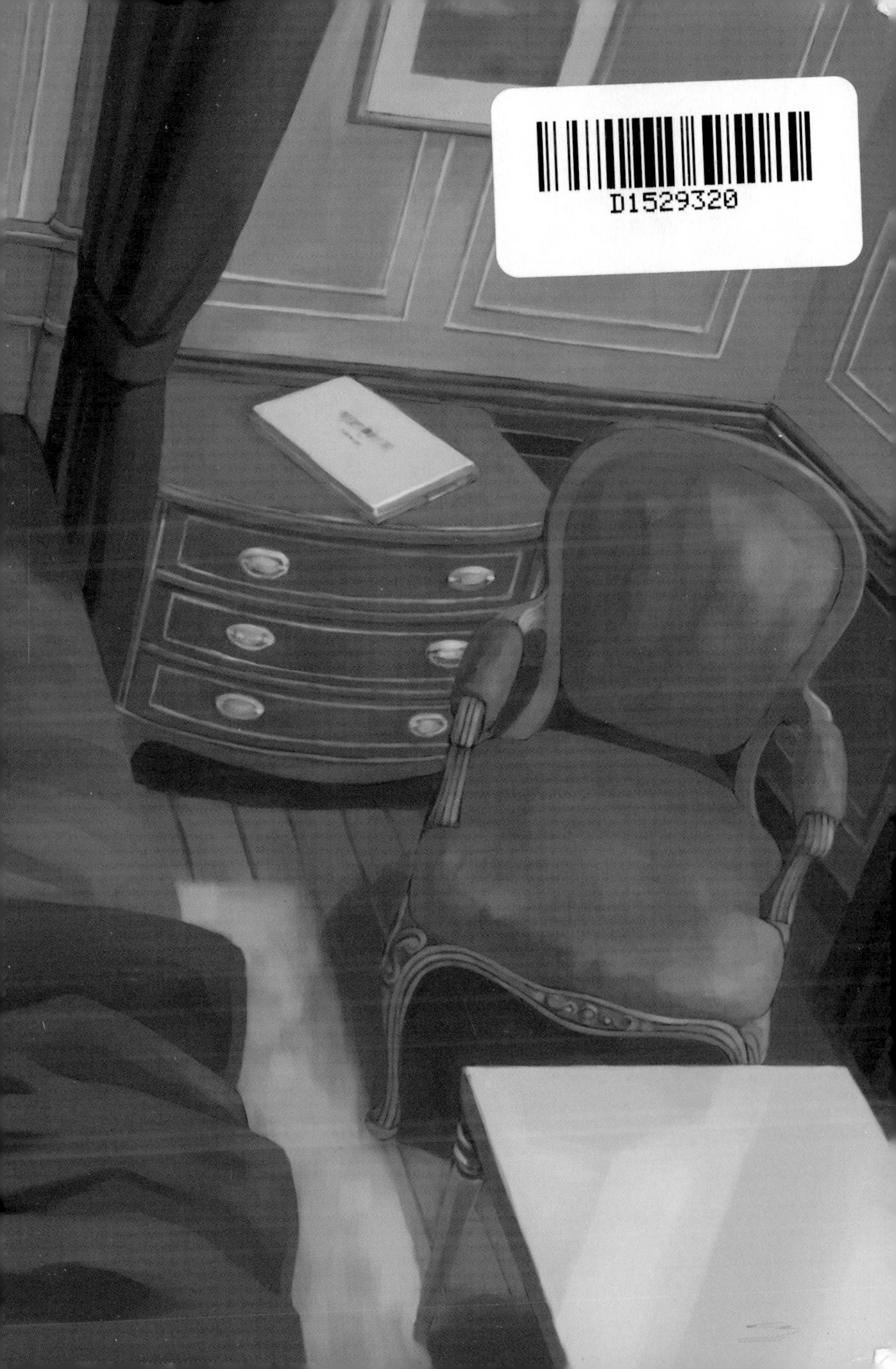